Crossing Waters, Crossing Worlds

Crossing Waters,

Crossing Worlds

The African Diaspora in Indian Country

edited by TIYA MILES *and* SHARON P. HOLLAND

Duke University Press   Durham & London   2006

© 2006 Duke University Press
All rights reserved
Printed in the United States of America
on acid-free paper ∞
Designed by C. H. Westmoreland
Typeset in Carter & Cone Galliard
with Quadraat Sans display
by Keystone Typesetting, Inc.
Library of Congress Cataloging-in-Publication
Data appear on the last printed page of this book.

Chapter 11, Tamara Buffalo's "Knowing All of
My Names" is reprinted from *International
Review of African American Art* 17, no. 1 (2000).

For Sun Old Man

CONSTANT, BRILLIANT, WISE

For Mary Scout's Enemy and Alfonso Ortiz

WHO WELCOMED ME

~~~~~~~~~

Contents

~~~~~~

Foreword

"Not Recognized by the Tribe"

SHARON P. HOLLAND

~~~~~~~~~

Chicago, June 2004

A beginning is always a failed enterprise, as much of what needs to be said — all that "counts" — is inevitably truncated, marginalized, or left behind altogether. With this in mind, I begin this text with an ending to a long journey in search of Elleanor Eldridge. In spring 2001, Jennifer Brody came to me with *Memoirs of Elleanor Eldridge*, a text written in 1838 by Frances Harriet Whipple Green McDougall. Eldridge claimed that her maternal grandmother, Mary Fuller, was Narragansett, while her grandfather was a former slave named Thomas Prophet. We were fascinated by both the intellectual and the pedagogical challenges this text would provide and began the arduous task of piecing together Eldridge's story — a journey that eventually led to our essay in this collection. What follows is a scene from one of those trips — a place where the "Indian" and the "African," to echo Whipple's language, haunt the edges of colonial history *and* herstory.

I arrived at the Providence, Rhode Island, airport at 10 o'clock in the morning after barely making my flight from Chicago's O'Hare. I waited in line for my Ford Focus, only to find that the rental-car company had no more compact cars available but could give me a brain-bucket Mazda Miata for the same price. If I wanted to wait ten minutes, I could have the Ford. I had played that game before — ten minutes is always thirty minutes, at least. I took the drop-top and headed south on I-95 to Charleston, Rhode Island. I was elated. I had not been on a road trip to Indian Country in about a decade. I had forgotten a few things; questions like, "How do you get to the — — reservation?" are often met with blank stares by rental-car employees. I figured out from the map that Route 138 eventually meets Route 112, and I would find the tribal offices somewhere on that last leg. As usual, I shot past the offices and inquired at Charleston Town Hall and then the Narragansett Indian Health Center before I doubled back to the tribal offices. I found it at the last junction I passed and pulled into the parking lot.

The front desk was empty, but a woman who looked like a childhood friend of mine told me that Shirley Champlin-Christy, tribal records administrator, would be in on Tuesday, Wednesday, and Thursday of that week. I thanked her and headed back to my car. I returned to the long stretch of road between the Narragansett Tribal Offices and Providence. Since the subject of our research, Elleanor Eldridge, had been born in Warwick, Rhode Island, on March 26, 1785, I decided to swing by the Warwick Town Hall to begin my search for any documentation of her birth. I found Prophets, Bakers, and Eldreges, but no Elleanor Eldridge or her maternal grandmother, Mary Fuller. I took a few random samplings of the deaths and marriages of several of the above and found that almost all of the "natural order" and "promiscuous" references to the name "Fuller" led me to the Reverend Edward T. Fuller, who had married an awful lot of people in Warwick's early days. The reverend was indeed promiscuous. I wrapped it up for the day and headed into Providence to meet Rebecca Schneider and follow her five miles out to her home, a bungalow at the end of a cove that looks onto the bay and the wider ocean beyond the point. I slept well, with a gentle breeze flowing through the window that reminded me of Cape Cod at night.

I returned to the Narragansett community to meet with Shirley Champlin-Christy, to check the tribal rolls, and to inquire specifically about Mary Fuller, reported by Frances Whipple (Eldridge's biographer) as the Narragasett grandmother of Eldridge. Previous experience with reservation rolls, and the stories of other scholars researching African and Native American confluences, had taught me that bringing my discovery to the attention of the official tribal records clerk would not be easy. I knew that the Narragansetts closed the rolls when they were formally recognized in 1987. I also knew that a recent casino deal in the making would make my attempt at "authenticating" Mary Fuller's Narragansett family all the more difficult. I decided to tell Shirley Champlin-Christy about my project and my purpose and let her do the talking. I would learn a lot about Narragansett family names and the current political climate from her response to my inquiry.

Our talk was illuminating. Although she could remember no one in the vicinity named "Fuller" or seeing that name in the rolls, she did remember that the tribe had researched the Prophet, Profit, or Proffit line. (Thomas Prophet was Eldridge's maternal grandfather.) We engaged in a little dance: Ms. Champlin-Christy simultaneously protected the tribal rolls with reiterations of the five family names (Wilcox, Champlin, Stanton, Noka, and Sekatau) and expressed a bit of fascination with the documentation about Fuller's self-identification that I had brought with me. She was so intrigued by Mary Fuller that she called the tribal historian, Ella Sekatau, who was at home sick that day. I also spoke with Ms. Sekatau, and she offered that the tribe had indeed researched the Prophet/Profit/Proffit line through a Susannah who had the "Profit" surname but could find no definite relation. Ms. Champlin-Christy and I continued our discussion, focusing on the proliferation of claims to Narragansett bloodlines that turn out to be false, or undocumented. I floated the possibility that Mary Fuller might have been taken from a Narragansett or Wampanoag family, placed in foster care or an orphanage, and raised by Baptist missionaries. She said that the scenario was a remote possibility, but if that were the case, it would be the first. We were guarded and intrigued. We liked talking to each other, so we eased into a conversation, sharing bits of our family narratives and getting to know each other. She then asked me about my family, and I told her about my grandmother's secret and her revelation to me: that my grandfather's mother was an "Indian from Alabama" and that he left Georgia one day and passed for black for the remainder of his life. She asked me what my grandmother looked like, and I replied, "She looked like you: same hair texture, same almond-shaped eyes, same brown skin, and I loved her dearly." Ms. Champlin-Christy paused, smiled, and nodded. Across decades and generations, we silently acknowledged our losses. I left with promises to share my subsequent findings and with the hope of a return to her offices sometime in the early fall.

Unwilling to go home immediately, I found Federal Hill, a predominantly Italian neighborhood in old Providence. I got a thinly sliced sopressata, a good Italian cheese with bite to it, and crusty bread at Roma's. I walked down the block to the wine shop and bought a nice Italian blend — sangiovesse, merlot, and cab. Rebecca and I ate a light dinner with salad and salmon and firmed up dinner plans for Wednesday night: dinner for four at 7 o'clock, William Yellow Robe, Wendy Walters, Becca, and me. I slept well under an open window with a Cape breeze.

Our dinner that night was magical: good weather, good food, good talk. William (Bill) Yellow Robe and I smoked and talked at length about African and Indian connections, about our families and the persistence of racism at home and abroad. Piqued by the project I was in the early stages of investigating, he told me about Debbie Spears-Moorehead (Narragansett) who could help me with my research. He dialed her on his cell phone, and Debbie and I began to chat. We agreed to meet the next day at the Warwick Public Library in the early afternoon.

Why I didn't get directions to my destination, I'll never know, but I arrived about an hour late. Who knew that the access road by the airport would also lead to the library? In any event, I apologized to Ms. Spears-Moorehead ("Call me Debbie"), and we set to our task. I showed her the document from 1753 with Mary Fuller's name on it, and we looked for "Thomas Green Burying Place" in the index of historic cemeteries of Rhode Island. We set off to find numbers 115 and 31, among others. As we traveled from one poorly marked and totally obscured gravesite to another, I witnessed a small part of Debbie's endless fight to protect the burying place of her family members. One construction crew had excavated a new housing development and placed a wall of dirt fifteen to twenty feet high at the border of one gravesite, casting a shadow over headstones, as if a storm were hovering in that place and nowhere else. We investigated the locations of a few gravesites near the airport. Many of the historic cemeteries are located *behind* private property and required us to knock on doors to gain access to them.

We finally hit the access road that circled the airport. The houses directly across from the airfield were abandoned and boarded, with signs saying "Property of TCG Airport" on front doors and windows. I felt as if we were trespassing twice — on the future property of the airport and on the memories of the families, then and now, displaced

Notice posted on a house on the perimeter of TF Green
Airport in Providence, Rhode Island. The airport sits on what
used to be Lincoln Farm, where in the nineteenth century a
community of Afro-Native peoples lived and worked.

by the word "expansion." We then drove around to cemetery number
31, which was located on airport property. Debbie parked her car pre-
cariously on the side of the narrow road, and we walked to the fence to
take a closer look. We stood in silence as we linked our hands in the
fence and tried to decipher the writing on the gravestones. Debbie
explained that we needed the airport's permission to visit the cemetery.
Our look was a bit forlorn until we noticed an opening in the gate. We
were elated; we rushed up to the entrance and almost simultaneously
stopped dead in our tracks. When we looked down, our brown arms
signaled a specific warning to us both: We were brown people about to
trespass on airport property in Bush's America. Post-911, post–Patriot
Act, we could be detained indefinitely if we trespassed on government
property. The feeling was overwhelming. Although we tried to laugh it
off — "What were we thinking?!" — it was bittersweet, and I wanted
to cry.

On the way back to my car at the public library, we passed the houses
with the airport-property signs pasted across their thresholds, and the
feeling came back to both of us. The next morning, I entered airport
property with my government-issued driver's license in hand and
boarded a plane for Chicago. I realized that the only *free* access I would

ever have to the mystery of Mary Fuller's burial would most likely be from the air, moving at a hundred miles per hour with the scene below me a complete blur and the G-force of the Airbus 320 pulling me back to the ground.

Note

The title of the foreword is taken from a phrase in Ann McMullen's ground-breaking essay "Blood and Culture: Negotiating Race in Twentieth-Century Native New England" (Brooks 2002, 261–91). My meditation is in conversation with that piece and its claims, in particular, as well as with the collection as a whole. My respect for the work of that collection and the insight that McMullen's essay offers is great.

Preface

Eating Out of the Same Pot?

TIYA MILES

~~~~~~~~~

Ann Arbor, Michigan, March 2004

In 1998, I was a dissertation fellow at Dartmouth College working on a historical project about an African American slave named Doll and her Cherokee owner and "husband" called Shoe Boots. Although I had turned to supportive senior scholars for advice and counsel, I often felt intellectually isolated at this time of my life, as though working on the overlapping experience of people from two marginalized populations located me on the outskirts of academic discussion, even in African American studies and Native American studies. I yearned for conversation with thoughtful colleagues who could offer intellectual companionship as well as critique, and I discovered, after sharing a panel at an American Society for Ethnohistory meeting with another graduate student working on Afro-Cherokee history, that I was not alone. Soon thereafter, with the steadfast partnerships of that fellow student, Celia Naylor, and the local community organizer Stephanie Morgan; with the support of a committee of advisers made up of Dartmouth faculty and staff; and with inconceivably generous funding from Dartmouth College, I co-organized a national conference titled, "'Eating Out of the Same Pot': Relating Black and Native (Hi)stories."

The name of the gathering was derived from an interview conducted in 1940 by a University of Oklahoma master's student Sigmund

Sameth. In the interview, a black man formerly held as a slave by Creeks compared his experience with that of African Americans enslaved by whites, saying, "I was eating out of the same pot with the Indians, going anywhere in this country I wanted to, while they was still licking the master's boots in Texas" (Sameth 1940, 56). Although I did not foresee it when I selected the quotation for our title, this Creek freedman's expression of intimacy with Indians, the very people he had been enslaved by, foreshadowed an aspect of tension, contradiction, and deep feeling that would mark the conference. Equally surprised, I suspect, were the scholars, artists, activists, community members, and students who attended the event from across the United States and from Canada and Mexico.

Many of the attendees were people who identified as "black Indians" and were seeking new knowledge as well as a community of belonging. A small minority of people within this black Indian group introduced themselves with names like Chief Sitting Sun and Little Arrow and wore clothing and accessories that approximated various forms of American Indian apparel: headdresses, deerskin, beads, and feathers, thus enacting stereotyped performances of Indian identity that would contribute greatly to an underlying discomfort shared by most in attendance. Many other participants were academics in the fields of African American and Native American history, literature, and political thought. A number of the attendees identified as African American or Native American and had long held a personal interest in the topic. And, of course, a significant number of the two hundred persons present occupied subject positions in more than one of these categories. The combined presence of so many different kinds of people with discrete orientations to and stakes in the subject of study sparked impassioned debate, subtle rebukes, impromptu soliloquies, and refined academic questions.

There were moments during this gathering in which participants arrived at public epiphanies that revealed emotional undertows of understanding and connection, but just as often, suspicion and resentment arose between "black Indians" and "red" Indians; academics and community folk; scholars of color, white scholars, and scholars of color who "looked white"; "wannabes" and "should-have-beens"; and, in the words of one participant and contributor to this book, "Super Indians" who felt they had the authenticity and authority to define the identities of others. One such moment became emblematic for me of the depths of division between some Native and Afro-Native people.

In a plenary-session lecture, a renowned Cherokee studies scholar described the history of Cherokee slaveholding while offering the example of an exceptional black slave who was freed and adopted by Cherokee clan members. Immediately after making her remarks, the speaker left the conference to keep a prior commitment. During the discussion that followed the lecture, and in the absence of the speaker, a Cherokee graduate student engaged in debate a woman who expressed an Afro-Native identity and was wearing a shawl and feather in her hair. The woman voiced the concern that the lecture deemphasized the injustice of Cherokee slavery. While she was speaking, the graduate student stood and interrupted, asking, in what was clearly an antagonistic tone, "Where are you from?" The graduate student then proclaimed that he was a Cherokee from Oklahoma. He raised his voice and pointed a finger at the woman while admonishing her not to speak about "his people." The woman answered in a rather unusual form, asking repeatedly, "Why do you want to hurt me? Why are you trying to shut me up? Tell me your story." The man responded to her by shouting, "We did not sell our own people; we did not sell our own people. Don't speak about my people." When an Afro-Cherokee woman in the audience stood and proclaimed that the graduate student was not the only person who had the right to speak about Cherokees and that his story was not the only story, the graduate student cursed and stormed out of the meeting hall. The woman who had made the original comment began weeping. The audience was stunned.

After I had recovered from my own shock, I interpreted this scene as encapsulating key and recurring tensions between Native Americans and "black Indians." The woman had adopted a mode of Indianesque dress that, while probably well intentioned, suggested a lack of close and current cultural knowledge of a particular Native tribe. The graduate student refused to entertain the idea that this woman who appeared to be African American could also be a Native American person. He also seemed uninterested in the documented history of Cherokee enslavement of blacks and denied that blacks could ever be considered part of the Cherokee populace. And finally, both the Indian man and the Afro-Indian woman were at odds with each other over a historical reality encouraged and coerced by white settlers and U.S. Indian agents and a retelling of that history by a Euro-American scholar. While the conflict seemed to be bilateral, it was in fact triangular, holding in tension Indian experience, black experience, and an invisible, structuring white presence.

I was not the only person to be startled and saddened by this heated exchange. Afterward, I felt all the more determined to lay bare the landscape of black and Indian relationships and the impact of oppressive systems of colonialism and slavery on those relationships. In the four years since that gathering, I have sought to understand what it is that draws African Americans to Native America in the past and the present, that divides Afro-Native people from other Native Americans, that propels blacks to claim Indian ancestry while at times dishonoring living indigenous peoples and cultures, and that leads some Native Americans to refuse a response to the call of their African-descended kin.

The writings in this book, contributed by presenters and audience members of the Dartmouth conference, as well as by scholars and creative artists who submitted pieces at a later date, continue a conversation begun many months ago. It is my hope that the work collected here will lend insight, immediacy, and a greater depth of understanding to the intersectional and interdependent lives of "the first and forced Americans" (Moraga 2002 [1981], xvi).[1]

Note

[1] The feminist theorist Cherríe Moraga uses this phrase in a parenthetical comment and attributes the wording to a friend: "We recognized and acknowledged our internally colonized status as the children of Native and African peoples ('the first and forced Americans,' as a friend once put it)."

Acknowledgments

〜〜〜〜〜〜

The seed for this book was planted at Dartmouth College, and I remain deeply grateful to the faculty and staff there for the freedom and support I received as a graduate student fellow-in-residence to conceptualize and plan the Dartmouth conference. The ideas sparked at that event took several years and many conversations to germinate. I am likewise grateful to the African American Studies Department and the International and Area Studies Program at the University of California, Berkeley, which invited me to attend intensive workshops on the African diaspora. I am thankful to the faculty and graduate student participants of the Westerbeke Ranch Diasporas workshop, especially David Chariandi, Gina Dent, Ruthie Gilmore, Bethuel Hunter, Pablo Idahosa, Suzette Spencer, and Rinaldo Walcott, who took my thinking in new directions. Thank you, also, to Sara Kaplan for her research assistance at the start of this project. I am appreciative also for Judith Byfield, Phil Deloria, Robin Kelley, and Amy Stillman who have no idea how important their thoughts and actions have been to the formation and completion of this project. Thank you, most importantly, to the talented and dedicated contributors who made this book possible.

I am thankful beyond words to my dear husband, Joseph, whose input never fails to enliven and sharpen my ideas. Thank you to my darling babies, Nali Azure and Noa Alice, for coming right on time, and to my generous family, who gave so much of their own time to help care for the girls in their infancy.

And finally, thank you to Auntie Sharon for saying yes, for taking care of business, and for nurturing this book along through difficult times.

TIYA MILES

This book began with my first essay in the field, "'If You Know I Have a History, You Will Respect Me': A Perspective on Afro-Native Literature" (1994). It has been a decade since that work began, and along the way I have been grateful for the encouragement and support of several: Paula Moya and Robert Warrior in those early years; Melinda Micco for her kind support during the early stages of my research in the field; Dartmouth College for hosting the first scholarly gathering of Afro-Native Americanists; the University of Illinois at Chicago for its generous support with research funds for trips to archives and to Ann Arbor for collaborations; and Robyn Wiegman, whose critique is always welcome and never fails to enrich. I am also grateful for the support of family and friends: Mr. and Mrs. Clifford Crowder (mom and dad), who encourage me to keep it up; Lila Karp, who is always the voice in my ear; the Chicago crew, who provide the meaning of the word "community"; and finally, Jennifer D. Brody, who helps me keep it together and who tolerated the long nights and the times when I just had to say it out loud.

When we began this project, we thought that the book was going to be the "baby." Little did we know that our intellectual endeavors had their own tiny orbit. A big thank you to my coeditor, Tiya Miles, for bringing us the next generation, literally and figuratively. This work would not have been possible without your meticulous care and your patience. Thanks for bringing this project to me.

SHARON P. HOLLAND

Crossing Waters, Crossing Worlds

~~~~~~~~

Muskogee Reds Baseball Club, an African American sports team in Indian Territory, 1907. *Used by permission of the Western History Collections, University of Oklahoma Libraries.*

Introduction

Crossing Waters, Crossing Worlds

TIYA MILES AND SHARON P. HOLLAND

~~~~~~~~~

The African Diaspora in Indian Country

No outsider knows where Africa ends or America begins.
— LESLIE MARMON SILKO (1991, 421)

In the eyes of neighboring slaveholders, Diamond Hill was a splendid plantation — glistening with fields, gardens, livestock, springs, outbuildings, a store, a school, and a pillared, two-story brick home that was the first of its kind in the region. Two of the enslaved black women who lived and labored there in 1811 attracted the notice of a nearby European missionary. In a diary, the missionary told the following story about Betty, "an African woman" who "had the misfortune fourteen days ago of having her house burned down in the absence of her husband. . . . A deeply rooted superstition caused her not to hurry and put out the fire even though she saw it right away in the distance. Betty claimed that in her country such appearances of fire are often created by witchcraft, and if one looked at it, it would all disappear." Betty's relative, named Crawje, was similarly described by the missionary as "a poor, completely ignorant heathen from Africa [who] did not even understand English."[1] While the diarist, a devout Moravian Christian named Anna Rosina Gambold, saw these two women as unfortunate due to the evidence of their African subjectivity, as twenty-first-century thinkers interested in cultural continuity, change, and exchange across the African diaspora, we might interpret the women's fractured stories in a different light. Betty's and Crawje's experience, though filtered through Western eyes, reinforces our realization that African beliefs and practices persisted in North America, even as they were transformed and reconstituted in the gristmill of forced displacement and enslavement.

The African women described here did not live in the slave quarters of a Southern plantation on the U.S. mainland. Nor did they live on the Georgia or Carolina sea islands, recognized for their protective encircling of African cultural ways. Rather, Betty and Crawje lived their lives among Native Americans in the Cherokee Nation of the Southeast. They were members of a community of nearly one hundred black slaves, some of whom spoke African languages to the exclusion of English and Cherokee, and many of whom acted in ways that the ethnocentric missionaries described as "crazy" and "wild." (Norton 1970 [1816], 67–68).[2] Black men and women on this plantation, one of the largest in the Cherokee Nation before Indian Removal, did things in an "African manner."[3] In so doing, they had a subtle but discernible influence on the Cherokees around them. Cherokee adults sometimes attended dances in the slave quarters, and Cherokee children who were being educated at the mission school socialized with black children, "riding around the bush with the Negro boys" to the extent that the missionaries feared the Indian children would be led astray.[4] The adaptation of Cherokee cultural ways by enslaved blacks on Diamond Hill is even more apparent, in their fluency in the Cherokee tongue and their use of Cherokee healing techniques in times of illness.[5]

The death of Crawje, Betty's relative, is a moment that encapsulates the Afro-Indian border crossings that occurred in this place and in many elsewheres that traversed Native America. At Crawje's burial, a stricken Betty "wailed terribly according to the customs of *this* country."[6] Betty, a woman who is described in the missionary diary as African by birth and behavior, apparently expressed her mourning as a Cherokee would at the loss of a loved one.

The example of Diamond Hill, a famous Cherokee plantation that has been restored today as the Chief Vann House State Historic Site in Georgia, illustrates ways that people of African descent transported and transformed cultures, created intersectional communities, and built metaphysical as well as physical homes on Native lands and within

Native cultural landscapes. In the process, they altered their interior worlds as well as those of Native peoples. Africans in Indian Country, like Africans in other parts of the Americas, have "exchanged their country marks" with the indigenous peoples with whom they came into contact (Gomez 1998). However, the persistent presence, symbolic resonance, and multifaceted meanings of African-derived peoples and cultures within the spaces of Native America often go unrecognized.[7]

Over the course of four centuries, thousands of black people, dispersed from Africa through the traumatic vehicle of the transatlantic slave trade, were relocated to Native lands and among Native populations in the "New World." In the aftermath of slavery in the United States, many others freely migrated to Indian Territory of present-day Oklahoma to escape racial injustice and violence. Indian country became, for these displaced Africans, both a literal and a metaphorical home.

The major purpose and goal of this book is to articulate in new ways this space where black experience meets Native experience — to live in it, so to speak. Our proposal is simple: that Native America *has been and continues to be* a critical site in the histories and lives of dispersed African peoples. Indeed, the very language of "New World" communities and "New World" cultures that has become commonplace in African diaspora studies as a means of differentiating peoples of the diaspora from peoples who remained in the African homeland takes as an implicit and undertheorized given the European colonization of Native America.[8] By focusing on the (re)production of personal and tribal histories and the production of cultural forms in the context of African diasporic presence in indigenous North America, *Crossing Waters, Crossing Worlds* provides a means to unpack this assumption, as well as others.[9]

As African Americanists in the main, we also wish to open a dialogue with scholars in Native American studies, to ask not only how Native place and presence have affected black life, but also how black people and cultures have influenced indigenous America, for better and for worse. We are interested in discovering what intimate conversations and negotiations took place between blacks and Indians in the long years after their first encounters; what political issues, strategies, and conflicts emerged out of their shared experience; and what creative works and cultural productions were inspired by their coming together. Overall, we seek in this book to raise and engage the central question: What happens when key issues in African diasporic experience, such as migration, freedom, citizenship, belonging, peoplehood, and cultural retention and creation, and key issues in Native American experience, such as tribalism, protection of homelands, self-determination, political sovereignty, and cultural-spiritual preservation and renewal, converge?

Freedom Dreams: African Americans in Indian Territory

> As slaves they had long been aware that for themselves, as for most of their countrymen, geography was fate. . . . And they knew that to escape across the Mason-Dixon Line northward was to move in the direction of a greater freedom. But freedom was also to be found in the West of the old Indian Territory.
> — RALPH ELLISON, "Going to the Territory" (1979)

Perhaps more than any other space in the United States, Indian Territory, broadly defined, has held out the promise of home to black slaves and their descendants. By the late nineteenth century and early twentieth century, many African Americans had come to see the Western lands called Indian Territory as a refuge in America, and more, as a potential *black space* that would function metaphorically and emotionally as a substitute for the longed-for African homeland. (If we also consider the African diaspora in New England, we have the making of an expansive understanding of African subjects and Indian country that might shift the prevailing understanding of Indian Territory's psychic location in the "West" rather than in the East.)

With the abrupt conclusion of Reconstruction in 1877, thousands of blacks made their way from the South to the West, heading for Kansas, Arkansas, Oklahoma, and Indian Territory. Nell Irvin Painter, Norman Crockett, and other historians have demonstrated that these migrants were seeking escape from the onslaught of white racial violence in a period of escalating attacks and sought to resettle in a location where they could find economic opportunity, preserve their dignity, and make new homes (Painter 1992 [1977]; Crockett 1979). Some migrants headed directly for Indian Territory. Others made their way there after facing disappointments in Arkansas, and later in Oklahoma Territory, where white settlers refused to share the most productive lands and organized violent attacks to prevent blacks from homesteading. Many of these migrants traveled in desperate circumstances: They were poor, hungry, and besieged by inclement weather as they walked what the historian Lori Bogle has called the "black Trail of Tears" (Bogle 1994, 169).

For black sojourners, Indian Territory shone like a beacon at the end of a long tunnel of racism and exploitation. Out of twenty-eight all-black towns that were founded in the region of present-day Oklahoma, twenty-four were located in Indian Territory on land allotted to former slaves of Indians, while only four were located in Oklahoma Territory in the aftermath of land runs (Carney 1998, 151). The majority of these Indian Territory towns were based in the Creek (or Muskogee) Nation. It is here, in the development of all-black towns in Indian Territory at the end of the nineteenth century, that the language of Indian Territory as the black paradise begins to emerge. It is also here that the few examples of blacks drawing connections between Africa and the Indian Territory can be found.

Black newspapers published in the Creek Nation prior to Oklahoma's statehood, as well as a rare extant brochure published to attract new settlers to the all-black town of Red Bird, also in the Creek Nation, offer a glimpse into African American views of Indian Territory between 1880 and 1907. As the historian Kenneth Hamilton has pointed out, black towns were business ventures as well as cities of refuge, and newspapers and booster sheets were published by land speculators and town companies to promote the towns and attract new settlers. We can surmise, then, that many of the published representations of Indian Territory found in these sources were edited to project an especially positive view. Nevertheless, the theme of Indian Territory as a liberating space for black people that emerges in these sources is revealing. In a June 23, 1904, article in the black newspaper the *Muskogee Comet*, titled "Unequal Advantages in the B.I.T. [Black Indian Territory]," one writer asserted that "the Creek Nation may verily be called the Eden of the West for the colored people." Another article in the same newspaper observed: "The Indian Territory is the only place now in the South where the colored voter has a chance to exercise the right of franchise" (*Muskogee Comet*, July 14, 1904). The Kansas newspaper the *Afro-American Advocate*, based in the town of Coffeyville, adjacent to the Creek and Cherokee nations, also emphasized the attraction of Indian country, encouraging black people from the South to "come home, come home. . . . Come out of the wilderness from among those lawless lynchers and breathe the free air" (as quoted in May 1996, 225).

In keeping with this invitation, the town of Coffeyville adopted the slogan "Coffeyville—The Gate City to the Indian Territory" (May 1996, 225).

In 1905, the Red Bird Investment Company published a fifty-page brochure with photographs to boost its all-black town and encourage new settlement. The company's representation of Indian Territory repeated and exaggerated the utopian image presented by black newspapers. The brochure begins: "A Message to the Colored man. . . . Do you want a home in the Great Southwest—The Beautiful Indian Territory? In a town populated by intelligent, self-reliant colored people?" (Red Bird Investment Company 1905, 1). The brochure later describes the physical location of Red Bird, insisting that "there cannot be found a more fertile location in the beautiful Indian Territory than the country tributary to Red Bird. . . . To ride through on the railway and watch the panorama unfold itself to your view, is like the realization of a cherished dream of a new home in the great and beautiful southwest" (Red Bird Investment Company 1905, 17).

In preparation for the publication of the brochure, the Red Bird Investment Company invited black professionals from across the Creek Nation and neighboring areas to comment on life in Indian Territory. Although the letters may have been edited, and negative letters are likely to have been rejected, the surviving testimonies open a window on the way that individual African Americans viewed and represented the Indian West. The first testimony, by the Reverend Jason Meyer Conner, who held a Ph.D. from Little Rock, Arkansas, and was an officer in the African Methodist Episcopal church, stated: "This is to certify that I have made a personal visit to the Indian Territory, and know it to be the best place on earth for the Negro" (Red Bird Investment Company 1905, 2). Dr. J. M. Davis, a physician from Muskogee, Indian Territory, reported that "this country is the Paradise for the colored man" (Red Bird Investment Company 1905, 36). And A. E. Patterson, an attorney-at-law also based in Muskogee, asserted:

In no section of this great land of ours do the colored people have a better opportunity to accumulate wealth and simultaneously develop individual characters and strong minds, than in Indian Territory. Here, where nature has so generously provided for the comforts of all people who are fortunate enough to have found their way to this earthly Paradise, every man is recognized according to his merit. (Red Bird Investment Company 1905, 36)

These newspaper articles and letters represented Indian Territory not just as a region where African Americans could thrive politically and economically, but also as an idealized Promised Land. In two examples, the writings of black town settlers suggest that they imagined Indian Territory as a surrogate for an African home. In an attempt to discourage thoughts of emigration, the *Afro-American Advocate* posited that any black person "who can't live in Indian Territory, need not go to Africa" (as quoted in May 1996, 225). Thomas Haynes, manager of the black town of Boley in the Creek Nation, compared his town to Egypt, claiming that Boley, like that ancient kingdom, was "an imperishable attestation of the power, might and intellectual genius of a race" (Crockett 1979, 46).

In imagining their paradisiacal home, black town settlers envisioned a place where Indians were necessary but peripheral. They were necessary because it was the Indian presence that differentiated Indian Territory from the states, and it was also the complex history between Indians and their former black slaves that had opened the door for African American settlement; they were peripheral because blacks located Native people at the margins of their new communities. Similar to Frederick Jackson Turner's concept of an American frontier in which an Indian *influence* makes white Americans distinct, but Indian *people* must give way to white progress, the concept of a black Indian Territory transformed Indians into a vehicle for black identity formation and racial uplift. For, as Norman Crockett has observed, the founders and settlers of all-black towns in Indian Territory sought a place where, by showing the values of race pride, self-reliance, moral fortitude, and industry, they could demonstrate their fitness for equal inclusion in the broader U.S. republic. It is perhaps telling that in the black town of Clearview, located in the Creek Nation, the two social organizations were the Patriarchs of America for men and the Sisters of Ethiopia for women — Africa and America jointly invoked against the unspoken backdrop of Indian land (Crockett 1979, 31, 66).

Several letters in the Red Bird brochure suggested that Native people were or should be marginal in the black Indian Territory and repeated the value of having a town "for colored people alone" (Red Bird Investment Company 1905, 36). A. E. Patterson, the attorney quoted earlier, described the population of the Creek Nation for would-be black settlers, emphasizing its mixed-race character and implying the absence of Native people of unmixed heritage. Patterson wrote: "Our population is largely cosmopolitan, being made up of Indians of mixed blood, educated colored and white people from the various States, the latter two races predominating" (Red Bird Investment Company 1905, 36). Mrs. J. Orlando Mitchell, the wife of an Indian Territory businessman, wrote:

> The time of the painted Indian on the war path, and the desperado, has gone to make way for the income of civilization, culture and refinement. The Indian Territory of today is as free from the taint of the wild, barbaric life as is the city of Boston. . . . Social conditions here need have no terrors for those who contemplate making the Indian territory their home. (Red Bird Investment Company 1905, 5)

Not until the last two pages of the Red Bird brochure is the Creek Nation, the site for Red Bird, acknowledged in any detail. In these final paragraphs, the brochure explains how black towns were founded on Indian land. But then, in a rhetorical erasure of Native presence, the brochure expresses the hope that all of Indian Territory will soon be dissolved into the new state of Oklahoma. The brochure ends with the call: "Soon there will be another star added to 'Old Glory' and it is then, when the Indian Territory is ushered into the sisterhood of States, the real boom will come. Get a start in time" (Red Bird Investment Company 1905, 25).

Despite the dream and rhetoric of black town members, turn-of-the-twentieth-century Indian Territory was not the ideal place that African Americans imagined it to be. Native residents viewed the stream of black settlers as intruders in their nations, and many blacks who had formerly been enslaved by Indians and had lived in Indian Territory for decades resented the new arrivals. As it would happen, the vision of Indian Territory as a haven for African Americans was not to be realized for former slaves of Indians or for new black settlers. As more blacks poured into the Indian nations, tribal governments began enacting de facto segregation policies, lumping together their former slaves with new black settlers. And when Oklahoma became a state in 1907, subsuming Indian Territory within it, the first act of the legislature was to pass Jim Crow laws segregating blacks from whites and Indians. What was arguably the last imagined space of refuge for blacks in the United States no longer existed. As one black Oklahoman, Clarence Love, remembered in an oral history: "My parents had decided to leave Muskogee, just like they had left other places before, because they had not found the Promised Land that they expected" (Gates 1997, 141). Indeed, in the years that followed statehood, hundreds of African Americans in the former Indian Territory began a desperate attempt to emigrate to Canada, Mexico, and Africa, ever in pursuit of their "dreams of an elsewhere" (Holt 1999, 37).

Seeing Red: Native America in the African American Imaginary

> 'Cause I'm goin' to the Nation, goin' to the territor'
> Say I'm bound for the Nation, bound for the territor'
> I got to leave here, I got to get the next train home.
> — BESSIE SMITH, "Work House Blues" (1998 [1930])

The words of Bessie Smith speak to an experience of coming and going, of nations and territories — a trajectory of experience shared by black and Indian peoples in the forging of a place called the United States. Indeed, this and other African American cultural and colloquial expressions suggest the importance to black experience of Indian presence, Indian relations, and Indian locales. African American resistance strategies, social worlds, and subjectivities have long been inflected by the idea of immigration to Native American spaces and of literal and metaphorical relationships with American Indian peoples, even as indigenous societies and cultures have been influenced by the arrival of these newcomers. In fact, one might argue that the very notion of a visionary politics in African American culture is inextricably tied to an idea (imaginary or realized) of Indian nations and territory as open and even marginal space, a psychic territory where black subjects find safety, solace, autonomy, and family. In essence, part of the idea of freedom in black experience includes the space for a powerful imaginary — a place where Indian presence is felt and often realized.

African Americans' idealized images of Native lands and Native people are not without foundation. The black historians Carter G. Woodson and Kenneth W. Porter began documenting the fact of black and Native interrelations in the *Journal of Negro History* as early as the 1920s and 1930s.[10] They found, as have scholars of both African American and Native American history who have pursued this question since, that Africans and Indians forged bonds with one another while jointly enslaved in the Americas and West Indies in the seventeenth century and eighteenth century; that some enslaved African people successfully escaped to Indian countries; that major figures in black historical life have been both black and Indian in racial and cultural background; and that African American and Native American individuals and groups have joined forces to challenge European imperialism, colonialism, and slavery.

At the same time though, African American projections of liberation, economic success, community belonging, and ease of life onto Indian lands and peoples have not been free from logical flaws and exploitative gestures. Often these projections incorporate and reiterate broader American colonialist presumptions that Native lands and Native people, particularly Native women, should be made accessible to outsiders for purposes that do not serve the needs of American Indians themselves. The lyrics of "The Faking Blues" (1925) by Papa Charlie Jackson have just such a problematic effect when they express the following intention of the speaker: "Lord I'm going to the nation / Buy me an Indian squaw. / I'm going to raise me a family / Got me an Indian ma" (Jackson 1925). These lyrics not only suggest that racism was part and parcel of the interracial imaginary; such pronouncements also draw attention to the impossibility of safety, family, solace, or autonomy in a country where the twin forces of removal and slavery continue to bring the nation's imaginary self in direct conflict with its lived history. In other words, we are well aware that words like "family" and "community" conjure a romance of past and present that can never be achieved or realized, as the dream constantly comes undone through the relentless presence of the real.[11] Black expressions of alliance with Indians often sideline the parallel history of adversarial relations between African Americans and Native Americans, in which Southern Indians owned blacks as slaves and black buffalo soldiers served in the U.S. military as a unit charged with crushing Native resistance movements and enforcing Native detention on reservations.

Although African Americans have met rejection as often as acceptance in Indian communities, and although African American and Native American historical relations have been characterized by a range of negative as well as positive interactions, a celebratory invocation of Indian peoples and places has persisted in African American cultural life. For if white America has been a wilderness of biblical proportions for African slaves and their descendants, Indian physical and relational landscapes have represented a new Eden for blacks, characterized by the possibilities of transformation. As the African studies scholar Pablo Idahosa has observed, thoughts of Indian country have functioned like a salve for black people, who have been "hit with every sharp, jagged edge of every stick and sword" in North America (Idahosa 2000). Dispersed from their countries of origin and perpetually homeless on this continent, African Americans have imagined into being a Promised Land that is located both within and outside the national boundaries of the United States. In the realm of the black imaginary, then, the site of the Indian has been present, persistent, and paramount.

Indeed, the idea of and desire for connectivity with Indians and Indian spaces has found expression in a variety of African American cultural forms, including song, story, and visual art. In particular, the oral and written tradition in African America includes a predominant narrative of black and Native interrelations: that during slavery and the unpredictable climate of Reconstruction, blacks found safe haven, enlivened hope, and spiritual renewal by resettling in Indian territories and, whenever possible, becoming members of Indian families. This narrative has been expressed and re-expressed in multiple forms: in everyday speech acts in which African Americans assert Native ancestry; in children's stories such as Angela Medearis's *Dancing with the Indians* (1991), in which a black family makes a ritual pilgrimage to the Seminole Indian community that had sheltered their grandfather from slavery; and in the writings of African American authors.

The fiction of the Pulitzer Prize–winning novelist and feminist theorist Alice Walker, for instance, is punctuated by Native American characters and themes. Walker's second novel, *Meridian*, about a young black woman's personal and political awakening during the Civil Rights Movement, includes a meditation on the spiritual meaning of Indian lands for a displaced and often despised African American people. Her fourth novel, *The Temple of My Familiar*, features mixed-race Afro-Native characters whose ancestry spans the South American and African continents and includes a chapter on the Seminole leaders Wild Cat and John Horse. Walker has suggested in her memoir, *The Way Forward Is with a Broken Heart*, that her representation of Native American characters and themes is an essential expression of her own identity:

In Mississippi I began to crave arrowheads. It came upon me suddenly as the desire, years before, to write poetry. I hungered for the sight of them. I ached for the feel of them in my hand. . . . Our child has never known her mother without arrowheads, without Native American jewelry, without photo-graphs of Native Americans everywhere one could be placed. Craft and art and eyes steadied me, as I tottered on the journey toward my tri-racial self. Everything that was historically repressed in me has hungered to be ex-pressed, to be recognized, to be known. . . . Indians are always in my novels because they're always on my mind. Without their presence the landscape of America seems lonely, speechless. (Walker 2000, 36–37)

Walker's articulation of the "lonely, speechless" landscape of an America without a Native presence challenges earlier and existing notions of the "vanishing" or, in the case of Indian women, "dead" Indian at the same time that it reveals a special, albeit problematic, attachment to Indian peoples and places.[12] The fiction of the Nobel Prize laureate Toni Mor-rison is likewise concerned with the emancipatory possibilities for Afri-can Americans of recognizing Native ancestry and nurturing relation-ships with American Indian people. Parallels between Indian Removal and African enslavement permeate Morrison's masterpiece, *Beloved*, in which the spirits of Indians violently removed from the Southern land-scape join in the chorus of loss and pain with the baby ghost, Beloved, herself.[13] As the literature scholar Catherine Griffin has astutely ob-served, the representation of indigenous Americans has been a trope in African American imaginative expression because Indians might offer a homeland in place of the stolen Africa and extend the promise of ances-tors in place of severed family lines (Griffin 2000, 214). Griffin explains that in a context in which "Black history in the U.S. is an endless tale of exile and alienation," images of Indians have become critical to the African American reinvention of self, family, community, and place (Griffin 2000, 162).

The foregoing discussion of black imaginings of Indians raises the question: How do Native Americans view African Americans, imagine blacks and black culture, and interpret the points of overlap between African American and Native American histories? Comparatively few Native intellectuals have taken up this subject matter in the past. Those who have — namely, the Powhatan-Renape scholar Jack Forbes, the Modoc-descended writer Michael Dorris, and the Laguna-Pueblo nov-elist Leslie Marmon Silko — have articulated theories that recognize the joint impact of European colonialism, slavery, and racial hierarchy on indigenous American and African American subjectivities, commu-nities, and resistance strategies. Through his character Rayona in *A*

Yellow Raft in Blue Water, Dorris indicates the complexities of Afro-Native "dual heritage" in a Montana Indian community that reproduces aspects of U.S. racial prejudice (Dorris 1988 [1987], 63). Silko introduces the prospect of cultural and spiritual fusion from the perspective of the African American character Clinton in *Almanac of the Dead*, writing: "From the beginning, Africans had escaped and hid in the mountains where they met up with survivors of indigenous tribes hiding in remote strongholds. . . . Right then the magic had happened: great American and great African tribal cultures had come together to create a powerful consciousness within all people" (Silko 1991, 416). It is this vision of shared experience and joint creation that the Lakota artist Francis Yellow embraces in his piece that graces the cover of this book, a pictograph-like drawing of Africans entering indigenous American lands, titled, "First They Made Prayers, and They Sang and They Danced and Then They Made Relatives." The work of Forbes, Dorris, Silko, and Yellow represent only a segment of Native interpretations of black and Indian relationships. There is much more to be said from the perspective of Native thinkers, and we hope to extend and invite that dialogue through the works collected here.

Summary of Collected Essays

In the spirit of interdisciplinary openness and in the hope of fostering unexpected and productive dialogues, this book is divided into two loosely organized, nonchronological halves that cross disciplinary lines. Chapters 1–8 are primarily concerned with the themes of race, place, belonging, citizenship, and historical memory. Chapters 9–15 are particularly interested in explorations of presence, identity, and intimacy through narrative, performance, and visual art.

We begin with the evocative "A Harbor of Sense," in which the veteran poet and literature professor Eugene B. Redmond conducts an introspective interview with the Creek poet and musician Joy Harjo (Mvskoke/Creek). Widely recognized for her many books of poetry, including *She Had Some Horses* (1983), *The Woman Who Fell From the Sky* (1994), and *How We Became Human: New and Selected Poems* (2002), Harjo speaks in the interview about becoming a musician, about the new musical form of "tribal jazz," and about sources of inspiration, from a grade-school classroom to her saxophone-playing grandmother and the history of black and Native shared traditions of music and dance.

In the first essay of the volume, "An/Other Case of New England Underwriting: Negotiating Race and Property in *Memoirs of Elleanor Eldridge*," the literary and cultural studies scholars Jennifer D. Brody and Sharon P. Holland provide one of the first extended readings of Eldridge's story. The memoir, first published in 1838 by the prominent Rhode Islander Frances Harriet Whipple Green McDougall, offers a window onto the complex metaphoric negotiations of African and Indian subjectivity in early-nineteenth-century New England. Brody and Holland return to the archive to investigate Eldridge's maternal grandmother, Mary Fuller (reputed to be Narragansett), and to trouble the terms of such an investigation. What they find is a narrative that, although written by a white woman, engages the articulation of race, gender, and sexuality. As such, the piece proves illuminating for scholars of the era and area.

In "Race and Federal Recognition in Native New England," the attorney Tiffany M. McKinney questions the impact of historical Afro-Native intermarriage on the makeup, identity, and federal categorization of certain New England Indian tribes. McKinney asserts that racial complexity within Indian kinship circles and citizenries has contributed to contentious debate within tribal communities. She takes as her point of focus the Eastern Pequot and Pautucket Pequot bands and the Mashantucket Pequot tribe of Connecticut and Rhode Island, which have encountered internal dissention and external criticism due to the presence of "phenotypically black" tribal members. In a survey of government regulations and legal cases that serves as an instructive overview of the intersecting racial and legal dimensions of federal tribal recognition, McKinney suggests that the United States' history of federal intervention and recognition have contributed to tensions around race and belonging in contemporary Native communities. The result, McKinney posits, has been the construction of new tribal definitions of membership and citizenship that disenfranchise community members based on their racial categorization and physical appearance.

The next essays carry the historical debate about community boundaries, belonging, and citizenship out of New England and into the Indian Territory of present-day eastern Oklahoma, to which certain tribes of the Southeast were removed in the 1830s and 1840s. By focusing on the aftermath of black slavery in Indian nations, these three authors import into Native locales key questions about the meaning of freedom and the practice of politics in post-bellum black life. The historian David Chang's essay, "Where Will the Nation Be at Home? Race, Nationalisms, and Emigration Movements in the Creek Nation," redirects the post-emancipation discussion to the meaning of nationhood for Creek Indians, Creek freedmen and women, and other Native peoples in late-nineteenth-century Indian Territory. Chang argues convincingly that the notion of the nation held a particular power for both black and Native communities. He then demonstrates the complexities and contradictions for these groups in claiming a national paradigm during a historical moment in which Native governments were under threat of dissolution by the U.S. government, Native tribes were excluding ex-slaves and mixed-race Afro-Native people from the national body, and both black communities and Native tribes were launching independent plans to emigrate to Africa, Mexico, and Canada in parallel attempts to find new homelands for their communities. In this exploration of national discourses and emigration projects, Chang shows how it was possible — and, indeed, consistent — for former slaves of Creek Indians to assert definitions of their community that embraced an Afrocentric nationalism, respected and identified with Creek nationalism, and implicitly opposed the racialized nationalist projects of the United States.

The historian Barbara Krauthamer continues this discussion in her essay, "In Their 'Native Country': Freedpeople's Understandings of Culture and Citizenship in the Choctaw and Chickasaw Nations." Krauthamer offers an overview of the experience of black slaves in the Choctaw and Chickasaw tribes and an assessment of their forty-year struggle for the rights of citizenship following the Civil War. Rather than focusing on the slaves' formation of syncretic Afro-Indian identities, as some scholars of this era have done, Krauthamer explores the political life of these communities. She argues that in their attempt to define the meaning of freedom for themselves, former slaves focused on civic inclusion and the attainment of land in Indian Territory based on their history of cultural identification with Indian tribes. By tracing the shifting strategies that freedpeople engaged in, sometimes pressing for citizenship within their respective Native nations and at other times vying for citizenship within the United States, Krauthamer reveals a political conviction as well as a sense of peoplehood that was both linked to and separate from Native American tribal bodies.

The final essay in this trio, " 'Blood and Money': The Case of the Seminole Freedmen and Seminole Indians in Oklahoma," by the ethnic studies scholar Melinda Micco (Seminole/Creek), traces the history of black Seminole and Seminole Indian relations since the Seminole Wars and examines contemporary ramifications of this history—namely, the present-day court cases concerning civil rights and the disbursement of federal monies within the Seminole Nation of Oklahoma. Micco's work reveals the ways in which structures of military alliance and social organization that developed in the earliest moments of black and Seminole interaction continue to shape tribal politics and intertribal relations. She argues that while external factors—namely, American territorial expansion, European categorization and control of indigenous Americans and transplanted Africans, and the codification of racial identity through the concept of blood quantum—have been critical to the fragmentation of the Seminole people, internal structures and tensions underlie the conflicts between black Seminoles and Seminole Indians. Micco's interpretation of the past and present state of Seminole politics is enlivened and complicated by interviews with black Seminoles collected over a ten-year period. These interviews, together with her historical research, lead Micco to conclude that black Seminoles and Seminole Indians have a connection that is enduring and a history that cannot be collapsed into the broader category of black Indian experience.

The historian Celia Naylor takes our study farther west in "Playing Indian: The Selection of Radmilla Cody as Miss Navajo, 1997–98." Here Naylor explores Afro-Native identity claims and contestations through a case study of the 1998 Miss Navajo Nation contest. The winner of this cultural pageant was the singer Radmilla Cody, the daughter of a Navajo woman and African American man, whose right to reign was questioned by other Navajos. In dialogue with the scholars Rayna Green and Philip Deloria, who have written about the phenomenon of "playing Indian," Celia Naylor begins her study by asking whether African American claims of Indian heritage are treated with greater skepticism by Native people than are European American claims. In addition, through a compilation of letters to the editor in the *Navajo Times* and personal interviews with Cody, Naylor traces the reception of the mixed-race Miss Navajo among Navajos both on and off the reservation. She finds that internal community dialogue about the relationships between race and nation, between race and culture, and between blacks and Indians was multivalent and contradictory rather than singular and cohesive. She concludes, based on this finding, that the racial dilemmas highlighted through the Miss Navajo Nation contest are indicative of a new problem of the twenty-first century: not that of the color line itself as W. E. B. Du Bois portended, but rather, the indeterminacy of racial boundaries.

Deborah Kanter's "'Their Hair Was Curly': Afro-Mexicans in Indian Villages, Central Mexico, 1700–1820," concludes the first part of the volume by transporting questions about perceived difference and the dynamics of African acceptance into the understudied location of colonial Mexico. She traces the history of African and Indian relations within and across the borders of indigenous communities, addresses the central issues of how kinship lines and the racial categorizations and signifiers of Spanish colonial rulers affected African and Afro-Indian belonging in indigenous communities, and considers ways in which blacks and black Indians engaged in the act of "passing" as Indian to improve their status among Indians as well as before Spanish officials. Using land-tenure cases to illustrate the uneasy position of Afro-Mexicans in Indian pueblos, Kanter considers the complex negotiation of perceived ethnicity and status in colonial communities. She finds that the ambiguous position of Afro-Mexicans in colonial Mexico came from within and from without—that identity and identities were imposed by both Indian and colonial officials. For Kanter, only a study that recognizes the animated nature of identification can comprehend the early period of racialized relationships and subjects.

The second half of the book begins with an essay by the Native American studies scholar and cultural critic Robert Warrior (Osage), who focuses on the ever important late nineteenth century and early twentieth century. In his essay, "*Lone Wolf* and Du Bois for a New Century: Intersections of Native American and African American Literatures," Warrior laments the facile comparisons that are sometimes made between Native American and African American experiences and calls instead for a careful method of conducting comparative work in the field of Native American studies. Offering this essay on the intellectuals W. E. B. Du Bois, Charles Eastman, Luther Standing Bear, and others as a possible model, Warrior constructs a comparative analysis of black and Native intellectuals and their views on racial uplift through education after first establishing the distinct turn-of-the-twentieth-century historical context for Native America. He concludes that while oppositional discourses existed in both the African American community and the Native American community, these discourses took subtle and unexpected forms in the writings and oral expressions of Native people.

In "Native Americans, African Americans, and the Space That Is America: Indian Presence in the Fiction of Toni Morrison," the literature scholar Virginia Kennedy offers an evocative, original reading of three of Morrison's major works. In conversation with the literary criticism of R. Radhakrishnan, Renee Bergland, Sharon Holland, and others, Kennedy explores *Song of Solomon*, *Beloved*, and *Paradise* to trace the contours of a third space in which African American and Native American experience meet. She finds not only that this space is embedded in the landscape and an intersecting history of dispossession, but also that the American nation cannot be at peace until it fully owns the atrocities committed against African slaves and indigenous peoples. Toni Morrison, Kennedy argues, is a writer uniquely conscious of the lasting imprint of the past on the present and the critical importance of American Indian nations, spirits, and lands to African American remembrance and resistance.

Tamara Buffalo (Ojibwe) is one of several select visual artists whose work was exhibited at the Two Rivers Gallery in the 1999 Minneapolis-based Intermedia Arts series "Red and Black: Sisters and Brothers to the Bone." In her personal essay reprinted here, "Knowing All of My Names," Buffalo describes her journey of self-realization through the discovery of her Ojibwe birth family and African ancestry and through the eventual naming of contested aspects of her multifaceted self. She expresses both the pains and pleasures of embodying an identity that deviates from expected monoracial, monocultural norms. In her accompanying pieces of visual art, *A Blind I Can C* (mixed media) and *The Singer* (acrylic on canvas), Buffalo interprets stereotyped images of black and Native people in tandem and creates her own icon of personal renewal and cultural connectedness by embracing the image of the mask.

The performance artist and literary critic Wendy S. Walters provides a groundbreaking examination of two First Nations Canadian plays in her essay, "After the Death of the Last: Performance as History in Monique Mojica's *Princess Pocahontas and The Blue Spots*." Placing performance at the center of her inquiry, Walters attempts to coin a new kind of performance theory that she terms "performance of history." In her fascinating effort, Walters asserts that "performances of history are didactic representations of past public events and human affairs that address the intricacies of the human experience typically not accounted for in written history or folklore." Given the reshaping of colonial events through creative narratives, Walters argues, the very concept of "diaspora" for Indian and black peoples is substantially challenged and revised through performative work. Evaluating the work of the Native playwright Monique Mojica (*Pocahontas and the Blue Spots*) while bringing in the texts of the African American playwright Suzan-Lori Parks as a point of comparison, Walters draws connections and contrasts between Native and African American histories of racism and colonialism and collective and individual identities. Her essay makes a significant contribution to the field of performance studies by challenging prevailing ideas in performance theory while simultaneously offering persuasive explications of primary texts that illustrate the shifting landscape of the personal and the political.

The next essay, by the anthropologist Robert Keith Collins (Choctaw), is an ethnographer's look at life-history interviews with Afro-Choctaws that draws out the critical themes of cultural acquisition, identity formation, and socialization. In *"Katimih o Sa Chata Kiyou* (Why Am I Not Choctaw)? Race in the Lived Experiences of Two Black Choctaw Mixed-Bloods," Collins poses the following central question: What happens when understandings of social viability in U.S. culture are multifaceted: split between race and culture? After conducting a two-year study with Choctaws of multiracial ancestry, Collins discovered that many interviewees defined their own identity formation by recounting verbal interactions with their Choctaw grandmothers. Collins's relentless analytical pursuit of this phenomenon redirects the accusation of the "Indian-grandmother complex" that is often hurled at mixed-race Afro-Native people who claim Native forebears and arrives at a new possibility for theories and practices of Indian identification (Deloria 1969, 3). In the end, Collins insists on a dynamic concept of the self — one in which processes of identity formation are interrelated and therefore not homogeneous; one in which "life strategies — like those from *sapoki anumpa* — are used to answer the question, "Who am I?"

Competing identities and nationalities converge in the provocative essay by the literary scholar ku'ualoha ho'omnawanui (Native Hawaiian), titled "From Ocean to O-shen: Reggae, Rap, and Hip Hop in

Hawai'i." From the perspective of a composer-poet, ho'omnawanui traces the growth of contemporary Hawaiian music in the last decade of the twentieth century, with a focus on its incorporation of Afro-diasporic musical forms and sensibilities. ho'omnawanui offers a cultural-studies critique that interprets the development and lyrics of the music, as well as the aims of its producers, and shows that hip hop and reggae are put to new artistic, social, and political uses within a Hawaiian context. "From Ocean to O-shen" includes a methodological mix of analyses of creative sound producers, audience response, and radio-station production to arrive at its primary conclusion. ho'omnawanui cautions scholars and consumers against a facile reading of contemporary cultures, especially where nations and borders are concerned. For this chapter, borrowing or sampling may or may not apply, as African and Native cultures move together and at the same time apart, on a simultaneous and parallel journey in which genre, language, and culture meet but do not melt.

In the short story, "Heartbreak," the poet and literary scholar Roberta Hill (Oneida) narrates the psychic life of losing and leaving as a woman witnesses her sister's disintegration after a painful breakup. As the narrator recalls, "She was balancing on the edge of catastrophe, unimaginable and deadening, the catastrophe of our colonization." "Heartbreak" is both poignant and humorous. It finds breath and life in the space between nations, peoples, marriages, and love affairs. Hill's narrative enfolds micro-fictive elements as it travels in the space of an afternoon but depends on lengthy histories, personal and national, to tell more than one story. As it mines the provocative boundary between stereotype and authenticity, "Heartbreak" provides another opportunity for literary scholars to explicate the connection between Indian and black peoples, especially in terms of gender. In the end, the women are "*bloka*, ready for anything, anything at all."

The concluding chapter is by Robert Warrior (Osage), whose epilogue reflects on issues raised by the collection — namely, the themes of place, loss, sadness, silence, ambiguity, instability, and the continual movement and transformation of blacks and Indians and their interrelations.

In the pages that follow, we have attempted to assemble an array of interdisciplinary contributions that illustrate the long history, as well as the cultural and political importance, of African diasporic experience in

Indian locales and of African and Native American intersectional lives. These scholarly and creative works investigate the permutations of historical interaction between Indians and blacks; the complex identities, cultural formations, memories, and aesthetic creations that arose out of those histories; and the reverberations of these historical exchanges and productions in contemporary African American, Native American and Native Hawaiian, and Afro-Native subjectivities, cultures, and communities. The historical chapters take up critical themes in African American studies and African diaspora studies in the context of Native American places, examining slavery, racialization, migration, displacement, the quest for belonging, the struggle for emancipation, and the battle for citizenship. The chapters of literary explication show the meaning of Indians in the African American imaginary, the intersectional nature of colonialism and racism in the Native American imaginary, and the contested terrain of Afro-Native narrative self-representation. The chapters on identity, both claimed and disclaimed, reveal the fluidity and complexities of Afro-Native subjectivities and performances thereof. The original fiction, visual art, and interpretations of contemporary music point the way toward establishing a new aesthetic capable of envisioning the transformation and even combination of seemingly disparate cultures. And all of these works explore conditions in which key issues in black experience confront similarly key issues in Native experience—namely, the designation and defense of a people and a homeland, the creation and protection of independent cultural ways, and the assertion of political dignity and autonomy.

Notes

1 Springplace Mission Diary 1811 (McClinton, forthcoming).
2 Ibid. 1807.
3 Ibid.
4 Ibid. 1816; letter dated July 22, 1806, Spring Place Letters, Cherokee Mission Papers, Moravian Archives, Winston-Salem, N.C.
5 Spring Place Diary, 1802, and letter dated July 22, 1806, both in Cherokee Mission Papers, Moravian Archives, Winston-Salem, N.C.
6 Springplace Mission Diary 1811 (McClinton, forthcoming); emphasis added.
7 For more on the enslaved black community of the James and Joseph Vann plantation of the Cherokee Nation (Diamond Hill), see Miles 2005; Perdue 1979.

8 The intellectual project of African American studies has been enriched by a revived transatlantic focus, which allows for comparative analyses of black populations, documents a vast array of survival strategies and cultural formations, traces retentions of Africanisms, and considers the cultural consistencies and inconsistencies that have made the peoples and cultures of the African diaspora cultural kin and at the same time strangers. But while de-centering the United States and adopting the particular paradigm of the black Atlantic has breathed new life, theoretical acumen, and political urgency into the field of black studies, it has also produced new invisibilities. The focus on the Atlantic Ocean diverts attention from other critical sites of cultural formation and exchange, such as the Indian Ocean, the Mediterranean Sea, the Pacific Ocean, and the lands of Latin America (Byfield 2000, 2001; Chrisman et al. 2000, 3; Kelley 2000, 33). In addition to overlooking black diasporic sites and experiences in these regions, the resurgent field of African diaspora studies has consistently neglected a salient location at the heart of the Atlantic world: indigenous lands, communities, and nations across the Americas. These Native American locales might be described as "third space[s]" of African diasporic displacement, as Michelle Wright (2004, 7) employs the term, which are the original homes neither of colonizing whites nor of captured blacks. Furthermore, just as the study of black experiences in locations as diverse as the United States and the Caribbean crosses and collapses national boundaries in keeping with a transnational, comparative frame, the study of black experiences in the Indian nations of the Americas crosses and collapses national boundaries. The populations and governments of Native America recognize themselves as separate peoples and independent nations and are recognized by the (post)colonial governments of the United States, Mexico, and Canada as distinct political entities and cultural bodies. As states within states, Native nations are prime locations for the study of the phenomenon that the historian Earl Lewis (1999, 5) has called "overlapping diasporas" or "dispersed communities," in which black peoples who have undergone a series of displacements have created multifaceted cultures and identities.

9 It is also a goal of this book to expand the conversation about African and Native American interaction and exchange beyond the fields of American Indian history and ethnohistory and into the fields of African American studies and American studies. Much of the academic work on relations between African Americans and Native Americans published since the 1970s has been produced by scholars of American Indian history. Primary examples are Brooks 1998, 2002; Forbes 1993; Littlefield 1977; Merrell 1984; Perdue 1979; Saunt 2005; and Wright 1981.

Few major works of this recent body of scholarship originated with scholars of black studies, American studies, or comparative ethnic studies, with the notable exceptions of Brennan 2003, one of few texts that presents frameworks for the study of an Afro-Native literary tradition; Holland 1994; Katz 1986, a foundational book in this field though geared to young adult readers; May 1996; Miles 2005; and Porter 1996.

10 See Porter, 1932, 1933; Woodson 1920.

11 Miranda Joseph (2002) offers a brilliant critique of "community."

12 For more on Native American themes and images in Alice Walker's work, see Brennan 2003, esp. 31–32. See also Riley 2003.

13 For more on Native American themes and images in Toni Morrison's work, see Virginia Kennedy's essay in this volume and Pasquaretta 2003.

CHAPTER ONE

A Harbor of Sense

An Interview with Joy Harjo

EUGENE B. REDMOND

~~~~~~~~~~

In early spring of 2004, Eugene B. Redmond, African American poet, editor of Drumvoices Revue, *and professor of English at Southern Illinois University, Edwardsville, invited the adventurous Creek poet and musician Joy Harjo to speak with students in his "Literature of the Third World" course. During her visit to the campus, Harjo conversed with Redmond about music, poetry, land theft, Indian-African camaraderie, rhythm, and the spirit.*

Eugene B. Redmond: [We're] on Interstate 255; we've just left East Saint Louis and are heading north, past the historic Cahokia Mounds. I'm fortunate enough to be chauffeuring sister and poet, musician, visual artist, storyteller, repository of ancestral wisdom, and walker of "ancestrail" Joy Harjo.

Joy, you've taken on other mantles or burdens — healthy, artistic burdens, if you will, since I last saw you. There's your music, all the awards that you've won; the professorships; the endless list of publications; the moving about and the soul journeying across this nation and the globe. So what do you feel you've wrought? What things stand out for you?

Joy Harjo: Right now, what shines is my experience yesterday at Miles Davis Elementary School. I was excited about being in Miles Davis country. His trumpet sound is indelible in my music memory. I always remember when I was about the age of some of the youngest students, how his horn came through the car radio, to the outside, around and inside of me as I stood on the floorboard, perched behind my father who smelled of Old Spice. I traveled freely in that sound into the future, beyond the body. When I returned, I was a kid standing behind her father in Oklahoma, in his car bought with what was left of his family's Creek Indian oil money.

I thought of all this as we drove to the school, and of how Miles's horn was one of the only trumpets I've ever really loved. Most are too raucous and brassy. I was pretty jetlagged and had no idea what in the world I was going to do when I walked into the school. Then there we were in an auditorium full of little children, beautiful little children, and that's really what the music is really all about—those beautiful souls. I could see some of them had already been through hell; many were still shining and open, and most had a lot of questions. I was impressed by their willingness to sing and improvise.

I'll always remember one young man, so focused, watched every nuance, hearing every sound—a young Miles Davis there. So that's really what it's about.

I've had a lot of opportunities in this passing fast life, and I've also failed a lot along the way. Anytime I'm introduced with a long recounting of my accomplishments, I mention my resume of failures, which [is] many, many times longer. The list would go out the door, and the ink would be fresh. The trick is using the stuff of failures to construct something beautiful. Miles did that with his horn: took the nastiness of racism and braided it into songs.

Redmond: Do any of those [failures] come to mind, and are they of any value to our discussion?

Harjo: Oh, sure. I used to have terrible stage fright. My first musical performance, I panicked—just stopped playing. Never did pick the horn back up. When I left the stage, I was shaking with shame and humiliation. After I calmed down, I told myself I had a choice. I could learn to get past it, or I didn't have to get on stage with a horn ever again. There was a choice. So every time after that, I took my horn with me and played, even just a lick or two. I'm sure I was horrible. But I kept at it.

I also learned a huge lesson by watching Faye Carol, a wonderful jazz singer who lives and works out of the [San Francisco] Bay area. We were in a performance of songs by Carolyn Brandy. I had a little eight-bar solo, along with a reading part. The reading was easy. I imagined failing the horn part over and over again, so guess what happened in the first rehearsal: I played out of tune, out of time, and nothing that made sense. There's nothing like the stab of utter failure. I wanted to run and almost did. Faye didn't say anything; neither did I. She just let me be. I realized that I had programmed myself for failure. So I turned it around, slowly, and had another rehearsal to redeem myself. Then, the night of the performance I watched Faye. What I learned from . . . her that night as I watched and listened is that she was totally inside the music, and the music was about sharing with the audience, being *with* them and *inside* the music. I'd been so worried about being perfect, I'd quit hearing the music. It was about serving the music, the audience. Maybe some people wouldn't relate to this at all. But it was my experience, and I offer it because it could help someone who's going through it now.

I've had to learn how to listen. That was one of poetry's first lessons to me, too. And poetry continues to teach me. Rewrites and revisions aren't failure; they're part of the process. I also think about the difference of being inside my native culture, where music isn't a spectator sport; rather, everyone sings. Music, art, dance belong to everyone, and everyone is involved in it. It's in the house, not just on CDs, computers, or radios. So much has changed and is changing. . . . In the earliest years, my favorites were Nat King Cole, Patsy Cline, Ray Charles, and Hank Williams. Later, [they were] the Four Tops and other Motown groups.

Redmond: You've spoken several times of your grandmother who played the saxophone. Can you say a little bit about that, and was that in the back of your mind when you took up the saxophone? Did you know, for example, since you were little that your grandmother played saxophone?

Harjo: Yes, my grandmother Naomi Harjo played the sax in Indian Territory at the turn of the century. She was Indian, female, and thus blows away (literally and figuratively) stereotypes of native women and music. . . . We're not even seen as musicians! I didn't know she was a horn player until after I'd been playing sax for a few years. My Creek-Seminole cousin from Holdenville, Oklahoma, told me about her, even tried to locate her old saxophone for me.

Redmond: John Jacobs?

Harjo: That was his name. He was a father figure to me. He was a cousin but more like an uncle; he was one of the people in the world who loved me without question. I've taken my saxophone everywhere to practice, including the stomp grounds of my tribal town there. I wasn't given much encouragement when I started learning. For one, I was in my late thirties, usually considered too late to start something new, and I had a poetry career. So why was I muddying it up or ruining it or distracting myself with the saxophone, everyone would question. I have a wonderful mentor and translator from Italy who took me aside and said, as anyone in her position would say (especially after hearing my early horn practices), "Why are you doing this? You are a poet. That's your gift." My head knew it didn't make sense. My heart knew better. Common sense went with my head. My bravado went to the horn. But I've always known that poetry did not come into the world by itself. Poetry came in with music on one arm and dance on the other; they came in together. They remain together in our root indigenous cultures, whether we're from this continent or Africa or South America or Australia or Europe. I picked up the saxophone because I wanted to sing. The horn sounds like a human voice, a crying and laughing human voice. Poetry on the page wasn't enough for me. The horn was a way to allow myself to sing.

It's amazing to think of grandmother playing horn. I never got to meet her. She died right after my father was born. She was an older mother, and I always had the sense that this life didn't make sense to her. I was close to her sister, my great-aunt Lois Harjo. Both Lois and my grandmother were painters. I have paintings by both of them in my home. The one by my grandmother is a three-quarters life-size of Osceola, who is still admired by us. On behalf of his people, the Seminole, he never surrendered to the U.S. government. Most people don't know that his mother was Creek. She painted it in 1916. By then, Oklahoma had become a state. In her short lifetime, she watched much of the land promised in perpetuity west of the Mississippi of the Creek Nation stolen. Oklahoma will be celebrating the land run soon, which was a theft of Indian lands. The state calls itself the "Sooner State." A sooner is someone who stole ahead of the others, lining up to stake land claims before the others. The state still glorifies the sooner. So to paint Osceola in this time was to make a major statement.

Redmond: Are there specific ways in which the music has changed or reconfigured your approach to poetry outside of the collaborations within yourself, between the various genres that you express yourself in? [Are there] ways music has altered you as a poet?

Harjo: I think so. I've been considering how this change has been an ongoing process with tribal music as well as my own sensibility of music as I move between this outside world and the inside world of my tribal ceremonial grounds. I wonder what our music was like before the arrival of European governments (we dealt with Spain, France, England, and now the United States) and Africans. The movement of our stomp dances is around the fire, counterclockwise. I understand that is the direction of dances in some of the West African tribes who were forced here. I can imagine camaraderie between our peoples. We provided a harbor of sense. Early on, though, the connection between Africans and Indians was broken by fearful state governments. They realized that if the Africans and Indians got together, they'd be fiercely outnumbered. Georgia was the first state to make a law against fraternization. But when I hear our music, I always think of Africa announcing itself as part of the mix. And it also goes the other way. The root of blues, rock, and jazz is around that stomp-dance fire, too, and it's never, ever mentioned. One day, the saxophone will be a Mvskoke (Creek) traditional instrument. That's how these things work! So all that's at the root of my sense of music and poetry. And at the root of that is rhythm. And rhythm is at the root of form and sense in this earthly world, maybe in all the worlds. It holds the physical body together, literally. In fact, rhythm holds the whole world together. Rhythm and vibration hold it together.

Redmond: Can you talk about the project that is currently under way — the new CD, *Native Joy for Real*?

Harjo: Yeah, *Native Joy for Real*. The CD has been in the works since sometime after the last one I did, the *Poetic Justice* CD, which was released by Silver Wave in '97. It's been quite a ride. Not long after the *Poetic Justice* CD, I left Albuquerque to be a visiting writer at the University of California, Los Angeles. [I] kept doing gigs with the band. Then, after nine months in L.A., [I] moved to Hawai'i. That basically ended the band. It would have ended anyway, because most of the band members were involved in a native reggae band with Skeme Garcia called Native Roots, and they were heavy into reggae. I wasn't. I love and appreciate Bob Marley but wanted a music that blended from my musical loves. I also wanted music I could dance to, a blend I haven't heard before. Since I didn't know exactly how to say it, it was difficult to translate. I kept performing the old *Poetic Justice* stuff with one of the original PJ band members, Richard Carbajal, then added and subtracted other players. We made one attempt to record a couple of songs, but it fell apart; [it] wasn't working. Richard has the band the Caribbean Cruisers in Phoenix. I then worked and practiced on my own, decided to not go out with a band for about a year until I got new material put together. Then [I] was led to an independent studio in L.A. It was disastrous. I lost a year's worth of work. But now I'm thankful for it, because from that I learned what I didn't want and had to turn back inside. Also, Band-in-the-Box, Garage Band, and my little Bose recorder helped me construct the shape and feel of this next CD. Recently, I premiered some of the new tunes in Vancouver, with Mary Redhouse. We were very well received. It was the first band gig where I've felt the music was my soul. I could be inside it, dance around in it, fly. How to describe it? It's hard to categorize, really. That's both positive and negative. There's really no easy place to fit it in when selling it in a music store. I guess it most often gets put in American Indian, Native American, yet it's not just that. The poetry in the last album made it a harder sell, but this is mostly singing, with some poetry. Responses have included [that it] sounds like Sade. That's the horn and voice. Other people have mentioned Suzanne Vega. Again voice. I mix hip-hoppish kinds of loops with native rhythms and sounds. People hear the saxophone, and they say jazz. I love jazz, but I know jazz well enough to know better than to call myself a jazz player. I'll improvise sometimes, but I'm not really in a straight tradition of jazz. Non-jazzers say, jazz. And there's the native music influence, from my tribe and others. I've called it, in the past, tribal jazz.

Redmond: What drives you to be on the road? What do you get out of it?

Harjo: Sometimes I wonder. I guess what pushes me are events like that class this morning, seeing those students and knowing that my place is to bring certain ideas together for pollination. I'm just the crafter of the place of the poem or song so the spirit can have a place to live. . . . There's part of me that would just like to hide out. I'd rather hang out and converse with mystery than be running to catch airplanes. But, you know, that's just part of it. . . . That's part of the job.

CHAPTER TWO

An/Other Case of New England Underwriting

Negotiating Race and Property in *Memoirs of Elleanor Eldridge*

JENNIFER D. BRODY and SHARON P. HOLLAND

~~~~~~~~~~

The question of the archive is not, we repeat, a question of the past. . . .
It is a question of the future.
—JACQUES DERRIDA (1998, 36)

Archive Fever

The publication of *Memoirs of Elleanor Eldridge* in 1838 marked a significant moment in the (re)production of Afro-Native subjectivity. Written by the distinguished Rhode Island resident Frances Harriet Whipple Green MacDougall (1805–78), the text chronicles the life, toils, and legal wranglings of one Elleanor Eldridge (1784–1865?),[1] a black and native freewoman who was a whitewasher, weaver, dairymaid, and entrepreneur.[2] Fifteen years Eldridge's junior, Frances Whipple "identified with her subject at some psychological level, despite their difference in color and class. Each of them lost a parent early in life and was forced by adverse circumstances to earn her own livelihood. In girlhood, both Frances and Elleanor worked very hard and were recognized as high achievers. As adults, they supported themselves as independent single women during an age when women's ordained social position was considered to be one of dependency on men" (O'Dowd 2004, 21). This chapter offers up Eldridge's memoirs, written by Whipple, as a text whose premise is the promise of collaboration. As such, we are aware of certain parallels between this narrative, rewritten in the here and now, and that earlier text that was conceived as a kind of insurance/underwriting for Eldridge's future. Thus, we begin our engagement with the Whipple text by remembering again that representation is an open(ing) process.

Indeed, eight editions of *Memoirs* were published between 1838 and 1847.[3] During the various publication cycles of the narrative, Whipple would marry (1842) and divorce (1847) her first husband, Charles Green, making her an anomaly in the "Victorian" society of Rhode Island. Despite the paucity of critical attention to Eldridge's narrative, both *Memoirs of Elleanor Eldridge* (1838) and *Elleanor's Second Book* (1839) were reprinted and widely read in the mid-nineteenth century (O'Dowd 2004, 19).[4] The first and only scholar to write a full-length biography of Whipple, Sarah O'Dowd notes that the text of Eldridge's *Memoirs* "can be read not only as a biographical narrative, but also as a literary text" (O'Dowd 2004, 21). The particulars of the literary text are indeed intriguing, if only because their drama is so dependent on one detail of her *Memoirs* that intrigues the contemporary Whipple and piques the interest of her twenty-first-century explicators.

Early in the account of Eldridge's life, Whipple reports that "[h]er maternal grandmother, Mary Fuller, was a native Indian, belonging to the small tribe, or clan, called the Fuller family; which was probably a portion of the Narragansett tribe. Certain it is that this tribe, or family, once held great possessions in large tracts of land; with a portion of which Mary Fuller purchased her husband Thomas Prophet; who, until his marriage, had been a slave" (Whipple 1838, 20). This detail about Eldridge's mixed heritage not only fuels Whipple's scripting of Eldridge's life but also provides the nexus for our investigation.[5] Was Eldridge, heralded as one of Rhode Island's most notable *African American* citizens,[6] also of Native descent? This question posed additional queries for us: how to speak to the life of someone who acknowledged, at least to Whipple, her dual heritage? What shape would such an exploration take? How to conduct such research without falling into the quagmire of racial and ethnic authenticity without justifying ideologies such as blood quantum?[7]

Black and Indian passages in New England have been painstakingly articulated in the work of scholars such as Jean O'Brien, Daniel R. Mandell, and Ann McMullen. In particular, McMullen reads C. Matthew Snipp's catalogue of census data and concludes that "descent [in the twentieth century] may be more important than tribal membership for many" (McMullen 2002, 269) who identify as American Indian.[8] In other words, an investigation of Eldridge's communication to Whipple *and* Whipple's interpretation of her ancestry recalls ongoing debates in contemporary scholarship on multicultural, ethnic, cultural, and racial communities. McMullen writes that "intermarriage has reduced the importance of blood quantum somewhat, and being Indian is now more often seen as a matter of descent and community participation, or blood and culture" (McMullen 2002, 269). Mandell's research indicates that the contemporary perception of "Indianness" had its complicated and complicating precedent in attitudes among those who intermarried in southern New England between 1760 and 1880, the period in which Eldridge's African grandfather and Indian grandfather saw their grandchildren move into the eighteenth century. Moreover, Mandell's research exposes the "fundamental flaws of a bichromatic view of racial relations in American history" by offering complicated readings of changing relations among intimately interrelated people such as the Narragansett, the Irish, and African Americans.[9]

O'Dowd contextualizes Fuller's marriage to Thomas Prophet by writing that their union was "a type of interracial alliance that was not unusual at that time. Narragansett women tended to see African-American men as more desirable husbands to Narragansett men, who looked upon hunting as their proper work and thought it beneath them to help women in the home" (O'Dowd 2004, 22). O'Dowd cites no scholarly source for her claims about the Narragansett people, and about Narragansett men in particular. Moreover, her account rehearses stereotypical perceptions about the innate motivations of Indian men and their female counterparts. O'Brien finds that "some Indians [of Natick] found African American spouses by the mid-eighteenth century. . . . Indian women with African American husbands seem to have been more common, which seems logical given the apparent decline in the male Indian population, coupled with the demography of African American slavery in New England" (O'Brien 1997a, 201). Mandell concurs, offering that, in eastern Massachusetts, "in the wake of the colonial wars, an increasing percentage of Indians within and without the refuges were the 'mixt posterity' of intermarriages, as many widows and young women found African American husbands" (Mandell 1996, 165).[10] In noting the phenomenon of intermarriage, scholars offer an array of causes: tensions between enslaved and freed subjects in New England, demographic pressures caused by British occupation during the Revolutionary War, forced consignment onto seafaring vessels, and shifting legal and rhetorical ideologies about land ownership and Native sovereignty.

At issue, as well, are prevailing attitudes toward "land" and community that work to define what it means to be Indian as much as what it means to *belong* to Indian communities, a controversy that persists into the twenty-first century. For Indian women in particular, O'Brien notes that "individuals could no longer count on thick networks of relatives to care for them when they were in need of shelter, sustenance, or support" (O'Brien 1997b, 151). The result was that, in the early to mid-eighteenth century, Indian women who relied on the care of white patrons often liquidated their land holdings to "pay" for their care. In *Dispossession by Degrees*, O'Brien remarks on a complex negotiation of land and Indian identity in Natick, Massachusetts, as she simultaneously marks the obstacles for the researcher:

> Indian individuals and families responded variously to the contest of cultures in Natick. Many of them used their land resources in English ways, selling off parcels of land, building English-style farms, furnishing frame houses with English goods. However, in doing so, they managed to perpetuate their families and retain claim to their place even though they no longer enjoyed exclusive occupancy of the land. . . . Telling stories about Native peoples whose lives have long been obscured, marginalized, and erased from histories of colonial New England involves a fair amount of detective work, and at least as much frustration when terse documentary evidence fails to answer pressing questions. . . . Even when relatively abundant, it never answers all the questions that need explication. (O'Brien 1997a, 126)

At the onset — for us, at least — the most important and enduring question was more practical in nature: How to document through existing archives, Eldridge's claim that her grandmother was indeed an "Indian." While O'Dowd and other scholars do an adequate job of articulating the particulars of Eldridge's life, they often take Whipple's account of her *genealogy* at face value, assuming that Eldridge's redaction of her grandmother's tribal affiliation is correct.[11] As O'Brien insists, the evidence (even when overwhelming) is spotty and does not answer; rather, it often poses more questions. Since Eldridge's maternal grandmother was born and married before the first federally sponsored census in 1790, and unions between people of color were recorded haphazardly in county record books, tracing the eighteenth-century life of the Prophet–Fuller union proves difficult.

When we began work on this project, we had archive fever, to gloss Derrida: We wanted to "find" Mary Fuller. And find her we did—in a record book for the Six Principle Baptist Church in an entry dated October 18, 1753, Warwick, Rhode Island:[12]

> Wee whose names are hereunto subscribed being members of the Church of Christ in Warwick formerly under the pastoral care of Elder Martin and Elder Hammett and Elder Martain [*sic*] by reason of old age and other infirmities is so impaired both in body and mind that he is not capable of serving of us as an Elder and Elder Hammett being taken from us by death so that wee are not in capacity to act as a Church and therefore have concluded to put our selves under the pastoral care of Elder John Gorton until such time it may please God to raise up another Elder amongst us or wee be otherwise provided for as it may please God to order for us.[13]

There are twenty-three witnesses to the changing of the guard at the Six Principle Baptist Church, among them is "MARY FULLER INDIAN."[14]

No other scholars of Eldridge's narrative have unearthed such a signatory, and we were elated at such "proof of life." We had an indication (but certainly, no *proof*) that Mary Fuller (Indian) did exist and in the time period in which Eldridge's narrative places her. Whipple's account of Eldridge's familial diaspora places an aunt in Adams, Massachusetts, a clear indication that the Eldridge–Prophet union encompassed relations in both states. While we cannot ascertain Mary Fuller's tribal affiliation, we can surmise that she might be related to Narragansett, Mashpee, Pequot, Wampanoag, or Nipmuc peoples, with the Narragansett, given Whipple's scripting noted earlier in our essay, as the most logical affiliation. Present scholarship on colonial New England supports this contention. As Colin Calloway remarks, "The diaspora of New England peoples that began with King Philip's War [1675–76] continued in its aftermath. Indians from New England migrated north and west, mingling with other tribes and building new communities" (Calloway 1997, 6). Furthermore, the imbrication of black and Indian identities and communities served another purpose in official Rhode Island records. As Ruth Wallis Herndon and Ella Wilcox Sekatau conclude, "The evidence points to a deliberate redesignation of native people as Negro or black, as officials replaced cultural description with physical description" (Herndon and Sekatau 1997, 127). Radically speaking, such a "redesignation" interpolates the "record" as the quintessential modern tool for genocide.

Significantly, what we had was a church record rather than a document generated by a state or federal agent or agency — documents that routinely truncate surnames and identify individuals according to the whim of the agent rather than the desire of the subject being read and inscribed. Preliminary research also unearthed an oral history of Lincoln Farm, now T. F. Green Airport in Providence, but formerly the place where peoples of African and Indian descent are reported to have lived together. Whipple notes that Eldridge's grandmother, "having witnessed the departing glories of her tribe, died in extreme old age, at the house of her son, Caleb Prophet; being 102 years old. She was buried at Thomas Green burying place in Warwick, in the year 1780" (Whipple 1838, 20). As with many nineteenth-century New Englanders, Whipple was inclined to believe that native populations were simultaneously witnessing "departing glories" and a kind of vanishing, a discourse that met with substantial revision in Americanist scholarship produced during the late twentieth century.[15] A search of the historic graveyards of Providence and Warwick, Rhode Island turned up no such burial ground, but a trip to the outskirts of the airfield did yield historic cemetery number 31. While there is no evidence to suggest that Mary Fuller is buried in cemetery number 31, we suspect that her gravesite might be unmarked and on or near airport property.

Literary Labors

In light of these twenty-first-century archival findings, consider the Library of Congress subheadings under which Elleanor Eldridge's 1838 narrative *Memoirs of Elleanor Eldridge*[16] are given to us: African-American — Rhode Island — Social conditions — 19th century. Absent from these subheadings are New England Women, Laborers, Courts, and Narragansett Peoples. In contrast to twenty-first-century bibliographic nomenclature, the text was introduced to its contemporary readers by classifying them as "the feeling and humane," in particular, "the colored population" who then become "the colored people [who] will be proud to assist in sustaining one, who is both an honor and an ornament to their race" (Whipple 1838, 3). Hers is a life that has "merit" (Whipple 1838, 3); hers is a body that is still "valuable to her numerous employers" (Whipple 1838, 6). While the brief preface to Eldridge's story is by no means unique — Eldridge's situation is akin to that of Philis Wheatley's male signature — the politics of patronage are written literally all over the body of the text.[17] In addition, like her transatlantic "sister" (of Caribbean Afro-Native descent) Mrs. Seacole, who wrote *The Wonderful Adventures of Mrs. Seacole in Many Lands* ([1857] 1988), Eldridge sought economic stability via the publication and distribution of her book after her property had been confiscated.

What brings the contemporary reader to this somewhat quotidian text is its introduction — and, perhaps, its laboring author. A. G. Dorrance, one of Eldridge's many supporters in the first narrative, states her objective in the following manner: "The object in publishing her life is to help raise a sum of money which MUST BE PAID, or she never can clear her property from its present incumbrance [*sic*]" (Whipple 1838, 7). In brief, through her industriousness Eldridge was able to secure property in Providence, according to Whipple, sometime in 1822. While on the way to visit family in Adams, Massachusetts, where Eldridge's maternal aunt lived on the western edge of the state line, she became ill and postponed her journey for a few days. Rumor of her illness reached Providence, where the sheriff, William Brayton Mann, seized the property and swiftly sold it to Benjamin Balch after circulating a rumor of Eldridge's death.[19] As Whipple writes, "Like a gathering snow-ball, [the story] grew as it went the rounds of gossip, into exceedingly dangerous illness — to the point of death; and finally, by the simple process of accumulation, it was resolved into death itself" (Whipple 1838, 72). O'Dowd finds that Whipple's recounting of the events is both "inconsistent with Court Records and as a literal record of history, problematic" (O'Dowd, 2004, 27). Our aim here is not to correct the "historic record," as Court of Common Pleas (CCP) documents indicate that preserving the "record" of events was far from the goal of social actors of the time. Instead, what we find are warrants, deeds, and summonses but no transcriptions or testimonies given on behalf of either plaintiff or defendant. CCP clerks were far more diligent in the recording of court costs than they were in documenting its proceedings.[19]

The *mystery* of how Eldridge's property became encumbered provides the impetus for the reader's curiosity, as the laboring identity of the main protagonist (Elleanor) provides for both the success of labor and its absolute failure. Resembling the story Barbara Ehrenreich tells in *Nickel and Dimed: On (Not) Getting By in America* (2001), it is impossible for this woman, who "may be found, daily at work, from sun-rise until sun-set for good wages" to make ends meet without "the assistance of friends to humanity and justice" (Whipple 1838, 7). So like Tennessee Williams's Blanche DuBois, she must rely on "the kindness of strangers." Ultimately, this book (the first of two) — another kind of labor altogether — fails. In the next year (1839), Whipple published *Elleanor's Second Book*, which was also undersigned by a portion of the elite white female population of Providence, who "cheerfully give our individual and united testimony, in favor of Elleanor Eldridge, the proprietor of this little book, for the purpose of assisting her to extricate herself from the difficulties into which she has been plunged . . . (Green 1842, 5). Interestingly enough, *Elleanor's Second Book* is not opened or offered to the "colored population"; there is no mention of this group in the public address, undersigned by eleven women from Providence.[20] Instead, the appeal in the second book is made more urgent by the direct appeal "To the Public." The *mystery* surrounding Eldridge's loss of title to her land is unveiled abruptly with the words, "a singular series of misfortunes and wrongs . . . occasioned by men" (Green 1842, 5). In this second account, it is the women who are to rescue Eldridge from a patriarchal plot.

The public address continues by delineating the source of such wrongdoings that "were occasioned by men, who, taking advantage of her ignorance of business, and her situation as an unprotected colored woman, were instrumental in depriving her of a handsome estate" (Green 1842, 5). In this appeal for Eldridge's plight, the women close ranks and "call then, upon the benevolence, the charity, the justice of the community; and especially upon the female part of it" (Green 1842, 5). In less than a year, we move from a *raced* appeal to a *gendered* appeal. Gone is the appeal to the "colored population" of *Memoirs*. The failure is twofold: The first book as an enterprise fails to move Eldridge from a state of near indigence to solvency; the specific public that the book addresses, by association with the first endeavor, also fails to rise to the occasion. The call is issued, but there seems to be no response. It is now up to the "female part" to produce the capital necessary for Eldridge to retain her title.

The opening appeal in Eldridge's narrative brings together gender, race, property, and labor. What is at stake is ownership, as we learn that

Jennifer D. Brody and Sharon P. Holland

Drawing of Elleanor Eldridge: Flypiece to
1842 edition of *Elleanor's Second Book*
(authors' private collection). The drawing
was also published in the 1838 edition of
Memoirs of Elleanor Eldridge.

Eldridge has had her property taken from her by the felonious efforts of
three individuals: the local sheriff, a prominent gentleman of the community, and an auctioneer. But ownership also implies responsibility,
and Eldridge's almost superhuman industriousness, her hyper-respon-
sibility, is put on the market before two publics — gendered and raced
— who must endeavor to aid their stricken sister, who must labor for
her. The conditions of the narrative's publication and production are
tied to its various publics, all of whom *labor* under conditions of exchange in which property and identity make economic claims in both
senses of the term "economic."

Nothing better illustrates the connectedness of labor, property, and
identity than the opening flypiece of the 1838 text, which depicts a
rough drawing of Eldridge holding a broom upright in a singular

muscled arm that makes a fist around the broom's pole. She sports a simple white shawl, shortly shorn hair, and wide-set open eyes. Her stance, demeanor, and representation as a whole suggest her capacity for work and her determination in the face of adversity. In an important intervention into the discourse of the frontispiece, Lynn A. Casmier-Paz argues that "author portraits of slave narratives offer a representative likeness of former slaves in order to provide a graphic point of reference for the title characters. . . . The portraits become meaningful when readers bring to them an ability to read the signs of race and class, privilege, and bondage" (Casmier-Paz 2003, 91). The ideological and rhetorical function of slave portraiture is to produce a readable and authenticating narrative. While Eldridge's portrait is certainly not in the same genre of portraits of authors, Dorothy Sterling writes, "it was one of the earliest pictures of an Afro-American woman" (Sterling 1984, 90). What is most notable here is that the portrait is not engineered to illustrate " 'proof' of writing . . . as rhetorical strategy for the relocation of African being" (Casmier-Paz 2003, 97); Eldridge labors precisely because, as Whipple states, she could not write. For Whipple, the perpetually suffering and laboring Eldridge finds solace in "occupation, . . . the best remedy for sorrow" (Green 1842, 55).

Eldridge's portrait is one of the first of a free black woman in the early nineteenth century, and her laboring posture appears in *Memoirs* (1838) bookended by a portrait of Wheatley (1773) and a photograph of Sojourner Truth (1864), two of the most famous representations of black women. Eldridge's posture — as a laboring free "colored woman" — is repeated in another scene of valuing women's labor: The "We Can Do It" poster from the campaign for the recognition of women's contribution in the World War Two effort depicts the same forearm as evidence of women's capacity to work, women's strength, and women's resolve.[21] Might Eldridge's portrait — her proof of laboring capabilities and of labors lost — be the precursor to protofeminist portraiture of postwar women in the workplace?

(E)racing Elleanor

The second chapter of *Memoirs* introduces readers to Elleanor as someone upon whom "the wrongs and persecutions of both races [have] fallen" (Whipple 1838, 12). Whipple explains that, "on the one hand, [she] is the inheritress of African blood, with all of its heirship of wo and shame; and the subject of wrong and banishment by her Indian maternity on the other" (Whipple 1838, 11). Such a claim is made despite the fact that, leaving "questions of romance and love aside, blacks and Indians who married found mutual advantages" (Mandell 1998, 469). What is stunning here is how Eldridge, in the eyes of the writer of her biography, *becomes* black.

As stated in this chapter's opening section, Eldridge's paternal grandfather was a native African who "was induced, with his family, to come on board an American slaver, under pretence of trade" (Whipple 1838, 12). He had one daughter, Phillis, and three sons, Dick, George, and Robin; Robin was the father of Ellen.[22] At the commencement of the American Revolution, Robin Eldridge and his two brothers received an offer of freedom, with the promise of an additional premium of 200 acres of land apiece in the Mohawk country, as an inducement to enter the lists and do their duty as soldiers.[23] As they had no funds, they could not take possession of the land, which was never secured to them. Robin Eldridge settled in Fulling Mills, in Warwick, marrying and purchasing a small house and plot of land. He had nine children, of whom Ellen was the last of seven successive daughters.

Eldridge's "African blood" is held from her "Indian maternity" by two emotional spheres — "wo and shame" and "wrong and banishment," respectively. Her blackness is a matter of public record, as the chronicle of "wo and shame" is articulated to the reader as an absence, an assumption on the narrator's part that the interested public will know how to interpret "wo and shame." Her African blood makes her an "inheritress" and is produced as belonging to the public sphere, a place long thought to be inhabited by men. Indeed, Elleanor Eldridge's Africanness is given to her by her "paternal grandfather, . . . a native African" (Whipple 1838, 12), suturing her black inheritance to *two* fathers — her African grandfather and her biological father — rather than one, as opposed to her Narragansett lineage, which is circumscribed *solely* by the life of Mary Fuller. In the private sphere, her Indian maternity slumbers, a space from which she has been banished but a place that makes her "the subject of wrong" (Whipple 1838, 11). What she gets from her Indian mother is abjection, a state of being less than blood, while being African entitles her to an inheritance, albeit a beleaguered one. The familiarity of her "African" origins makes her legible to the reader by placing her in a generic genealogy popularized by tales such as that of Equiano.

The first story is that of Eldridge's paternal grandfather (Dick) — his tragic middle passage is rife with romantic and fecund imagery. Whipple's odd juxtaposition of his subjugation ("he stretched out his arms . . . in the agony of desperation") with a detailed description of flora and fauna in "his own beautiful Congo" not only paints a romantic picture, but also marks "the African's" rapidly receding homeland as a mixture of the real and the fantastic. Home, for "Dick," is always already *unreal and open* to another kind of mastery, both anthropological and biological. In the face of this fantastic challenge, Dick is someone whom Whipple believes still "felt and acted as a man" (Whipple 1838, 17). The seat of slavery's "wo and shame" is also reproduced as a masculine burden, as the plight of "Dick" is tied to the land and an enduring masculinity. In contrast, the unnamed female ancestor's rage is produced in the present in nineteenth-century language that is also stereotypical and familiar: "The wife was more violent. With the most fearful cries she flung herself at the captain's feet and embracing his knees, begged for mercy. Then successively she embraced her weeping children; and at last, sank exhausted into the arms of her husband" (Whipple 1838, 16). The scene produces a narrative fit for the often printed and circulated image of the supplicating black woman in chains.

The focus on a masculine narrative of "wo and shame," coupled with the outstanding issue of inheritance, is continued in the story of Eldridge's father and his brothers. In a homage to the three Eldridge men, Robin, Dick, and George, who fought in the American Revolution, where liberty was the goal and the premium, the added bonus would be "200 acres of land in the Mohawk country, apiece."[24] The companion narrative here — the memoirs' interstitial moment — is the part of Mohawk (Six Nations) history that documents this liberty as a loss. What makes this story of three brothers and their enslaved counterparts so compelling is what they leave behind: "They literally left footprints of blood upon the rough flint and the crusted snow" (Whipple 1838, 18). Blood makes a claim on the land that supersedes any title Mohawk peoples might have had to it. Furthermore, the three (African American?) brothers labor for "the pure air of liberty" alongside white men (Whipple 1838, 18). This allegiance further legitimates their claim to 600 acres of land in the Mohawk country, as it also produces *blood,* the substance of toil, which is shadowed by sacrifice and national be-longing. After the African blood narrates its legitimacy, "Elleanor's maternal ancestry" is relayed as "a glance" in the *Memoirs*. In the story of the three brothers, inheritance is put aside for the loftier goals of "FREEDOM" and "LIBERTY." The historian Benjamin Quarles finds that "the New England States, despite their relatively small Negro population, probably furnished more colored soldiers than any other section. . . . The Rhode Island First Regiment enrolled some two hundred Negroes" (Quarles 1961, 73). Enslaved blacks serving in the Revolutionary War "had difficulty in obtaining the land grants which had been promised them" (Quarles 1961, 200). In 1784, the Rhode Island General Assembly granted gradual emancipation to enslaved men who fought in the Revolutionary War.

Pursuing Elleanor

Hannah Prophet died when Eldridge was ten. The narrator moves through elaborate musings about "home" as she describes in sentimen-tal language suffused with affect how "little Elleanor" left her home in Warwick to work for the Baker family. Whipple even credits Eldridge with negotiating her own contract with the family.[25] Eldridge ventured forth as the perfect servant, especially where the animals were con-cerned, her grace with them attributed to "the sang froid of her Indian character" (Whipple 1838, 28). The biographer remarks, "Not only the family, but every living creature about the house and the farm, loved little Elleanor" (Whipple 1838, 29). Her first human/animal family paves the way for more admirers: All become smitten with Ele-anor. Whipple makes Eldridge both invincible and irresistible, a com-bination that follows the contours of a laboring and sexual subjectivity: "The new relation into which Elleanor had entered tended to produce mutual satisfaction to the parties sustaining it" (Whipple 1838, 26). As Eldridge makes the transition from a body bounded by a blood con-tract to a body bound by a labor contract, Whipple takes pains to articulate how "the serving and the served generally become identified; and the heart quickens and strengthens the hands in the performance of duty" (Whipple 1838, 27). Finally, this *new* relation is analogized as productive and reproductive, as the feeling parties engage in a "perfor-mance" that renders labor inconsequential as labor itself, as work.

The sexualized body of Eldridge proves too seductive for Whipple: "About the period of her nineteenth year, Elleanor became quite a belle; and her light foot in the dance, and her sweet voice in song, made her an object of great interest among the colored swains" (Whipple 1838, 31). Included among the enthralled is our narrator, who attempts to extract information about a particular suitor, only to have her desire frustrated by Eldridge's withholding of such information. Whipple remarks, "Sometimes, with a low, quick breath, — I could almost imagine it a sigh — she would say 'there was a young man — I had a cousin — he sent a great many letters.' But further our deponent saith not. Not a syllable more could I ever extract from her. I have asked her for the letters; which, being her veritable biographer, *I had a right to do*; but she always tells me they are in a great box, with all the accumulated weight of her household stuff resting upon them" (Whipple 1838, 31; emphasis added). The metaphor of the box, the letters, resting under "household stuff" again puts labor over love, even as Whipple reads them together. Whipple then promises, in a direct address to the reader, "if I ever extract aught further touching this delicate and pleasing subject, I will not fail to make you acquainted with it; or if I can, by any persuasion, get a *peep* at any letters from the cousin afore-mentioned, I hereby pledge myself that you too shall be advised of their contents" (Whipple 1838, 32; emphasis added). What we have is the pleasure of a promise. As the narrator revels in *imagining* an affair, she also participates in its possibility: The effort of extraction so exhausts the vicarious onlooker/*flaneur* that, she notes, "as darkness is closing fast around me, I beg leave to retire from your pleasant company" (Whipple 1838, 32).

Whipple is compelled to "fulfill the promise tendered in the last chapter" (Green 1838, 35) and produces the aforementioned letters. Their acquisition is a mystery, and so the letters are *purloined*, even though she states that the "portion of the correspondence has been laid before me" (Whipple 1838, 35). But to recount the tale imbedded in these letters, our narrator needs "to descend, at once, from the language of metaphor, to that of plain, sober fact" (Whipple 1838, 35). It is the language of metaphor that binds the reader and the author to the pleasure, literal and figurative, of the text. Moreover, Eldridge's biographer arrogantly remarks, "I shall, in no wise, feel myself bound to explain anything in regard to the circumstances by which I became possessed of them" (Whipple 1838, 35). The reader is entrusted to view the second trespass — if authorizing Eldridge's text can be seen as a first act of transgression—as an act of rightful ownership. Here the pleasure of obtaining the letter, as well as the knowledge of its contents, puts the sexual life of the text's heroine on display. Sensing a readerly disapprobation, the biographer sutures her discourse to that described in Orientalist tales of "Blue Beard" and "Aladelin [*sic*]," such that the letters move from being placed before her to being "unveiled" (Whipple 1838, 37) before her.

Eldridge's desire becomes the imaginary plaything of the narrator. The reader is cajoled, almost like a lover to "where . . . we may indulge in an hour of repose; turning, meanwhile, to the simple story for amusement. Having thus so comfortably established ourselves, wich [*sic*] no evil-minded eaves-dropper to make us afraid; bend now, dear reader, thy most earnest and delicately adjusted eat [*sic*]; for I am going to tell thee A SECRET" (Whipple 1838, 36). The secret is a rather banal letter from one Christopher G., who expresses a desire to be with "Ellen" (Elleanor) again, but his chief concern is with the "astonishing and disgusting behavior of the whites" (Whipple 1838, 40).

The question of Eldridge's eligibility for conscription into a heterosexual union returns in the penultimate paragraph of the narrative. Whipple concludes, "Some of our young and romantic readers, may feel curious to know why Eldridge never married. When questioned on the subject, she says that she has determined to profit by the advice of her aunt, who told her never to marry, because it involved such A WASTE OF TIME; for, said she, 'while my young mistress was courting and marrying, I knit five pairs of stockings'" (Whipple 1838, 100). The reference to "stockings" here suggests the coded eighteenth-century euphemism "bluestocking," a cover for "lesbian" intellectual women. The emphasis throughout the narrative on the value of work and on Eldridge's fortitude recurs in this final paragraph. Labor serves as an ethical cover for the lack of (heterosexual) desire, while specific, inter-racial female friendships are foregrounded. The only marriage in the text is that of Eldridge's brother George, whose "bride-elect" is their cousin Miss Ruth Jacobs. One senses that Whipple tries to manage the desire of her "young and romantic" readers to see Eldridge's narrative end happily with a marriage. Whipple covers for Eldridge's "lack" with, "This is the reply that Ellen generally gives; but she has had several good offers, WE can look back to the records of the past, and think of a tenderer, and deeper reason" (Whipple 1838, 100). That "reason" is both explanatory and intellectual.

Eldridge's ambiguous reply opens another interpretation: She might have preferred the companionship of her protectors — the "female part," such as "the benevolent Miss C—. During her first bout with typhus, Miss C— nursed Elleanor back to health and "PAID HER THE FULL AMOUNT OF HER WAGES FOR THE WHOLE TIME, as if she [Elleanor] had always been in actual service" (Whipple 1838, 65). As the text recalls, "Pleasant as a perfume distilled from roses, and indestructible as the purest gold, will be the memory of Jane C—; for it shall be written in the bosoms of many, and inscribed in burnished characters on the brightening tablet of Humanity" (Whipple 1838, 66). Eldridge first went to work for Miss C. in New York and "liked Miss Jane C.—very much/ . . . The kind Miss C—treated her with the most generous and affectionate attention; indeed, as if she had been one of her own family. She had an excellent nurse provided, and two of the most skillful physicians the city afforded; with every delicacy that gives comfort to the chamber of the sick" (Whipple 1838, 64). The debt that many of the white women who *employed* Eldridge were willing to *forgive* for her services is extraordinary.[26]

For a time, Eldridge worked with her oldest sister, Lettise, "in miscellaneous business, of weaving, spinning, going out as a nurse [like Mary Seacole], washer &c, . . . and soap boiling" (Whipple 1838, 62). They sold the soap in the Providence market. There is little doubt that Eldridge's respectability was enhanced by her participation in these "cleanliness is next to godliness" tasks. She did this work from the time she was twenty-seven, in 1812, to the time she was thirty, in 1815, when with another sister she "commenced a new business, viz. — whitewashing, papering, and painting; which she followed for more than twenty years, to the entire satisfaction of her numerous employers" (Whipple 1838, 63).

All this fine work and hard labor gave Eldridge the opportunity to purchase a house — or, as the text says tellingly, "a happy home" (Whipple 1838, 69). The distinction between a house and a home is significant. At that time, as in present, the latter served as a metonym for "family." That Elleanor shared the home with a renter again could have led to disparagement of her character; however, in the text she is again lauded for her industry and the attentive care she devotes to her environs.

Judging Elleanor

The signal event that brings supporters to Eldridge's defense, and future scholars to her life story, is the seizure of her property. Eldridge's house, valued at 4,000 dollars, is sold at a hastily staged auction a few months later "for the pitiful sum of two hundred and forty dollars" (Whipple 1838, 83).[27] The narrator comments, "There seems to be a spirit of willful malignity, in this wanton destruction of property, which is difficult to conceive of existing in the bosom of civilized man" (Whipple 1838, 83). Later in the same passage, however, she adds that such avarice and boldness is the result of the fact that: "THE OWNER OF THE PROPERTY WAS A LABORING COLORED WOMAN" (Whipple 1838, 88). The association between the owner's devalued status and that of her property, sold at "little more than one third its value, for only 1,500 dollars" (Whipple 1838, 84) is clear. Thus, the so-called honorable men feel free to "unceremoniously eject [Elleanor's family] from their comfortable home" and "[compel] them to find shelter in barns and out-houses, or even the woods" (Whipple 1838, 86). Although he (identified in CCP documents as George Carder) is "a PROFESSED friend of their race [and] AN HONORABLE MAN," he nevertheless says that he merely "followed the advice of his lawyer." What is legal is not always ethical. Whipple vigorously defends Eldridge as someone who "has traits of character, which, if she were a white woman, would be called NOBLE. And must color so modify character, that they are not still so?" (Whipple 1838, 85). This is the crucial (racial) question of the text. The narrator adamantly critiques such racist prejudice while nevertheless, as the rhetoric requires, imagining "color" as the problem. She continues: "But the subject of this wrong, or rather of this accumulation of wrongs, was a woman, and therefore weak — a COLORED WOMAN — and therefore contemptible. No MAN ever would have been treated so; and if A WHITE WOMAN had been the subject of such wrongs, the whole town — nay, the whole country, would have been indignant: and the actors would have been held up to the contempt they deserve!" (Whipple 1838, 91).

Eldridge consults the State's Attorney (Mr. Greene) and finds that she can bring a case against the purchaser of the property on the grounds of "Trespass and Ejectment" (Whipple 1838, 87). Whipple reports that the case against the sheriff (identified in court documents as William Mann) was brought before the CCP in January 1837. According to CCP documents, a warrant for the arrest of Benjamin Balch, the gentleman to whom Sheriff Mann "auctioned" Eldridge's property, was not sworn until May 6, 1839.

A warrant for Eldridge's arrest was sworn on January 20, 1835, referring to her as "a Woman of Color Laborer." The case against Eldridge (*John Carder v. E. Eldridge*) was not decided in her favor; Whipple then offers that she determines to use more of her own resources to prove the law wrong. "Ellen" hires two men whom she "fee'd liberally" (Whipple 1838, 88) to investigate the unscrupulous events that precipitated the loss of her property. Whipple's phrasing and redaction of the events indicate that she understands the imbrication of discourses of freedom, justice, and liberty and their dependence on economic structures. For Eldridge—and, indeed, for other "colored" New Englanders—land, property, ownership are always already bound to the loftier discourses of freedom, liberty, and justice. The social, psychic, and legal realms reside together in the text as both material and symbolic properties.

The "whole affair, from beginning to end, in all its connections and bearings was A WEB OF INIQUITY. It was a wanton outrage upon the simplest and most evident principles of justice" (Whipple 1838, 90). This language draws on the discourse of illicit sexuality—"wanton outrage" was a nineteenth-century euphemism for "rape." Moreover, the phrase "wanton outrage" gets truncated in William Faulkner's cosmos as "outrage," an entanglement that signifies the combined violence to *land* and *body*, and therefore connects economic exploitation with gendered dynamics that underwrite Whipple's account of Eldridge's position.

Leaving Elleanor

If Eldridge's legal trials rely on the failure of justice in the face of color, caste, and gender, then Whipple's staging of her drama takes part in abolitionist discourse that champions colored subjects and can radically discredit white (men's) testimony and authority. Such sentiments are borne out in the appendix of the text that contains, as was customary, several "subscriptions" (underwritings and appeals) written in verse by white women who wished to advertise (for) Eldridge's cause.

Several of the subscribed appeals, unlike the larger narrative, are written in the first person—as if mimicking Eldridge's voice. The first, penned by E. C. J. is entitled, somewhat erroneously, "The African's Appeal." This short, eighteen-line poem written in heroic couplets speaks for the "African" subject and asks, "Why rejected? Wherefore base? / Is our long degraded race? / Are we not of human kind? / Have we not the gift of mind?" (Whipple 1838, 106). This verse clearly bears the mark of monogenetic liberal discourse. It asks again as an interrogatory, "Am I not a brother or a sister?" a phrase that, for all its good work, nevertheless undermines itself by not being declarative. The *question* of relation here brings us back to our beginning, as Eldridge's chief underwriter and her white female audience extract, if not demand, an intimate relationship with her *story*. When numerous wrongs are relayed, the poem pleads, "And shall our hard earned labors fail / And white men our dear rights assail?" (Whipple 1838, 106). In this instant, the speakers seem to eschew raced connection for the righteousness of a gendered relationship. But the suture is disrupted by the subsequent appeal to "thou God of Love" to "forbid" injustice.

In the E. C. J. piece, Eldridge is not mentioned specifically; the poem, "Hard Fate of Poor Ellen" by "A Lady of Providence," presents a contrast. Written in quatrains with an abab rhyme scheme, "Hard Fate" refers to Eldridge's thirty years of labor and is more of a ballad that narrates events of her loss:

> A house and home, were now her own;
> By honest industry, 'twas reared;
> She dreamed of happiness, alone —
> She knew no foes, no *fraud*, she feared. . . .
> But, too secure, in evil hour —
> The wily snare, for her, was laid,
> Her absence, gave it legal power,
> Her home was seized, and she, betrayed! (Whipple 1838, 108)

These passages make Eldridge into the passive victim of a "wily snare," suggesting that she was "trapped" by evildoers. In so doing, the second stanza presents a moral indictment against "legal power" that has might if not, in its ethical view, right. Even after the narrative's official close, the women who support Eldridge continue a debate about her industriousness and vulnerability crafted in figurative language: It is as if they cannot decide on how to leave Eldridge. The poetry contained in the narrative's last pages is a reminder to the audience of the issues at play, and at risk, in telling her story.

The next subscription is a prose piece that mentions Eldridge's ancestry. It begins by noting the "wrongs of the distant Indian and the Southern slave" that take away from "the afflicted in our own vicinity" (Whipple 1838, 109). Such an argument for the "local" separates out two causes that Ellen's case enjoins — namely, violations against Afro-Native subjects. The piece criticizes the law that would allow her property to be stolen, calling it "chicanery" without compassion. It notes how Ellen "accumulated and husbanded her property," which was then "incontrovertible proof of her moral character." This racial (and deeply gendered) characterization notes that, in contradistinction to the myth of black and Indian laziness, Ellen was industrious — a manager able to increase her capital. This industriousness is psychically tied to Puritan concepts of working the land, because land that is not cultivated is underutilized, and therefore uninhabited. The prose piece also rehearses the "nurture over nature" argument by stating, "It is worthy of consideration, that if Ellen, with her limited improvements, and under all the disadvantages of colour, could achieve so much as she has, what would she have done if those disadvantages had not been in the way" (Whipple 1838, 111).

Again, such a twisted or backhanded compliment catalogues Eldridge's disadvantages even as it tries to dispel them. The statement indirectly takes aim at changing the conditions under which such subjects were limited by laws and customs. This aspect is undercut, however, in the next paragraph, whose author, C. R. Williams, notes, "Finally, in befriending Ellen, we have the pleasure of assisting one who carries in her veins not only the blood of some of the Aborigines of our own State (the unfortunate and extinct race of the warlike Pequots) but of that much wronged and abused people, who have been sold in slavery on our Coasts" (Whipple 1838, 111). Whipple includes an editor's correction, stating that the author "meant to say the Narragansetts." She does not bother to correct the more erroneous fact: that neither tribe was extinct.[28]

Whipple's editorial correction is very interesting. She observes, "Elleanor is descended from the noble race of Canonicus and Miantonomo, who were for a long time, the generous protectors and friends of Roger Williams — HER fore-fathers, then, nourished and protected OURS" (Whipple 1838, 111). We find this allusion to history stunning for its reversal not only of the text to which it is subscribed, but also for its radical writing of early colonial history that often obfuscates the mélange of whites, blacks, and Native peoples who inhabited the area. In essence, the debt that white women *owe* Eldridge is substantial, but its payment is to be made not in economic terms here but, rather, in the historical relation — the archive of the future. It makes the *desire* to protect Eldridge more of a payback than a charity case. While some of those who undersigned her book no doubt did so as an act of charity, one that would be inscribed for posterity, others sought to endorse Eldridge's endeavor as an enterprise. The latter viewed selling a product as an appropriate remedy for the loss of property — a remedy that the text's various conclusions, or leave takings, do not and cannot support.

Notes

This essay is the beginning of a larger collaborative project about two Afro-Native women of the nineteenth century: Elleanor Eldridge (1785–1865) and Edmonia Lewis (1846–90). This work would not have been possible without the help of Andrew Smith at the Rhode Island Supreme Court Records Building; Rosemary Cullen and John Brown at the John Hay Library, Brown University; and Jan Marshall in the County Clerk's office and Paula Garbett and Judy Wild (Probate Division) in the Office of Vital Records, both in Warwick, Rhode Island. We also thank Mike Pincus of Bolerium Books in San Francisco, one of the best antiquarian booksellers in the business, who was instrumental in providing connections to bibliophiles in Rhode Island and at Brown University. We thank William Yellow Robe and Deborah Spears-Moorehead, who helped us negotiate the complex oral histories of community formation in contemporary Rhode Island among the Pequot, Narragansett, and Wampanoug, for their generosity and interest in this project. We also thank Rebecca Schneider, who provided a place to stay and an agile mind with which to play out the day's research findings. Finally, we dedicate this essay to Georgine and William Shedrick Willis, who did so much to further research on Afro-Native subjects.

1   Whipple recalls that, "during her mother's life, it had often been her practice to follow washing, at the house of Mr. Joseph Baker, of Warwick; a daughter of whom, Miss Elleanor Baker, gave her·own name to the little one she often carried with her" (Whipple 1838, 21). Vital records for Warwick indicate that Eleanor Baker married William Tillinghast on March 12, 1797, about the time that Whipple reports the young mistress to whom Eldridge was first indentured left the household. Although Whipple, and then O'Dowd, note that Elleanor Eldridge lived to be almost eighty, the date 1845 is still reiterated in popular encyclopedic entries and scholarly essays.

2   Frances Harriet Whipple Green MacDougall (hereafter noted as Frances

Whipple, although she published under the surname Green, except for her *Memoirs*, which were published under the name of Whipple) wrote the first appeal for Eldridge, modestly titled *Memoirs of Elleanor Eldridge*, in 1838. For clarity, we will use Whipple to refer to the 1838 text, and Green to refer to the 1842 text. Frances Whipple was quite the iconoclast: She hailed from one of the first families of Rhode Island (the Whipples) and spent much of her life championing the rights of ordinary laborers. Whipple was familiar with Eldridge because Eldridge was employed by many of Providence's most prominent citizens, including the Greens and the Bakers. Eldridge went to work as an indentured servant for the Baker family at age ten and worked at various occupations until her death. The exact date of her death is unknown, as Providence directories dating back to 1836 indicate that "Eleanor Eldridge/Eleanor Eldredge" did live at 22 Spring Street at least until 1853. Spellings of Eldridge's name vary in court and informal documents. We have decided to use "Eldridge" because that is the spelling that previous scholars have used. For a more detailed account of Frances Whipple's life, see O'Dowd 2004.

3 Ibid., 19, fn. 1.

4 While several encyclopedic collections mention the work and life of Elleanor Eldridge, there are few scholarly treatments of her narrative or her history: see n. 11, below.

5 We are aware that our investigation of Eldridge's Indian ancestry might convey a bias on our part, as the inquiry into her grandfather's ancestry appears to be undervalued. In essence, we are aware that the assumption works both ways. A search of vital records in Providence and Warwick indicates that Prophets lived in both towns; the name appears as early as 1745 and as late as 1852. In his 1883 memoirs, William J. Brown noted that he descended from the Prophet line, a well-known African American family in Providence throughout the nineteenth century (Rosalind Wiggins, telephone interview, May 2004). Ironically, Brown also mentioned that his Narragansett grandmother had bought her African American husband around 1770 "to change her mode of living" (*The Life of William J. Brown* [Providence, 1883], as quoted in Mandell 1998, 184). Likewise, Sarah Muckamugg moved to Providence, where she married Aaron Whipple, "a Negro servant" (as quoted in Mandell 1998, 189).

6 O'Dowd (2004, 19) notes that Eldridge's name was one of the first among thirty-five women who were proposed to the Rhode Island Legislature for statues honoring their contributions.

7 The exhaustive research of Jack D. Forbes has been invaluable to scholars researching the early lives and narratives of people of African and Indian descent in the Americas. In particular, his explication of early court records, census data, ledgers, and ships' logs reveals that terms such as "black," "Negro," "colored" and "mulatto/a" did not often correspond accurately to the peoples such terms sought to define. As Forbes concludes, "This is a matter of consider-

able significance for the scholar seeking to understand the actual ethnic or racial identity of non-white persons in the slave trade, in the American colonies and in the United States over the centuries" (Forbes 1993, 91).

8 See Snipp 1989.

9 The quote is from Mandell (1998, 466), a superb article that treats complex issues of property, race, gender, and generation in the sociopolitical-geopolitical context of colonial America. He notes the larger hardening of racial difference with the incursion of Enlightenment thought and shifts to a patriarchal notion of property, law, and citizenship.

10 At the time of publication, we were able to find no record of Fuller's purchase of Prophet's freedom, although the practice was not uncommon in the North or the South in the eighteenth century. Fuller did have a female counterpart in the Wampanoag Ruth Moses, who in 1746 married Kofi, "a freed African" (Mandell 1996, 173).

11 For scholarly treatments of Eldridge's story and Whipple's narrative, see Loewenberg and Bogin 1976; Sterling 1984. Still one of the most important scholarly treatments of black women's literary production, Hazel Carby's *Reconstructing Womanhood: The Emergence of the Afro-American Woman Novelists* (1987) does examine narratives of slave and free women before emancipation. But the prevailing methodology in the period of its publication was to unearth self-authored African American narratives, providing evidence that black peoples did participate in the tradition of letters so central to the making (and unmaking) of the United States. Carby's text, therefore, leaves no room for the potential (il)legitimacy of a voice like Eldridge, a "free" woman laboring under adverse conditions, and the voice of a white author. One of the earliest and most extensive encyclopedic entries for Eldridge is in Dannett 1964.

12 Preliminary research at the Rhode Island Historical Society and the John Hay archives at Brown University reveals that the Six Principle Baptist Church does have a significant history in Rhode Island.

13 Church records, Six Principle Baptist Church, mss. 145, series 3 (loose volume), Rhode Island Historical Society (RIHS) Archives, series 2, vol. 2 (discrepancy between the RIHS's labeling and the actual cover of the journal). We also found reference to a Mary Fuller in a transcription of the original vital records of Rhode Island: "Mary Fullers [*sic*] Earmark of her Creatures is Two slits in the underside the left Eare. — Recorded Jany the 26th 1762" (signed manuscript document in the vital records of Rhode Island, 235). At the time of publication, we were unable to verify any connection between this Mary Fuller and the "Indian" identified in 1753.

14 The only other racial category noted in the list is "Negro."

15 For an extensive discussion of this issue, especially in the New England region, see Calloway 1997; O'Brien 1997a. Published only a year earlier, Mandell's *Beyond the Frontier* (1996) engages the discourse of "vanishing" as a paradigm and at times, repudiates it; see also Bellin 2001; Deloria 1998; Konkle 2004. For an examination of invisibility in the context of connections between Native studies and African American studies, see Brennan 2003; Brooks 2002; Perdue 2003.

16 O'Dowd notes that eight editions of *Memoirs* were printed between 1838 and 1847. All citations are from the 1838 edition, unless noted otherwise. The second edition appeared in 1845 with a lengthy preface written by Whipple. Brown University's John Hay Library has the 1838 and 1845 editions of *Memoirs*.

17 In the first narrative, *Memoirs of Elleanor Eldridge* (Whipple 1838), the title page features a quotation from Shakespeare's *Merchant of Venice*. The quotation speaks to the politics of patronage and reads:

> O that estates, degrees, and offices
> Were not Derived corruptly! and that clear honor
> Were Purchased by the merit of the wearer!
> How many, then, should cover, that stand bare?
> How many be commanded, that command?
> How much low peasantry would then be gleaned
> From the true seed of honor? and how much honor
> Picked from the chaff and ruin of the times,
> To be new varnished?

The author or authors of Eldridge's narrative mark the peculiar situation that creates the occasion for their outcry: the racial difference that allows for Eldridge's loss of land; the class injustices that speak to the impoverishment of the "low peasantry" as much as these injustices speak to the continued privilege of the wealthy; and the extent to which these crimes of race and class are "new varnished" and thus repeated in the vicious cycle that is history.

18 Whipple conceals the identity of the men involved, but court records show that a deed to "lot no. 55," the property in question, ironically was witnessed and signed by Mann on September 16, 1835: William B. Mann to Benjamin Balch, *Carder v. Eldridge*, Court of Common Pleas (hereafter, CCP), May term 1835. Records show that the initial problem began on January 20, 1835, with Mann's arrest warrant for Eldridge, "a Woman of Color Laborer" on the complaint of the estate of George Carder, deceased, on behalf of John Carder, "Executor of the last Will and Testament of George Carder." The story about Elleanor's rumored death seems to be an invention of Whipple's or an afterthought on the part of Mann, who feared that his scheme might be discovered. Whipple records the interaction with the baker's son in the following manner:

> With the most querulous and misgiving tones, he called out: "Is that you Ellen? — Why I thought you was — dead!"
> "No, I am not dead;' replied Ellenor [*sic*], 'but I am hungry. Give me some bread, quick!'" . . .

The boy still retreated, and still holding out his hands, as if to ward off danger, he cried out: "Don't come any nearer! — don't Ellen, if you be Ellen — cause — cause — I don't like dead folks!"

It was some time before Elleanor could assure the poor little fellow of her real, bona fide, bodily presence, so strongly was he impressed with the belief that she was actually "departed." (Whipple 1838, 76).

The debacle was not fully resolved until 1839, when the sheriff of Providence swore out a warrant for the arrest of Benjamin Balch, "Baker, alias trader, alias Gentleman": *Eldridge v. Balch*, CCP, May term 1839. Could this be the same baker whose son witnessed Eldridge's return from the dead?

19 CCP (1789–1893), Judicial Archives, Supreme Court Juridicial Records Center, Pawtucket, Rhode Island. O'Dowd attempts to correct the discrepancies in Whipple's account of Eldridge's legal difficulties by using CCP documents: see *Carder v. Eldridge*, CCP, Providence, May term 1835; *Eldridge v. Balch*, CCP, Providence, November term 1836, May term 1839.

20 The women who authorized the second narrative, again told by Whipple, were "Harriet Lee Truesdell, Francis Harriet Whipple, Mrs. Elizabeth G. Chandler, Mrs. Amey A. Arnold, Ms. Mary A. Earle, Mrs. Harriet Chandler, Mrs. Abby Thurber, Mrs. Sarah Olney, Elizabeth Elliot, A. G. Dorrance, Mrs. Anne Arnold" (Green 1842 [1839], 6). By 1839, Whipple had put her name to the volume but only as one of many authors rather than as the single author of the narrative. A copy of the second book, published in 1842, is in our possession. All references to it are from the 1842 edition, unless noted otherwise in the text.

21 For a study of the classic feminist figure, see Honey 1984.

22 Whipple later tells us that "his African name was Dick" (Whipple 1838, 17). Her articulation of the events surrounding "Dick's" capture are interspersed with botanical references, highlighting Whipple's own employment as a "dedicated botany teacher" (O'Dowd 2004, 26). The scene draws heavily on the discourse of travel narratives about Africa, as well as on accounts of the Middle Passage, which were widely read and available in the nineteenth century.

23 Rhode Island census data from 1790 report that "Robin Eldrich" lived in Kent County, Warwick. At least five other "free persons" of color lived with him: "Heads of Families at the First Census of the United States Taken in the Year 1790," RIHS, 15.

24 See Quarles 1961.

25 Not only was Hannah Prophet's death distressing to Eldridge; it could not have come at a worse time. During the 1780s, a severe depression hit the just liberated former colonies. The historian Ruth Wallis Herndon reports that "Warwick councilmen, for example, conducted their first auction in 1788, when they disposed of 'sundry poor children' to the lowest-bidding households" (quoted in Herndon 2004, 151). In addition, Herndon notes that the last two decades of the eighteenth century, the period in which Eldridge was born and reached adolescence, were the last in which Rhode Island's poor were visible. "Within a few decades, the poor would be segregated in farms, orphanages, and other institutions, no longer a daily presence in the homes of community members and no longer mentioned by name in the council minutes" (Herndon 2004, 157). O'Dowd muses that Whipple's account of Eldridge's industriousness is suspect: "Whipple was a literary writer — not a journalist or a historian — and wrote a moral fable to persuade her readers of what she believed was the truth" (O'Dowd 2004, 28).

26 In her redaction of Eldridge's property seizure, Whipple writes that "Elleanor was able to procure twenty-one hundred dollars, upon her own credit, at such a time, in the space of six weeks, of itself shews the esteem in which she was held, as well as the energy and perseverance, for which she has always been remarkable" (Whipple 1838, 89). *Elleanor's Second Book* continues to record Eldridge's extraordinary sway with her employers. In one example, Eldridge appears at the foot of the bed of one employer, Nora. Whipple writes, "The sun is a laggard to Elleanor . . . when she appeared in my bed, saying, "Come Miss Nora, wake up and I'll tell you something; and so I rose and listened to her" (Green 1842 [1839], 11). Later, Eldridge, the women's "dark protégée" (Green 1842 [1839], 15), hails and then lures her supporters by offering them "a rose" from her garden.

27 In the 1845 edition of *Memoirs*, Whipple notes with an asterisk that "it has been disputed that Ellen's property was valued at so much. She was always taxed for 4000 dollars, at any rate; whether her estate was worth that or not, her papers will testify": *Memoirs*, John Hay Library, Brown University.

28 Mandell (1998, 478) notes that "intermarriage posed a potential threat to a Native community's resources and power, particularly as the once fluid Anglo-American attitudes toward race and gender roles hardened into new, more threatening forms. Those who shaped the region's laws drew increasingly rigid lines between racial groups, labeled the offspring of intermarriages as mulattoes or blacks, and therefore saw New England Indians as vanishing."

CHAPTER THREE

Race and Federal

Recognition in Native New England

TIFFANY M. MCKINNEY

~~~~~~

Historical encounters between American Indians and African Americans in the United States have resulted in an ongoing and contentious debate in current Indian politics. Given the potential political and financial gains of federal tribal recognition, Indian communities have begun to stringently review their membership rosters, with the hopes of increasing their chances for such recognition (Beinart 1999, 3).[1] The result of this, at times, has been for Indian communities to cast phenotypic black Indians as non-Indians for purposes of tribal membership. Several tribes, such as the Mashantucket Pequots of the State of Connecticut, have been accused of instituting such racialized membership criteria.

The current racial divide in several Indian communities illustrates how racial ideologies have traveled between the national and local levels and how they are internalized and, at times, manipulated by certain Indian communities, as the anthropologist Circe Sturm (2002, 224) has outlined in her work on the Cherokee of Oklahoma. In this essay, I trace the development of racial tensions in Pequot communities of New England and explore ways in which these preexisting conflicts are exacerbated by the federal-recognition process. Interweaving ethnohistory and legal history to further this analysis, I highlight the past racial divide between the Eastern Pequot and the Paucatuck Pequot Indians and the current racial divide between the Mashantucket Pequot Indians

and the Simonds family to demonstrate the racial politics that are taking place in some New England Indian communities.

Ethnohistorical View of Indian–African American Relations

New England Indian Communities and Slavery

By the inception of the Civil War, New England Indian communities
had experienced several generations of intermarriage with African
Americans. In particular, members of the Mashpee of Cape Cod, the
Narragansett of Rhode Island, the Mohegans and Pequots of southeastern Connecticut, and the Montauks and Shinnecocks of eastern
Long Island enjoyed significant population increases as a result of the
influx of African Americans to these communities (Barsh and Steel
2000, 6–7). Russel Lawrence Barsh, director of the Center for the Study
of Coast Salish Environments for the Samish Indian Nation, writes: "By
1832, coastal New England Indians had intermarried and occupation-
ally integrated with black Americans to such an extent that the social
boundaries between them began to dissolve, and they began to conceive
of themselves collectively as 'people of color' with a shared political
struggle" (Barsh and Steel 2000, 4). Given the open society inherent in
Indian communities, both free African Americans and fugitive slaves
sought membership in these groups. Other large contributors to the
alliance between Indians and African Americans were state antimiscegenation laws and occupational discrimination, both of which led to
collective mobilization around similar plights (Plane 2000, 30). Fugitive slaves, for instance, were largely attracted to Indian communities
that "recognized their right to share in the use of tribal property, and to
vote in local elections" (Barsh and Steel 2000, 4).

Miscegenation among Indian and African American communities
was so widespread that in 1849 a Massachusetts state inquiry found that
over 99 percent of the Indians in the state were "of mixed blood; mostly
Indian and African" (Barsh and Steel 2000, 5). This liaison between the
two groups informed political mobilization, familial ties, and one's
overall perception of oneself and one's community. Indian communities with African American populations, for instance, never questioned their Indian authenticity yet welcomed African Americans into
their fold. For instance, as James Clifford (1988, 306) notes, "Children

with one Indian parent could become full members" of the Indian community. Moreover, many Indian communities viewed the African American plight as an intrinsic component of their own and vehemently advocated for change within the racist American social order. The union between the two groups had particular significance during the abolitionist movement and activities surrounding the Civil War.

Prominent Afro-Indian abolitionists such as Paul Cuffe, William Apess, Gad Apes, and Armstrong Archer all brought the abolition message to mixed New England Indian and African American communities (Barsh and Steel 2000, 6–9). Between 1863 and 1864, Connecticut formed two colored Union regiments in which a half dozen Mohegans and Mashpees were soldiers (Barsh and Steel 2000, 17). Moreover, it has been reported that nineteen of the men who fought in the Civil War for the Union were Mashpee, and the much celebrated 54th Massachusetts Regiment, formed in Boston in 1863, had at least a half dozen Afro-Indians from the New England area, according to Barsh and Steel.

The result of this early mixing of the two communities has had a lasting impact on Indian politics. Nowhere is this impact felt more than in the past tribal conflict between the Eastern Pequots and the Paucatuck Pequots and the present tribal conflict between the Mashantucket Pequots and the Simonds family.

The Pequots of Southern New England

Precolonial History

In the seventeenth century, the Pequot community was the strongest economic power in Southern New England.[2] The tribe's land base began at West Niantic, which is near New London, Connecticut. The territory continued northward to the mouth of the Thames River, eastward to the present Connecticut–Rhode Island border, and south along that border to the eastern end of Long Island. The total area of Pequot territory was approximately 2,000 square miles, much of which had been gained through warfare (Hauptman and Wherry 1990, 34).

During this time, much of Pequot subsistence revolved around horticulture (O'Brien 1997a, 16). The tribe planted diverse crops such as corn, beans, squash, and tubers (Hauptman and Wherry 1990, 35).

Hoes for cultivation were manufactured from the shells of horseshoe crabs, clams, and other shellfish (Hauptman and Wherry 1990, 35). The Pequot diet also included fish and wild animals, obtained from fishing and hunting. Women conducted a majority of the planting, while men were responsible for harvesting tobacco and hunting (O'Brien 1997a, 18–19). Both groups participated in fishing activities. Pequots generally lived in small villages with ten to twenty houses, hamlets, farmsteads, or simple isolated dwellings. The Pequot living arrangement mirrored that of a seasonal transhumance community: The Pequots often migrated during the change of seasons to find more suitable living conditions.

In political terms, members of the Pequot community could be categorized as (1) the sachem (civil officers who provided day-to-day community leadership basis) and members of the esteemed family;[3] (2) ordinary members of the community; or (3) resident nonmembers (usually captured during war) who were servants. Under this sociopolitical order, most Pequots were ordinary members of the community. Membership in the sachem or esteemed family often involved lineage or personal achievements that impressed the entire community. In noting the power and influence of village sachems, Jean M. O'Brien (1997a, 20) writes: "Though sachems were [often] born into their positions as village leaders, their power and following depended on their charisma, power of persuasion, and demonstrated skill in securing the best interests of the group."

Decision making and other governmental affairs were based on consensus. In describing the interworkings of Pequot government, Laurence Hauptman and James Wherry observe:

> Each sachem received counsel from other high-status individuals, including the pnieses [one who after receiving a supernatural vision was regarded as a special person] and powwows [part-time magical-religious specialists who acted as intermediaries between the physical and spiritual worlds]. In addition, influential or well-regarded warriors had input into the political process, along with members of the community, such as elders and other respected persons, who formed councils or caucuses. (Hauptman and Wherry 1990, 43)

Pequots generally lived healthy lives. With the arrival of the Europeans, however, came incurable diseases and other afflictions. Ailments once unknown to the community, such as smallpox, measles, malaria, yellow fever, chicken pox, and whooping cough, became widespread epidemics (Hauptman and Wherry 1990, 45). In 1633, after European settlement in this region, the Pequot community experienced a smallpox epidemic. The years following the epidemic saw a Pequot mortality rate of 77 percent (Hauptman and Wherry 1990, 46).[4] The deleterious effects that disease brought on the population made the community vulnerable to European attack.

The Pequot War

The killing of Tatobem, a Pequot sachem, by Dutch traders ignited the flames of the conflict that would escalate into the Pequot War. In retaliation for Tatobem's death, Pequots attacked the Dutch trading post. Shortly thereafter, the Western Niantics, a tribe that paid tribute to the Pequots, killed John Stone, a Virginia trader. In an effort to prevent further killings, the Sassacus (or the chief Pequot sachem) negotiated a peace agreement between the tribe and the Massachusetts Bay officials. However, when unknown Indian assailants killed the English trader sent to the Pequots as a condition of the peace agreement, full-scale retribution by the colonial officials ensued.

In 1637, English colonists and their Mohegan[5] and Narrangansett allies militarily crushed the New England Pequots, killing as many as 700 men, women, and children at the tribe's principal village, in what is now Mystic, Connecticut.[6] After the Pequot defeat, many members of the group came under Mohegan control. In addition, a significant number of defeated Pequots came under Narrangansett control. However, within a generation a number of Pequots in the latter group had escaped captivity and joined members of the tribe who had not become subjugated to either the Mohegans or the Narrangansetts. Other members of the tribe were sent to Bermuda as slaves. The war ended in 1638 with the signing of the Treaty of Hartford. The tribe was officially declared dissolved, and colonial administrators outlawed the use of the name Pequot. Hence, three factions of splintered Pequots existed in New England: (1) those under Mohegan control; (2) those under Narrangansett control; and (3) those who were fugitives.[7]

Given the Pequots' strong resistance to remaining under subjugation to any group, English colonists eventually awarded two groups land parcels in the center of the former Pequot homelands (Hauptman and Wherry 1990, 118). The group that had escaped Narrangansett control was given land in North Stonington, Connecticut, and became the Eastern Pequots. The colonists granted the group that was formerly under Mohegan control adjacent land in Ledyard, Connecticut. That group became the Western or Mashantucket Pequots.[8]

Present-Day Racial Divide among the Pequots

In the 1930s, an intra–Eastern Pequot dispute began to unfold. In 1933, J. R. Williams, an inspector for the Connecticut State Park and Forestry Department (the organization that administered Connecticut Indian reservations until 1941), released a report that described the racial divide between light-skinned and dark-skinned residents on the Eastern Pequot reservation. According to the report, in the 1930s, Atwood I. Williams,[9] known as Chief Silver Star, challenged the right of some dark-skinned members to live on the reservation. Chief Silver Star's main assertion questioned the legitimacy of that group's ancestry, which traced to both Tamar Brushell, a documented resident of the Pequot Reservation in the early nineteenth century, and Manuel Sebastian, a sailor from the Azores.[10] The grievance asserted that Tamar Brushell was a darker Indian who had married Manuel Sebastian, a recorded Portuguese, and thereby delegitimized her own and her descendants' right to obtain Eastern Pequot membership and remain on the reservation.[11] In 1973, the Connecticut Indian Affairs Council was established to provide services to the state's Indian reservations. Helen LeGault, a descendant of Chief Silver Star, sought to become the group's representative on the council. However, when descendants of Tamar Brushell and Manuel Sebastian began to oppose her campaign, LeGault revived the question of whether any Sebastian had the right to live on the reservation.[12]

The Eastern Pequots began seeking federal tribal recognition in 1979. In 1990, a splinter group of about ninety members (known as the Paucatuck Pequots) contemporaneously began to pursue federal recognition. The Paucatuck Pequots claimed that they were the only true descendants of the Eastern Pequots and that about 770 members of the group calling itself the Eastern Pequots (comprising mostly descendants of Tamar Brushell) were not legitimate Eastern Pequots.

The Mashantucket Pequots face a similar racial divide. In 1983, when congressional approval of Mashantucket Pequot recognition was imminent, President Ronald Reagan granted the group federal recognition through an Executive Order (Hauptman and Wherry 1990, 80). The Simonds, who allege to be a family within the tribe, claim that they were purposefully excluded from the Mashantucket membership list because of their darker skin color. Exclusion from the list has disqualified the family from government benefits that federal recognition brings.

Bureau of Indian Affairs Review Process

Legislative Analysis

Before 1978, requests from Indian groups for federal recognition as tribes were determined on an ad hoc basis. Some tribes gained recognition through congressional action; some gained recognition through various forms of administrative decisions within the executive branch; and some gained recognition through the judiciary. With the increase of requests for federal recognition in the 1970s, the Department of the Interior created the Federal Acknowledgment Project (FAP). Through FAP, the federal government prescribed rules governing the administrative process for federal recognition. The rules, which became effective on October 2, 1978, were designed to provide a uniform process to review Indian petitions for federal recognition. When FAP was first established, the regulations were designated Part 54 of Title 25 of the Code of Federal Regulations. The regulations were officially redesignated Part 83 of Title 25 of the Code of Federal Regulations (25CFR83) on March 30, 1982, and amended in 1994.[13] The Branch of Acknowledgment and Research (BAR), an office of the Bureau of Indian Affairs (BIA), administers the regulations. BAR reviews applications to assess whether petitioning Indian groups meet criteria established pursuant to 25CFR83.

There are three alternative methods through which Indian communities can obtain federal recognition. First, Congress has the power to acknowledge tribes through legislation. Second, through an Executive Order, the president has the ability to grant federal recognition to Indian groups. However, since 1978, presidents have largely relied on the BIA and its recognition process to determine Indian groups' tribal status. Third, through the judiciary, courts may grant Indian groups federal recognition. However, once the federal-recognition process was formally established, courts began directing Indian petitioners to exhaust their administrative remedies through BIA before commencing litigation.

Federal recognition by the Department of the Interior is a prerequisite for the protection, services, and benefits the federal government grants to recognized tribes. In addition, recognition entitles Indian groups to certain immunities and privileges by virtue of their government-to-government relationship with the U.S. government (25CFR83.2). The privileges accorded to acknowledged groups under the Indian Gaming Regulatory Act are arguably the most lucrative aspect of federal recognition.[14] In *California v. Cabazon Band of Mission Indians*,[15] the U.S. Supreme Court held that federally acknowledged tribes located in states that permit gaming, regardless of whether the gaming is highly regulated, are entitled to license and operate gaming without state regulation. In response to this decision, Congress passed the Indian Gaming Regulatory Act in 1988, which states:

> Indian tribes have the exclusive right to regulate gaming activity on Indian lands if gaming activity is not specially prohibited by Federal law and is conducted within a State which does not, as a matter of criminal law and public policy, prohibit such gaming activity.[16]

The act has allowed several Indian communities to operate extremely profitable gaming activities, such as casinos and bingo halls. Foxwoods Casino, owned by the Mashantuckets of Connecticut; Mohegan Sun Casino, owned by the Mohegans of Connecticut; Silver Star Resort and Casino, owned by the Choctaws of Mississippi; and Spirit Mountain Casino, owned by the Grand Ronde Confederation of Oregon are just a few of the Indian casinos that gross millions in profits per year.[17] Consequently, federal recognition provides not only the possibility of cultural validation, but also the potential for economic independence for Indian communities that successfully complete the recognition process.

The Recognition Process

An Indian community begins the process of federal recognition by writing a letter to the assistant secretary of Indian affairs, stating its intent to petition (25CFR83.4). Once the assistant secretary receives the letter, BAR will arrange publication in the *Federal Register* concerning the group's intention. BAR will also publicize in a local newspaper of the group's residence and notify the governor and attorney-general of the group's home state that the group intends to petition. In addition, BAR will send the group an official petition packet, which the petitioning group must complete to be considered. The package requires the group to provide substantial supporting data regarding its tribal status.

The petitioning group has unlimited time to submit the petition packet. A preliminary decision on federal recognition usually takes place within one year of receipt of the package, with a possible 180-day extension.[18] The preliminary decision is posted in the *Federal Register*. After receiving comments from any interested people concerning the preliminary decision, BAR schedules a meeting with the petitioner and such interested persons to assign a date for the final decision. The assistant secretary of Indian affairs issues the final determination within 60 days of the negotiated date. The final determination becomes effective 90 days after publication of the "Notice of the Final Determination" in the *Federal Register* (25CFR83.9[h]).

Criteria for Recognition

Tribal-recognition authority under 25CFR83 is limited to Indian tribes indigenous to the continental United States. Moreover, the provisions of the section are intended to apply to those Indian groups that can demonstrate a "substantially continuous tribal existence" and that have "functioned as autonomous entities throughout history until the present" (25CFR83.3). Section 83.7 provides seven mandatory criteria that Indian groups must meet for federal tribal recognition:

(a) The petitioner has been identified as an American Indian entity on a substantially continuous basis since 1900.[19]

(b) A predominant portion of the petitioning group makes up a distinct community and has existed as a community from historical times until the present.[20]

(c) The petitioner has maintained political influence or authority over its members as an autonomous entity from historical times until the present.[21]

(d) The petitioner must provide a copy of the group's present governing document, including its membership criteria. In the absence of a written document, the petitioner must provide a statement describing in full its membership criteria and current governing procedures.

(e) The petitioner's membership consists of individuals who descend from a historical Indian tribe or from historical Indian tribes that combined and functioned as a single autonomous political entity.[22]

(f) The membership of the petitioning group is composed principally of people who are not members of any acknowledged North American Indian tribe. However, under certain conditions, a petitioning group may be acknowledged even if its membership is composed principally of people whose names have appeared on the rolls of, or who have been associated with, an acknowledged Indian tribe. The conditions are that the group must establish that it has functioned throughout history until the present as a separate and autonomous Indian tribal entity; that its members do not maintain a bilateral political relationship with the acknowledged tribe; and that its members have provided written confirmation of their membership in the petitioning group.

(g) Neither the petitioner nor its members are the subject of congressional legislation that has terminated or forbidden the federal relationship.

Successful petitioners must meet all seven criteria. Failure to meet even one criterion results in a negative decision. Hence, the burden of proof is on the group seeking federal recognition. During an Indian community's active consideration period, BAR personnel assigned to the group will make field visits to the area in which the group is located. These visits often include interviewing various members of the community and gathering additional information. If BAR gives a group a negative finding, the group is not allowed to reapply. It must, instead, commence action in federal court under the Administrative Procedures Act (APA).

Given the intensity and importance of the review process, many Indian groups hire costly counsel to assist in preparing the petition. Several commentators have argued that the federal recognition process favors groups that have the financial wherewithal to provide elaborate, intensely researched, and well-prepared petitions, creating an economically biased result in tribal recognition (Beinart 1999, 11).

The Pequot Conflicts and the Federal Recognition Process

Eastern Pequot Petition

On March 17, 1993, Roy Sebastian (acting president of the Eastern Pequots) wrote a letter to President Bill Clinton requesting a grant of federal recognition through an Executive Order. Concurrently, the group continued its federal recognition process through BAR. The group petitioned that there was one Eastern Pequot tribe in which both they and the Paucatuck Pequots were members. In addition, the Eastern Pequots' 296-page petition asserted that the group had fulfilled the seven criteria established by the BIA. First, the petition stated that the group had evolved from a portion of the historic Pequot tribe of southeastern Connecticut and existed at the time of the first sustained contact with non-Indian settlers. Second, the petition asserted that the group had been continuously identified as an Indian tribe, was a distinct community, and had maintained political authority over its members, and that its present-day tribal members were descendants of members of the historical tribe (Beinart 1999, 1–8). Third, the petition stated that the Eastern Pequots fall outside the definition of a Mohegan tribal community. This definition was established by the 1994 federal recognition of the Mohegans and required that a majority of the group live on or near the Mohegan reservation and have family ties to other members of the Mohegan reservation.[23]

Although the group demonstrated its tribal lineage through several Indian families in the petition, its primary lineage was through Tamar Brushell and her descendants. The petitioning group sought to establish this lineage through vital records of various members of the Brushell family, including seaman records for Moses Brushell (Tamar Brushell's father) during the 1820s and 1830s. A record of the 1820 census of Waterford, Connecticut (uncovered during BAR research), cited Moses Brushell as a free colored man. The Eastern Pequots asserted, however, that both of Moses Brushell's wives were Eastern Pequots, providing Pequot ancestry to Tamar Brushell, the daughter of one of the wives.[24] The Eastern Pequots also provided BAR with a list of Eastern Pequots living on the reservation in 1825, which recorded the first Brushell family listing, and the 1889–91 overseers' report, which specifically included Tamar Brushell.

The Eastern Pequots regarded Tamar Brushell's 1915 obituary as further evidence of her Pequot ancestry. The obituary stated:

> The passing of Tamer Sebastian deserves more than slight mention in the obituary column. She had the pure blood of the Pequot Indians in her veins, and is almost the last of that historic race, whose reservation has been at Lantern Hill. Her marriage 63 years ago in the town of Stonington was to a

Portuguese, Manuel Sebastian, who was brought from the island of Porto Rico by one of the Mystic captains, tradition has it. . . . For 73 years of her 94 she was a member of the Union Baptist church. . . . Besides the children mentioned elsewhere, there survive 32 grandchildren, 24 great-grandchildren, and one great-great-grandchild.[25]

In its initial finding, BAR was unable to establish that the Eastern Pequots and Paucatuck Pequots represented one tribe with political factions.[26] BAR found that the Eastern Pequots met the requirements of Section 83.7(a), (c), (d), (e), (f), and (g) but decided that more information was needed to determine whether the petitioners met requirement 83.7(b).[27] BAR also opined that it desired to recognize a successor to the historic Eastern Pequot tribe but that it was not sure whether the members of the Eastern Pequots or of the Paucatuck Pequots were the appropriate successors.

Paucatuck Pequot Petition

The Paucatuck Pequots represented about ninety members of the Eastern Pequots who had seceded from the larger group. The Paucatuck Pequot petition asserted that the group met the seven criteria necessary for federal recognition. The Paucatuck Pequots' secession from the larger group was based on the belief that, pursuant to Pequot ordinances, Tamar Brushell's descendants had been granted tribal membership illegally. Unlike the Eastern Pequot petition, the Paucatuck Pequot petition rejected the use of the 1889–91 Overseers' report because, they claimed, the report inaccurately included Tamar Brushell. Despite the Eastern Pequots' traditionally matrilineal society, the splinter group's primary objection to Tamar Brushell's inclusion in the report was her marriage to Manuel Sebastian,[28] a non-Pequot, which the group believed excluded her and any of her descendants from inclusion in the tribe. This rejection amounted to the only substantive difference in the two petitions. Otherwise, both petitioners provided the same historical background and relied on the same vital statistics for those families that were not in dispute.[29]

Furthermore, the Paucatuck Pequot petition argued that certain Eastern Pequot family lines (in particular, Tamar Brushell's) could not be traced to the eighteenth-century Pequot records, indicating that the Eastern Pequots did not represent a continuation of the historical tribe as defined by 25CFR83. Conversely, the Paucatuck Pequots' petition asserted that their lineage could be traced to the eighteenth century and did not include Tamar Brushell.

This divide between the two groups had extreme racial undertones. An article in the *Hartford Courant* summarized the familial factions among the Pequots by saying that the divide "results from an 150-year old struggle in which two factions of the tribe have been at odds over whether one side which has habitually married blacks and Portuguese is as equally Eastern Pequot as one [that] habitually married whites."[30]

Hence, the central issue in the divide between the two groups was which group, according to the federal recognition process, is more Indian and therefore worthy of tribal benefits: those that have intermarried with African Americans or those that have intermarried with whites.

On June 24, 2002, Assistant Secretary of Indian Affairs Neal A. Mc-Caleb announced his decision to grant federal recognition to both the Eastern Pequots and the Paucatuck Pequots. The BIA's decision to recognize the two groups was predicated on their uniting as a single tribe.[31] Because of the factious, and at times acrimonious, history of the two groups, administrators at BIA have pledged to work with them to develop governing guidelines and procedures for the newly recognized and united Eastern Pequot tribe.[32] Commentators expect this process to be quite challenging, since the former Paucatuck Pequots had established governing guidelines, relationships with financial backers, and plans for economic development.

Mashantucket Pequot Indian Claims Settlement Act and the Simonds Family

On October 18, 1983, President Ronald Reagan signed into law the Mashantucket Pequot Indian Claims Settlement Act.[33] The act determined that the Western Pequot tribe, which was represented by the Mashantucket Pequot Tribal Council, was the "sole successor in interest to the aboriginal entity generally known as the Western Pequot Tribe which years ago claimed aboriginal title to certain lands in the State of Connecticut."[34] The act further acknowledged the grant of land (located in Ledyard, Connecticut) made by the State of Connecticut to the Western Pequot tribe and extinguished any competing land claims to the area by either citizens or other Indian tribes.[35] In addition, the act established the Mashantucket Pequot Settlement Fund, which sought to assist the promotion of economic development within the tribe.[36]

As a result of federal recognition, the Mashantucket Pequot tribe benefited from the Indian Gaming Regulatory Act. In 1992, the Mashantucket Pequots opened the Foxwoods High Stakes Bingo and Casino, currently the largest casino in the world and the most profitable Indian casino in the United States.[36]

The act limited constitutional challenges to its provisions by only recognizing those "pleadings contained in a complaint filed before the end of the one-hundred-and eight-day period beginning on the date of the enactment of this Act."[38] Consequently, anyone who desired to seek redress under or to challenge the act had to act promptly. Furthermore, the act never addressed the basis for the Mashantucket Pequot Tribal Council's authority or analyzed the framework in which the tribe determined tribal membership.

Recognized members of the Mashantucket Pequots include the descendants of Martha George and her four daughters, who now total more than 370 people living on or near the reservation.[39] The Simonds family, a group that has been denied Mashantucket membership, claims Mashantucket Pequot ancestry through Immanuel Simons, whom Hauptman and Wherry identify as an important political leader in the eighteenth century, and Susan Simons, whom they describe as a leader of one of the core Mashantucket families (Hauptman and Wherry 1990, 127).[40] Paradoxically, the Mashantucket Pequots consider Hauptman's and Wherry's *The Pequots in Southern New England* their official book.[41] However, in 1976, when Mashantucket Pequots residing on the reservation called a tribal meeting to discuss the direction of the tribe, the descendants of Immanuel and Susan Simons (the present-day Simondses) were not invited.[42] As a result, members of the Simonds family were omitted from the tribal membership roll and consequently did not benefit from the act. The Simonds family, being dark skinned, suspect that race played a pivotal role in their exclusion by other tribal members.

Mashantucket Pequots currently listed on the membership roll deny that race had anything to do with their decision to omit the Simonds family. Instead, they insist that the Simonds family did not meet membership requirements, which were amended in 1984. The 1984 amendment in membership criteria dictates that a person seeking tribal membership must demonstrate that his or her ancestors were on the 1900 and 1910 tribal censuses. The Simondses' ancestors, who had left the reservation to find work sometime in the 1860s, are listed on the 1858 census and every surviving census before that date, but they are not on the 1900 and 1910 censuses. The criterion before the 1984 amendment was whether one could prove through a birth certificate or other legal record that he or she was directly related to an Indian who had been genealogically recorded as a Western Pequot Indian by the State of Connecticut. The Simondses claim that they could have met the earlier requirement easily.[43]

Consequently, the Simondses assert that membership qualifications were amended solely to prevent them from obtaining tribal membership. Moreover, Mashantucket Pequot censuses dating from 1855 to 1888 (in which Simons family members are listed) were the basis for the act, which, according to the Simondses, makes the 1984 amendment even more egregious.[44]

Although the federal government did not mandate the 1984 amendment, it did accept the change in membership criteria for the act's purposes. Hence, the Simonds family hired lawyers who were prepared to argue in federal court that the membership rules that exclude the family were the result of collective actions by the federal government and the Mashantucket Pequot tribal government. In particular, the Simonds family's lawyers were set to argue that, by recognizing those currently listed on the Mashantucket Pequot roll through the act, the federal government violated the Simonds family's civil rights. In addition, the Simonds family's lawyers were prepared to argue that the federal government was aware of the amendment to the tribe's membership laws, which, according to the Simonds family's claim, created further governmental culpability in the deprivation of rights that they experienced.[45]

The Simonds family has delayed moving forward with the lawsuit in hopes of reconciling with the larger Mashantucket Pequot community. In light of possible reconciliation with the tribe, the Simondses have decided to no longer publicly discuss their grievances against the larger group. Instead, they have decided to wait on the promises of the chairman of the tribe to allow them entrance into the fold.[46]

It has not been alleged in either Pequot case that the federal government openly encouraged the racial divides. However, it is difficult to divorce past government practices, such as the use of blood quantum in determining whether one is Indian, from the racialized practices found in some Indian membership policies. Further, it has been argued that the racial practices found in certain Indian communities have root in policies and practices advanced by the U.S. government throughout the years. Laura Lovett, for instance, writes that during Jim Crow, Indian communities such as the Lumbees, the Pamukeys, and the Monacans disassociated themselves from their African American kinsmen and neighbors in attempts to curry favor with dominant society (Lovett 2002, 192). The Lumbees of North Carolina, who were federally recognized in 1956, for example, resisted their classification as "Colored" in the American system, which caused tension between them and their once friendly African American neighbors (Lovett 2002, 212). The Pamunkeys of Virginia carried membership cards to ensure that they would not be forced to sit in the Colored railway coach; some members of the tribe also wore their hair long and straight to ensure that they would not be mistaken for African American (Lovett 2002, 213). Finally, the Monacans of the Blue Ridge Mountains, having been classified as Colored because of historical intermarriages with African Americans, chose to remain illiterate rather than attend a Colored school and stopped intermarrying with African Americans, hoping to further isolate themselves from their African American neighbors (Lovett 2002, 213).

Consequently, although the federal government may not directly encourage New England Indian communities to institute racially discriminatory membership policies, the role that race and power have played historically in wider American politics should not be diminished or ignored when discussing racial politics in present-day New England Indian communities. It can be argued not only that past practices by the federal government have encouraged New England Indian communities' seeming preoccupation with race, but also that decisions in several court cases — and, in particular, the Mashpee trial — reflect the judiciary's emphasis on race in determining the existence of tribes and the rights of individuals within these tribes.

American Indian Case Law

Mashpee Tribe v. Town of Mashpee et al.

In 1977, after significant purchases of property in the Cape Cod area by non-Indian residents, the Mashpee Indians of Cape Cod, Massachusetts, brought action in a Boston federal court to thwart what they perceived as continuing encroachment on their land. In *Mashpee Tribe v. Town of Mashpee*, the Mashpees based their claim of recovery on the Indian Trade and Intercourse Act of 1790.[47] The act provided, in part, that "no purchase, grant, lease, or other conveyance of lands, or of any title or claim, thereto, from any Indian nation or tribe of Indians shall be of any validity in law or equity unless the same be made by treaty or convention entered into pursuant of the Constitution." Between 1842 and 1870, unilateral acts of the Massachusetts government resulted in the Mashpees' loss of significant portions of land in Cape Cod, actions that the Mashpees claimed were in violation of the Intercourse Act. Through government action, for example, land formerly held in common by the tribe was divided among its members, who were permitted to sell their individual holdings. Members who had not sold their land were subject to local taxes and soon lost their holdings through tax sales. By 1870, the year that Mashpee land was incorporated into a town, a majority of landowners in the area were non-Indian. The defendants in the suit, non-Indian residents and others with economic interests in the area, countered the petitioners' claim by arguing that the Mashpees were not a tribe and therefore were unable to seek redress under the Intercourse Act (Campisi 1991, 27–28).

Since the Mashpees were not federally recognized and did not have preexisting treaties with the U.S. government, the critical issue in the case became whether the Mashpees constituted a tribe and could, as a result, seek redress under the Intercourse Act. Consequently, the presiding judge separated the two issues of tribal existence and land ownership and set trial to first determine the issue of tribal existence. Ironically, in *United States v. Maine*, the U.S. government brought the interests of the Pasamoquates, a lighter-skinned Indian community, before the court without the group's first having been federally recognized as a tribe. Since the Mashpees had previously filed a petition with BAR for federal recognition, their attorneys objected to the judge's instructions and argued that the federal recognition process should resolve the issue of tribal existence. The judge overruled the objection, and the trial began (Campisi 1991, 18–19).

The majority of Mashpee Indians have dark complexions.[48] At various times during the trial, the defense counsel attempted to discredit anthropological evidence offered by the petitioners demonstrating that the group was Indian by referring to the Mashpee as an *African American* community (Campisi 1991, 27–28). In asserting the racial composite of the group, the defense stated, "You will find evidence rather clearly showing that there was a significant influx of other people of other racial backgrounds, so that by [the time the Mashpee became incorporated as a town in the State of Massachusetts] they were referred to as Indians, mulatto and *black* people" (Campisi 1991, 27; emphasis added). In demonstrating the defense counsel's emphasis on the racial makeup of the Mashpee, Clifford (1988, 285) writes:

> The image of Mashpee Indians, like that of several other eastern groups such as the Lumbee and the Ramapough, was complicated by issues of race. Significant intermarriage with blacks had occurred since the mid-eighteenth century, and the Mashpee were, at times, widely identified as "colored." In court the defense occasionally suggested that they were really blacks rather than Native Americans.

In addition, the defense counsel used the U.S. census of 1870, which recorded 86.5 percent of the Mashpee population as African American and less than .05 percent of the population as Indian, to further buttress this position (Campisi 1991, 28). The petitioners countered that during the 1870 census, enumerators recorded an individual's race based on their own perception rather than on the history or personal attestation of the individuals they counted. Hence, the crucial issue during the trial became whether the core Indian community had absorbed the African American outsiders or were themselves absorbed into the African American outsiders (Clifford 1988, 306).

The allegation that the Mashpees were an African American community and thereby absorbed into the African American outsiders was an assertion that the petitioners could not overcome. Although the petitioners introduced a great deal of evidence, ranging from expert anthropological testimony to historic documents, that strongly supported the Mashpees' tribal claim, the jury found that the Mashpee Indians did not constitute a tribe and thereby eliminated any hopes of land recovery for the group (Campisi 1991, 59–60). The decision also ended the federal recognition process taking place at BAR.

Conclusion

As federal funding for Indian programs becomes less available and appeals against the continued development of Indian casinos become more vocal, BAR has begun to review applications for federal recognition more stringently. The result is that Indian communities have become even more attuned to racial differences among their community members and, as a result, have begun to make undefined distinctions based on race among community members with the hope of securing federal recognition. Consequently, those phenotypic black residents of Indian communities who have lived among and intermarried within tribes for generations, and who at times have deeper cultural roots and connections than their "pure blood" counterparts, are faced with the ever increasing possibility of being disenfranchised within and abandoned by their own community.

Notes

1   Federal recognition entitles a tribe's members to a host of special services — including business loans, subsidized housing, scholarships, and health care — and it exempts them from some state and federal laws.

2   "Pequot Tribe Seeks Recognition," *New York Times*, December 20, 1998.

3   The term "esteemed family" demonstrates the complexity of Indian politics. The "esteemed family" in Indian communities, for instance, has been used to legitimate to the outside world individuals in the community who embody the traditions and customs of the tribe. Therefore, use of the term does not necessarily connote birth into a royal, superior family.

4   During the years preceding the smallpox epidemic, the Pequot community numbered 13,000 persons. After the epidemic, this was reduced to 3,000. Following the Pequot War of 1637, the population was further reduced to 1,000.

5   The Mohegan tribe currently owns the Mohegan Sun Casino in Connecticut.

6   "Pequot Tribe Seeks Recognition."

7   Ibid.

8   "The Big Gamble: Have American Indians Found Their New Buffalo?" *Fortune*, October 2, 2000. The Mashantucket Pequots own the Foxwoods casino, which is located on their reservation in Ledyard, Connecticut. The casino grosses more than one billion dollars a year and is currently the world's largest casino.

9   U.S. Bureau of Indian Affairs, Paucatuck Pequot Petition, 138–39. In a 1941 interview, his niece, Mrs. Calvin Geer, expressed a similar disdain for African blood. The interviewer recorded: "Mrs. Greer wanted it understood that there was not a drop of Negro blood in her. She was indignant at the 'Indians' on the reservation at Lantern Hill who she says are a bunch of Negroes. Her aunt, a

Mrs. Atwood Williams, of Mystic is married to another part Indian and they were active some years back in the 'Indian Federation' but have since dropped since so many Negroes came in."

10 "Pequot Tribe Seeks Recognition."

11 This conflict will be discussed further in the section dealing with the Eastern Pequot and Paucatuck Pequot petitions for federal recognition.

12 "Pequot Tribe Seeks Recognition."

13 Part 83, Title 25, Code of Federal Regulations, available online at www .access.gpo.gov/nara/cfr/waisidx_03/25crf83_03.html (accessed April 4, 2003). Bureau of Indian Affairs, Department of Interior, Part 83, Procedures for Establishing that an American Indian Group Exists as an Indian Tribe. Code of Federal Regulations.

14 Interview with Renee Kramer, Ph.D. candidate, Department of Politics, New York University, November 8, 2000. Kramer's dissertation will provide an anthropological and sociopolitical critique of the federal recognition process.

15 *California v. Cabazon Band of Mission Indians*, 480 U.S. 202 (1987).

16 *Brantley Willis v. The Honorable Kirk Fordice, Governor of the State of Mississippi*, 850 F. Supp. 523 (1994).

17 "The Big Gamble," 233–34. The majority of Indian gambling enterprises are not as successful.

18 However, this process often takes much longer.

19 Evidence to be relied on in determining a group's Indian identity may include one or a combination of the following, as well as other evidence of identification by someone other than the petitioner itself or its members: (1) Identification as an Indian by federal authorities; (2) relationships with state governments based on identification of the groups as Indian; (3) dealings with a county, parish, or other local government in a relationship based on the group's Indian identity; (4) identification as an Indian entity by anthropologists, historians, or other scholars; (5) identification as an Indian entity in newspapers and books; and (6) identification as an Indian entity in relationships with Indian tribes or with national, regional, or state Indian organizations.

20 (1) This criterion may be demonstrated by some combination of the following evidence and/or other evidence that the petitioner meets the definition of community set forth in paragraph 83.1:

Significant rates of marriage within the group, and/or, as may be culturally required, patterned-out marriages with other Indian populations.

Significant social relationships connecting individual members.

Significant rates of informal social interaction that exist broadly among the members of a group.

A significant degree of shared or cooperative labor or other economic activity among the membership.

Evidence of strong patterns of discrimination or other social distinctions by non-members.

Shared sacred or secular ritual activity encompassing most of the group.

Cultural patterns shared among a significant portion of the group that are different from those of the non-Indian populations with whom it interacts. These patterns must function as more than symbolic identification of the group as Indian. They may include, but are not limited to, language, kinship, organization, or religious beliefs and practices.

The persistence of a named, collective Indian identity continuously over a period of more than 50 years, notwithstanding changes in name.

A demonstration of historical political influence under the criterion in paragraph 83.7(c) shall be evidence for demonstrating historical community.

(2) A petitioner shall be considered to have provided sufficient evidence of a community at a given point in time if evidence is provided to demonstrate any one of the following:

More than 50 percent of the members reside in a geographical area exclusively or almost exclusively composed of members of the group, and the balance of the group maintains consistent interaction with some members of the community;

At least 50 percent of the marriages in the group are between members of the group;

At least 50 percent of the group members maintain distinct cultural patterns such as, but not limited to, language, kinship organization, or religious beliefs and practices;

There are distinct community social institutions encompassing most of the members, such as kinship organizations, formal or informal economic cooperation, or religious organizations; or

The group has met the criterion in paragraph 83.7(c) using evidence described in paragraph 83.7(c)(2). (Code of Federal Regulations, paragraph 83.7 (b) (1) — (b) (2) (v)).

21   (1) This criterion may be demonstrated by some combination of the evidence listed below and/or by other evidence that the petitioner meets the definition of political influence or authority in paragraph 83.1.

The group is able to mobilize significant numbers of members and significant resources from its members for group purposes.

Most of the membership considers issues acted upon or actions taken by group leaders or governing bodies to be of importance.

There is widespread knowledge, communication and involvement in political processes by most of the group's members.

The group meets the criterion in paragraph 83.7(b) at more than a minimal level.

There are internal conflicts that show controversy over valued group goals, properties, policies, processes and/or decisions.

A petitioning group shall be considered to have provided sufficient evidence to demonstrate the exercise of political influence or authority at a given point in time by demonstrating that group leaders and/or other mechanisms exist or existed which:

Allocate group resources such as land, residence rights and the like on a consistent basis.

Settle disputes between members or subgroups by mediation or other means on a regular basis;

Exert strong influence on the behavior of individual members, such as the establishment or maintenance of norms and the enforcement of sanctions to direct or control behavior;

Organize or influence economic subsistence activities among the members, including shared or cooperative labor.

A group that has met the requirements in paragraph 83.7(b)(2) at a given point in time shall be considered to have provided sufficient evidence to meet this criterion at that point in time. (Code of Federal Regulations, paragraph 83.7 [cjc1]–[c] [3]).

22 (1) Evidence acceptable to the Secretary which can be used for this purpose includes but not limited to:

Rolls prepared by the Secretary on a descendency basis for purposes of distributing claims money, providing allotments, or other purposes;

State, Federal, or other official records or evidence identifying present members or ancestors of present members as being descendants of a historical tribe or tribes that combined and functioned as a single autonomous political entity.

Church, school and other similar enrollment records identifying present members or ancestors of present members as being descendants of a historical tribe or tribes that combined and functioned as a single autonomous political entity.

Affidavits of recognition by tribal elders, leaders, or the tribal governing body identifying present members or ancestors of present members as being descendants of a historical tribe or tribes that combined and functioned as a single autonomous political entity.

Other records or evidence identifying present members or ancestors of present members as being descendants of a historical tribe or tribes that combined and functioned as a single autonomous political entity.

The petitioner must provide an official membership list, separately certified by the group's governing body, of all known current members of the group. (Part 83 of Title 25 of the Code of Federal Regulations).

23 "Pequot Tribe Seeks Recognition."

24 Bureau of Indian Affairs, Eastern Pequot Petition, 89–90.

25 Ibid., 90–91.

26 Paucatuck Pequot Petition, 50.

27 Eastern Pequot Petition, 48–49.

28 Many anthropologists are of the opinion that Manuel Sebastian was an African from Azor, a Portuguese colony off the coast of West Africa, and that he arrived on the East Coast of the present-day United States as a result of his seafaring on behalf of the Portuguese empire.

29 Eastern Pequot Petition, 7.

30 "Pequot Indians Suing State for Representation," *Hartford Courant*, September 4, 1976.

31 U.S. Department of the Interior, Office of the Assistant Secretary, Indian Affairs, "McCaleb Issues Final Determination to Acknowledge the Historical Eastern Pequot Tribe," available online at www.doi.gov/news/020624c.html (accessed March 28 , 2004).

32 "Pequot Recognition Is Only the First Step," *New York Times*, June 30, 2002.

33 Mashantucket Pequot Nation in Connecticut, Public Law 98–134 (S. 1499), enacted October 18, 1983.

34 Ibid., sec. 2(e).

35 Ibid., sec. 4(a–b).

36 Ibid., secs. 5(a), 5(b)(3).

37 "The Big Gamble."

38 Public Law 98–134, sec. 7(a)(1).

39 "Who Is an Indian and Who Decides?" *New York Times*, January 14, 1996.

40 Ibid.

41 Ibid.

42 Ibid.

43 Ibid.

44 Ibid.

45 Ibid.

46 "Those Unrecognized as Members of Tribes Work to Prove They Are the Real Thing," *Hartford Courant*, July 7, 2003.

47 Indian Trade and Intercourse Act of 1790, 1 Stat. 137, codified as 25 U.S.C., sec. 177, available online at www4.1aw.cornell.edu/cgi-bin/thm_hl?DB= uscode25&STEMMER=en&WORDS=177+&COLOUR=Red&STYLE= s&URL=/uscode/2 5/177.html#muscat_highlighter_first_match (accessed April 4, 2004).

48 The community has a history of intermarriage with African Americans.

CHAPTER FOUR

Where Will the Nation Be at Home?

Race, Nationalisms, and Emigration Movements

in the Creek Nation

DAVID A. Y. O. CHANG

~~~~~~~

In June 1898, a group of men gathered in the town of Wewoka, capital of the Seminole Nation, to found the Inter-national Afro-American League. With an eye toward impending changes in the political and social landscape of Indian Territory, they dedicated themselves to mobilizing African Americans to defend their interests.[1] The name of the league is worthy of close examination. The term "Afro-American" proudly proclaimed the enduring identification of these black Americans with Africa. In the word "Inter-national" we are tempted to hear a related affirmation: that the struggle of African Americans was part of a worldwide struggle of people of African descent. Although this interpretation is possible, another is more likely and more instructive. In the context of Wewoka in the 1890s, "international" often referred to relations among the principal nations of Indian Territory: the Cherokee, Chickasaw, Choctaw, Muskogee, and Seminole nations. The founders of the league were inhabitants of these nations. By organizing across national lines and by claiming the name "Afro-American," the founders of the organization affirmed the racial unity that bound them together. By asserting that this was an international organization, the founders of the league also asserted that the Cherokee, Chickasaw, Choctaw, Muskogee, and Seminole nations were indeed nations, and this at a time that the federal government of the United States was threatening to abolish those nations' political existence. Read in this way, the name of the Inter-national Afro-American League signals the power that the idea of the nation held in late-nineteenth-century Indian Territory.

The power of the idea of the nation becomes even more evident when we consider that the same year that the league was formed, many residents of Indian Territory were discussing moving their nations to other parts of the world. In 1898, Cherokees, Choctaws, and Muskogees (commonly known as "Creeks") were debating whether, given the fact that the government of the United States was threatening to do away with their existence as nations, it might be better to relocate south of the Rio Grande. Meanwhile, black citizens of these nations (often referred to as "Freedmen" at the time) were following with interest plans for emigration to Liberia. In recent years, various Creek Freedmen had already taken that path. Now African Americans (that is, black settlers who had formerly lived in the southern portion of the United States) were planning to leave Oklahoma Territory for Liberia.

From the 1880s to the 1940s, nationalist and emigrationist movements repeatedly captured the imaginations of people of indigenous and African descent in Indian Territory and eastern Oklahoma. The trials of these tumultuous years refigured and reinforced nationality in the region. This essay will use a discussion of nationalist and emigrationist movements among Creeks, African Americans, and others to trace how the idea of the nation became so powerful in this region at a moment when the boundaries and sovereignty of Indian nations were very much in doubt. This exploratory survey asks what these nationalist and emigrationist movements mean in the context of the histories of Indian Territory and especially of Creek people of African descent. This story demonstrates that these national discourses always related to ideas of race, but that the nature of this relationship could vary considerably. The specificities of history gave different shapes to the links between race and nation. Before turning to the issue of nationalist and emigrationist movements, however, it is worthwhile to consider the nature of the collective identity of Creeks of African descent.

In the 1890s, a common English-language designator for Creeks of African descent was "Freedman." The word, which was equally applicable to women and men, both revealed and concealed much about the group. On the one hand, it correctly expressed the condition of the former slaves of the Creek nation: They had been slaves; now they were freed. On the other hand, the word was a powerful tool that implied that

Freedmen were readily discernable from other Creeks. When applied to all Creeks of African descent, the term implied that they all had been slaves to Creek masters before 1866, when the government of the Creek Nation was forced by the federal government of the United States to abolish slavery. But not all "Freedmen" were freed Creek slaves or descended from freed Creek slaves. Free men and women of African descent had been members of the Creek Nation since its emergence in the eighteenth century, although they had not always been accepted as equals in the nation. In the years preceding the Civil War, the Creek Council had passed legislation that sought to restrict the number and influence of free people of African descent, proclaiming, for example, that Creek slaveowners could free their slaves only if they removed them from the territory of the nation. But despite all the hostility they had faced in their nation, free black Creeks were part of the nation even during the days of slavery. In the late nineteenth century, when non-African Creeks applied the term "Freedmen" to all black Creeks, they relegated all black Creeks to the status of freed slaves and descendents of slaves. They thereby erased the free Creeks of African descent from the history of the Creek nation and remapped its racial boundaries (Chang 2002, 77–78, 106–7; Debo 1941, 126–127).

When we look at the word "Freedman" in this way—as a term imposed from without—it drew a sharp line between Freedmen and Creeks. Creek Freedmen were, following this logic, not truly Creek. The mark of slavery, their African ancestry, made them something other (Todorov 1987, 185–201). This process of naming also implicitly defined the unmarked category of "Creek." "Creek" meant non-slave, non-black. It included only Creeks of exclusively indigenous ancestry or of mixed indigenous and European ancestry. In the case of certain notable Creek families, such as the Perrymans, many other Creeks politely ignored the fact that they were believed by many to have some African ancestry. The Perrymans had been among the Creek Nation's antebellum plantation-owning elite. After the Civil War, the family supplied sons who held judgeships, seats in the House of Kings, and the chieftaincy of the Creek Nation (Meserve 1937). The selective omission recognized that these families' social, political, and economic stature in the Creek Nation made the reputed African element in their genealogies irrelevant. Much as in parts of Latin America and the Caribbean, in the Creek Nation in the late nineteenth century wealth and status had the power to remove the liability of African ancestry, a liability that was captured in the term "Freedman" (Harris 1964; Skid-more 1972).

The term, however, was not only imposed from without but also claimed from within: Creeks of African descent came to claim the name of Freedmen for themselves. When they did so, they also redefined their relationship to the Creek Nation. The term had the power to assert unity among Creeks of African descent. "Creek Freedman" had become a term of self-reference at least by the turn of the twentieth century. By calling themselves Creek Freedmen, people asserted a common identity, something shared and apart from other groups — indigenous, white, and black. As will be seen later, people in Indian Territory, and later in the State of Oklahoma, would not use the term for African Americans who had come to settle from the states to the east. Creek Freedmen asserted (among other things) both that they were members of the Creek Nation and that they had a special and separate place within that nation.

In this same period, as Creeks were renegotiating the social boundaries of their nation, the U.S. government was working to abolish the existence of the Creek Nation as a political entity. This goal was inseparable from the intention to divide the lands of the Creek Nation into private parcels. Both of these changes were necessary to ready the area for the imposition of statehood — redefining the area into part of the "American" nation. In 1887, Congress passed the General Allotment Act, usually known as the Dawes Act. The law provided for the dividing of Indian peoples' lands in preparation for extinguishing tribal government. Its champions declared that private property would bring "civilization" to American Indians. The vehement objections of the "Five Civilized Tribes" (the Cherokee, Chickasaw, Choctaw, Creek, and Seminole Nations) won an exemption from the act for Indian Territory. The ironies in the exemption were multiple. Few other Indian peoples had embraced private property, Christianity, the English language, schooling, or the other trappings of the reformers' brand of civilization to the degree of the "Five Civilized Tribes." These very attributes and skills, however, initially permitted them to fight off a threat to their sovereignty and system of land tenure (Prucha 1984, 669, 737, 746). In the years after the passage of the act, however, Western legislators and businesses interested in land speculation militated for the allotment of lands in Indian Territory (Debo 1940, 52–53). These demands for more allotment legislation came to fruition in

1893, when Congress created the Commission to the Five Civilized Tribes. Congress empowered the commission to negotiate agreements with each of the five tribes to provide for the allotment of Indian lands and the end of tribal political sovereignty. The commissioners met, however, with the resolute refusal of Indian governments to consider the allotment of lands and the end of national existence (Debo 1940, 22; Goble 1980, 72). Fed up with the intransigence of the Indian governments, Congress decreed that if the Creek, Chickasaw, and Choctaw nations had not negotiated and ratified an agreement for allotment by October 1, 1898, then the entire authority of their courts would be transferred to the U.S. courts. This was a powerful incentive for the Indian governments to capitulate on allotment. In February 1899, the Creek National Council finally ratified an allotment agreement (Carter 1999, 43).

As the debate raged over the fate of Creek national sovereignty and Creek lands, some Creek Freedmen looked for their future abroad. In 1887, several groups of Creek Freedmen left the area of Muskogee for Liberia. Just how many emigrated is unclear, but the migration would go on for several years. More Creek Freedmen left for Liberia in 1889 and 1890. Those who contemplated the voyage were encouraged by the reports of such emigrants as Moses Cade. Cade had settled with his wife Clarissa in the region of the St. John River in Liberia and reported that the happiness he had found had well warranted the forty days of travel from Muskogee. The Cades' labor had led to material comfort. Cade boasted, "My land is drawn, my house is built," and not only were the crops in the ground but "breadstuffs are coming up plentifully." Cade assured his friends that what he had found, so, too, could they, for "there is plenty of land here, and good land it is." He intimated that prosperity awaited the emigrant.[2] But ultimately, what Cade advocated was not emigration to Liberia but *return* to Africa. Cade did not call his friends out of Indian Territory and to Liberia for the simple sake of material success. Rather, he called them as part of an explicitly nationalist project. He enjoined them to "come home to Liberia," for it was "our home where we can truly praise God who made us under the flag of liberty." Cade made clear that this banner was not the Stars and Stripes but, rather, the "lone star of Liberis." Cade's was a specifically racial form of nationalism: He proclaimed that he had arrived in "the land of the Negro Race." For Cade, this was what gave meaning to the material gains he had made in Liberia. After returning to his African home, he could declare, "I am happy under my own vine and fig tree."[3]

Not all of the emigrants sent back reports of such glowing success, and yet for some the movement retained its appeal. In 1888, a Muskogee newspaper reprinted letters supposedly sent from former residents of the city who had emigrated to Liberia. They warned potential emigrants not to make the move, reporting that they were hungry and wished they had never left Indian Territory.[4] The experiences they recounted did not differ greatly from those of many men and women who returned to Africa from the diaspora. Some found the success that Cade trumpeted, but others suffered the poverty that the second group reported was their lot. The emigration movement nonetheless continued to gather adherents, with the Creeks' neighbors also participating. In 1892, a group of twenty-five families struck out for Liberia from the Sequoyah district of the Cherokee Nation but were unable to secure the transportation they needed from New York.[5] In 1899, newspapers reported that two rail cars full of African Americans from Oklahoma Territory had set off for Liberia.[6] The number that emigrated may not have been large, but the desire to emigrate to Africa was something that Creek Freedmen shared with other people of African descent in the region.

Other Creeks, Cherokees, and Choctaws (that is, those who were not of African descent) were also considering group emigration at the time, but not to Africa. Mexico beckoned to these people. By 1895, some Creek leaders were calling for a southward migration. For more than a decade, reports circulated in the area that Creeks and other American Indian people were debating an exodus to Mexico, laying out plans for selling lands in Oklahoma, sending exploratory parties to Mexico to investigate the possibilities for American Indian settlement there, even seeking to negotiate the terms of land sales with Mexican authorities.[7]

The idea of a migration of Indian nations together to Mexico bears a resemblance to the impulse behind the founding of the Inter-national Afro-American League in 1898. Like the league, it continued to affirm the reality and importance of the separate nations. And like the league, it nonetheless indicated a belief in a common purpose and in some way a common identity. The idea of cooperation among different Indian nations was well established in the relations between indigenous peoples, especially in Indian Territory. From the Pueblo uprising of 1680 and King Phillip's War in 1675–76 to Tecumseh's confederacy in the early nineteenth century, Indian leaders had sought to build Indian military unity in the opposition to European and Euro-American invasion (Dowd 1992; Edmunds 1983, 1984). In Indian Territory, the effort to build Indian unity had often taken a diplomatic cast. In the 1870s, the Creeks hosted a series of councils in which members of the "Five Civilized Tribes" attempted to bring their Plains neighbors into a cooperative alliance and ultimately to create "a federal union similar to that of the United States." The plan foundered due to the concerns of the smaller Indian nations that they would be overwhelmed by the larger groups and opposition by whites fearful of the potential power of a unified and independent Indian authority (Debo 1941, 205–10; Nolen 1980). In the 1880s and the 1890s, representatives of the Cherokee, Choctaw, Chickasaw, Creek, and Seminole nations had worked together to resist allotment legislation, this time more successfully overcoming national divisions between them. The idea of a joint Indian emigration to Mexico could draw nourishment from this long but sometimes contentious history of international relations in Indian Territory.

In the 1890s, much of the energy behind a migration to Mexico came from the resistance to the changes that the Dawes Act was forcing on Indian Territory. In the Creek Nation, advocates of emigration to Mexico included the most famous opponents of the allotment of lands and the dissolution of the Creek government. In 1895, the principal chief of the Creek Nation, Isparhecher, announced that he would rather that his people emigrate than accept allotment. He was joined in this statement by Cherokee and Choctaw leaders.[8] Isparhecher had campaigned for the office of principal chief largely on the power of his firm and established opposition to allotment and defense of Creek political autonomy (Debo 1941, 361).[9] Ultimately, Washington succeeded in forcing Isparhecher to accede to a plan to allot Creek lands and dissolve the Creek government. When Isparhecher accepted the U.S. government's demands, Chitto Harjo emerged as the most prominent foe of allotment. By 1901, he, too, was reported to be considering the emigration of his people to Mexico.[10] Chitto Harjo became a leader of Creek "irreconcilables" whom authorities and pressmen dubbed the "Snakes" (a term derived from the English translation of Chitto Harjo's name, "Crazy Snake"). For Chitto Harjo and the "Snakes," the primary line of action was the defense of Creek lands and Creek sovereignty at home, but emigration to Mexico retained its appeal for them for years to come. Indeed, newspapers reported in 1905 that the "Snakes" were planning for emigration to Mexico. Creeks and members of other Indian nations had convened near Tulsa to hatch a plan to sell the lands they had been allotted to purchase land in Mexico.[11] Tobe Berryhill took a place of leadership in these plans, reportedly sending a delegation of Creeks to Mexico to look into the possibilities of resettlement there. He was apparently pleased by their reports, as he announced in 1904 that conditions in Mexico were better suited to the needs of American Indians than the situation they knew at home.[12] Allotment and the impending dissolution of Indian governments had convinced many that their options were better abroad. For some, emigration to Mexico seemed the only possible choice. Bird Harris, a Cherokee, had already concluded in 1895 that it was impossible for Indians to "exist as a race under allotment of lands and Statehood." It was in this spirit that the Choctaw Jacob B. Jackson petitioned the federal government to assist Indians in moving to Mexico. Jackson noted that among the rights that "the Great Father of all men" had granted to Indians was "the right to exist as a race." Emigration was necessary to preserve this right.[13]

Jackson's words remind us that race was intimately related to the issue of Mexican emigration and to the fate of Indian lands, Indian sovereignty, and Indian nationhood. Press reports consistently referred to those who favored emigration as "Indians," a term that in the parlance of the region excluded Freedmen. Often, reports were more specific, claiming that "full bloods" provided the bulk of support for emigration to Mexico. While the term technically described people of exclusively indigenous heritage, it was also used as a marker of political and cultural orientation. In late-nineteenth-century Indian Territory, a "full blood" was assumed to be "traditional" and therefore particularly resistant to allotment and statehood. In reality, matters were considerably more complex: Ancestry did not correlate so neatly with political beliefs. Just as families like the Perrymans were considered "mixed blood" (i.e., mixed European and indigenous) despite their reputed African ancestry, some Creeks were considered "full bloods" despite some nonindigenous ancestry. Furthermore, some people who were apparently of entirely indigenous ancestry (including Isparhecher) came to accept allotment and statehood (Chang 2002, 67–68, 88–91).

The term "full blood" is better understood as a marker of cultural and political orientation than of biological heritage and points to the ways that nationhood was marked by race. In short, "full blood" described a person's beliefs more than her "blood." Among those beliefs might figure a dedication to the Muskogee language rather than English, Creek religion rather than (or alongside) Christianity, Creek land tenure rather than allotment, and Creek political autonomy rather than U.S. statehood. Thus when news reports tell us that "full bloods" favored emigration to Mexico, it tells us that the sort of people who opposed the incorporation of the Indian nations into the Anglo-American political and land-tenure system were the same sort of people who looked for relief in Mexico. In the Creek Nation, Isparhecher and Chitto Harjo, leaders of supposedly "full-blood" factions, were vocal proponents of Creek emigration to Mexico.

The fact that these men favored emigration should help to undermine the notion that they were the conservative champions of "tradition." Anglo-American contemporaries often portrayed the opponents of allotment as tragic figures stubbornly holding fast to a passing order. The willingness to pull up roots and head to Mexico indicates that Creek people were willing to embrace significant change in the defense of what they were trying to protect. The migration to Mexico would have been a dramatic change in the lives of Creek people. Even considering that the Creeks had arrived in Indian Territory only beginning in the 1830s, they had made the area their home. This is where they had established their farms, their ranches, their ceremonial stomp grounds. Almost two centuries of contact with Scots, Englishmen, and Anglo-Americans had created a familiarity with (if not necessarily an affection for) Anglo-American culture, Protestantism, the English language, and the U.S. government. This was true even of Creek people who were hostile to political incursions by the United States. The move to Mexico would have been a true emigration. Creeks who favored the move were not mired in the past but seeking a better future. Just as some Creek Freedmen were making a nationalist "return" to Africa to build a different tomorrow, some Creeks perceived Mexico to be the place they could find their future.

But did nationalism play a role in the Mexico emigration movement, as it did for the advocates of a return to Africa? The question is a complex one, and it indicates differences between how some Freedmen and some other Creeks drew the boundaries of nation. For at least some Creek Freedmen, Africa meant a homeland for what Moses Cade called "the Negro Race." In other words, it was a homeland that Freedmen shared with other black people — including black citizens of the United States and the emigrants from the Cherokee Nation. This racial unity and the racial nationalism that it supported had the power to override the national differences that might have divided the emigrants into Creek Freedmen, Cherokee Freedmen, Choctaw Freedmen, and African Americans from the Southern states. Emigration to what Cade termed "the land of the Negro Race" thus suggested the refiguring of race as a basis of nationhood. For the non-black Creeks (that is, the "Indians"), it is more difficult to argue that there was a direct relationship between the emigration movement and a pan-Indian nationalism — a nationalism that transcended the boundaries that divided Creeks from Cherokees from Choctaws. When Bird Harris called for emigration to Mexico on the grounds that Indians could not "exist as a race under allotment and Statehood," he affirmed that being Indian was a racial identity. He did not, however, imply that Indians were one nation. When Creeks and Cherokees and Choctaws came together to plan for emigration, they did so as Indians together, but they also did so as nations apart.

Indeed, some Creeks believed that Mexico was the land of origin of the Muskogee Creek people. From the late eighteenth century until today, some Muskogee Creek people have said that their ancestors migrated to what is now Alabama from an earlier home in Mexico (Milfort 1956, 161–63).[14] Emigration to Mexico may thus have appealed to some Creeks as a return to an ancestral Creek land. This must remain a hypothesis deserving of further archival and oral-history research. But if Creeks looked at emigration as a return to a national homeland, they did so in a different way from Freedmen who looked at emigration as a return to the homeland of the whole "Negro race." Even if Creeks moved to Mexico with Cherokees and Choctaws and other Indian people, they seem not to have looked to this as a national project that transcended the lines between them.

In the pivotal 1890s, a distinctive Creek Freedman national identity similarly existed alongside the sort of pan-African nationalism expressed by some who championed a return to Africa. The celebration of Emancipation Day in the Creek Nation provides a glance at the complexity of nation for people of African descent in the region. Since the end of the Civil War, African Americans in many places have marked the anniversary of the time that news of emancipation reached a particular area. This is most famous in the celebration of June 19 as Juneteenth Day, the day that some enslaved people in Texas learned that they were now legally free. Juneteenth Day functions in many ways as an African American Independence Day, a national holiday for the African American nation. In the 1890s, newspapers in the Creek Nation reported that "the Negroes" celebrated Emancipation Day on August 4. Celebrants would gather near a creek for a barbecue and games — a picnic to celebrate their freedom. In some ways, the Emancipation Day picnics bore a resemblance to the Green Corn festival, the annual summer festival at which members of Creek towns purified themselves and participated in rituals that affirmed the bonds between them. Unlike the Green Corn festival, Emancipation Day was not explicitly sacred. Nevertheless, the picnics were an annual ritual that celebrated a transformative moment in the history of Freedmen. The Green Corn festivals and other festivals of Creek towns took place at a stomp grounds, the ceremonial locus of the dispersed Creek towns. Freedmen celebrated Emancipation Day in analogous locations of symbolic power: the banks of creeks — Cane Creek in 1893, Adam's Creek in 1894. Because these bottomlands were rich, Creek slaves and their Freedman descendants had centered their communities on the water's edge for decades. Freedmen gathered for Emancipation Day at places that were central to their history. The celebration of Emancipation Day in the Creek Nation thus marked a holiday that African Americans around the United States would have recognized, but it marked it in a distinct manner. The celebrations were even separate from those of other Indian Territory Freedmen. In 1893, for example, Creek Freedmen and Cherokee Freedmen both celebrated Emancipation Day on August 4, but at separate events. If we see the celebration of emancipation as in some way a national holiday for African Americans, we should also recognize that Emancipation Day in the area of Muskogee suggested an affirmation of the Creek Freedmen's national distinctiveness from other African Americans.[15]

Different forms of national celebration point to other differences that would be the basis of conflicts between Creek Freedmen and African Americans from the Southern states. The rapid migration of African Americans to Indian Territory placed strains on the kind of racial pan-Africanism that some advocates of a return to Africa endorsed. This migration opened a rift between black settlers and Indian Territory Freedmen, a rift often expressed in terms of national identity. The

David A. Y. O. Chang

development of African American towns highlights the social distance that separated the African American immigrants from the Creek Freedmen. Between 1890 and 1907, the African American population of Indian Territory increased more than fourfold, surging from fewer than 19,000 to more than 80,000. African Americans tended to settle in the Creek and Seminole nations in areas that would make up Oklahoma's "Black Belt." Faced with impediments to farming and attracted by the commercial opportunities in the towns and cities of the rapidly growing region, many African Americans settled in some twenty smaller communities that had been founded as "all-black towns." Miles of territory separated most immigrant towns from the Creek and Seminole Freedmen settlements. Some towns, such as Boley and Clearview, were founded quite close to or even on lands that Freedmen had chosen for their allotments, but the social distance between the African American settlers and the Freedmen remained great despite their physical proximity. The conflict sometimes spilled into violence. Boley residents complained that Freedmen not only disrupted their church services but also even periodically rode through town at night, terrorizing the population by shooting out windows. One report maintains that the attacks ceased only when Boley's security officer killed several of the Freedmen in an altercation, but the animosities remained. National identity continued to separate Creek Freedmen from African Americans who had come from the states to the east. The division between the groups is nowhere more apparent than in the terms they used to refer to each other. The newcomers in Boley and other towns called the Freedmen "natives." Freedmen similarly set themselves apart from the immigrants by referring to them as "State Negroes" (Bittle and Geis 1964, 22–23; Crockett 1979, 28–29; Hamilton 1991, 126; Sameth 1940; Teall 1971, 167).

Judging from news reports, African emigration movements quieted at the turn of the twentieth century. Although it is risky to venture a guess why, this period coincided with massive transformations in the region. When they moved to Indian Territory, newly arrived African Americans from the southeastern states had just completed a major act of emigration in hopes of bettering their lives. Perhaps this made them less likely to pick up and move again, this time across the Atlantic Ocean. Meanwhile, the changes that the area was undergoing — allotment was all but completed by 1907, when the new state government of Oklahoma replaced the governments of the Indian nations — may have occupied the attention of many of the Freedmen who otherwise would have looked for their future in Africa. Finally, the influx of African Americans from the southeast, and the resulting tensions between Freedmen and black newcomers, may have placed strain on the racial pan-Africanism that underlay appeals for a return to Africa. Whatever the reason, African American emigrationist movements in the area seem to have quieted during the first decade of the twentieth century.

They gained new intensity after 1909. That year, Dr. P. J. Dorman, an African American teacher from Mantee, Oklahoma, founded a society to favor the emigration of African Americans to Africa. That society apparently included only a few members. Those members, however, followed the news of African emigration movements elsewhere in the country. In 1913, Dorman learned about Chief Alfred Sam, an African who was organizing a trading company and intended to lead African Americans to settle in Africa. Dorman and his fellows put themselves in correspondence with Chief Sam and arranged for him to come to Oklahoma. By May 1913, Chief Sam was in Oklahoma, speaking in small towns, making quite a stir in the area of dense African American settlement that stretched through the lands of the old Creek and Seminole nations.

One can judge the confluence of race and nation in a speech Chief Sam gave in October 1913 in a church in the town of Weleetka. Chief Sam informed the crowd that he came from Apaso in the western Akyem district of the British colony of Gold Coast (present-day Ghana). He announced that that there was "more than ample room in Africa for the American Negro to settle." African Americans who moved there, he told the audience, would find unequaled opportunity. Chief Sam offered his listeners the chance to be part of this enterprise. Chief Sam said he had purchased forty-five square miles of fertile land in the region and had founded the Akim Trading Company. Anyone who bought a share of this company would receive passage to the Gold Coast and the chance to start over on that land. Many who were present knew about this opportunity to emigrate to Africa and had already decided to follow Chief Sam there. When Chief Sam finished speaking, they took the pulpit and testified not only that his plan was not only solid, but that it offered the chance for individual prosperity and the redemption of "the Negro." The testimonials continued the next day, when the manager of the Akim Trading Company announced that shares in the company would be sold in front of the church for twenty-five dollars apiece. In a matter of hours, the company sold over $6,000 in stock, more than 240 shares. By the end of the emigration effort, the company would sell $72,000 in shares (Bittle and Geis 1964, 79–81).

Chief Sam drew the interest of men such as R. C. Lee, a minister in Nuyaka. The secretary of a local club of Chief Sam supporters, Lee summed up the appeal of emigration to the Gold Coast: Chief Sam told African American Oklahomans that "they will have a home there always without price and without taxation and that the Government is run absolutely by negroes." The nationalist idea of linking land and self-government was compelling in this context. Many African American farmers in Oklahoma were landless, and the grandfather clause and repression had instituted white political supremacy in the seven years since Oklahoma had become a state. One of the hopes that had convinced so many African Americans from the southeastern states to settle in Oklahoma was the belief that they could secure a fuller measure of justice there than in the South. C. G. Samuels, a resident of the all-black town of Boley, pointed out that, instead, "the ballot box has been taken from us and we can not act as a man and [our] peoples are treated so crual . . . , lynched for most any little frivulus crime with the cord of law and . . . jim Croed in the courthouse and in all publick places." Given such a disappointment, Samuels decided, it would be better to "make it to our native land" (Bittle and Geis 1964, 75–78).

Africa was, of course, the "native land" not only of African Americans who had recently settled in the area but also of the Creek Freedmen. Indeed, the emigrationist nationalism of Chief Sam's movement brought together Freedmen and newcomers. African American newcomers spearheaded Chief Sam's organization, but the legitimacy of the emigration effort gained a boost when it won the endorsement of J. Coody Johnson, a widely respected Creek Freedman attorney. One newspaper reported that Johnson, "one of our noblest attorneys, . . . made the speech of his life" in favor of emigration. The discourse "brought tears and groans from the audience." Johnson's stamp of approval led even the skeptical editor, a newcomer to Oklahoma, to believe that exodus to Africa was inevitable.[16] Thus, for all the divisions between them, some Creek Freedmen and some recently arrived African Americans could come together in the hope of building a nation far from American shores. Indeed, the ways that people of African descent understood their national identities were being refigured and reinforced in Oklahoma in this period. In the African return movement,

Creek Freedmen and African American newcomers embraced the idea that a nation rooted in Africa bound them together. Moving from the particular nationalisms that had divided them toward the common nation that joined them together did not erode the power of the idea of the nation but, rather, lent it fresh vigor.

The emigration effort ended in failure for most. By February 1914, hundreds of would-be emigrants gathered to make camp at Weleetka and then at Galveston, Texas, the port of departure. Difficulties with hostile port authorities and the antiquated steamer Chief Sam had bought meant months of waiting, during which time many would-be emigrants exhausted their supplies and funds. The ship was far too small to carry all who held stock in the company, and only sixty passengers were aboard the *Liberia* when it left port on August 20, 1914. After a difficult voyage and a delay of several months in Sierra Leone (imposed by the British authorities), the ship finally arrived in Gold Coast on January 13, 1915. Contrary to the skeptics' predictions, Sam did in fact have land ready for the immigrants to settle, and they were well received by Sam's people. The crops, tools, and methods of agriculture were unfamiliar, however. Sam disappeared, according to reports, into "self-exile" in Liberia. Although a few settlers stayed in Africa and thrived as planters and business operators along the Bight of Benin, the bulk of the settlers returned to the United States. Reports of the emigrants' failure reached Oklahoma even before the settlers returned home, reports that featured prominently in the newspapers that had opposed the plan (Bittle and Geis 1964, 173–212; Hill 1983–95, 1:542–46).[17]

Despite this disaster, which had cost families their farms and shareholders over $72,000, pan-Africanism and emigrationism would retain their force in Oklahoma for years. Oklahoma was a Western stronghold of Marcus Garvey's Universal Negro Improvement Association (UNIA). The largest African American mass movement of all time, the UNIA endorsed (along with the building of black economic strength in the United States) the return of African Americans to Africa. Histories of the Garvey movement tend to emphasize its administrative center in Harlem, but the organization's success in Oklahoma serves as a reminder that its appeal extended well beyond the Hudson River. Between 1921 and 1933, thirty-one chapters of the association were active in the state. This was far more than Texas's ten, and even more than existed in Southern states such as South Carolina and Alabama, which had substantially larger African American populations. Small all-black towns such as Lincoln City, Red Bird, and Tullahassee sustained UNIA chapters in this period (Hill 1983–95, 7:991–95). The central place of Africa as a homeland and destination for people of African descent in Oklahoma would seem to be secure by the 1920s.

Africa, however, did not have an exclusive hold on the emigrationist plans of African Americans from the area of the old Creek Nation. At the very moments that some were planning to migrate to Africa, others favored moving elsewhere in the Americas. Between 1909 and 1911, while Dorman and others in Oklahoma were communicating with Chief Sam, other African Americans from the area were migrating to the prairies of the Canadian West. Some African Americans made the move from eastern Oklahoma to Alberta. More might have headed northward if the Canadian government had not acceded to racial fears that the migrants would transform Alberta into "the homeland of the Negro race." Canadian border authorities selectively enforced immigration requirements to block the entry of people of African descent, using the pretext that African Americans' tropical constitutions made them ill suited for Canada's climactic rigors. Migration to Canada therefore waned (Troper 1972). But calls for emigration within the Americas arose again a decade later, coinciding this time with the height of the Garvey movement. In the early 1920s, some African Americans in Oklahoma were preparing to emigrate to Mexico. In 1922, the Afro-American Mexico Colonization Association held a state convention at which it elected commissioners who were charged with investigating the possibilities for African Americans in Mexico (Williams 1996, 288). The next year, newspapers reported that fifteen African American families had left Okmulgee, the capital of the old Creek Nation, to settle in Mexico.

These migration movements must complicate our understanding of the recurrent calls by African Americans in Oklahoma for a return to Africa. First, in many ways the emigrants' hopes for Canada and Mexico may have been analogous to the hope that Oklahoma had once held out for the migrants who had arrived from farther to the east. Mexico and Canada may have represented both an economic and a political opportunity for landless and disfranchised farmers. Seen in this light, emigration to a bordering nation does not seem so far afield from westward migration to Oklahoma. Nevertheless, there was an important difference: The move to another country, even a neighboring country, meant turning one's back on the United States and the disappointments and injustices that it had brought to African American people. Isparhecher's and Chitto Harjo's calls for the emigration of Creeks to Mexico in the 1890s marked a willingness by Creek people to abandon one country to find a new home for their nation. So did the willingness of African Americans in the 1910s and 1920s to countenance migration to Canada or Mexico.

In fact, the name of the Afro-American Colonization Association recalls the name of the organization whose founding opens this essay, the Inter-national Afro-American League. For both groups, founded roughly twenty years apart in very different historical circumstances, the name "Afro-American" claimed an identity defined first by African heritage and second by birth in the United States. For both of these groups, and for the African American emigrationist organizations discussed in this essay, this identity was both racial and national. It was racial in the sense that the political and economic context of the Creek Nation and the State of Oklahoma had made African ancestry a racial mark. This was a mark that non-black Creeks imposed from without with the term "Freedmen," and a mark that the State of Oklahoma imposed from without with the law and custom of white supremacy. That racial identity was also embraced from within, however. Freedmen of different Indian nations built movements and identities that spanned national boundaries. Later, Freedmen and African American settlers worked together on a variety of political projects, including the projects of emigration that this essay examines.

Movements for emigration point also to the national meaning of this racial identity. Emigrationists believed that moving to Africa, establishing homes there, and, most important, establishing a government there would be the means of achieving political liberation. This kind of African emigration movement was a nationalist project in that it was an attempt to bring the boundaries of the state and the boundaries of the people into congruence. The African American movements for emigration to Mexico and to Canada were not nationalist in precisely the same sense. The lands they turned to were not the African homeland. Nevertheless, the would-be emigrants to Mexico and Canada, like Chief Sam's advocates, sought a place where African Americans could enjoy a higher level of political and economic self-determination. These movements demonstrate the great flexibility of the nationalist and emigrationist impulse that brought Freedmen of different nations together, that encouraged African Americans from the American South to settle in the Creek Nation, and that led Creek Freedmen and African American settlers and their children to countenance pulling up stakes for Africa, Canada, and Mexico. Whatever the intended destination, the unifying power of this nationalism can be heard in the name "Afro-American." In each case, the national affiliation with Africa was powerful enough to override the pull of an American nation — whether that was the United States or an Indian nation.

Here we return to the important differences between the nationalism of Creek Freedmen and African Americans who called for emigration, on the one hand, and the nationalism of Creek Indians who called for emigration, on the other. The nationalism of the Freedmen and African Americans emphasized the unity of people of African descent. Creek Indians did not emphasize to the same degree the unity of people of indigenous descent. The emigration movement toward Mexico brought Creeks together with Indians from other nations. It did not, however, assert their essential unity as much as it suggested a common interest. Advocates of Indian emigration to Mexico sometimes gave voice to a strong sense of racial unity for Indian people but not one that overrode their national differences.

The distinctions between Creek Freedman nationalism and that of other Creeks, however, exist within a much more significant similarity. At a time when powerful forces were re-drawing the boundaries of power and wealth, at a time when the federal government was declaring that they were no longer a nation, the residents of the Creek Nation (and the region of Oklahoma it became) refigured what it meant to be a member of a nation. They decided who was a member of the nations they created and re-created, often making this decision in terms of race. The fluidity and complexity of national boundaries accompanied an intense dedication to the nation as a project. One would be mistaken to conclude that, when emigrants moved to another nation-state, they demonstrated their detachment from nationalism and national identity. Rather, they made clear that they believed deeply in the idea of the nation but also believed that the future of the nation they cared most about lay beyond the boundaries of the United States. The national projects of Creeks, Creek Freedmen, and African Americans existed within the context of a complex web of nations: American Indian, Anglo-American, pan-African, Mexican, and Canadian. Nationalists in the region found new ways to situate themselves in this changing world of nations. When Creek Freedmen emigrated with Chief Sam to Africa, they signaled the weakening of their attachment to the Creek Nation and their disregard for the idea of seeking a future as part of the "American nation" of the United States. Most of all, however, they made manifest their dedication to a nation rooted in African soil. When these emigrants walked away from Indian Territory, they were not turning their back on the nation as an idea but looking for a place where the nation would be at home.

Notes

1 "The Inter-National Afro-American League," *Muskogee Pioneer*, June 24, 1898, 2. See also *Muskogee Phoenix*, June 4, 1898, 4, as cited in Muskogee Newspaper Index, Newspapers Room, Oklahoma Historical Society, Oklahoma City (hereafter, MNI), s.v. "Negroes, Afro-American League."

2 "Letter from Liberia, West Africa," 1996.

3 Ibid.

4 "Liberia," *Muskogee Phoenix*, November 8, 1888, 1.

5 "Territory News," *Muskogee Phoenix*, February 25, 1892, 1; see also *Muskogee Phoenix*, February 25, 1892, 4.

6 *Twin Territories*, March 1899, 79, as cited in MNI, s.v. "Negroes, Emigration to Africa."

7 "Bird Harris' Dream," *Muskogee Phoenix*, June 8, 1895, 2; "Full-Blood Colonization," *Muskogee Phoenix*, October 14, 1897, 1; "On the Road to Mexico," *Muskogee Phoenix*, November 4, 1897, 4; "Will Surely Emigrate," *Muskogee Phoenix*, February 17, 1898, 1; *Muskogee Phoenix*, March 3, 1898, 1; "Grandest Government on Earth," *Muskogee Phoenix*, July 13, 1899, 2; "Current Comment," *Muskogee Phoenix*, August 3, 1899, 6; "Copy of Letter from Secretary of Interior to Rev. David L. Berryhill," January 21, 1908, Masingale Papers folder, Creek Documents M–Z box, Creek Council House Museum, Okmulgee, Okla. See also the following articles cited in MNI, s.v. "Indians, Movement to Mexico": *Muskogee Phoenix*, June 5, 1895, June 22, 1895, 1, 2, June 29, 1897, 4, June 15, 1904; 8; *Muskogee Democrat*, August 24, 1904, July 14, 1905.

8 *Muskogee Phoenix*, June 5, 1895, 2.

9 This opposition was not new to Isparhecher, who had also sounded this theme in his 1891 bid for the post of principal chief: see "Letter of Isparhecher," in *Our Brother in Red*, August 8, 1891, typescript copy in folder 1, box 1, Isparhecher Collection, Western History Collections, University of Oklahoma, Norman (hereafter, WHC).

10 *Cherokee Advocate*, August 3, 1901, 2, as cited in Oklahoma Newspaper Index, Newspapers Room, Oklahoma Historical Society, s.v. "Mexico, Removal."

11 *Muskogee Democrat*, July 14, 1905, 1, as cited in MNI, s.v "Indians, Movement to Mexico."

12 Ibid., August 24, 1904, as cited in MNI, s.v. "Indians, Movement to Mexico."

13 *Muskogee Phoenix*, June 5, 1895, 2, as cited in MNI, s.v. "Indians, Movement to Mexico"; Debo 1991, 60.

14 See also "Traditions of the Creeks: Story of Their Trek from Mexico More Than Three Centuries Ago," *Indian Journal*, February 22, 1901, folder 26, Creek Nation Collection, Western History Collections, University of Oklahoma, Norman. Thanks to Joseph Hall for the Milfort reference and a discussion of twentieth-century Creek beliefs regarding origins in Mexico.

15 "Local Paragraphs," *Muskogee Phoenix*, August 3, 1893, 5; "Trouble at an Indian Celebration," *Muskogee Phoenix*, August 10, 1893, 8; "Local Paragraphs," *Muskogee Phoenix*, August 9, 1894, 5; ibid., August 8, 1895, 5; Lawrence Lay, James Bruce, Willie Allen, J. S. Thomas, and Classie Oden, "The Negro in Oklahoma: A Manuscript Prepared for the Oklahoma State Guide," November 1936, Negro Studies Project, Oklahoma Contemporary Culture, folder, box A887, Works Progress Administration Federal Writers' Project Papers, Manuscript Reading Room, Library of Congress, Washington D.C., 17. On Juneteenth, see Wiggins 1993, 28–31.

16 "African Delegation Meets," *Wewoka and Lima Courier*, November 21, 1913, 1.

17 See also "Chief Sam's Party Can't Stay in Liberia," *Clearview Patriarch*, September 12, 1914, 1, as cited in Teall 1981, 286–88.

CHAPTER FIVE

In Their "Native Country"

Freedpeople's Understandings of Culture and

Citizenship in the Choctaw and Chickasaw Nations

BARBARA KRAUTHAMER

~~~~~~~

In the months and years after their emancipation from slavery in 1866, the 3,214 African Americans held in bondage in the Choctaw and Chickasaw nations sought to infuse their freedom with meaning. Freedpeople in the Choctaw and Chickasaw nations understood the ways in which the laws and practices of slavery had maintained hierarchies of race and legal status. Emancipation disrupted that order, and former slaves pursued their own definitions of freedom rather than remaining subject to the continued subordination that Choctaws and Chickasaws attempted to impose on them. Immediately after emancipation, Choctaw and Chickasaw leadership enacted legal codes designed to replicate the dehumanization and coercion of slavery and, for nearly four decades after emancipation, continually denied their former slaves the status and rights of citizenship. Yet the freedmen and women in the Choctaw and Chickasaw nations assessed the extent of their freedom primarily in relation to their status as recognized citizens of these Indian nations. As they pursued citizenship in the nations over the course of almost forty years, freedpeople articulated cultural and political arguments to justify their inclusion in the Choctaw and Chickasaw nations.

Rather than offering entirely new understandings of citizenship, freedmen and women relied on Choctaw and Chickasaw ideas, images, and history to depict their lives in the nations. They illustrated their familiarity and affinity with the Choctaw and Chickasaw peoples to highlight their long-standing presence in the nations. Freedpeople argued that they had lived and labored in the nations for generations, sharing the rituals and practices of daily life with the Choctaws and Chickasaws. They and their ancestors, moreover, had endured the trauma of removal from the Southeast. Memories of the past and knowledge of contemporary mores constituted the basis of the freedpeople's demands for inclusion as citizens in the Choctaw and Chickasaw nations. Prevailing distinctions of race and previous divisions of status, they argued, threatened to eclipse their history in and cultural affinity with the Choctaws and Chickasaws. Freedmen and women thus called for an expansion of the category "citizen" to accommodate their cultural identification with the Choctaws and Chickasaws, but also to cement the rights that lay at the heart of their conceptions of freedom.

Freedpeople's quest for Choctaw and Chickasaw citizenship lasted for nearly forty years while they navigated both the internal politics of the Choctaw and Chickasaw nations and the broader realm of U.S.–Indian relations. While their freedom had been guaranteed in 1866, when the Choctaw and Chickasaw nations entered a new treaty with the United States, the treaty addressed the question of freedpeople's citizenship in the Indian nations only in hypothetical and conditional terms, calling on the Indian nations to extend the rights of citizenship to their former slaves but leaving room for the possibility that the nations would refuse to do so. For almost forty years after ratifying the 1866 treaty, continual conflicts between the Choctaw and Chickasaw nations and the United States over the treaty's validity left the African Americans in the Choctaw and Chickasaw nations with no clear citizenship in either the Indian nations or the United States. Had they simply left the Indian Territory and relocated to states, presumably the freedmen and women of the Choctaw and Chickasaw nations would have become citizens of the United States, although the treaty did not explicate any administrative means for naturalization. The treaty's provisions reflected Congress's assumption that the Indian nations, rather than the United States, should extend citizenship to the black men and women who had lived and labored among them. The treaty indicated that Congress expected the Indian nations to treat their former slaves in the same fashion that the federal government was treating the freed slaves of the United States. Choctaw and Chickasaw leadership perceived the treaty's provisions regarding freedpeople's status as an arrogation of their authority to determine eligibility for Indian citizenship and as a clear indicator of Congress's nascent plans to undermine Indian sovereignty. Here lay the conundrum at the heart of the treaty: It pulled the Choctaw and Chickasaw freedpeople into the orbit of Reconstruction policy and sentiment toward former slaves in the states, but it could not overcome the force of the Indian nations' sovereignty in the Indian Territory.

From the outset, freedpeople's status in the Indian nations was deeply embedded in the increasingly tense relations between the United States and the Indian nations. As relations between the Choctaw and Chickasaw nations and the United States grew ever more strained through the second half of the century, neither party abided by the treaty provisions concerning the freedpeople's citizenship. The matter was resolved only in the early twentieth century, when the nations' sovereignty was terminated, and the freedmen and women acquired U.S. citizenship. From the earliest moments after emancipation through the end of the century, African Americans in the Choctaw and Chickasaw nations continually invoked, and often reinterpreted, the treaty's provisions in their call for resolution of their citizenship. While freedmen and women changed their tactics and arguments over the course of forty years, the core of their demands for Indian citizenship remained largely unchanged.

Contemporary scholarship on slavery and emancipation in the Indian Territory has highlighted freedpeople's cultural identification with Native Americans. Sources such as the Works Progress Administration (WPA) narratives recorded in the 1930s have offered a wealth of detail about the conditions of African Americans' daily life in the Indian Territory, as well as about memories of slavery, emancipation, and family history in the Indian nations. As the historian Celia Naylor-Ojurongbe (2002, 161) has shown, African Americans understood the ties to Native Americans in terms of "specific cultural markers — namely clothing, language, food, and knowledge of herbal remedies." This and other studies, furthermore, have argued strongly for a keener awareness of the intricate, and often intimate, relationships forged between African Americans and Native Americans from the mid-eighteenth century in the southern colonies through the antebellum period in the southern states and Indian Territory (May 1996; Mulroy 1993; Perdue 1979; Saunt 1999; Wright 1986). Freedpeople in the Indian Territory are now taken seriously as historical actors, and this emphasis on the lives of enslaved and free African Americans offers critical insights into the complexity of North American slavery and freedom. Yet historians have centered African Americans' cultural and familial ties with Native Americans without fully interrogating the political valences of freedpeople's articulations of their identity and history in the Indian nations.

Absent from current studies of emancipation and the transition from slavery to freedom in Indian Territory is a critical analysis of freedpeople's efforts to obtain citizenship in the Native American nations under the provisions of the 1866 treaties. While a few historians have concentrated on assessing the treaties, specifically their implications for Native American sovereignty and Indian leaders' reactions to them, freedpeople's interpretations of the treaties have gone unexamined. In the only book-length study devoted to U.S. Reconstruction policies directed at the Native American nations, M. Thomas Bailey's *Reconstruction in the Indian Territory* (1972), emancipation and freedpeople's citizenship are discussed in brief sections and are presented only in relation to larger issues relating to the extension of U.S. power into Indian Territory. In a 1996 article, Daniel F. Littlefield presented the treaties and their provisions for freedpeople's citizenship as a deliberately calculated effort on the part of Congress to use the former slaves as "a wedge to factionalize the tribe, [and as] a means of sapping their resources and energy" (Littlefield 1996b, 102). In his conclusion, Littlefield argues that by the end of the nineteenth century, the federal government had little interest in protecting freedpeople's rights and was far more committed to "[using] them simply as a convenient tool to help dismantle the tribal nations" (Littlefield 1996b, 107). Littlefield certainly offers a compelling critique of Congress's arrogation of the authority to bestow citizenship in the sovereign Native American nations. His rendering of the freedmen and women in Indian Territory as little more than anti-Indian ordinance in the congressional arsenal, however, elides their sustained participation in the conflicts over citizenship and sovereignty and raises the specter of earlier scholarship's racist portrayal of former slaves as unwitting dupes of Northern politicians and speculators (Debo 1961). The 1866 treaties' provisions regarding freedpeople's citizenship require careful attention and evaluation, and any appraisal must account for the treaties' multiple goals — protecting the rights of former slaves while undermining the autonomy of Native American nations — and the context in which they were formulated. By focusing on freedpeople's interpretations of the treaties and their interactions with Native American and congressional leaders, we can discern how freedpeople's conceptions of their cultural identity and history in the Choctaw and Chickasaw nations informed their expectations of freedom and their efforts to secure citizenship in these nations.

Freedpeople's commitment to securing their status as citizens in the Choctaw and Chickasaw nations rested on both their personal history of enslavement in the nations and their determination to control their own lives as free people. African Americans had lived in the Choctaw and Chickasaw nations as slaves since the late eighteenth century. Choctaws and Chickasaws purchased slaves from local white slaveholders and traders with the intention of exploiting slaves' labor to produce cotton for sale in the American market (Carson 1999, chapter 4; Gibson 1971, 125; Littlefield 1980, 10). From the outset, human bondage in the two nations maintained clear distinctions of status and race within the nations. Blackness was equated with servitude. Slavery was a permanent condition that passed from mother to child, regardless of the father's status. Slaves, moreover, were worked, purchased, and sold as chattel.[1] Choctaw and Chickasaw laws and customs maintained the hierarchy inherent in chattel slavery. Slaves were prohibited from owning property such as livestock and weapons, and slaves' testimony was not accepted in the nations' courts unless the matter involved only African Americans (Littlefield 1980, 13–15).

The categories of race and status that structured relations between enslaved African Americans and free Choctaws and Chickasaws did not preclude their ongoing exchange of ideas and information. Slaves owned by Choctaws and Chickasaws labored to produce surplus for the market and to supplement women's agricultural labor, and enslaved women consequently learned the patterns of food production and preparation that were specific to the Choctaw and Chickasaw peoples and were the province of Choctaw and Chickasaw women. Long after emancipation, African American women who had been enslaved in the nations and provided interviews to WPA field workers underscored their knowledge of Choctaw and Chickasaw food production and consumption. Kiziah Love was but one of the former slaves interviewed in the 1930s who told of eating " 'Tom Pashofa' an Indian dish." Polly Colbert similarly recalled, "We cooked all sorts of Indian dishes: Tom-fuller, pashofa, hickory nut grot. . . . Tom-fuller was made from beaten corn and tasted sort of like hominy" (Baker and Baker 1996, 87, 259). Jane Battiest (1937) explained that freedwomen "beat our corn to make meal just like the Choctaws did."[2] African American women, like Choctaw and Chickasaw women, understood that their ways of producing, preparing, and consuming food constituted important elements of Choctaw and Chickasaw identity and distinguished them from other societies (Carson 1999, 77–85; Debo 1961, chapter 1; Hudson 1939; Kidwell 1995, 163; Wright 1958). While slaves had little choice but to adapt to Choctaw and Chickasaw labor patterns, including the production of food, their articulation of their memories and knowledge in the decades after emancipation operated on a symbolic level to communicate their presence in, and identification with, a particular society (Kalèik 1984; Scholliers 2001).

In other contexts, the exchange of knowledge flowed back and forth between masters and slaves in the Choctaw and Chickasaw nations. Consequently, slaves could occupy positions of relative autonomy and authority when they served as sources of important information. Nineteenth-century observers of Native American slaveholding practices saw enslaved African Americans moving and speaking seemingly at will and noted that Native American slaveholders did not practice the systematic violence and dehumanization embraced by white slaveholders in the Southern states. Recognizing the relative freedoms enjoyed by slaves in Native American nations, however, should not diminish the ways in which law and custom allowed for their exploitation. The dehumanization of slavery may have been mitigated by particular conditions and circumstances in the nations, but it was never entirely effaced. The relationships that took shape between missionaries, Choctaws, Chickasaws, and slaves illustrate the tensions between the liberties and constraints of slavery in the nations.

Before removal, slaves in the Choctaw and Chickasaw nations were permitted enough mobility and control over their time to attend the religious services conducted by missionaries to the Indians. The relationships that developed out of slaves' contact with missionaries allowed African American converts, conversant in English as well as the Choctaw and Chickasaw languages, to serve as interpreters for their Native American masters (Kidwell 1995, chapters 4–6). The sparse records of these three-way conversations reveal the complex workings of slavery in the Native American nations and point us to the distinctive features of slaves' lives in the nations.

Necessity and proximity facilitated the exchange of language and information between masters and slaves, and bilingual slaves, in their capacity as interpreters, stood in a position of autonomy and authority in relation to their masters. Choctaw and Chickasaw leaders, steadfast in their commitment to slavery, kept a close watch on the interactions between their slaves and the abolitionist missionaries in the nations.[3] When slaves served as interpreters and lay preachers, the divide between master and slave may have narrowed temporarily, but the distinction was one that slaveholders guarded carefully (Kidwell 1995, 79–83; Littlefield 1980, 13–18; Perdue 1979, 56–59, 84–89). At the same time, however, enslaved African Americans shared with their Native American masters the Indian language that branded them inferior in the eyes of white Americans and marked them as targets of the "civilizing missions" endorsed by the federal government and carried out by religious missionaries. After emancipation, when they pursued citizenship in the nations, former slaves cited these experiences of living both as property and as people identified as members of Choctaw and Chickasaw communities.

African Americans enslaved in the Southern Native American nations again existed as property and as people-like-Indians during the period of Removal in the 1830s and 1840s. Choctaws and Chickasaws brought what property they could, including their slaves, with them on the 350 mile forced trek west to Indian Territory. Enslaved African Americans, like their Native American masters, found themselves torn from the region they had known as their home. Indeed, for slaves whose community and kinship ties extended beyond the boundaries of the Choctaw and Chickasaw lands in Mississippi to nearby white-owned farms and plantations, the trauma of removal replicated that of being chained to the slave traders' coffles (Debo 1961, 50–56; Foreman 1932, 56–104, 193–226). The enslaved also endured the privations of Removal. The diseases and starvation that plagued the recent arrivals in Indian Territory knew no bounds of race or status. Two decades later, when the Civil War broke out and the Choctaw and Chickasaw nations sided with the Confederacy, African Americans fully comprehended both the meanings of their status and lives as slaves and the ways in which the conditions of their lives were culturally and historically bound to the Native Americans among whom they lived and labored.

Neither the end of the Civil War nor the subsequent resumption of treaty relations between the Choctaw and Chickasaw nations and the United States offered African Americans enslaved in the Native American nations any reason for jubilation. They were not freed when Union troops retook Indian Territory in 1863, and they were not emancipated when the war ended in April 1865 or when the Choctaw and Chickasaw nations surrendered their troops in June and July 1865 (Gibson 1971, 241). The nearly 3,000 African Americans enslaved in the Choctaw and Chickasaw nations — there were approximately 1,000 slaves in the Chickasaw Nation, and between 1,700 and 2,000 in the Choctaw Nation — were formally and finally liberated in autumn 1865, after Choctaw and Chickasaw leaders returned from Fort Smith, Arkansas, where they and other Native American leaders met with delegates from the treaty commission sent by the U.S. federal government (Debo 1961, 221; Gibson 1971, 273–74). The U.S. commissioners presented the nations' leaders with the terms of the new treaties they would have to enter with the United States. The treaty provisions put before the Choctaw and Chickasaw leaders were generally the same as those presented to the other Southern Indian nations. The United States insisted on the abolition of slavery and the extension of citizenship to the freed slaves; it also required the cession of land for the creation of a U.S. territory.

In October 1865, six months after the Civil War ended, the Choctaw Nation enacted legislation emancipating its slaves, and the Chickasaw Nation implemented a policy of gradual emancipation. Both nations' legislators approved laws, akin to the Southern states' Black Codes, restricting freedpeople's mobility and compelling them to work as sharecroppers (Abel 1993 [1925], 286–89; Debo 1961, 99–101, 289; Littlefield 1980, 23–25). Freedmen and women who did not enter a labor contract were subject to arrest as vagrants, and their labor was auctioned to the highest bidder (Choctaw National Council 1865).

The following spring, in April 1866, the Choctaw and Chickasaw nations entered a joint treaty with the United States establishing connections between tribal sovereignty and freedpeople's citizenship that set the stage for four decades of debate and discord over African Americans' status in the Native American nations. Under the 1866 treaty, the nations permanently ceded the Leased District, the area west of the Chickasaws' territory, in return for $300,000 that would be held for them in trust at 5 percent interest.[4] The money would be paid to the nations only if they enacted legislation adopting, and thus granting citizenship to, their former slaves (Debo 1961, 221; Gibson 1971, 247).

Adopted freedmen and women, the treaty indicated, were to receive the full rights, privileges, and immunities, including suffrage, of Choctaw and Chickasaw citizens, although they would not have an interest in the nations' annuities. The only freedpeople eligible for citizenship were those residing within the nations at the time of the treaty's ratification in April 1866. Any freedperson living within the nations by April 1866, however, could opt to remove voluntarily from the nations, and anyone who did so would receive a $100 per capita payment that would be deducted from the nations' $300,000 trust. In the event that the Choctaw and Chickasaw nations did not incorporate their former slaves as citizens within two years, by April 1868, the United States would then use the $300,000 to remove and relocate the freedpeople to the Leased District (rather than disbursing the money to the nations) within ninety days, by July 1868 (Kappler 1904, 919–20). Although the treaty is mute on the question of freedpeople's status in the latter case, they presumably would have received citizenship in the United States. The treaty implied, however, that the Choctaw and Chickasaw freedpeople belonged in Indian Territory, even if they did not reside among the Choctaw and Chickasaw people.

After the treaty was ratified, freedmen and women in the Choctaw and Chickasaw nations probably expected to be removed from the nations and relocated to another site in Indian Territory. Almost immediately after the treaty's ratification, the nations' leaders informed the federal government that they would not adopt their former slaves and called on the United States to remove them. Between 1866 and the 1868 adoption–removal deadline, freedmen concurred with the Choctaw and Chickasaw leadership's insistence that they be removed from the nations and located elsewhere in the territory. After the ratification of the 1866 treaty, the freedpeople of the Choctaw and Chickasaw nations recognized that they were on particularly precarious footing. Although free, they lived from day to day without the protections and benefits of citizenship in either the Indian nations or the United States. In the wake of emancipation, despite their lack of citizenship, freedpeople had established themselves as self-sufficient farmers, sharecroppers, and wage laborers in the nations (Gibson 1971, 251). Yet lacking formal citizenship left them without legal rights to claim and farm tracts of land, which was collectively owned by the nations and their citizens, making their improvements, livestock, and personal property, as well as their lives, prey to thieves and attackers. In the months and years immediately after emancipation, freedmen and women routinely notified federal officials when they were assaulted and their property was threatened by individual Choctaws or Chickasaws. As late as 1868, the Indian agent for the nations informed the Office of Indian Affairs that the freedpeople were industrious and self-reliant but still came to him with reports of abuse. Their "unsettled condition," meaning their lack of rights, he noted, fostered a turbulent atmosphere in which murders were not unusual (U.S. Office of Indian Affairs 1868, 280). In the months and years immediately after emancipation, consequently, freedpeople wanted to be relocated within Indian Territory because they feared that the post-emancipation wave of violence against them would not subside, not because they considered themselves a people distinct from the Choctaws and Chickasaws.

The freedpeople were aware of the provisions, including the loophole, in the 1866 treaty. The treaty had framed the issue of their citizenship as a matter of Indian sovereignty and land dealings between the two nations and the United States, effectively denying them any direct participation in determining and securing their citizenship in the Choctaw and Chickasaw nations and placing U.S. citizenship just beyond their reach. Unlike the Creek freedpeople, those from the Choctaw and Chickasaw nations were not given any time to return to the nation; neither were they allowed to make individual requests for adoption. The Choctaw and Chickasaw treaty placed all responsibility and possibility for action with the nations' governments and with the United States. Despite their exclusion on paper from the process of determining their citizenship, freedmen and women closely monitored the actions of the Choctaw, Chickasaw, and United States legislatures.

Once the 1868 adoption–removal deadline had passed and neither the Choctaw and Chickasaw nations nor the United States had acted according to its provisions, freedmen went into action to resolve the question of their citizenship. Freedmen held mass meetings, sent delegates to Washington, D.C., and petitioned Congress with their demands. Although they had initially supported the plan of relocating within Indian Territory, the freedpeople had shifted their position by 1868 and then insisted on their right to remain within the nations. In their letters and petitions, they identified themselves as former slaves and African Americans but also as people wholly identified with Choctaw and Chickasaw culture and history, and they drew on their history in the nations to fuel their efforts to obtain citizenship.

In August 1869, over three hundred freedmen "representing their people from all parts of both nations" responded to a call by Indian

Agent George T. Olmstead to attend a public meeting to discuss the issue of their citizenship. Governor Harris of the Chickasaw Nation, Principal Chief Allen Wright of the Choctaw Nation, and various other leading men from the two nations also attended the meeting. Harris and Wright each addressed the freedmen, and Olmstead invited them to "express their sentiments" regarding the options of removing or remaining in the nations. The freedmen, Olmstead reported, considered their "many and various" opinions and "decided in a body" that they wanted to remain in the nations because "they preferred being with the people among whom they were raised than among others whom they did not know" (U.S. Office of Indian Affairs 1869, 408–9). The freedmen also indicated to Olmstead and the others that, even though they wanted to reside within the nations, they wanted the rights and protections of U.S. citizenship rather than inclusion on the citizenship rolls of the Choctaw and Chickasaw nations.

One month after this meeting with Olmstead and the leaders of the Choctaw and Chickasaw nations, the freedmen organized their own mass meetings. The first was convened in September 1869 in Scullyville, a town in the Choctaw Nation. At that meeting, the freedmen drafted a platform in which they articulated their positions on the citizenship question and on the future of Indian Territory, and they sent their resolutions to the Indian agent and Congress. The freedmen decided that because the nations had failed to adopt their former slaves, the terms of the 1866 treaty no longer provided valid or appropriate criteria for resolving the issue. The Choctaw and Chickasaw freedmen who assembled at Scullyville in autumn 1869 stated that they considered themselves "full citizens of those nations," entitled to all rights and privileges in the nations, "the same as any citizen of Indian extraction." Arguing that the matter of citizenship was also a matter of cultural identity, the freedmen stated that they could claim no other land as theirs and that they had little inclination to leave their "native country" (U.S. Congress 1870, 2–3).

Only one month after expressing to Olmstead and the Choctaw and Chickasaw leadership their desire for U.S. citizenship, the Choctaw and Chickasaw freedmen reversed course. They declared at the Scullyville meetings and in their petition to Congress that they considered themselves "full citizens" of the Choctaw and Chickasaw nations (U.S. Congress 1870, 2). What had changed in the span of one month to bring about this shift in opinion? At the Scullyville meeting, the freedmen convened on their own rather than in the company of the Indian agent and the Choctaw and Chickasaw leaders, men known to be antagonistic to the freedmen's political mobilization. When they met alone, the freedmen voiced a different set of opinions and demands regarding their cultural identity as well as their proposals for dealing with their uncertain legal status. Whatever disagreements they may have had among themselves, the freedmen who participated in the Scullyville meeting issued unequivocal demands for citizenship in the Choctaw and Chickasaw nations.

Freedpeople throughout the two nations shared this sentiment, and in the months after their first mass meeting, freedmen attempted to organize a second convention. The freedmen's mass meetings emerged from a network of communication that reached across the Choctaw and Chickasaw nations. The freedmen from the eastern portion of the nations who attended the September 1869 meeting hoped to convene a similar meeting in December for their peers in the western portion of the nations. Two of the organizers, James Ladd and Richard Brashears, sent a letter to the freedman Lemon Butler in Armstrong, a town on the western border of the Choctaw Nation. They told him about their meeting at Scullyville and informed him of their plans to hold a convention in the town of Armstrong for freedmen from the western region. They asked Butler to spread the word among the freedmen in his area, and they encouraged him to "see that there be a full attendance." Choctaws and Chickasaws who opposed freedpeople's citizenship and activism prevented the second meeting from taking place. They tore down the posters announcing the convention and threatened to kill "any colored man attempting to meet at the appointed place and time" (U.S. Congress 1870, 5). The second convention finally took place in January 1870, but it was held in Scullyville again, not in Armstrong, as originally planned.

The freedmen who attended the second Scullyville meeting affirmed the positions taken by the attendees of the September meeting and made their demands for Choctaw and Chickasaw citizenship known to the federal government through their contact with the Freedmen's Bureau agent assigned to Indian Territory. They underscored the urgency of securing their citizenship in the nations by describing the severe limitations imposed on them by individual Choctaws and Chickasaws as well as by the nations' governments. The freedmen complained that their freedom was almost worthless because they enjoyed "few, if any, of the benefits of freedom." Lacking any meaningful rights, they explained, the freedmen and women in the Choctaw and Chickasaw nations remained entirely under the power of their former masters, "who were almost a unit on the side of the rebellion." Forced into this position, they contended, the freedpeople in the Chickasaw and Choctaw nations found themselves in a "helpless condition," suffering "many ills and outrages, even to the loss of many a life" (U.S. Congress 1870, 1).

Describing the Choctaws and Chickasaws as disloyal Confederates and barbarous Indians allowed the freedmen to gain the attention as well as the support of those in Washington who sought to establish a U.S. territorial government in Indian Territory and then open the lands to white settlers. Bringing images of lawlessness — the refusal of the Indians to implement the provisions of the 1866 treaties and their subsequent, and often violent, denial of freedpeople's property rights and access to education — to the attention of U.S. authorities played well to that audience. Freedmen and women understood the treaties' implications for Native American sovereignty, and they appreciated the sense of mission inherent in congressional Reconstruction legislation that worked to protect the rights of newly freed slaves (Foner 1988, 462; Prucha 1994, 272–85). The federal government's position toward the Native American nations opened an avenue for the Choctaw and Chickasaw freedpeople to pursue their interests as former slaves. They made their demands that the United States resolve their citizenship and protect them from violence commensurate with the United States' mission to stamp out "savagery" as well as the vestiges of Confederate rebellion in Indian Territory.

How could the freedmen reconcile this stance with their other resolutions from the Scullyville meetings, specifically their desire to remain within their "native country" (U.S. Congress 1870, 3)? For the freedpeople, their cultural affinity with the Choctaws and Chickasaws was only part of the equation in shaping their lives as free people. They wanted to protect their improvements and their investments of time, money, and labor in the land. Leaving the nations, even for a new location in the territory, would have deprived them of the fruits of three years' labor, everything they had accomplished since emancipation. Indian agents and other federal authorities who took stock of the freedpeople's situation arrived at a similar conclusion. When Indian agents assessed the freedpeople's prospects, they viewed them from the vantage of Reconstruction's ideological commitment to freedmen's property rights in their labor and households.[5] In this regard, the freed-men and women in the Choctaw and Chickasaw nations who had succeeded in establishing themselves as independent farmers or as hired workers appeared as model former slaves who had adapted to the principles and realities of the free labor system. Indian agents, however, also recognized freedpeople's long-standing cultural affinity with the Indians.

In the years after emancipation, civilian visitors to the territory and military personnel stationed in the West took note of freedpeople's shared cultural practices with the Choctaws and Chickasaws. In 1872, a congressional investigation committee visited Indian Territory to in-quire into the affairs of the various nations. The visiting congressmen hoped to ferret out information regarding the degree of "civilization" attained by the Choctaws and Chickasaws, which in their view could be measured by rates of literacy, Christianity, and commercial industry. They inquired about the Indians' religious practices, their education, and the relations that had developed between Native Americans and African Americans. Lemon Butler told them that some freedmen and women had Indian ancestry and "talk[ed] the language of the Choc-taws. I saw one freedman at the barbecue to-day who was talking the Choctaw language." When asked if the freedpeople generally had learned Choctaw when they were enslaved, Butler replied that "some did and some did not," and that the exchange of language had also gone in the other direction (U.S. Congress 1873, 466). Although the visiting congressmen were more interested in the course of Native Americans' so-called advancement than in African Americans' conceptions of cul-ture and identity, they shared Butler's appreciation of the importance of language as a marker of cultural distinctiveness.

By the middle of the nineteenth century, neither the Choctaws nor the Chickasaws relied on interpreters when they conducted their busi-ness with the U.S. government. Increasingly in the late nineteenth century, the nations' leaders had been educated in the states and were fluent in English, and through the end of the century it was these men who served as interpreters when needed (Debo 1961, 60–65). That freedmen and women spoke the Choctaw and Chickasaw dialects of the Muskoghean language no longer distinguished them as critical intermediaries between Indians and Anglos, as it had earlier in the century. Instead, it marked them as both different from African Ameri-cans and former slaves in the States and akin to Choctaws and Chickasaws (Kidwell 1995, 30; Littlefield 1980, 5–9). The notion that the freedpeople had some legitimate claim to land and rights in the Indian nations because of their past labor and personal history among the Choctaws and Chickasaws resonated with the Indian agents and the U.S. politicians who faced the task of resolving the citizenship issue. One Indian agent, for example, understood that freedmen and women based their claims for citizenship on the fact that they "were born upon Chickasaw soil, are well grounded in the customs and usages of that people, and speak the language as fluently as the natives themselves" (U.S. Congress 1896, 112).

It was this sense of cultural identification with the Choctaws and Chickasaws that informed the actions and declarations of the freedmen who met first with Olmstead in the late summer of 1869 and then attended their own meetings in September 1869 and again in January 1870. Yet the freedpeople did not necessarily see themselves and their interests as identical to the Choctaws and Chickasaws and their priorities. Freedpeople saw themselves as culturally and historically tied to the Choctaws and Chickasaws, but they also recognized their particular history of enslavement. The legacy of slavery, specifically the continued degradation of African Americans, informed freedpeople's conceptions of their identity and their demands for meaningful freedom and citizenship in the Choctaw and Chickasaw nations. When the freedmen at Scullyville planned in September 1869 to organize a meeting in the western portion of the nation, they wrote to Lemon Butler, who lived in the western town of Armstrong. The letter Butler received asked him to inform the freedmen in his region of the upcoming meeting and urge them all to attend. Butler and his peers knew that despite their identification with the Choctaw and Chickasaw cultures, they constituted a distinct community of former slaves, and they had specific demands and needs. His fellow activists must have known that he would appreciate their closing line, "If we do not work for ourselves, who will?" (U.S. Congress 1870, 5).

Throughout 1869 and 1870, freedmen became increasingly vocal in their determination to secure Choctaw and Chickasaw citizenship for all former slaves in the nations. In the summer of 1870, now two years after the adoption–removal deadline had passed, the freedmen stated publicly — to Choctaw and Chickasaw leaders and to Agent Olmstead — their refusal to relocate outside of the nations. Freedmen at an August 1870 mass meeting in Boggy Depot "declared unanimously that they wished to remain." Allen Wright, principal chief of the Choctaw Nation, attended the meeting and noted that freedmen "from all parts" of the two nations were in attendance and that they were the "leading characters of every farm and plantation and neighborhood." These freedmen listened to Wright's proposal that they "leave the country and go to Liberia, where there is a home provided for freed people" (U.S. Congress 1873, 564). Unlike some freedpeople in the states, those in the Choctaw and Chickasaw nations did not consider Liberia a potential future home. The freedmen informed Wright that they had no interest in his conversations with missionaries interested in African colonization because they had no desire to leave their homes in the Choctaw and Chickasaw nations.[6] After the adoption–removal deadline had passed, freedpeople unequivocally asserted their right to remain within the nations. They identified with the Choctaw and Chickasaw culture, and they maintained that their cultural identity entitled them to citizenship in the nations.

In 1885, the Choctaw Nation, acting without the cooperation of the Chickasaw Nation, finally adopted and extended citizenship to the African Americans it had held as slaves. Chickasaw freedmen continued to present their demands to the U.S. government, and they routinely protested the efforts of the Chickasaw legislature to check their personal and economic opportunities. In 1886, for example, Chickasaw freedmen met at Stonewall in Pontotoc County, where African Americans outnumbered the Chickasaw population, and put together a memorial that once more affirmed their ties to the Chickasaw Nation. They argued that they had not removed from the nation in 1866 because they had "lived with the Indians all the days of our life and do not know the rules of no body else but the Indians" (Littlefield 1980, 144). The fault lay squarely on the shoulders of the United States, the freedmen contended, because they had long been waiting for "the strong arm of the Government to rescue them in accordance with the spirit and intent of the treaty of 1866" (U.S. Congress 1897, 33–35).

By the time the Choctaw freedpeople were recognized as Choctaw citizens, U.S. Indian policy imperiled their standing in the Choctaw Nation, along with the Chickasaw freedpeople's hopes for citizenship. Thirty years of congressional strivings to put a territorial government in place in Indian Territory culminated in the 1887 passage of the Dawes Act, authorizing the president to compel reservation Indians to relinquish their common land title and accept land allotments in severalty. Although the five slaveholding nations in Indian Territory — the Cherokee, Chickasaw, Choctaw, Creek, and Seminole nations — were exempt from the Dawes Act, they came under continual pressure to relinquish their nations' land in exchange for individual allotments. The Dawes Commission thus met with Choctaw and Chickasaw delegates in Atoka (in the Choctaw Nation) in spring 1897 (Debo 1961, chapter 11; Gibson 1971, chapter 13; Littlefield 1980, 163–65). After the commission determined the amount of land that would be granted to the Indian citizens of these nations, the subject of freedpeople's land claims arose. Under the Atoka Agreement, the adopted Choctaw freedmen and women were each granted only forty acres, and everyone in the nation, Choctaw and African American, agreed to accept U.S. citizenship.

Chickasaw freedpeople promptly protested their exclusion from the Atoka Agreement, and once more, freedmen organized a mass meeting (Debo 1961, 260–68; Gibson 1971, 272–75; Littlefield 1980, 172–73). The Chickasaw freedpeople were not alone in their dissatisfaction with the Atoka Agreement's provisions. The Choctaw freedpeople had their own complaints about their situation.[7] Choctaw freedmen and women demanded that they be treated as equal citizens in the Choctaw Nation and thus not be limited to forty-acre claims during the process of allotment. Charles Fields, a Choctaw freedman, informed the Dawes Commission that he was worried that he would not receive "equal rights" during the allotment process. Fields merited this equality, he explained, because "the Indians raise me from a boy" (U.S. Congress, Senate, 1886, 298). Freedpeople thus continued to reject the racial categorization and hierarchy embraced by both Choctaw and Chickasaw leaders and the Dawes Commission, who sought to draw a clear line between "Indians" and "blacks." Freedmen and women in the Choctaw and Chickasaw nations, like Charles Fields, continued to insist that shared culture and history rather than dominant notions of race should prevail in identifying individuals and determining their attendant legal status and rights.

Not until the early years of the twentieth century did the United States resolve with certainty the standing of the Chickasaw freedpeople and their descendents in relation to the Chickasaw Nation. The question of land allotment, for Indians and freedpeople, was finally put to rest on June 29, 1898, when Congress passed the Curtis Act, which transferred questions of citizenship, allotment, and property rights to the federal courts and effected the termination of the Indian nations' land title. The Curtis Act included an amended version of the Atoka Agreement that provided for land allotments to Chickasaw freedpeople.[8] By 1903, the Dawes Commission had compiled the rolls of everyone in the Choctaw and Chickasaw nations, creating separate lists of "Indians" and "freedmen," and finished issuing their land patents. The final roll of Chickasaw freedpeople enumerated 4,662 men, women, and children; the roll of Choctaw freedpeople totaled 5,994 (Debo 1961, 276; Littlefield 1980, 204). Catalogued as "freedmen," freedpeople's cultural affinity with, and history in, the Choctaw and Chickasaw nations was eclipsed by prevailing and rigid categories of race that allowed no room for fluidity, despite numerous freedpeople's testimony to the Dawes Commission about their Native American ancestry. Just over forty years after emancipation, the freedmen and women of the Choctaw and Chickasaw nations completed a full transition from slavery to freedom and became citizens of the United States. This occurred, ironically, at the very moment that extreme racial violence and Jim Crow took hold in the Southern states. Oklahoma's first state legislature convened in December 1907, and both houses immediately passed a bill erecting Jim Crow laws, including a grandfather clause designed to disfranchise African American men (Littlefield 1980, 225–27, 1996b).

For almost thirty years, freedpeople in the Choctaw and Chickasaw nations worked to resolve the question of their citizenship. The treaty of 1866 did not bestow citizenship on former slaves but instead put into place procedures for Indian governments to follow, enabling freedpeople to obtain citizenship. Choctaw and Chickasaw freedmen and women held firmly to the belief that they belonged in the Indian nations in which they had previously been enslaved and resolved to secure their status in the nations despite continued opposition. Their sense of connection to the Choctaw and Chickasaw nations stemmed from two related factors: First, they shared certain cultural patterns and practices with their Indian masters and, second, they had lived and labored, often for successive generations, in the nations. They valued their ties to the nations as a homeland and simultaneously sought to protect the land they had cultivated and claimed as their own.

In their quest for citizenship, freedpeople advanced their own ideas about their place in the nations and their eligibility for formal inclusion — citizenship — rather than operating solely within the confines of the 1866 treaty. The freedmen who petitioned and provided testimony to various congressional committees had precise understandings of the federal government's intention to open the territory to white settlement. Freedmen appealed to the federal government with postwar rhetoric that castigated former slaveholders and offered images of savage and heathen Indians to contrast their depictions of themselves as loyal veterans and freedmen eager to embark on a course of industry and self-sufficiency. The language of their petitions should not obscure the logic. Freedmen's petitions distinguished between freepeople and the Indians who had been their former masters for the purpose of obtaining federal action that would secure their citizenship and rights in the Indian nations. Drawing on American conceptions of freedom and individual rights and on indigenous markers of social and political inclusion, freedpeople in the Choctaw and Chickasaw nations navigated the increasingly tense relations between the Indian nations and the United States by charting their own course.

Even at the various times when freedmen expressed their willingness to remove their families and communities from the nations to another site in the Territory, or when they indicated that they wanted U.S. citizenship, they never attempted to diminish or elide their ties to the Choctaw and Chickasaw nations. Many had survived the trek west earlier in the century when the nations were removed from the Southeast. They had lived and labored in the new country where the hunger and diseases that punctuated the early years in the West knew no boundaries of race or status. Born and raised in the Chickasaw and Choctaw nations, the freedpeople had no intention of organizing a mass migration away from the region, culture, or land that had defined their lives and their family histories in slavery and freedom. The meanings of these ties sustained the freedpeople throughout almost half a century between emancipation and citizenship.

Notes

1 The historian Daniel Littlefield (1980) has described Chickasaws' buying and selling of enslaved African Americans. Archival sources illuminate some

Choctaws' slave trading activity: Letter to Peter Pitchlynn, September 29, 1824, box 1, folder 4, Pitchlynn Papers, WHC.

2 Jane Battiest was born a slave in the Cherokee nation and moved to the Choctaw nation after emancipation: Jane Battiest, interview by Johnson H. Hampton, September 21, 1937, Indian Pioneer Papers, microfiche 43, WHC.

3 By the late 1830s, the Choctaw nation had legislation proscribing Choctaws from cohabiting with slaves and prohibiting teaching slaves to read or write without the owner's permission. The Choctaw national council was forbidden from emancipating any slave without the master's permission. Chickasaw laws passed in 1857 forbade Chickasaws from harboring runaway slaves and made it a crime for slaves to own property such as livestock or weapons. Chickasaw law also barred African Americans and their descendants from holding office or voting in the nation. Law and legal systems, of course, do not exist on their own but reflect the social, political, and economic conditions, and power struggles, in a particular society. The limited number of sources discussing the law and slavery in the Choctaw and Chickasaw nations makes it especially difficult to assess the circumstances under which slave laws were generated. Clara Sue Kidwell (1995), for example, lays the groundwork for the supposition that the limitations on educating slaves may have been directed more at curbing missionaries' autonomy than barring slaves from acquiring literacy. The development of laws to maintain the hierarchies embedded in slavery points to the increasing awareness of the distinctions between enslaved and free people.

4 The two nations had merged under an 1837 treaty. In 1855, however, a new treaty granted the Chickasaws the right to organize their own government. Under the 1855 treaty, the two nations ceded the land lying between the ninety-eighth and one-hundredth meridians, bounded on the north by the South Fork of the Canadian River and on the south by the Red River. The nations granted the United States a permanent lease on this land for $800,000, and the area became known as the Leased District. Although they had technically separated their governments in 1855, the Choctaw and Chickasaw nations ratified a joint treaty with the United States in April 1866 (Debo 1961, 74–75; Gibson 1971, 196–99; Littlefield 1980, 12).

5 For a thorough discussion of Reconstruction-era conceptions of men's property rights in their labor and in their wives, see Stanley 1998, especially chapters 1–2.

6 For a discussion of former slaves from the Oklahoma-Kansas region who left the United States for Africa in the post-emancipation period, consult Bittle and Geis 1964; Painter 1992 [1977], 87–95, 124–30.

7 In 1897, a committee of Choctaw freedmen wrote to Indian Agent D. M. Wisdom. They protested their treatment by the Dawes Commission and both the Choctaw and Chickasaw leaders in the Atoka agreement (U.S. Congress 1897, 2–6).

8 The U.S. Court of Claims decided in 1903 that the Chickasaw freedmen in

fact had no rights to Chickasaw land, as they had never been made citizens of that nation. The federal government was thus ordered to compensate the nation by adding the value of the lands allotted to the Chickasaw freedpeople to the tribal funds distributed in per capita payments. On February 23, 1904, the Supreme Court upheld this decision (Littlefield 1980, 177, 191, 199–203).

CHAPTER SIX

"Blood and Money"

The Case of Seminole Freedmen

and Seminole Indians in Oklahoma

MELINDA MICCO

~~~~~~~

In *Seminole Nation v. Gale Norton* (2002), the U.S. District Court issued a decision to determine the legitimate principal chief of the Seminole Nation in Oklahoma,[1] as well as the status of Seminole Freedmen (tribal members of African descent) in the wake of a 2000 election that disenfranchised the Freedmen.[2] The 2000 election and subsequent federal case are but two examples of the Seminole Nation's attempts to define its membership and maintain control over its internal organization. The crux of the legal justification for such actions delineated in the District Court decision is again one of sovereign rights and whether the Seminole Nation had exceeded its authority with a referendum election that disenfranchised the Seminole Freedmen, thereby superseding the 1866 treaty that incorporated Seminole Freedmen into the tribe. The 2000 election proposed nine amendments to the Seminole constitution as revised in 1969 and included, among its points, the institution of a blood-quantum requirement for membership in the nation, in addition to the exclusion of Seminole Freedmen from membership. The exclusion aspect of the amendments received the majority of the media attention. The legal decision concerned the Seminole Nation's sovereignty and the obligation of the Department of the Interior (DOI) to protect its fundamental principles. One measure of a nation's sovereignty is the ability to determine membership, and this essay focuses on this dimension of the case.

Unlike other ethnic groups in the United States, American Indians predated the U.S. Constitution and are distinct groups for whom sovereignty is "the supreme power from which all specific political powers are derived. Sovereignty is inherent; it comes from within a people or culture. It *cannot be given* to one group by another" (Kickingbird et al. 1999, 1). The U.S. Constitution, therefore does not grant sovereignty to indigenous nations because they already possess it. Before the influence of governmental agencies such as the DOI, membership in a nation remained within the realm of inherent sovereign powers of American Indian people to determine their constituents. While seemingly championing "sovereignty," bureaucratic regulations imposed by the DOI through the Bureau of Indian Affairs (BIA) have complicated the process of membership decisions, thereby undermining traditional considerations and methods of indigenous self-government.

For Africans who escaped from plantation slavery and fled to the Native-held regions, their acceptance ran the gamut from slavery under Indian masters to the free and autonomous villages in Seminole country. Several internal factors in the Seminole Nation have a bearing on the relationship between black and Indian people and include (1) acknowledgement of the importance of military alliances in the past; (2) a reassessment of tribal membership more suitable to current conditions; and (3) limited economic resources. It is also imperative to note that coterminous external factors were prime conditions for the unraveling association between Seminole Indians and Freedmen. One of the more deleterious factors was considering them a conjoined "nation" in the Southeast so both groups could be dealt with under a single policy of removal to the West.[3] Treaties promised freedom for African members and a homeland for Indian ones. Neither promise was fully kept. In addition, in offering freedom to African members, the federal government affirmed a racialized notion of who was slave or free. The ongoing controversy of membership in the Seminole Nation is compounded by the DOI's attempts to limit sovereign rights of a Native nation.

The Seminole Nation's 2000 election results highlight issues about blood quantum and about whom, in the future, will be tribal members. It also raises the underlying and often debated query of who will benefit financially from tribally funded programs. Although prior to the 2000 election Seminole Freedmen were tribal members, they could not apply for any programs paid by the Judgment Fund, monetary resources that are derived from a 1976 settlement between the Indian Claims

Commission and the Seminole Nation. In part, the impetus for the 2000 election was for the Seminole Nation to remain an "Indian" tribe. There was concern that once the Judgment Funds were distributed in 1990, people previously uninterested in membership would be driven by economic greed. So strong was this idea that in 1994 the Constitution Revision Committee raised the issue when it indicated that "enrollment figures which show that increasingly persons with small Seminole blood quantum have joined the tribe, probably due to available judgment fund benefits." The benefits were not excessive and included a one-time per capita payment of $1,000 for young members and $3,000 for members older than 55. Also included in the benefits were educational, clothing, burial, and housing awards. Even though the sums were modest, it was evident that a two-tiered membership system excluded Seminole Freedmen from benefits.

The determination to exclude Seminole Freedmen from the Judgment Fund was decided by the DOI exclusively, which was thoroughly discussed in the Senate document "Distribution of Seminole Judgment Funds," (U.S. Congress, Senate 1978, 2) for the allocation of funds. Seminole Nation members who received benefits from the Judgment Fund were members of the Seminole Nation as defined in 1823, prior to the 1866 treaty in which Seminole Freedmen were formally incorporated. The conundrum that sparked the 2000 election controversy is whether Seminole Freedmen had been members of the Seminole Nation in 1823 and, as such, were entitled to judgment funds. I maintain that ancestors of Seminole Freedmen were indeed tribal members, though not necessarily by present-day conventions, particularly within the confines of DOI requirements. In 2000, to outsiders — and in some cases, to tribal members — it appeared that two basic issues centered on blood and money: what quantum was sufficient for membership, and who would receive monetary benefits of such membership?

Seminole Nation v. Gale Norton

The suit to decide the fate of Seminole Freedmen and tribal leadership was filed by Jerry Haney, who was principal chief at the time of the 2000 vote. Haney asserted that the 2000 election had no bearing because elimination of Seminole Freedmen countermanded the 1866 treaty. Subsequent to the election, in a letter dated September 29, 2000, DOI

Assistant Secretary Kevin Grover stated that he "would not approve the nine amendments to the Seminole constitution because they sought to exclude the Freedmen and had not been submitted to the DOI for approval."[4] The letter from Grover demonstrates two important points: (1) that Seminole Freedmen were and are a constituent element of the Seminole Nation; and (2) that an external body, the DOI, exerts considerable control over the internal affairs of a sovereign nation. A thorough analysis of the language of the legal decision maintains that matters conducted by the Seminole Nation General Council (minus the two Freedmen bands, Dosar Barkus and Bruner) are considered illegal. Hence, the justification for a statement such as, *"We will not recognize any future resolutions or actions of the General Council without the participation of the Freedmen."*[5] In the decision, Judge Reggie B. Walton described the lawsuit as "but one chapter in the ongoing saga between the plaintiff, the Seminole Nation of Oklahoma . . . and the defendants, the Secretary of the United States Department of the Interior . . . and its officials." The final decision also upheld Haney's claim that he would remain principal chief until a legally held election that included Seminole Freedmen determined the next principal chief. Although a runoff election in July 2001 elected Ken Chambers principal chief, the ballots of Seminole Freedmen were not counted by the tribe, prompting Judge Walton to declare the election invalid. In a personal conversation in August 2003 with Haney, Judge Walton confirmed that Chambers remained in office as principal chief despite the orders from the District Court. Although the matter of principal chief was left unchanged, as of September 2003 both the Dosar Barkus and Bruner bands were reinstated in the Seminole Nation.

Even Judge Walton noted that "the Court is confident that, no matter what it decides, or for that matter what the Circuit Court may ultimately decide since it is inevitable that this case will be appealed, that internal rifts within the Seminole Nation and friction between the Seminole Nation and the DOI will continue."[6] Judge Walton's words specifically identify and particularly focus on the DOI. This is significant, for while it may appear that the situation between the Seminole Nation and Seminole Freedmen is irreparable and that all parties are contentious and permanently litigious, I posit that the current rifts among the various bands did not arise from continuous conflict. Rather, they are indicative of previous town formation and indeed reflect the position of members of African descent in the tribe.

Maroon Communities

An analogy to ethnic communities in contact and often in conflict with European powers observed by the South African scholar Grant Farred is that the reconfigured communities emerge and create new histories. Africans and Seminoles constituted hybridized entities who occupied liminal spaces in metaphorical and physical senses. Specific African tribal origins had been erased from the Middle Passage on,[7] and Seminole identity was a byproduct of an amalgamation of aboriginal tribal remnants. Together, Africans and Seminoles made up a New People, a multiracial alliance that threatened the neat black–white racial categories of the slaveholding South. As Farred noted, "As hybrid communities reproduce themselves and produce their own (abbreviated or expansive) histories, their violent origins are subsumed by the larger struggle of making, or maintaining, their marginal place in societies where 'racial purity' holds sway" (Farred 2000, 3). "Racial purity" was never more evident than in antebellum society. Black Indians were both a creation of and a challenge to the color line. With racial signifiers that reduced people into either–or categories and relegated African people to the status of property, a black Indian occupied an untenable space in racial ideology. As discussed later in this essay, "blood quantum" among Seminole people did not exist prior to 1896. Therefore, multiracial people who constituted hybrid or — more correctly in the Southeast — maroon communities were incorporated at the discretion of the town's leaders.

Seminole Indians were themselves remnants of aboriginal groups (including Timucua, Apalachee, Oconee, and Yuchi) who had fled into the swamplands of Florida and later welcomed runaway Africans (Sturtevant 1971, 102–3). Indeed, their origins could be considered violent as slave catchers marauded throughout the region to recapture escaped "slaves" who were actually closely connected to Seminole Indians. Although Africans had become affiliated with the Seminole Nation, many lived in autonomous villages, as did Seminole Indians under the leadership of a *micco* (Wright 1986, 86).[8]

Today, the Seminole Nation is the last of the Five Tribes (the others are Creek, Choctaw, Chickasaw, and Cherokee) to retain members of African descent. To understand this retention, it is crucial to look at aboriginal patterns of autonomous leadership in the Seminole Nation as one explanation for the current struggles. According to the Seminole

Nation's constitution, there are two elected representatives from each of the fourteen Seminole bands.[9] Each band elects its representatives without interference from other bands. In this structure, an elected representative, regardless of his or her own sentiments, must vote as instructed by a consensual decision of band members. Not only does this structure allow for a manageable forum to evaluate tribal matters; it also reflects some of the original townships of the Southeast.

Ethnic Identity of Seminole Freedmen

The distinct identity of Seminole Freedmen was evident during one of my annual trips to Oklahoma. In summer 1998, I asked a young tribal member to describe his ethnic background. He quickly replied, "black Seminole." With further questioning, he explained that he considers himself not African American but specifically black Seminole. In the ensuing discussion with his other relatives, what first appeared to be a denial of black ancestry became an attempt to elucidate a little re-searched but vastly important aspect of the founding of the American nation and the construction of black Seminole identity. An assortment of names applied to Africans associated with Seminole Indians, includ-ing black Seminole, Seminole Freedmen, and *estelusti*, demonstrate the difficulty of identifying their specific status. Some of the seminal points of Seminole tribal history include the role of black and Indian people as military allies, the frequency of intermarriage between the two groups, and the way in which the "peculiar institution" of slavery was practiced in the Seminole Nation.[10] Various scholars of black and Indian studies have attempted to extricate a precise history of the two groups, par-ticularly that within the Seminole Nation. One of the earliest scholars documenting the relationship between black and Indian people in the Southeast was the anthropologist Laurence Foster, who began field-work in 1929 and interviewed several people in Oklahoma and Texas for a 1935 doctoral dissertation. Foster traced the history of black and Indian peoples in Latin America but focused primarily on the Seminole Indians and black Seminoles who originated in the Floridas and then traveled to areas that promised greater freedom, including Indian Ter-ritory in Oklahoma, Texas, and, finally, Mexico.

Cooperation based on the exigencies of war in the Southeast allowed black and Indian people to present a formidable challenge to colonial forces. It also contributed to the establishment of maroon communities that operated autonomously. During wartime, each group fought under its own leaders (Foster 1935, 27). As Foster notes, when he last interviewed black Seminoles in Oklahoma and Texas, their previous close alliance with Seminole Indians had evaporated under the segregation laws Oklahoma enforced at statehood in 1907. Some descendants from Freedmen bands over the years had not retained ties to the Seminole Nation, including identical twin brothers I interviewed in the early 1990s, Lawrence and Lance Cudjoe. Although Lawrence's and Lance's participation with the Seminole Nation occurred later in their lives, they were formidable Freedmen band leaders until their deaths in 1994. In a personal conversation with Lawrence Cudjoe in 1993, he supported Foster's earlier observation as he recalled growing up in racially segregated Oklahoma with limited life opportunities for African American people and traced some of the antagonism to statehood when Indians were classified as "white" and Jim Crow laws were widespread. Indian Freedmen who moved away from Seminole communities were more commonly accepted by African American ones. Severing those ties also eliminated a distinct ethnic identity as Indian Freedmen.

Two other scholars, Kenneth Wiggins Porter and Daniel F. Littlefield Jr., wrote extensively about the alliances between African and Indian people during colonial and American battles and when both groups were removed to Indian Territory. Begun in the 1940s, Porter's research documented the stories of descendants from Florida who had continued their journey into Mexico but in the mid-1800s returned to Texas, where a black Seminole community still exists. Littlefield concentrated on the relationship between the two groups through the end of the Civil War and the signing of the 1866 treaty. Both monographs illustrate the reliance of each group on the other during times of war and the use of *estelusti* as interpreters and guides in the three Seminole Wars fought from 1817 to 1858, but they do not clearly delineate the rate of intermarriage or the adoption of Africans into clans by Indian peoples, let alone Seminoles (Littlefield 1977; Porter 1996).

Rebecca Bateman (1991) and Kevin Mulroy (1993) do pay close attention to intermarriage, noting that it was the exception rather than the rule. Each scholar points to the lack of inclusion in clans and to the establishment of separate settlements for black and Indian towns as a reason for infrequent intermarriage between Africans and Indians. Bateman and Mulroy both document cases in which some African leaders were adopted into Indian clans. In addition, they maintain that under usual circumstances the clan and kinship system was matrilineal, and a child of a black woman without a clan or a band was outside Seminole society (Bateman 1991, 253–59; Mulroy 1993, 20–22).[11] However, the child of a Seminole woman and a black man would be in the mother's clan. Although there is evidence that maroon settlements were indeed separate, I suggest that this pattern of town structure followed the organized settlements modeled after the Creek Confederacy. Leaders of those towns would operate in an autonomous manner and would not necessarily come together until ceremonial events or in the event of outside warfare. As Littlefield (1977, 6) notes, the system of slavery adopted by Seminole Indians had more to do with political cooperation than with an inherent position of blacks as inferiors. I contend that twin factors of freedom for runaway slaves and the maintenance of an aboriginal homeland for Indians led to shared cultural practices, intermarriage to some degree, and recognition of their futures as intertwined. Although clear and consistent accounts of their allied communities are unavailable, Jack Forbes (1993, 61) observes: "Needless to say, one must also acknowledge considerable African impact upon Native Americans in the Americas. Up to four or five centuries of contact cannot be without cultural interchange." As to whether Africans and Indians saw themselves as constituting a "nation" is extremely debatable, since the towns often functioned as independent units. Regardless, and most important here, outsiders viewed Africans and Indians as a conjoined threat to the expansion of the American nation and as a refuge for runaway slaves. After the turn of the century, Florida's Governor William DuVal "was more and more Convinced that the Slaves belonging to the Indians are a Serious nusance [sic]" and "have by their art and Cunning the entire Control Over their Masters" (Carter 1958, 454). If Africans were feared for armed insurrections and Indians for unprovoked savagery, a coalition between the two required the utmost condemnation. To prevent such an occurrence it became incumbent upon military or government officials to determine the ethnic identity of both groups. This was accomplished through various efforts, as the American government sought to treat the two disparate groups as an organized entity. The next section details this emerging empire and simultaneous governmental categorization and control.

Forging an American Empire

In *The Rising American Empire*, Richard Van Alstyne (1960, 1–2) considers the first application of the term "a rising empire" by George Washington in imagining what would be encompassed by territorial expansion and conquest of Indian people in various regions. Van Alstyne explains that "the declared purpose in fighting the War for Independence was to create a new empire or, to put the thought in words hardly familiar at the time, a *new national state*" (emphasis added). What this overarching strategy meant to Africans and Indians in the Southeast was an imperiled existence that would be obliterated, as they knew it, by this new nation. Following the War for Independence, the new Americans sought to incorporate regions held by England by removing all traces of political control by the former Colonial power. In the diplomatic negotiations that arose, Africans and Indians in the Floridas, if considered at all, were viewed as impediments to territorial acquisition, but race was a factor only inasmuch as it potentially hindered the process.

Determining the ethnic identity of African and Indians in the Seminole Nation was a crucial part of regulating Indian subjects in the emerging republic. The terms that legally defined blacks, regardless of various admixtures, undergirded plantation slavery as an enduring institution and relegated blacks to perpetual subordination. As Ian Lopez (1996, 119) notes: "The very practice of legally defining Black identity demonstrates the social, rather than natural, basis of race. . . . In the name of racially regulatory behavior, laws *created* racial identities." Not only were black Indians a challenge to binary racial designations, they also confronted coercion and control by white colonizers. Black Indians were part of the creation of racial identities by virtue of a new "body." European colonizers in the eighteenth century imported the notion of "racial" categories that not only sorted physical types according to superior and inferior classifications, but also provided the foundation for laws as to who would be slave or free (Spickard 1992, 13). By the vagaries of imprecise laws, blacks have often been reduced to a fraction of their identity by the "one-drop rule" of descent. However, Indians needed a requisite amount of "pure blood" to substantiate their identity claims. With either category, the designation devolves into a fixed biological determination that either confirms or denies one's connection to a tribal group. Furthermore, such designation is taken out of the hands of the Native people and of blacks to decide for themselves.

The early eighteenth century was a crucial period in American legislative history in the formulation of racial divides. Paul Spickard (1992, 118) notes that Virginia, for example, passed the first legal ban on interracial marriage in 1705, one that "constituted the first statutory effort to define who was Black." Thus, Indian lands in proximity to slave territories were sensitized to distinctions between diverse groups. Furthermore, as Indians were aware, laws supported and emphasized these differences. Designations for various groups were reduced to black, Indian, or white. Such strict categories did not favor a multiracial composition of the Seminole Nation, just as it denied the historical legitimacy of similar communities in regions of the Eastern seaboard (Forbes 1993, 189).

As opposed to this "divide-and-conquer" strategy, collaboration between Indians and blacks supported a multiracial group, creating a cultural situation in which Seminoles (black and Indian) vacillated between borderlands of identity that subverted notions of who was clearly either black *or* Indian. As communities that were closely associated and faced invasions from white settlers, intermarriage between the groups forged ties based on the extension of clan affiliations to Indian mothers and through the children of such unions. From the first law banning intermarriage to the final Virginia antimiscegenation statute overturned in 1967,[12] the central imperative of the United States and state governments has been "to prevent intermixture between peoples of diverse origins so that morphological differences that code as race might be more neatly maintained" (Lopez 1996, 117). Since longstanding familial ties linked blacks and Seminoles, racial designations articulated by outsiders were effectively ignored and superseded by clan obligations. Moreover, distinctions based on white naturalists' notions of "race" were not part of Seminole cosmology.[13] Several Indian leaders, including Osceola, were less than "pure."

Civil War Treaties

When discussing membership and identity issues today, tribal members — both Seminoles and Freedmen Indians — frequently refer to the 1866 treaty that ended the Civil War and at the same time incorporated

Seminole Freedmen into the tribe. This treaty recognized that all Seminoles, black *and* Indian, would be united as one nation. In the Senate bill "Remonstrance of the Seminole and Creek Delegates,"[14] proposed to offer Indians citizenship in 1878, Seminole and Creek delegates elaborated points of the 1866 treaties that incorporated Indian Freedmen in both tribes. Article 2 of the treaty "required the Seminoles to give the Freedmen among them all the rights of native citizens, and enacted the stipulation that the laws of said nation shall be equally binding upon all persons, *of whatever color*, who may be adopted as citizens or members of said tribe" (emphasis added). This was further stipulated in the revision of the Seminole constitution in 1969 that included Freedmen but did not have a blood-quantum requirement.

In contrast to separate and distinct black and Seminole towns that existed in the Southeast, the treaty provisions formalized the relationship and bound each group to its obligations. This is a variant to the previous arrangement in the Southeast whereby towns were organized and controlled by Seminole leaders from certain clans — for example, the Wind clan based on kinship ties. The 1866 treaty replaced the kinship structure with a politico-legal arrangement.

After the move to Indian Territory, the Seminole Nation at times was also affected by the dominant society in its relationship to black Seminoles. As Lewis Johnson expressed in regard to external influences when I interviewed him in 1999:

> Sometimes we hear it from different levels of government, of our tribal government and the citizenship that try to make it a black and Indian situation. What I feel like, personally, is that I think as Indians we have taken on characteristics of our environment, too, of the larger society, their philosophies, their ways of thinking. I'm not saying we've totally assimilated. I know we haven't. But I do know that our ancestors before us thought differently about the people that sided with them in conflict and perhaps had good friendship relationships and things of that nature.

This "friendship relationship" was reflected when treaty negotiations were in progress. The stipulation imposed by the federal government that slavery be abolished was a stumbling block for others of the Five Tribes (Cherokee, Chickasaw, Choctaw, and Creek), but "this condition gave the Seminoles less concern than it did the leaders of the other tribes because *little adjustment* was required by them for meeting it" (Henslick 1970, 281; emphasis added). This statement demonstrates that incorporating Seminole Freedmen into the treaty was not difficult — and, indeed, Seminoles were the first to sign — but it does little to emphasize the contradictions that existed. The vision of a united nation, for example, did not acknowledge the animosity and factionalism of Seminoles who had fought on both sides of the war. Although the majority of Seminoles sided with the Union and left Indian Territory to seek protection in Kansas, a portion remained in Indian Territory and signed a treaty with the Confederate states at the end of 1861 (Abel 1992, 320). The treaty signed in 1866 was designed in part to punish Seminoles who had sided with the Confederacy, and although they were the first tribe to sign, the federal government exerted pressure to do so.

The 1866 treaty was an attempt to repair a fractured nation and to formally articulate the status of the Seminoles' black allies. Provisions of the treaty included that slavery "shall not exist, nor involuntary servitude, except for and in punishment of a crime [according to Seminole law]"; a portion of land was set aside for friendly Indians in Kansas; and all tribes in Indian Territory were to form a consolidated government (Kappler 1904, 203). To prevent freed slaves from other states from joining and overwhelming the Seminole Nation, John Chupco, principal chief of the loyal Seminoles, clarified in a letter to the Commission of Indian Affairs dated January 30, 1866, that only Seminole Freedmen could settle there:

> We asked [our] Southern brothers to return to homes and live again in peace and we wished some laws to govern us as before the War. . . . We have agreed in council to recognize the colored people formerly belonging to the Seminoles as a part of us, with equal rights among us in property protection and the enjoyment of all the benefits.[15]

Chief Chupco was repeating the practice of Seminoles who prior to Removal had returned fugitives slaves to colonial forces on threat of starvation but withheld 800 Seminole Freedmen who were their allies. White slaveowners — and, indeed, some of the Southeastern tribes — viewed black people as property, but after the Civil War a distinction was made between blacks associated with the Seminole Nation and those inundating Indian Territory from Southern states. Chief Chupco recognized the debt owed to black Seminoles for their assistance during various wars or based on kinship ties but could not be induced to include freed slaves who had no connection or legitimacy in the postwar nation. It may be argued that Chief Chupco's statement established that black Seminoles actually were property; it is, however, un-usual to extend equal benefits to those in a subordinate position. A more likely reading of this statement is that once incorporated into the nation, whether by intermarriage or through military alliances or both, Seminole Freedmen *belonged* in the sense that a place in the tribe was reserved for them.

Freedmen or Seminole?

Each time I interview Freedmen or Seminole Indians on any number of subjects, the issue of blood quantum arises without provocation. In an interview in July 1999, Sarah Thomas, a Seminole Freedman, recalled how her grandmother treated people in the nation:

> If my grandmother said you welcome in that door, you was welcome and it wasn't no turnin' nobody away. I ain't never knew my grandmother to turn anybody away from her door. And I think that's the way we should all be again, helping one another. Not because she's black. She's white; she's In-dian. But, you know, I went to the tribal complex down there, and I seen more white people get help than anybody, and they don't have no bloodline. They ain't got no Indian in 'em. All they did they married into an Indian [family] and they get everything!

Over time, blood quantum has become a symbol of who is or is not Indian and by what percentage. After the Dawes Commission was established, it was noted that before 1896 no tribal rolls had included "blood quantum." As Kent Carter (1999, 49), the National Archives' Southwest regional archivist, observes, "In cases of mixed Freedmen and Indian parents . . . the applicant was always enrolled as a 'freedman' and not given any credit for having any Indian blood." This is a carry-over from the "one-drop rule" that says one drop of black blood makes one black. The two separate rolls from the Dawes Commission, the "Seminole Freedmen" and the "Seminoles by Blood," are at the center of the most recent controversy over membership.

In *Goat v. United States*, decided in the Eighth Circuit Court of Ap-peals in 1912, it was noted of the Seminole Nation: "Indeed, it is essentially a nation of full-bloods, save as to its colored citizens, who, under treaty provision, are on an equal footing with the citizens by blood. About one third of the citizens of the Seminole Nation are

Freedmen, and while the law does not specifically require a separate roll of each of these classes, the commissions' data will enable it to *so separate them*."[16] As a result of the colonial government's determination to create divisions within the Seminole Nation, and its insistence on basing this on blood quantum, separation has certainly occurred and created a bifurcated funding system that provides benefits for Seminole Indians while denying them for Seminole Freedmen. We have not yet seen the end of its enduring impact on our tribe. The Dawes Commission also had a deleterious outcome for mixed-blood Indians because degree of blood by Seminole custom was traced through the mother's line and resulted in cases such as "the child of a full-blood Seminole father and full-blood Creek mother as one-half Creek, even though the child had '100% Indian blood'" (Carter 1999, 49). By instituting a blood-quantum requirement using these standards, each successive generation of Seminoles would decrease the amount of Indian blood, even to the point of making them ineligible for tribal membership.

Blood quantum also played an important role in determining when restrictions were removed from allotted land so it could be sold. Seminole Freedmen and "competent" Indians (those determined by the roll system to have less than one-half Indian blood) had restrictions removed quickly, which resulted in permanent loss of their land (Bateman 1991, 70–71). In the final analysis, imposition of blood quantum to determine who is Indian was dictated by the federal government as a strategy to secure the majority of tribal lands at the turn of the twentieth century. Furthermore, the exclusion of blacks from the Seminole rolls as rightful members was seen as a necessary step, since obtaining the land would be more difficult if there were more legitimate "Seminoles" who also held valid claims to it.

When I interviewed Lewis Johnson in 1999, then the youngest Seminole tribal council member, he articulated some key distinctions between Seminole Freedmen and Seminole Indians concerning their relation to blood quantum:

> A lot of people believe that we discriminate against ourselves [Seminole Indians] because we require a blood quantum against our own tribal people. . . . [But there is no] blood check on the bands of the Freedmen, which a lot of people feel like, you know, a Freedmen is not a race. . . . They are of *a* race, but Seminole Indian people are of a tribe. . . . If they [Freedmen] were held to the same [blood] criteria, . . . many would not be allowed into the tribe.

Johnson's argument supports the biological determination of "race" that is fixed and immutable and the idea that instituting blood-quantum rules helps ferret out people who are not entitled to membership. As scholars have argued, "race" is socially constructed and therefore shaped by many factors, including colonialism, taxonomic systems, religious institutions, and legal proceedings (Gregory and Sanjek 1996; Omi and Winant 1994).[17] To the federal government, whether one was on the Freedman roll or the Indian roll resulted in who would receive allotted land and what that share would encompass. Among the Five Tribes, Indian Freedmen were given various size allotments from as large as 120 acres to a mere 40 acres. Thus, the "racial" distinction between Seminole and Freedmen resulted in an unequal share of the tribal estates. More important, it gave the government the remainder, which in all fairness should have gone to members of either group.

Over the years, some Seminole Freedmen have actively pursued documents that would enable them to transfer to the Seminole Indian roll. In 1994, I traveled to the National Archives–Southwest Region with one of the Seminole Freedmen band leaders, Lawrence Cudjoe, who was searching the records for proof that some Freedmen had been erroneously and deceptively placed on the Freedmen roll but indeed belonged on the Seminole Indian roll. Lawrence was unsuccessful in uncovering any proof, but as noted earlier, the government's mission in taking rolls of mixed-blood Indians and Freedmen enrollments were created as opportunities for inaccuracies to occur (Carter 1991, 41).[18] Transferring from one to the other would ensure a share of judgment funds but would also be an acknowledgment that "blood" supersedes cultural affiliation and historical connections for tribal membership. This is a crucial point whereby cultural ties provided the interconnected relationship of Seminole clans and towns and bound them to ceremonial and traditional customs that ensured their survival.

The Judgment Fund of 1990

Although monies were awarded in 1976 in the amount of $16 million to settle the dispute over lands illegally seized in 1823, it was not until 1990 that President George H. W. Bush signed Senate bill S.1096 dividing the now $56 million award, with Oklahoma Seminoles receiving a 75 percent share and the remaining 25 percent share going to Florida

Seminoles. The fund provides for members of the Seminole Nation as it existed on September 18, 1823. The award was to provide compensation for 24 million acres of aboriginal land taken by the United States (U.S. Congress, Senate 1978, 2). With reason, what has become a sticking point for Seminoles in Florida and Oklahoma is the precise composition of the nation in 1823.

A number of factors prevented an earlier distribution of the funds, including vigorous protests from Seminole Freedmen who would not share in the allocation and from Florida Seminoles who wanted a larger portion of the award (Micco 1995, 177–78). Statements submitted by Rick Lavis, Assistant Secretary of the Interior, in congressional documents for Senate bill S.2000 and S.2188 stated that "participation in the use of the funds involves only Seminole tribal members by blood. The bill [U.S. Congress, Senate 1978, 56] appropriately does not provide for participation by descendants of Oklahoma non-Indians who did not become members of the Seminole Nation until 1866. The Seminole lands were taken in 1823."

This decision follows a pattern begun with the Dawes rolls, whereby two classes of citizenship, freedman and Indian, were established and evoked earlier divisive strategies that drove wedges between Seminole tribal members. When I inquired during my interviews in 1999 whether Indians supported Freedmen, Dora Thomas, a Seminole Freedman, explained:

> It's some . . . that support Black Seminoles — it's some of 'em and then it's some of 'em that tell you right to your face on the [tribal] council board that they rather not participate with the blacks. Because, you know, I usually go to the meetings and I see how they do our [Freedmen band] chairman, Sister [Sylvia] Davis, and them. I know how they feel for you to get up there and, say, call names and say that they hate the blacks. It's not right.

This antipathy was also evident when various members, including the Dosar Barkus band leader Sylvia Davis, wanted to apply for benefits and programs available from the Judgment Fund. At the same time that I was conducting the interview with Dora Thomas, Sylvia Davis pointed out, "I went to enroll, and each time I applied for different programs in the nation, my application was denied, and I felt personally that by me having this [Seminole Freedmen] membership card, I should be entitled to the same benefits that all Indians are entitled to . . .

[and] I feel I'm a 100 percent member of the Seminole Nation. I still feel that way right now."

The connection of Seminole Freedmen to the nation has not diminished over the years, despite the two-tiered system of benefit allocation. Instead of assuming a position that unless Freedmen benefited directly from a program and therefore would not receive their vote or support in tribal council meetings, the Seminole Freedmen I spoke with felt that larger issues were at stake. Until the Judgment Fund was awarded in 1990, most Seminole tribal members were impoverished, and many remain so today. Land and oil loss through various swindles and frauds related to allotment titles left Seminoles, Indian and Freedmen alike, without property and with no means of financial support. As a small compensation for their multiple losses, the Judgment Fund provides educational awards, clothing allowances, community development, housing benefits, and health services. Although Seminole Freedmen do not receive any of these benefits, they continued to support the initiatives until they were disenfranchised in the 2000 election. Sylvia Davis maintains:

> We sympathize with the elders and with the young, and that's one reason why we sometimes go along with the votes to get those programs passed for the nation in order to help . . . even if we know it's not going to benefit [Freedmen] elders and young. . . . [B]ut it do hurt us because we be told on the council at times that the only reason they wanted us there was just to vote.

To date, all Seminole Freedmen's attempts to receive benefits from the Judgment Fund, including a lawsuit filed on behalf of Sylvia Davis's son, have failed to yield results in their favor. The final determination made on September 10, 2003, affirmed two previously appealed cases (1999 and 2002) holding that the tribe is an indispensable party to the case whose sovereign immunity protected it from being joined to the suit. The original case, *Davis v. United States*, was filed in 1998 by the law firm of Velie and Velie in Norman, Oklahoma.[19] The key point of the case is that Seminole Freedmen have been denied benefits based on their African ancestry and that Judgment Fund benefits are restricted to members with Certificate of Degree of Indian Blood (CDIB) cards issued by the Bureau of Indian Affairs. The suit also claims that the BIA "colluded with certain Tribal leaders to exclude the Estelusti from enjoyment of the Judgment Fund."[20]

In response to the allegations that Seminole Freedmen were kept from obtaining a CDIB, the BIA challenged that "if a Freedman band member or anyone else applies for a [CDIB] that cannot provide acceptable proof of relationship to a Seminole Indian by blood, they will be denied a [CDIB]."[21] Recall that in 1893 it was the federal government that insisted on separate Freedmen and Indian rolls, even though it was not required by law and despite the fact that it created inaccuracies for both mixed-bloods and Freedmen. Searching through records to document a switch to the Seminole by blood roll puts the onus on those least powerful and most directly affected by this ruling to somehow "recover" or "discover" documents that the government knows do not exist.

Mineral Rights Bill of 1999

While the *Davis* lawsuit has not rendered a successful outcome for Seminole Freedmen, another avenue remains for them to achieve some economic parity with other Seminole Indian tribal members. In an opportunity to address the unequal economic status between Seminole Indians and Seminole Freedmen, a bill was proposed in 1999 that would provide some relief. The impetus for this legislative solution originated in an 1898 document known as the "Original Seminole Agreement."[22] When it was apparent at the end of the nineteenth century that the Dawes Commission would go forward with enrolling citizens of the Five Tribes, the Seminole Nation negotiated the 1898 document. The language of the agreement could be construed as misleading in regard to Seminole Indians and Freedmen in that it states that "all lands belonging to the Seminole tribe of *Indians* shall be divided into three classes . . . and the same shall be divided among the *members* of the tribe so that each shall have an equal share thereof in value" (Kappler 1904, 663; emphasis added). Kappler also acknowledges that the three classes of allotment were inadequate; the tribe also insisted that "should there be discovered on *any allotment* any coal, mineral, coal oil, or natural gas, and the same should be operated so as to produce royalty, one-half shall be paid to each allottee and the remaining half into the tribal treasury until the extinguishment of tribal government" (Kappler 1904, 663; emphasis added).

The federal government fervently planned to end tribal government in 1906 and to impose Oklahoma statehood on Indian Territory. A year after statehood in 1908, Congress unilaterally, and without the advice or consent of the Seminole Nation, abrogated the Seminole Agreement of 1898, thereby terminating the 50 percent equalization fund that would have provided royalties to all allottees. With the torrential production of oil from the greater Seminole field in the 1910s, the present mineral claims are anticipated to exceed $100 million.[23] Realizing that a bill for mineral rights presented to Congress would not receive any support from the Black Caucus if Seminole Freedmen were excluded, the vote from July 1998 was tabled until more discussions within the bands could be completed. I presented testimony before the tribal council in November 1998 to explain the merit of including Freedmen in the distribution of mineral-rights claims, including a short history of Seminole and Freedmen alliances in the Southeast. In a close vote of the tribal council in December 1998, it was decided to submit the mineral-rights claims to Congress and not to exclude the Seminole Freedmen from membership in the tribe. On January 20, 1999, Principal Chief Jerry Haney signed "Royalty Claims: Proposal for a Private Relief Act for the Seminole Nation of Oklahoma." On several trips to Washington, D.C., over the past few years, representatives of Freedmen and Indian bands have presented the position of both groups relative to this bill.

Before many Freedmen or Indians had traveled to Washington, I asked a few of them what they hoped would be the outcome from the settlement of this claim. Sylvia Davis said, "I'm hoping to see better living conditions for both sides. I'm hoping to see unity be brought into the nation with both sides." Sarah Thomas regretted that elders who had passed away before the Judgment Fund was finally allocated had not received any benefits. She emphasized, "Not to be greedy or nothin' like that but if our ancestors, if this is what was due to them, a lot of them passed on, they done left, they didn't get to enjoy it. . . . So if it's for us to have and enjoy, then they should let us have it and enjoy it while we have a chance."

Lewis Johnson, however, expressed concern about portions of the 1898 agreement and what it actually meant to allottees. Were there different stipulations considered for Freedmen than for Indians, and would that sway the final resolution? There was also some question in his mind about whether it might ultimately affect enrollment of Freedmen bands:

If we get the settlement . . . we realize that the Freedmen was allotted, you know, properties, too. . . . [But] that could be the basis of the area of trying to stop the enrollment increase of those particular bands. . . . I think some were saying this as recently as a few days ago that Freedmen land was not restricted so that agreement would not apply to them simply because the agreement was done with tribal land that was in trust at the time, half, allottees, half to the tribe.

What this refers to is the removal by Congress on May 27, 1908, of restrictions of alienation or encumbrance on "all lands, including homesteads, of said allottees enrolled as intermarried whites, as Freedmen, and as mixed-blood Indians having less than half Indian blood, including minors"(U.S. Congress, Senate, 1930, 9). The blood-quantum distinction is a reference to the belief of policymakers that the more Indian blood one has, the less competent he or she is to make a decision regarding land. Mixed-bloods of one half of more Indian blood had their land held in trust for twenty-five years to prevent unscrupulous land swindles from occurring (Debo 1991, 32).

Points raised as to who should share in the resources of the Seminole Nation of Oklahoma bring stark reality to the socially constructed phenomenon of Seminole Freedmen identity. What it demonstrates is that both blacks and Indians are caught in a web of ethnic-identity verification. Seminole Freedmen must provide their historical association with the nation; at the same time, Seminole Indians must provide their connection based on ancestors enumerated on the Dawes rolls. If the mineral-rights claims for the Seminole Nation can be settled in the near future, this more than empty political rhetoric may demonstrate a trend to strengthen tribal independence. Since the tribe has faced other, more pressing issues in the past few years, including its 2000 and 2001 elections, the mineral-rights claim has not received the attention needed to pass in Congress.

The Seminole Nation in the New Millennium

In attempting to articulate the deeply felt connection Seminole Freedmen have to the Seminole Nation, those I interviewed in Oklahoma shared with pride their fight against the formidable United States and recounted their distinctive ethnic identity. The history of interaction between Seminole Freedmen and Seminole Indians is complex and convoluted and is not easily defined by lumping the former into the larger group of black Indians.

Newspaper and television interviews have been sharply critical of the Seminole Nation's seemingly recalcitrant position toward inclusion of Seminole Freedmen in the tribe. Two *New York Times* articles provided simplistic overviews of history and painted Seminole Indians as "mean spirited and immoral."[24] As I have shown in this essay, federal and military agencies, including the BIA and the DOI, exerted tremendous pressure on the Seminole Nation related to membership issues. It is important to acknowledge that Congress has plenary power over tribal affairs. Therefore, it appears that the answer to who gets to decide who is Seminole is the federal government.

The difficulty for outsiders in understanding the relationship of Seminole Freedmen to the Seminole Nation was evident in a 2002 article that featured Sylvia Davis. Davis, whom I have interviewed over a number of years, was depicted "as near to royalty as a Seminole Indian can get."[25] Davis has an identifiable and honorable connection to the Seminole Nation through her family's ancestry and has continued to maintain her duties as a band leader in difficult situations. I also know her to be a modest, hardworking, intelligent woman who, to my knowledge, has never referred to herself as "royalty." I fear that attaching such a label to any person in the Seminole Nation elicits visions of the mythical Indian princess. This image has done a disservice to all Native people, particularly Native women, because it unfortunately perpetuates the image of the Hollywood Indian and quite possibly exacerbates negative views of the Seminole Indians.

An interview by the television program *60 Minutes* taped in June 2001 but not shown until June 2002 also did not offer many perspectives to underscore the multifaceted connection between Seminole Indians and Freedmen. Although I had several conversations with the segment's executive producer, Wendy Krantz, and provided historical background to Chief Haney for the interview, the Seminole Indian viewpoint did not fare well when it was aired. The segment gave short shrift to the policies that eliminated funding opportunities for Seminole Freedmen. In addition, it did not describe our tribal organization and the independence of band decisions. This is a key point that provides an explanatory basis for the historical relationship of the two groups, as well as a window into our current political structure.[26]

"Blood and Money"   **141**

It is also just as inaccurate to portray our tribe as an "Afro-Indian" one. More precisely, the Seminole Nation recognizes its creation as the product of multiple ethnic threads. It may seem a semantic dance, but the name "Seminole" acknowledges our history of harboring runaway slaves and of creating a multiracial military force who became pioneers of racial tolerance long before mainstream society. Rather than "running from history," the Seminole Nation has privileged our history through the oral tradition that documents events from all sides. It also takes into account less than principled events that included harsh slave masters and narrow-minded individuals.

I maintain that the relationship between the two groups originated in the Southeast and certainly was solidified for military expediency, and the enduring connection cannot be easily dismissed by an unqualified election. In a 1993 interview, Lawrence Cudjoe explained:

> We belong to the Seminole Nation. There are fourteen bands. I tell them all the time. I didn't put myself in the band. Our forefathers put us there. They put us in there and wrote a constitution. We've got just as much right here as you. The constitution says as long as the water flows. But people change. It's a changing world. They become polarized. We are black Indians. . . . I said, when you refer to us in the Seminole Nation, refer to us as Freedmen because every black is not a freedman. It's a distinct category.

Our constitution does not precisely state "as long as the water flows," but the sentiment remains the same: Seminole Freedmen and their ancestors were a meaningful part of the Seminole Nation from its founding in the Southeast. This emotion was echoed in summer 1998 and again in 2002 when I spoke to a number of Seminole Freedmen who patiently explained the affinity between them and Seminole Indians that preceded Removal to Indian Territory. Based on those conditions, they are a distinct group of Seminoles. Several also emphasized that their complaint is not with the Seminole Nation but with the U.S. government, which has not provided benefits that befit their role in the tribe. The heart of the matter is that outsiders to the nation, including government officials, other tribal groups, settlers in Florida and Oklahoma, as well as racially divisive laws had a bearing on the final outcome between Freedmen and Seminole Indians. Seminole Freedmen now are demanding that the federal government make amends for the situation and provide an opportunity to move each group toward a resolution that honors and acknowledges their shared history.

Notes

I express my gratitude to Nimachia Hernandez for her insightful comments and keen attention to detail.

1 U.S. District Court, *Seminole Nation v. Gale Norton*, no. 02–0739 (RBW) (D.D.C. September 23, 2002). As a member of the Seminole Nation of Oklahoma, I have personal and professional interests in the legal decisions and tribal decisions affecting the Seminoles. My family has been involved in tribal politics for decades, and my cousin, Leon Lusty, was a candidate in the runoff election for principal chief in 2001. I am both an insider and an outsider to tribal politics by virtue of returning to California following my annual summer research travels in Oklahoma to research this essay and other projects. This personal connection provides resources that are not readily accessible to those who are unaffiliated with the Seminole Nation and offers insight into the complex issues of blood quantum, tribal history, and links between Seminole Indians and Freedmen.

2 Throughout the history of the Seminole Nation, people of African descent have been described by many names. Treaties referred to Indian Negroes; Muskogee speakers called them *estelusti* (black man); and the 1866 treaty with the Seminole named them Seminole Freedmen. Those who fled from Indian Territory to Texas and Mexico are known as Seminole Indian Negro Scouts, and contemporary writings refer to black Seminoles. The latter connects them to dispersed groups in the Bahamas, Mexico, and Florida not affiliated with the Seminole tribe. I have chosen to use "Freedmen" to indicate both genders and make the designation less unwieldy when referring to men and women.

3 I use "nation" here to signify that an external body rather than Seminole people made that decision.

4 *Seminole Nation v. Gale Norton*, 2.

5 Ibid., 15

6 Ibid., 41.

7 These are the sea cargoes that brought African people to be enslaved in the "New World."

8 The English translation of *micco* as "chief" is insufficient to explain the character of a leader. *Micco* more closely translates as keeper of the people who demonstrates responsibility for the community and prevents internal strife.

9 After removal in the 1830s, the Southeastern towns were the origin of the current band structure. Not every town from the Southeast is represented, and over time several were absorbed into the fourteen bands that currently exist.

10 The term "peculiar institution" was coined by the historian Kenneth Milton Stampp 1956.

11 Bateman's study presents a contemporary view of Seminole and Freedmen history with interviews conducted in the 1980s. An earlier master's thesis by Art Gallaher (1951) provided an update of Foster's in the 1930s. I began my own

in-depth interviews in the early 1990s. Through these various scholars, we have roughly covered the twentieth century.

12 The 1967 case *Loving v. Virginia*, 388 US1, 18 L ed 2d 1010, 87 S·Ct 1817, concerned the marriage of a black woman, Mildred Jeter, and a white man, Richard Loving. They were married in Washington, D.C., and when they returned to live in Virginia they were arrested and sentenced to a year in prison. The final decision by the Supreme Court ruled that "to prevent marriage between persons solely on the basis of racial classifications violates the Equal Protection and Due Process Clauses of the Fourteenth Amendment."

13 As noted earlier, Seminoles were composed of a number of indigenous groups. Intermarriage between aboriginal groups and white settlers also occurred when Spain and Britain controlled the Florida regions.

14 U.S. Congress, Senate. 1978. "Remonstrance of the Seminole and Creek Delegates." *Senate Misc. Doc. 18*, 45 Cong. 2d Sess., 1–2.

15 John Chupco to Commissioner of Indian Affairs, January 30, 1866, M234, National Archives Microfilm Publications, *Microcopy R23* (Office of Indian Affairs, Seminole Agency, Letters Received), Washington, D.C.

16 *Goat v. United States*, 224 U.S. 458; 32 S. Ct. 544, 56 L. Ed. 841 (1912) emphasis added.

17 Both volumes challenge the biological determination of race and examine systems of power that ensured inequalities traced along "racial" lines.

18 Carter 1991 discovered that inaccuracies occurred in the construction of the Dawes rolls, but the Seminole Nation was thought to be "relatively free from corruption" and more easily enrolled because of the high percentage of full-bloods.

19 *Davis v. United States*, 343 F.3d 1282 (10th Cir. 2003).

20 Ibid., 6.

21 Ibid., 3.

22 Original Seminole Agreement, 30 Stat. 567 (1898), which acknowledged a disparity between allotment values, and provided for the creation of an "equalization" fund, with money to come from one-half of all mineral interests from the allotted lands.

23 Attorney General's Opinion no. 98–3, ref. no. 7533.1, D. Michael McBride III, Attorney-General, Seminole Nation of Oklahoma, July 18, 1998, 3/12.

24 "Who Is a Seminole, and Who Gets to Decide?" *New York Times*, January 29, 2001; "The Seminole Tribe, Running from History," *New York Times*, April 21, 2002.

25 Ibid.

26 "A Nation Divided," *60 Minutes*, June 2002. I thank the producers of *60 Minutes* for honoring my book project of the same name when they chose a title for the interview.

CHAPTER SEVEN

"Playing Indian"?

The Selection of Radmilla Cody as

Miss Navajo Nation, 1997–1998

CELIA E. NAYLOR

~~~~~~~~

Critical studies by a number of Native American scholars have articulated the historical and sociopolitical foundations for "playing Indian" within European and European American cultural landscapes. Rayna Green's provocative essay "The Tribe Called Wannabee: Playing Indian in America and Europe" (1988) illustrated not only various manifestations of this "performance" grounded in the European context, but also the presentations embedded within the American imagination.[1] American history has been punctuated by a number of famous performances that reflect the infusion of a warped "Indianness" within the European American consciousness. Perhaps the most infamous, and often redramatized, presentation of "playing Indian" occurred on December 16, 1773, with the dramatic act of rebellion by American colonists commonly referred to as the Boston Tea Party. As Philip J. Deloria (1998) maintained, this demonstration in Boston was certainly not limited to the Revolutionary era but, in fact, has spanned several centuries of American history. In the late twentieth century, inextricably connected to the "playing Indian" discourse, pointed criticism has been leveled at individuals and organizations in the United States that have appropriated Native American cultures in copious behaviors and activities. A great deal of the dialogue has been presented in an erudite manner. However, overgeneralizations regarding Indian play and performance have mistakenly defined individuals and events in ways that

Radmilla Cody, Miss Navajo Nation 1997–98, accompanied by her grandmother at the Dartmouth conference "Eating Out of the Same Pot." *Used by permission of the photographer, Benny Miles, 2000.*

are strikingly problematic. This critical wave contesting Indian play has been swept up with currents of racialist (and, in some cases, racist) language and attitudes.

One expression of this misdirected impulse occurred in the aftermath of the selection of Radmilla Cody as Miss Navajo Nation 1997–98. This essay highlights some of the printed responses to Cody's reign to illustrate the mislabeling process sometimes associated with notions of "playing Indian," as well as to challenge the generic framework of the "playing Indian" diatribe. Central to the issue, and to this case in particular, is the contested position of people of African and Native descent within Native American communities and nations.

African Americans and Indian Play

The "expressive complex of behaviours" of playing Indian / Indian play, Green contended, reiterates itself freely across boundaries of race and class, gender and age group, regional and other affiliative groups, to find its various expressions in a range of media from traditional, orally transmitted texts (songs, stories, jokes, anecdotes) to formal, literary texts, to artifacts (clothing, toys, tools, drawings, paintings), to dramatic performances (games, gestures, dramas) and ritual enactments or reenactments. (Green 1998, 30)

As Green explained, there are some people who play Indian for a lifetime; others choose to do so for "brief, transient staged performances performed only in childhood or erratically and situationally over a lifetime. For some, it is a hobby; for others a semi-religious passion; for others still, merely one of many reference points that root them in an American identity" (Green 1998, 30). The frequency and specific acts of Indian play within the American context, however, also expose the multifaceted dimensions of European and Indian social, political, and military contacts. In *Playing Indian*, Deloria positioned Indian play within a complex, evolving struggle between the ideology and reality of Indianness, whiteness, and Indian–white relations. The array of Indian play and Indian–white interactions, he asserted,

have modeled a characteristically American kind of domination in which the exercise of power was hidden, denied, qualified, or mourned. Not surprisingly, Indian play proved a fitting way to negotiate social struggles within white society that required an equally opaque vision of power. The Revolution, in which Indian play transformed treachery to patriotism, is, of course, the first significant marker of this intramural use of Indianness. The New York Tammany Society used "the Indian" in building a powerful political party with specific class and ethnic inflections. Other working-class fraternal orders played Indian to address anxieties driven by their increasing distance from political power and the threatened loss of economic self-sufficiency. Lewis Henry Morgan's elite Indian fraternalism, on the other hand, allowed him to criticize exactly those people — working-class salt boilers who "profaned" the national landscape. For Ernest Thompson Seton, Indianness was key to an upper-class reformist impulse to nurture children placed in gender danger by the modern city. Boys were to be raised to masculinity through contact with Indianized nature, while Camp Fire Girls were to learn the timeless value of female domesticity. In Cold War America, Indian lore hobbyists sought to come to terms with an uneasy middle-class identity that was at once celebrated and attacked. Each of these enterprises found meaning and power on the contradictory foundations of Indian Americanness and Indian dispossession. (Deloria 1998, 187)

Even before the Boston Tea Party, European and European American colonists had begun the process of negotiating, as Deloria portrayed, how to "wield power against Indians — social, military, economic, and political — while simultaneously drawing power from them" (Deloria 1998, 191). Indian play demonstrates part of this synchronized and synergetic process of dispossession and appropriation.

Although playing Indian has been performed primarily by European Americans and Europeans, Green affirmed that "persons of Hispanic, Mediterranean and African/Afro-American background also play Indian in large numbers. Even Apaches, Sioux, and Cherokee 'Indians' play 'Indian'" (Green 1988, 30). When women, African Americans, or other "minority" groups play Indian, she alleged, they often do so as a means of circumventing rigid gendered and racial roles constructed from within the dominant society (Green 1988, 46–48). Although people of all cultural and racial backgrounds have professed to be Native American as part of their identity, Green argued that, for "Blacks and Hispanics, both in and outside of the United States, the claim is deeply rooted in racial politics" (Green 1988, 46). She also posited that African Americans frequently claim Indian blood, especially Cherokee blood and Blackfeet blood (Green 1988, 46). Deloria briefly mentioned African Americans playing Indian, maintaining that "African-American Indian play — especially the carnivalesque revels of Mardi Gras — follows white practices to a degree, but it also stems from a different history of Afro-Caribbean cultural hybridity" (Deloria 1998, 8). For Green, the assertion of African American claims to Indian blood, "unsubstantiated by any known familial or settlement pattern, simply appears to be a kind of folk alliterative device" (Green 1988, 46). Although Green admitted that more Native Americans and African Americans "had extensive relationships in the Southeast than are documented," she still questioned the authenticity of African American claims to Indian blood (Green 1988, 47). She declared that African Americans continue to play Indian and present these "unsubstantiated" pronouncements as a way of perhaps "connecting to a world that allows them to be first, to be other than Black, other than white, other than victims who did not fight their enslavement" (Green 1988, 48). Green's suspicion echoes critical discussions that understandably object to the appropriation of Native

American cultures by non–Native Americans. However, her overall rejection of African American claims to Native American cultures and identities not only unjustifiably denies the dynamic historical interactions between Native Americans and African Americans but also invalidates the existence of people who are rightfully Native American and African American.

Partially due to the complex racial dynamics in the United States, people of African descent who present themselves as genetically or culturally Native American may be viewed by self-identified and tribally affiliated Native Americans as more suspect than European Americans who make similar claims to an Indian identity. In her examination of "blood politics" in relation to Cherokee freedpeople in Oklahoma, Circe Sturm averred:

> At the center of this story is an absence, an exclusion, a silence where the Cherokee freedmen might have been. The reason for this absence is clear: when Cherokee citizens conflate blood, color, race, and culture to demarcate their sociopolitical communities, they often exclude multi-racial individuals of Cherokee and African ancestry, who are treated in both discourse and practice in qualitatively different ways from multiracial individuals with Cherokee and White ancestry. . . . Several centuries of social, political, and economic relations with Euro-Americans engendered Cherokee color prejudice, whose legacy means, among other things, that Cherokee identity politics has never been simply a question of blood or culture. Cherokee freedmen and other multiracial individuals who choose to identify as both Indian and Black challenge the prevailing racial ideologies that ask us to "choose one" racial or ethnic identity, often at the expense of another. (Sturm 2002, 224)

When people of African and Native American descent express their mixed racial and national identities, they are often denied, scrutinized, and neglected within the Native communities with which they identify. Often the physical manifestations of their Native identity are viewed as yet another form of appropriation of Native American cultures. In fact, their expressions of "Indianness" are often considered merely an aspect of one of the prevalent forms of cultural expression and performance in the United States, and even in parts of Europe — the act of "playing Indian."

The Miss Navajo Nation 1997–98 Debate in the *Navajo Times*

A clear example of the suspicion surrounding the authenticity and legitimacy of Native black people within Native American communities emerged after Radmilla A. Cody was selected as Miss Navajo Nation 1997–98 on September 6, 1997. Cody was raised by her maternal grandmother, Dorothy Cody, in Grand Falls, Arizona, on the Navajo reservation. Her grandmother taught her to speak Navajo fluently, weave rugs, and prepare fry bread, as well as to herd and butcher sheep. She also cultivated Cody's love of Navajo stories and songs. Even though Radmilla Cody impressed the judges of the 1997 competition and was selected from among the six other finalists as Miss Navajo Nation, some members of the Navajo Nation viewed the judges' selection of Cody as utterly incomprehensible and inappropriate. To date, however, this debate has not resulted in any critical examination of this case.

The controversy sparked by Cody's reign as Miss Navajo Nation revolved not around her ability to speak the Navajo Diné language, her understanding of contemporary Navajo politics, or even her talent in preparing fry bread or butchering sheep. Rather, her perceived inappropriateness centered on her phenotype — specifically, the fact that her father was African American and her physical features emphasized this biological reality. The judges of the contest did not mention Cody's multiracial background during the competition. However, discussions of Cody's ability to represent the Navajo Nation transpired not only in conversations throughout Navajo communities, but also permeated the pages of the Navajo Nation's weekly newspaper, the *Navajo Times*.

In a letter to the editor printed in that newspaper in December 1997, Orlando Tom, a member of the Navajo community residing in Blue Gap, Arizona, argued that "when the Navajo people select a person to represent their nation as 'Miss Navajo,' that person must possess the appearance and physical characteristics of the Navajo people. Miss Cody's appearance and physical characteristics are clearly black, and are thus representative of another race of people."[2] From Tom's perspective, Navajo members of mixed race represent a threat to the future of the Navajo Nation. "There is a duty and responsibility," Tom charged,

> to procreate within our own kind, so we can perpetuate our existence in the years to come. If we fail in this endeavor, within 200 years from now, there will be no Indian people. We will all be part of the melting pot, part this and

part that, yet never being anything specific. That is why inter-racial unions and the children it brings forth, is nothing other than ethnic genocide, and is the true enemy of Indian sovereignty.[3]

It is "the very essence of the genetic code," Tom claimed, "which is passed down from generation to generation that makes us who we are." Instead of being involved in Navajo affairs, Tom recommended that Cody focus on her African American heritage.[4]

Tom's letter generated several responses from Navajo people, many of whom self-identified as mixed-race Navajo members and expressed their support of the selection of Cody as Miss Navajo Nation. The week after Tom's letter appeared, the *Navajo Times* published four letters challenging Tom's remarks about Radmilla Cody.[5] Three of the four letters were written by people who self-identified as mixed-race members of the Navajo Nation. Rick Abasta, a "biracial" Navajo from St. Michaels, Arizona, affirmed that

> it's unfortunate that Navajos like Mr. Tom are willing to discredit the accomplishments of another tribal member due to their bi-racial back-ground. . . . Such a blighted view of people is an unadulterated example of racism, and to have a minority express contempt upon another minority (let alone an Indian upon another Indian), is absolutely ludicrous. Your ignorance Mr. Tom, obviously precludes your intelligence, sir.[6]

La Tanya Diaz Cortez-Curley, "[one-half] Navajo" whose father is Puerto Rican, asserted that mixed-race Navajos "are not the enemy. People who say things, like Mr. Tom, sometimes make us that way, but also makes us stronger and willing to be a part of it more. . . . We do not just think of ourselves, but want to be thought of as equally as anyone else on this earth. . . . We are Navajos too, and proud of it."[7]

A few of the letters to the editor challenged the whole notion of what it means to be Navajo, specifically accentuating Navajo people's multiracial and multicultural background. Daphne Thomas of Leupp, Arizona, maintained that

> if he [Mr. Tom] thinks that all Navajos are full-bloods, he's mistaken. Where do you suppose all the last names of Navajos who reside in Navajoland that are spelled in Spanish originate from? There have been many interracial marriages among Navajos with the Spanish, Paiutes, Utes and Hopis in the last century that genetically, a significant portion of the Navajo population has become a mixture of many tribal groups. It's the same with other Indian tribes as well.[8]

Raquel Casuse of Chinle, Arizona, further insisted that in the case of the Miss Navajo contest, "the subject of skin complexion or who was 'part this or part that' never held any relevance to the judges. Let me bring to your attention the fact that those of us nowadays do come in various complexions, whether dark or light."[9] Dorothea Lynch of Tempe, Arizona, stated that

> culturally, she [Cody] is Dine. If you haven't already forgotten, with her being a woman of our people, her clan will continue on through her children. So, it troubles me why you are disrespectful to one of our life givers. If I didn't know better, you appear to come from a European patriarchal background. . . . [W]here on the initial qualifications does it state that Miss Navajo has to "possess the appearance and physical characteristics of the Navajo people?" On what or whom will you base these characteristics on? If someone looks too dark or too light, are they to be immediately disqualified? . . . Tell me where does this end or where does it begin?[10]

In March 1998, after a two-month hiatus, Leona R. Begay of Kirtland, New Mexico, reignited the *Navajo Times* debate.[11] Her letter to the editor declared that she was

> quite disturbed, disappointed and very upset. Disturbed at the fact that our reigning Miss Navajo is bi-racial. The whole concept of having a Miss Navajo is just that, in the title itself, Navajo. Anyone can learn to speak Navajo, learn to butcher a sheep/goat, learn another's culture. But it takes a full-blooded Navajo to be hundred percent Navajo. This Navajo would then have every right to call herself Miss Navajo.[12]

Begay considered Radmilla Cody's reign "another slap in the face" for the Navajo Nation. Moreover, "a bi-racial Miss Navajo," she believed,

> is a change to the Navajo Culture. It is then not the true Navajo Culture. What changes are to come next? The cremation of bodies, changes as to which for [*sic*] mountains will be our Sacred Mountains, or perhaps a new mountain will be added? Our ancestors would turn over in their graves, as they would say. Call me a racist if you will. I am a racist for loving and defending my own race.[13]

Begay's comments sparked yet another battery of responses. Ryan Battles of Window Rock, Arizona, reiterated the legitimate position of biracial and multiracial people in the Navajo Nation. Radmilla Cody, he declared, is the epitome of the Navajo youth today because she is of mixed blood. Like many of us who are bi-racial, and in my case tri-cultural, she is forced to deal with the discriminatory attitudes of those who have the temerity to remain oblivious of the changing world. . . . Why must Navajo Purists, who really are not that pure, consider us to be the bastard children of the Dine. Are we to be considered illegitimate by other members of the Navajo tribe who refuse to recognize our status because we are not full bloods.[14]

Battles proclaimed that, "for all who share that individual's feelings that a bi-racial lineage causes one to feel disturbed, disappointed, and very upset, you should only be disturbed, disappointed, and very upset at yourself for being a hypocrite. Very few Navajos possess a full blood lineage and for an individual to claim as such makes them a hypocrite."[15] Although initially concurring with Begay's beliefs, Nathan J. Tohtsoni of Shiprock, New Mexico, realized that he could not agree completely, as his own great-grandfather was half-Hopi:

If we really want to get to the basis of the contamination and genocide of our culture, let us look at the thousands of years we inter-married and bore bi-racial Navajos with other native tribes. And let us not forget the Spaniards and their bi-racial offspring, the Mexicans, as they and we pillaged and traded our Navajo identity. But somehow we adapted and stayed Navajo.[16]

Tohtsoni, and others, rightfully pointed out that the mere fact that "we have a Miss Navajo Nation title is a change to Navajo culture."[17] Shirlee James-Johnson of Chinle, Arizona, who self-identified as Navajo and "half African-American," proposed that "we should regard all individuals as having the potential to bring healing to the sickness we are dealing with on the Navajo Nation, and encourage all children regardless of their features/blood — White, African American, Mexican or Indian — to succeed and be the best they can be to help bring healing to our world of fear, ignorance, and hatred."[18]

Others responded to the controversy by accentuating the interjection of racial and identity politics into the debate. Sean Walker, chairperson of the Legal Redress Committee of the NAACP Gallup Local Chapter in New Mexico, expressed that he

failed to understand Mr. Tom's reasoning as to why he feels that any mixed-blood person could not be representative of the Navajo Tribe. In the past, hasn't there been mixed-blood Miss Navajos? It wasn't a problem then, so why is it a problem now? Could it be because Ms. Cody is part African

American? Is he saying that all mixed-blood Navajo children coming up cannot possibly represent the Navajo Nation in any capacity because of their mixed blood?[19]

Tish Ramirez of Holbrook, Arizona, concurred with this sentiment, explaining that

> a 100% full-blooded Navajo does not exist. The Navajos, by virtue of their nomadic ancestors, are a mixture of many races: Pauite, Ute, Zuni, Hopi, Apache . . . the list is long. Bi-racial children are not a product of the 90's. Those very traditional Navajos who made the long walk to Ft. Sumner brought back some bi-racial children. I think their mothers loved them all the same. The Indian Agents of the 1800's left many descendants, many of whom still proudly carry their names. Are you to deny their offspring and their deeds? If so, consider that the Navajo reservation would not be as large as it is today. . . . I don't believe that the racist attitudes being expressed towards Ms. Cody are really about being "bi-racial" as it is about her being of African American descent. If it soothes you any, in comparison to other races, the African Americans have committed far fewer atrocities against the Navajos.[20]

For Ivis Daniel Peaches of Flagstaff, Arizona, Begay's opinion, and not Radmilla Cody's bicultural identity, threatened the future of the Navajo Nation. She argued:

> What is wrong with a bi-racial person representing his or her own people and wanting to express cultural identity with pride, strength? If these individuals who speak out against people such as Miss Radmilla Cody, feel that their traditional way of life is doomed, then they have already condemned the future of the Navajo people. . . . [W]hen a person like Miss Cody is discredited in representing the Navajo Nation just because she is not "100% Navajo," they might as well discredit our forefathers (i.e., Manuelito, Barboncito) and the great Native American athletes (i.e., Billy Mills, Jim Thorpe). If you have not noticed, the majority of our forefathers have Spanish names, what makes you so sure that they are not bi-racial? . . . Not all Navajos, such as myself, feel that Miss Cody is a threat to the future of the Navajo people, but is a blessing.[21]

Although the majority of the letters regarding Radmilla Cody's reign as Miss Navajo Nation 1997–98 focused on her biracial identity, it was not her biracialness that represented the overwhelming and underlying concern. Women who had been named Miss Navajo Nation previously had been biracial or bicultural—certainly not "100% Navajo." However, Radmilla Cody would be the Miss Navajo Nation who would always conjure up the image of biraciality in the minds of many Navajo people because she is of African descent. To some, Cody's "black blood" severed and erased any possible legitimate connection to the Navajo Nation. Others presented their essentialist position equating a person's degree of Navajo blood (their blood quantum) with their Navajoness. In a few letters, members of the Navajo Nation conflated notions of "race," tribal belonging, and culture. The letters vividly illustrate the degrees of mixed-raceness and acceptance, with a particular focus on Cody's phenotype as the determining factor for her supposed placement outside the Navajo culture and nation. In fact, all of the letters, whether in support of Cody or not, demonstrated the complicated nature of cultural, racial, and tribal / national identities. The complexity of these issues emerged not only in the letters in this debate, but also in Cody's responses to the controversy surrounding her reign.

Radmilla Cody Responds

With the variety of perspectives on Radmilla Cody's reign frequently highlighted in the *Navajo Times*, it is, of course, telling that the one viewpoint absent from this particular forum is that of Radmilla Cody. Her mother, however, wrote a letter of thanks and appreciation to those who had written letters of support concerning her daughter.[22] Although Radmilla Cody did not respond to the debate in the *Navajo Times*, she voiced some of her views on the matter in an interview published in the March 1, 1998, issue of the *Albuquerque Journal*.[23] In her interview with the journalist Leslie Linthicum, Cody expressed that she "was stunned" after reading Orlando Tom's letter. At twenty-three, she had "come to terms with being a curiosity among both blacks and Navajos and she had entered the Miss Navajo contest to make a statement that biracial people should not be judged as 'half' of anything."[24] In reaction to the controversy, Cody remarked that

> instead of looking at you as a human being and just another person, they want to look at you for the color of your skin. . . . And if you are half-black, they push you into that position where you feel you have to try to fit in when you're with either group. . . . I actually felt like I was a child again. . . . I was

dealing with all the feelings I had dealt with growing up, dealing with racial slurs from the black side as well as the Navajo side.[25]

Although the reason for the *Albuquerque Journal* interview was to explore the debate about Cody's reign, within the article Cody focused her comments on her early life and preparation for the Miss Navajo Nation competition. Her remarks about the controversy itself, including the letters in the *Navajo Times*, are limited to only a few general statements concerning mixed-race Navajo people.

In April 2000, two and a half years after being selected Miss Navajo Nation, Cody shared more of her sentiments about her controversial reign at a conference held at Dartmouth College. Cody explained that, after an initial "honeymoon period" at the beginning of her reign as Miss Navajo Nation, she became particularly upset by these letters. She specifically recalled Begay's letter avowing that as Miss Navajo Nation she "should be 100% Navajo and that basically anybody can learn how to bake fry bread, butcher sheep and know how to speak the language if they wanted to."[26] Although she said she was "very upset when the letter was brought to my attention and . . . did want to respond," she decided that, "due to my respect for my elders . . . the best thing to do was to leave it alone and just to hold my head up high."[27] After reading the letters, she said, she initially thought

> of all of our children on the reservation who were of mixed race[,] and I went before the Council and they gave me the time to speak and basically share my feelings about that. . . . I told them that we have a lot of children on the reservation who are of mixed race, who are of the Black race, White race, Native American of other tribes. . . . Instead of shunning them, we need to teach them to preserve our way of life and our culture.[28]

Cody chose to use the controversy not as an opportunity to validate or justify her Navajoness, but as a way to address broader issues related to the reception and treatment of mixed-race people within the Navajo Nation.

Perhaps one of the most revealing aspects of this controversy is the fact that some members of the Navajo Nation questioned Cody's "authenticity" and in effect charged her with "playing Indian," even though she had been raised on the Navajo reservation and identified completely with Navajo culture and traditions. Since Cody did not develop a significant relationship with her African American father or his family, her first contact with African Americans occurred when she left the reservation to live with her mother in Flagstaff, Arizona. At that time she was a junior at Coconino High School. As a result, Cody had a limited knowledge of African American culture and history.[29] Her decision to enter the contest was not based on personal reasons alone. Cody states openly that she "went into this competition with a goal, a goal that not only was I going to open eyes, but I was going to open doors."[30] Moreover, by entering the competition, she was going to "let my people know that I was proud of who I am, both Black and Navajo."[31]

In interviews I conducted with Cody in November and December 2002, she emphasized how her reign affected the understanding and reception of mixed-race Navajo people:

> I believe the controversy that surrounded my term as Miss Navajo Nation has made many people realize the existence of individuals who are of mixed ethnic backgrounds. My reign affected people (young and old) in different ways. There were individuals who disagreed with me holding such a title due to my outer appearance and others who were accepting of who I was as a person. As for the "black Navajos," I saw a difference in their sense of pride and position as biracial. . . . If there were one thing I would have changed in response to the controversy, it would have been to have a stronger sense of knowledge about my black culture [and] history so that I would have educated the Navajo people about African Americans and the similarities between the two cultures. Otherwise, no. Silence says a lot in itself. I relearned that ignorance is not going anywhere.[32]

Although there might not have been any resolution of this issue during the duration of Cody's reign, the controversy sparked by this matter underscores the necessity for ongoing discussion about the complicated nature of race and ethnicity in the United States in general, as well as the critical exploration of ideologies related to "Indianness" in particular.

Reclaiming Black Native Identities: Implications for the Twenty-First Century and Beyond

In the past few years, a number of forums and publications have begun to explore the relationships between African Americans and Native Americans, as well as to reclaim specifically black Native identities. In the academic arena, the *American Indian Quarterly*'s 1998 special issue titled "Confounding the Color Line: Indian–Black Relations in Historical and Anthropological Perspective" cultivated renewed interest in this area (Brooks 1998). Due to the growing interest in this subject, the University of Nebraska Press published an anthology on the same theme in summer 2002 (Brooks 2002). In March 1999, the Auburn Avenue Research Library on African-American Culture and History organized a lecture series titled "African Americans and Native Americans: Explorations in Narrative, Identity and Place." A year after the lecture series, in April 2000, the "Eating Out of the Same Pot" conference was held at Dartmouth. The conference represented a momentous meeting of the minds for many scholars and activists interested in this area of study. The gathering introduced participants to major themes and questions related to the study of black–Indian relations, with "the explicit purpose of encouraging curricular development, fostering dialogue between faculty, students, and independent researchers in Native American and African-American Studies programs, as well as supporting research and creative work in this growing field."[33]

Other projects, conferences, and associations continue to be organized to advance the understanding of black–Native relationships. On November 14, 2000, Wilma Mankiller (former principal chief of the Cherokee Nation) and Willard Johnson (professor emeritus at the Massachusetts Institute of Technology, founder and president of the Kansas Institute of African American and Native American Family History, and a descendant of a Cherokee freedman) convened a roundtable discussion at the National Congress of American Indians (NCAI) held in St. Paul, Minnesota. The discussion focused on the historical and contemporary connections between Native Americans and people of African descent.[34] The historical relationships between African Americans and Native Americans have also become a topic of interest for filmmakers and visual artists.[35] With the amplified use and development of the Internet in the past few years, websites focusing on black–Indian history have also increased interest in this topic.[36]

The growing attention focused on interactions between African Americans and Native Americans, particularly the appropriate "place" and identity of black Indians in Native American communities, problematizes the process of narrowly describing and defining Native Americans and, indeed, "Indianness." If, as W. E. B. Du Bois predicted, the problem of the twentieth century was the color line, then the

Celia E. Naylor

twenty-first century not only inherits this problem but also complicates it in terms of the definition of color lines. As the mixing and blurring of color lines, ethnicities, cultures, and heritages continue into the twenty-first century, for some the need to quantify and qualify who has which blood becomes even more pervasive and imperative. With a heightened sense of diluted Indian blood — and, by extension, cultures and heritages — for many Native Americans blood quantum serves as a palpable means of determining Indianness, no matter how ensconced that is within racialized and racist ideology.

Afterword

Five years after Radmilla Cody was selected Miss Navajo Nation, she became embroiled in yet another controversy about whether she could appropriately represent the Navajo Nation and whether she should be deemed a worthy and suitable role model for younger generations of Navajos. Although this quagmire did not center on her race specifically, it is difficult to deny that her African American racial background colored the tone of the public discourse. In January 2003, when Cody should have been celebrating her nomination for a Grammy Award for her compact disc *Seed of Life*, she began serving a twenty-one-month prison sentence at the Phoenix Correctional Facility and Federal Prison Camp for being an accessory to drug trafficking. In late December 2002, a few days before she entered the facility, I spoke with her candidly about the specific allegations and the deleterious ramifications to her personally and professionally. As in previous conversations, she disclosed how the abusive nature of her relationship with her ex-boyfriend had forced her involvement in this illegal activity. I was already aware of Cody's commitment to supporting groups and organizations dedicated to victims and survivors of domestic abuse. However, I had not fully comprehended the extent to which her ex-boyfriend's manipulation and control had altered her everyday life. Although apologetic for her involvement in a drug-trafficking operation, masterminded by her ex-boyfriend, she nonetheless seemed almost hopeful as she described her attempts to reconcile her past transgressions, present reality, and future aspirations.

In the months leading up to her sentence, an enormous amount of publicity surrounded Cody. Her conviction for being involved in drug-related activities became one of the major topics of discussion in Navajo country. Some believed that the Navajo Nation Council should rescind her previous Miss Navajo Nation title. In our conversations during this difficult period, Cody focused (understandably) more on preparing herself and her family for her imprisonment. From my view, as an outsider, the intensity of the attacks on her seemed to echo many of the racially charged statements that had appeared in the *Navajo Times* during her reign. Recognizing that the lives of many African Americans and Native Americans have been disproportionately affected by a racialized criminal-justice system, I could not help but wonder how Cody's biracialness trapped her in a different kind of web of suspicion and conviction.

As news of Cody's pending imprisonment proliferated throughout the Navajo Nation, her name — her image — became defined literally and figuratively as the "black sheep" of the Navajo Nation. Those who had vehemently conveyed their cynicism about her ability to represent the Navajos, and her authenticity as Navajo, were now even more convinced that her criminal actions signified her disconnection from the Navajo Nation. Just as criticisms of Cody's racial background jeopardized her reign as a "true" representative of the Navajo Nation, so, too, has the element of criminality served to solidify not only her supposed misplacement in the Navajo Nation, but also the stereotypical link between African Americans, crime, and corruption. It is uncanny how allegations of mistrust and deceit in relation to Cody's reign and her recent imprisonment mimic the notions of many Native Americans about the trickery and deception associated with others' "playing Indian." Cody's criminality exacerbates her contentious position within the Navajo Nation; her imprisonment reifies and reinforces her status as "other" — as outside the racial boundaries of the nation itself.

The positioning of black Native people within Indian communities presents a challenge not only to Native American conceptions of identity and nationality, but also to social, political, and ideological constructions of race in the United States in general. The controversy over Cody's reign highlights problematic ideologies grounded in the monolithic characterization and definition of racial, cultural, and national identities. The existence of biracial and multiracial people disrupts one-dimensional approaches to race, culture, and identity. With the ongoing establishment of gene-based centers in the twenty-first century — the burgeoning area of genomics is but one example of this development — it becomes even more essential to complement systematic analyses of genes with more sophisticated tools for enhancing societal understanding(s) and meaning(s) of race and culture. Moreover, as racial and ethnic lines continue to be etched in the political arena, it is also crucial to interrogate the position and placement of these racially engendered lines — and of the cultural boundaries themselves.

Notes

1 See also Axtell 1975; Calloway 1986; Drinnon 1972; Faery 1999; Strong 1999.
2 Orlando Tom, "Sense of Identity," *Navajo Times*, December 23, 1997.
3 Ibid.
4 Ibid.
5 Letters to the editor in response to Orlando Tom's letter regarding the selection of Radmilla Cody as Miss Navajo Nation appeared in the *Navajo Times* on December 30, 1997; January 15, 1998; January 22, 1998; and January 29, 1998.
6 Rick Abasta, "Disturbed by Racial Attack," *Navajo Times*, December 30, 1997.
7 La Tanya Diaz Cortez-Curley, "Equally Navajo and Proud," *Navajo Times*, December 30, 1997.
8 Daphne Thomas, "Interracial Marriages Have Deep Ties," *Navajo Times*, December 30, 1997.
9 Raquel Casuse, "Not Judging Material," *Navajo Times*, January 15, 1998.
10 Dorothea Lynch, "What's Your Beef?!" *Navajo Times*, January 15, 1998.
11 Leona R. Begay, "Times Are Changing," *Navajo Times*, March 26, 1998. Responses to Begay's letter continued in the April 2, 1998; April 9, 1998; April 16, 1998; and May 7, 1998, issues of the *Navajo Times*. The focus of the letters to the editor appears to have been redirected due to the growing concern regarding Navajo President Albert Hale's resignation. As a result, letters to the editor concentrated on the status and future of the Navajo Nation in light of Hale's situation.
12 Ibid.
13 Ibid.
14 Ryan Battles, "Superior Disgust," *Navajo Times*, April 2, 1998.
15 Ibid.
16 Nathan J. Tohtsoni, "Less Than 100 Percent," *Navajo Times*, April 2, 1998.
17 Ibid.
18 Shirlee James-Johnson, "Bring Healing not Hate," *Navajo Times*, April 9, 1998.
19 Sean Walker, "Sovereign Racism," *Navajo Times*, January 22, 1998.

20 Tish Ramirez, "Mothers Love Their Children, Who They Are," *Navajo Times*, April 16, 1998.

21 Ives Daniel Peaches, "Different Hogan," *Navajo Times*, April 16, 1998.

22 Margaret Cody, "Thank You for Support," *Navajo Times*, January 22, 1998.

23 Leslie Linthicum, "Queen of Two Cultures," *Albuquerque Journal*, March 1, 1998.

24 Ibid.

25 Ibid.

26 Radmilla Cody, remarks presented at the opening session of the "'Eating Out of the Same Pot': Relating Black and Indian (Hi)stories" conference, Dartmouth College, Hanover, New Hampshire, April 20, 2000.

27 Ibid.

28 Ibid.

29 For example, she recalled seeing an African American student wearing a T-shirt with a large "X" on it at her new high school but thought it was a fashion statement, "just another letter of the alphabet." When she said to the person wearing the shirt, "'You have an X on your T-shirt. I guess I'll go and get me an R for Radmilla," she recalls, his facial expression said, "What planet are you from?" Cody says that she did not have the "'slightest idea who Malcolm X was. The only person I was aware of as a black leader was Martin Luther King and that was just briefly.'" Since that experience, she has become more knowledgeable about African American culture and history, especially because the controversy over her reign has "put her in the position of a spokeswoman for black Navajos": Linthicum, "Queen of Two Cultures."

30 Ibid.

31 Ibid.

32 Telephone interview with the author on several dates in November and December 2002, as well as written comments from Radmilla Cody dated December 20, 2002.

33 Conference program, "Eating Out of the Same Pot."

34 The roundtable was moderated by Mankiller. Participants included Johnson; Daniel F. Littlefield Jr., historian, American Native Press Archives, University of Arkansas, Little Rock; Patrick Minges, historian; Deborah Tucker, librarian, Adamany Library, Wayne State University, Detroit; and David Wilkins, historian, American Indian Studies, University of Minnesota, Minneapolis.

35 In her short film *Real Indian*, Malinda Maynor (Lumbee) depicts her personal and familial connection to Lumbee culture and heritage (*Real Indian*, New York: Women Make Movies, 1996). The documentary *Black Indians: An American Story* (Dallas: Riche-Heape Films, 2000), as well as Robert Russell's documentary *Black Rivers, Red Valleys: The African Presence in Native America*, currently in the production phase, will undeniably contribute to future discussions regarding the historical and contemporary position of black Indians. The photographic essay *Native Americans: The Red–Black Connection*, by Valena Broussard Dismukes (black Choctaw), has also attracted attention to this subject area.

36 See, for example, Angela Walton-Raji's African Native Genealogy website at www.african-nativeamerican.com, and the Black Indian Mexico Web page at hometown.aol.com/fsln/index.htm. In August 1998, the Native Peoples Magazine, an online magazine, created a forum on "Black Indian Culture." This forum, one of many administered by the magazine, provides an opportunity for individuals to discuss the historical and contemporary relationships between African Americans and Native Americans, specifically addressing the position of black Indians in Native American communities. For information, see the Native Peoples Magazine website at www.nativepeoples.com.

CHAPTER EIGHT

"Their Hair Was Curly"

Afro-Mexicans in Indian Villages,

Central Mexico, 1700–1820

DEBORAH E. KANTER

~~~~~~~~

After the Indians of San Pedro Xolostoc held their annual elections for village officers in 1746, the priest and district mayor vetoed their choice of *fiscal* (community official who oversaw villagers' ecclesiastical requirements), proposing instead a man named Pasqual Antonio. The villagers opposed Pasqual's appointment, arguing that he was a mulatto and therefore could not legally hold office in an Indian village. Witnesses from Xolostoc attested that Pasqual Antonio was a mulatto, as were his parents. "Their hair was curly," the witnesses pointed out. Officials quickly checked the parish registry and found Pasqual listed as "indio." Pasqual agreed. His neighbors, however, tried to block him from a position of authority by stressing his African ancestry. This election marked the beginning of Pasqual's struggle with his neighbors over his ancestry and his rights within his home community.[1] Similar struggles were played out in Mexican Indian villages throughout the eighteenth century. This paper argues that Mexican Indians manipulated colonial law and racial stereotypes to jeopardize the security of their neighbors of African descent.

Afro-Mexicans held an ambiguous position in historical Indian communities.[2] In reality, long-term Afro-Mexican residents in Indian villages differed little from their Indian neighbors. Afro-Mexicans depended on their *milpas* (cornfields); they paid tribute; and they served in church and village offices (Gibson 1964, 162). Many spoke the native language of the community, such as Nahuatl or Maya. Their neighbors were often kin, either by common ancestors or by marriage. Given this shared blood, physical differences between Afro-Mexicans and Indians were not always obvious. Sometimes, a person's "true" race could be determined only by searching for a grandparent in a dusty old parish register or by a recollection of telltale curly hair.

From Black to Red: Rethinking Passing

Within a hemispheric context, scholarship and popular beliefs about racial variability generally look at people of African descent as moving toward whiteness and greater mobility. As summed up by Elaine K. Ginsberg, "the cultural logic of passing suggests that passing is usually motivated by a desire to shed the identity of an oppressed group to gain access to social and economic opportunities" (Ginsberg 1996, 3). For the United States, passing is usually discussed within a binary black–white model. The black–white model of passing does not adequately describe the social and demographic realities of colonial North America. The dichotomy is certainly too narrow to explain the pervasive racial diversity and mixture that characterized Mexico and Latin America in general. For Latin America, scholarship has often examined the possibility of mulattos passing as mestizo or any of the lighter-skinned, higher-status *castas*.[3] This perspective equates passing with "whitening." Frederick Bowser offered a classic summary of this view: "Intelligent Afro-Peruvians who had accumulated modest fortunes were quick to see that racial solidarity was all very well, but that "whitening" and "passing," culturally if not racially, was the key to socioeconomic advancement" (Bowser 1973, 321; see also Alberro 1981).

More recent works have critiqued common assumptions about racial variability. Herman Bennett, for example, questions the idea that blacks wanted to whiten, arguing instead that they preferred to marry within their own ethnic milieu (Bennett 1993). Based on economic considerations, Douglas Cope contends, "There is little reason to believe that numerous castas were actively attempting to 'improve' their racial status by passing," because "the material advantages of passing were limited" (Cope 1994, 78).[4] While these studies offer a more crit-

INDIAN AND AFRO-MEXICAN POPULATIONS:
TOLUCA REGION PARISHES, 1779

Parish	Indios	Afro-Mexicans[a]	% Total Population
Calimaya	6,355	192	2.2
Capuluac	4,702	0	0.0
Malinalco	3,829	289	5.5
Metepec	6,639	47	0.5
Ocoyoacac	4,174	228	4.8
Sultepec	8,533	729	4.0
Temascaltepec	3,331	788	12.4
Tenango del Valle	4,591	166	2.7
Texcaliacac	3,684	22	0.5
Toluca	13,591	589	3.0
Xalatlaco	3,571	165	3.4
Zacualpan	2,490	651	13.1
Zinacantepec	4,349	3	.04

Source: Archivo General de Indias, Seville, Varios 38, "Plano exacto de todas las personas del Arzobispado de México con distinción de clases, estado y calidades, formado en execución puntual de Rl Orn año de 1779." I thank Robert McCaa for sharing this source.

[a]Numbers for Afro-Mexicans include those listed as *negros, mulatos, lobos,* and *moriscos*. Sultepec, Temascaltepec, and Zacualpan were mining centers.

ical look at passing, the tendency remains to examine the trajectory of blacks and castas who might move "up" the caste system. Passing, as this paper demonstrates, occurred in multiple directions.

The Mexican judicial cases examined here allow a glimpse into the intriguing and under-studied phenomenon of blacks and mulattos who passed as Indians. As one high-ranking royal officer in Mexico astutely observed, "A Mulatto, for instance, whose color helps him somewhat to hide in another 'casta,' says, according to his whims, that he is an Indian to enjoy the privileges as such and pay less tribute, though this seldom occurs, or, more frequently, that he is a Spaniard, Castizo or Mestizo, and then he does not pay any [tribute] at all" (Mörner 1967, 69). Perhaps in the cities, Afro-Mexicans were more likely to pass (or to try to) as a person of higher status. In rural areas, passing as Indian brought the possibility of access to land, one of the few privileges held by Indians.

This essay discusses situations where people of African descent made up only a fraction of the local population. Most scholarship on Africans in Spanish America has examined areas with high concentrations of blacks (namely, cities and plantation zones). The cases analyzed here grew out of research on Indian communities in the Toluca region (just west of Mexico City), where Indians made up between 70 percent and 90 percent of the late-colonial population. Beyond mining centers and a few head towns, Afro-Mexicans and *gente de razón* (non-Indians) lived scattered among a clear Indian majority. Afro-Mexicans seldom constituted even 5 percent of the rural population (see table above). The only notable concentration of slaves in the region was Xalmolonga, a Jesuit sugar plantation. This study, then, suggests patterns for highland zones with a native majority, including central and southern Mexico, the Andean highlands, and Guatemala.

Protecting the Pueblos: The Evolution of Colonial Segregation Policies

The reality of Afro-Mexicans residing in Indian villages, regardless of their numbers, ran counter to colonial Spanish law. This policy of race-based segregation was rooted in the crown's desire to protect Indian subjects from others. Colonial rule began in Mexico with a plan for two distinct sociolegal groups: *la república de indios* (the republic of Indians) and *la república de españoles* (the republic of Spaniards). The Spanish crown mandated a strict separation of *las dos repúblicas* (the two republics) in part to protect and convert the Indians subjects to Christianity. The church established separate parishes for Indians and Spaniards; law mandated residential segregation. This system allowed Indians, via the pueblo, to retain a large degree of autonomy over local affairs. Indians gained an official, and in some ways privileged, status in Spanish colonial law. This goal of protecting native subjects arose from the influence of missionary ideologues, including Bartolomé de Las Casas. While history touts Las Casas as the protector of Native Americans, we tend to forget that his plan to save the natives' weak bodies and pristine souls involved promoting the importation of slaves from Africa. The forced arrival of Africans in Mexico — and simultaneously the birth of mestizo and other mixed-race children — shattered Mexico's de facto racial dichotomy. Yet the fiction of the two republics persisted in law.

The African presence in Mexico added to the justifications for the sheltering of Indian pueblos by law. The crown received reports of the noxious influence of Africans, mixed-raced individuals, and Spaniards on Indians. Spanish officials reserved some of their harshest words for Africans and their *criollo* (American-born) descendents. A judge in Guatemala in 1585, for example, described blacks and mulattos as vagabonds and reprobates who, "for the Indians, are worse than wolves among sheep, taking away their food, wives, daughters and the rest" (Mörner 1966, 340). In response, the Spanish crown issued laws that aimed to protect the rapidly declining native population. Efforts to limit African–Indian contact began as early as the 1540s, when law prohibited *encomenderos* (Spanish grantees) from sending slaves into Indian villages (Mörner 1966, 333–38). By 1578, the crown had mandated a formal ban on non-Indian residence in Indian villages throughout Spanish America (Gibson 1964, 147). Enforcement of the ban must have been spotty, at best. Although the viceroy of Peru declared in 1611 that few Afro-Peruvians lived beyond the cities ("due to constant efforts to remove them from the pueblos of Indians for whom they are the most noxious and dangerous neighbors"), no similar pronouncement would be heard from Mexico (Mörner 1966, 344). In sum, despite the emergence of a more varied racial situation, the Spanish crown upheld the notion of a separate and protected Indian republic. Enforcement aside, segregation remained on the books and served as point of reference in lawsuits throughout the colonial period.

By the late eighteenth century, however, crown authorities began to question the utility of a segregation policy. Bourbon officials, intent on the Hispanization of native subjects, argued that Indians would benefit by interaction with non-Indians (Mörner 1965). Indians, however, claimed — when it suited them — that their survival still required separation. As this paper shows, Indian communities used this sixteenth-century rationale to stave off eighteenth-century problems such as declining land availability in the villages.

Roots and Realities of Afro-Mexicans in Indian Pueblos

An Afro-Mexican presence took root in Indian pueblos to varying degrees, despite laws proscribing black residence. The eighteenth-century records I consulted seldom explain how people of African descent came to live in the pueblos of the Toluca region. Some may have been runaway slaves or the offspring of slave or free blacks from mines or plantations in nearby districts. Others may have come to know the region as they traveled through with the mule trains either to Mexico City or to the plantation lowlands of Morelos, both places with high concentrations of Afro-Mexicans since the early colonial period. Perhaps African ancestry can be traced within the Toluca region to several large haciendas that specialized in raising livestock. Records show little or no slave labor on this region's haciendas in the eighteenth century, but that may have differed in earlier times. Slave cowboys and herders worked under few restrictions, moving with their animals on expansive haciendas. They came into contact with Indians, including women such as the *molenderas* who prepared their food (Konrad 1980).

Gender imbalance in the slave trade from Africa is crucial to understanding how the colonial Afro-Mexican population grew. The surfeit of males in the African-born slave population in Mexico (and throughout the hemisphere) meant that many slaves had to find mates and sexual partners in the non-slave population. Male slaves more frequently found partners among Indian women than among *españolas*. As early as the 1540s, black ranch hands reportedly entered Indian homes and forcibly took women and hens, beating Indian men who protested (Bowser 1973; Mörner 1966, 334). While slaves were often said to have raped Indian women, a range of social and sexual contacts, including concubinage and marriage, led to mulatto children born free to Indian mothers. Especially in the countryside, Mexico's large mixed-African sector grew from interethnic unions that generally occurred between a black man and an Indian woman (Brockington 1989, 145–46; Forbes 1993). By the late-colonial era, most Afro-Mexicans were undoubtedly, in Forbes's words, "Red-Black people" with biological roots in both societies.

The settlement of Afro-Mexicans and other non-Indians in the pueblos benefited a number of parties and thus was tolerated, despite laws to the contrary. By 1572, the crown had ordered that mulattos pay tribute. Yet collection proved difficult unless mulattos were permanently settled, perhaps with access to land in a given place (Bowser 1973, 304–5; Forbes 1993, 165). This rationale, in fact, was similar to how the crown understood the need to protect Indians' land rights in their home communities. From the crown's standpoint, Afro-Mexicans and Indians had similar responsibilities and needs as tributaries. In general, royal authorities felt more in control of blacks and castas living within the structure of village life (García Martínez 1990, 113–14). Some Indian villagers also saw a benefit in having non-Indian neighbors. By renting parcels to outsiders, Indians could earn much needed cash. Indians must have been especially willing to lease unused lands with village populations at a low in the seventeenth century (Martin 1985, 164; Mörner 1967, 99). Finally, non-Indians realized that taking up residence in these villages offered them a chance to become settled farming people.

In many places in Latin America, Indians allowed the descendants of Africans and other gente de razón to settle in their communities (Mörner 1967, 100). In villages near Mexico City, non-Indians constituted between 10 percent and 25 percent of the population at the end of the eighteenth century. Cheryl Martin documented the permeation of "Indian" villages by Afro-Mexicans in late-colonial Morelos, a sugar-growing region. Indians formed a minority in many of their own villages there, as in other parts of Mexico (Martin 1985, 156–57).[5] The non-Indian presence in the Toluca region was much smaller.

The acceptance of Afro-Mexicans in Indian pueblos depended on a complex mix of biological and social factors. Birthplace and family ties were crucial. An Afro-Mexican born in the pueblo where he or she resided earned community acceptance. In this case, Afro-Mexicans might claim the privileges of *hijos del pueblo* (offspring of the village), a term that usually pertained to Indians in their natal village. Given that most Afro-Mexicans in the villages were partly Indian, they likely had kin ties with Indians in the village, as well. Marriage to an Indian was another way for Afro-Mexicans to establish kinship in a pueblo. Both Indians and royal authorities generally agreed that by marrying in, non-Indian residents could remain in the pueblos.[6] Royal authorities, however, tended to look more kindly on Spanish–Indian marriages than on African–Indian marriages.

While kinship ties allowed Afro-Mexicans to enter Indian villages, they fared best if they followed village rules: living settled lives, serving in the *república* (village government) or church, and obeying Indian authorities. Royal authorities seemed to ignore segregation laws if Afro-Mexicans living in Indian villages paid tribute. Unless non-Indians merited special complaint, in the late-colonial period authorities saw little reason to consider enforcing the old separation laws. Some Bourbon officials even proposed abolishing the laws, hoping that non-Indians would have a positive, "civilizing" impact on their neighbors (Beleña 1787, 37). The laws remained but were seldom acted on unless Indian villagers found sufficient cause.

Were Afro-Mexicans "Hijos del Pueblo"?

The status of Afro-Mexicans as "hijos del pueblo" faced serious challenges in late colonial Mexico. As in much of central Mexico, the Toluca region had become a crowded place by the late eighteenth century. The native population, so devastated in the first centuries of colonial rule, had recovered and was growing after 1700. Area haciendas encroached on village lands and took over forests and pastures once shared by all local residents. The number of Spanish and mestizo farmers also expanded in the eighteenth century. Pueblos that once had more than enough land for the use of the community found it increasingly difficult to allocate lands to all households (Kanter 1992).

As a result, competition over land, even house sites, became endemic in these pueblos. The conflicts divided families, pitting sons against daughters, legitimate offspring against bastards. At the community level, gender and other marks of status similarly colored contests for land. Married men challenged widows, while hijos del pueblo challenged outsiders.

Race became an important argument in these land cases, as well, as Indians questioned the ethnicity of their rivals for scarce village resources. The criteria for land tenure in Indian communities became more exclusive, as Indian repúblicas tried to preserve scarce village resources for certain community members: Indian men, born in the pueblo, of legitimate birth. This marked preference could effectively deny community lands to Indian widows, mestizos, and Afro-Mexicans — all of whom might consider themselves hijos del pueblo. In some of these cases, litigants mention race almost as an afterthought. But Indian litigants understood that race could prove a powerful tool, enabling them to call on the old Spanish laws that prohibited non-Indians from living in the pueblos. Individuals who could not deny their mixed heritage faced dispossession, even expulsion from the pueblos, notwithstanding their adherence to village ways.

Antonio Trinidad Molina, a mulatto, was a model community member whose position and livelihood was threatened in this time of tight-ened community membership. Molina had lived for at least two decades in Santa Cruz Atizapán. Then, in 1782 he faced destitution when an Indian who had earlier sold him a piece of land suddenly tried to revoke the sale. The Indian contended that the sale had been illegal because Molina was a mulatto. Molina countered that the sale had been carried out in good faith. The Indian had begged him to buy the land. Molina recalled how the transfer had been recorded, witnessed, and accompanied by food and beverage, "as these drinkers are so accustomed in such sales." (With that final detail, Molina oddly underscored his ethnic identity as distinct from his neighbors. At the same time, his condescending stress on the Indians as "drinkers" might have been a bid to ally himself with the Spanish judge.) Molina also contended that, because he paid tribute, he needed the land. Despite the appeal of these arguments, the district magistrate ordered Molina to vacate the parcel in question. The magistrate directed village officers to replace Molina with the neediest Indian in the village.

Molina, now with a lawyer, appealed this decision. Molina's lawyer stressed the man's status as a tributary, adding that Molina's Indian wife and five children also met tribute demands. The mulatto had served in the república, "ascending from *topil* (a low officer) to *regidor*, positions that although honorable are onerous." Because Molina had borne the burdens attendant with these positions, "it is not strange that he should solicit the conveniences the *naturales* (Indians) enjoy." This argument gained the court's favor: The court ordered the pueblo to assign Molina an unoccupied section of community land. The pueblo stonewalled, however, claiming (perhaps truthfully) that no land stood empty.[7]

This case demonstrates the complex ways that law could be manipulated on the local level. Antonio Trinidad Molina seems a model resident of Atizapán. Married, he worked hard to raise his family and to meet his tribute obligations. The fact that Molina served in public offices indicates that his neighbors accepted and probably respected him. In this service, he gave of his time to the community. Apparently, he spoke Nahuatl as well as Spanish.[8] As stated in the court case, the village had no reason to remove Molina other than land scarcity. The only way to remove him was by stressing his non-Indian status, yet Molina seems to have conducted himself within Indian norms. In the end, the Spanish court was less concerned with Molina's race than with his conduct and ignored the letter of the law on separation.

In similar cases, Indians often asserted that non-Indian individuals refused to live within village norms and to obey Indian officials. Antonio Navarrete was a self-declared *pardo* (person of part-African ancestry) resident of Santa María la Asumpción. In 1749, village officials challenged his tenure of two plots of land. Navarrete claimed he had inherited the land from his grandfather, an *indio principal* (Indian noble) of the village. As proof, he presented two witnesses and his grandfather's Nahuatl-language testament. He further argued that the land allowed him to maintain his family and to pay church fees, tribute, "and other things as a *vecino* (neighbor) of the pueblo."

Santa María's Indian officials had a different take on their pardo neighbor. They asserted that Navarrete had not inherited the land in question. First, he had rented the land; then, after the true owner's death, Navarrete usurped the plots. Worse, as a mulatto living in an Indian village, he resisted their laws. They concluded that the land should be divided among those of the village, implying Indians only. Hearing the case, the *alcalde mayor* (Spanish district officer) gave Navarrete six days to prove that he was the Indian's grandson and heir. If he could not, he should leave the village.[9]

Turbulent Blood: Stereotypes of Afro-Mexicans

Indian villagers deployed a barrage of negative labels and stereotypes to argue that Afro-Mexicans were not true hijos del pueblo. Indians might charge that these ethnic outsiders, including Spaniards, acted with pride and of their own authority rather than submit to village officials. One Indian town complained that mulattos and Spaniards influenced their pueblos with "pernicious customs" such as drunkenness, games of chance, and cards.[10] While all gente de razón might be accused of misbehavior, Indians and Spanish officers agreed that Afro-Mexicans created special problems. Viceroy Mancera, for example, contended that "the mestizos, sons and descendants of the Spaniards, are no less presumptuous than the Negroes and mulattoes . . . but in a somewhat more elevated manner. Their presumption is better controlled and more subject to reason" (Cope 1994, 26).

Indians, the perennial victims of a multitude of negative ethnic stereotypes in Mexico, did not hesitate to defame people of African descent when it suited their needs. In one Indian village, a hijo del pueblo tried to pass as an Indian, but parish registrars revealed him as the grandson of "mulatos y coyotes." Indian officers declared that this man had "*sangre revuelto*" (mixed-up, turbulent blood), adding that he "disturbs the public peace."[11] The Indian officers used stock phrases that fit well with how Spanish society viewed Afro-Mexicans. Mixed blood — part of which was African — signaled disorder and impropriety. Consider other ways that Indians described some of their Afro-Mexican neighbors: "*mulato expuesto y de perversas inclinaciones*" (perversely inclined mulatto orphan); "*lobo . . . de genio revoltoso y cabiloso*" (wolf, with a rebellious, ill-willed character); "*ser osado y de calidad mulato*" (impudent and of mulatto status); or "*una mulata revuelta . . . puta*" (disorderly mulatta whore).[12] When Indians described their black and mulatto neighbors as perverse, lazy, dishonorable, rebellious, and whore-like, Spanish judges likely nodded in agreement, since the colonial elite also disparaged people of African descent. Given that most Afro-Mexicans who lived in the pueblos were probably more like the hardworking, stable, and obedient Antonio Trinidad Molina, how did Indian villagers come to hold such negative stereotypes of Afro-Mexicans?

Circumstances of birth cast aspersion on many Afro-Mexicans. Illegitimacy was a strike against anyone in colonial Latin America. A person born out of wedlock might suffer attacks on character and doubts about his or her parentage, especially in terms of race. Many mixed-race children, in fact, were born of illegitimate unions. In the documents consulted, a number of Afro-Mexicans were orphans or bastards. (These terms were often interchangeable in popular usage in the eighteenth century.) Colonial society assumed that anyone of part-African descent must be illegitimate, unless proved otherwise. A number of marriage cases make it clear that Afro-Mexicans found it hard to marry since Indians and Spaniards alike considered them undesirable marriage partners.[13] Without a sizeable pool of potential spouses, Afro-Mexicans may have had little choice but to continue the cycle of illegitimacy.[14] Questionable parentage did more than limit marriage-ability. Illegitimacy, real or imagined, did not sit well with Indian village officials looking for ways to pare down the list of those eligible to receive community lands.

The misconduct of slaves and runaways also tainted Indian attitudes toward Afro-Mexicans. Xalmolonga, a Jesuit-owned sugar plantation near Malinalco, had the Toluca region's only significant concentration of slaves,[15] but these slaves cast a long shadow. Xalmolonga slaves and free workers had a bad reputation in the region's villages.[16] Jesuit administrators likely treated the slaves with a relatively even hand. After the Jesuit order's expulsion in 1767, conditions at Xalmolonga became more uncertain. Slaves responded by resisting new administrators, and many simply fled (Konrad 1980, 266). Slave flight may have been on the rise throughout Mexico in the mid-eighteenth century (Barrett 1970, 85).

By 1791, discipline at Xalmolonga had clearly eroded. A royal commissioner reported that the current administration hardly provided food and clothing for the slaves. "Insolent" slaves spent more effort planting their own milpas than working in the cane. A slave known as Capitana Eugenia (who had a talent for "fooling all the Administrators") led a wave of female slave insubordination. Slaves also attacked and stole from neighboring Indian villages. Xalmolonga slaves so frightened the Indians that "they barely dare to open their doors at the sight of them." In Malinalco, residents believed their women were not safe from the slaves.[17] The disorder that radiated from Xalmolonga intensified Indian suspicions of Afro-Mexicans in the region.

Since the early colonial period, Spaniards and colonial officers had perceived people of African or part-African descent similarly as shiftless and violent. Thus, in 1611 the viceregal government felt it necessary to order "free Blacks and mulattos to stay put to serve their masters, not go about as vagabonds, but rather to learn trades, serve, and not be idle" (Beleña 1787, 42). This view had not changed much by the eighteenth century. In fact, the Bourbons grew more concerned with vagabondage as a social and economic ill. A royal tax officer in Bourbon Mexico thus criticized free blacks and mulattos "as *gente extravagante* (outlandish people) who have never been stable."[18] Bennett describes how Afro-Mexicans did in fact move frequently "in their quest for work, higher wages, family, and friends." Yet in doing so, they gained the reputation as "chronic transients" (Bennett 1993, 107–8). Strangers, especially Afro-Mexicans, encountered suspicion and fear in rural Mexico.

Consider the situation of Victoriano Millán, an Afro-Mexican who served the priest of the Indian pueblo of Xalatlaco in 1806. Victoriano had come to Xalatlaco from the Xalmolonga plantation. Although part of the priest's household, Victoriano lacked family ties in the village. When an outspoken mestiza began a complicated feud with the priest, Victoriano stood in the middle, protecting his master. The servant's race and origins became central as she brought criminal charges against

Victoriano. The townswoman claimed that Victoriano had threatened to kill her. Unmarried, without parents or relatives or even his own house, this black servant could not be trusted to refrain from his violent threat. Under arrest, Victoriano denied the townswoman's charges and told how she had embarrassed him, shouting in the village streets for all to hear, "Here is the black bully (*negro garrotero*)." She further taunted, "Here come the blacks from Xalmolonga, they come breaking in (*amansando*) mules." Beginning with this apparently sexual provocation, she then proclaimed that the servant was the "priests' pimp and informer." In the end, the Spanish judge acquitted Victoriano of all charges.[19] Overall, the case suggests how the idea of Afro-Mexicans as rootless, lawless, and of unknown parentage could cohere into a powerful and negative stereotype.

Just calling a person black or mulatto could start a fight in colonial Mexico. Even if labeling someone a mulatto had no basis, the suggestion alone cast aspersion on an individual's status in the community. Judicial records throughout the colony demonstrate that villagers called one another mulatto to defame character or to appropriate lands (Martin 1990; Taylor 1979, 83). Such name-calling almost cost Marcelino Manuel the land once granted to his father by the village república. In 1760, a contentious Indian neighbor claimed Marcelino's holdings for himself, in part because of past family possession. He also declared Marcelino a mulatto who, as such, had no legal right to the land. The question of Marcelino's ethnicity led to a local investigation. Various witnesses flatly denied that Marcelino and his father were anything but Indians. With a quick check in parish registers, their opinion held sway: Marcelino was allowed to continue his possession.[20]

Persistent Notions of Race in the *Imperio Mixto*

If, to borrow Amy Robinson's phrases, "the manifest truth of melanin" had its limitations in the United States, the "visual as a guarantor of racial knowledge" proved particularly ineffectual in the *imperio mixto* (mixed empire) of late-colonial Mexico (Robinson 1994, 717). Telltale hair, as in the case of Pasqual Antonio, could still mark a person. But the skin of "Red–Black" people and other castas had developed into a rich and complex palette that included pardo, *amarillito*, *amembrillado*, *champurrado*, and *color quebrado* (yellowish, quince-colored, milky chocolate, and broken color). In the world of the castas, determining an individual's "true" race then rested on a whole host of variables, often subjective evidence including recollections of a grandmother's clothing or primary tongue or a look at a parent's baptismal entry. At the same time the tangible markers of race and ethnicity blurred, Bourbon authorities tried to deemphasize racial separation and distinctions in colonial society. But Indians and Spaniards clung to racial differences for as long as possible, in part because race granted certain legal and social prerogatives for both groups.

On the eve of independence, Indian villagers continued to seek the ouster of non-Indians. In one small village in 1819, a self-declared Spanish resident and his family entered into a street squabble with a neighboring Indian family. These neighbors claimed that the man insulted them as *indios carajos* (fucking Indians) and hired a lawyer to question the man's presence in the village. Their legal attack rested largely on the insinuation that he was not quite as Spanish as he claimed. The Indians' lawyer declared it "hardly credible that some Spaniards or *mulatos like them* could be insulted by Indians, when everyone knows how these castas oppress us." The Indians, with their lawyer, cited sixteenth-century laws, noting that this protective legislation had arisen from "the experience that existed of despotism and oppression, with which the other castas had treated the Indians since the conquest of these lands."[21] Their argument began with familiar, colonial Indian reasoning on the need for separation. But the stress on oppression and conquest exemplifies a new political rhetoric evident after 1810 that stressed Indians' background as a conquered people in need of mercy.

Despite decades of Bourbon (and then Mexican) rule that tried to downplay the importance of race, Indians continued to stress racial differences to protect their own interests. At the popular level, most Mexicans still saw "race" as a useful point of differentiation. Legal and policy changes had not changed deeply rooted, persistent notions of race.

Afro-Mexicans in Postcolonial "Mestizo Mexico"

The eventual disappearance of Afro-Mexicans as a distinct racial and social group remains a historical puzzle. Despite the substantial number of blacks in colonial Mexico, beyond the coastal zones of Guerrero,

Oaxaca, and Veracruz, their presence is no longer obvious.[22] Today, few Mexicans have any idea of the extent to which their colonial past included Africans and their descendants. This can be explained in part by the revolutionary state's invention and encouragement of a "mestizo Mexico" — a mixed Mexico that proudly claims an indigenous and Spanish heritage. Yet on both the official and the personal level, mestizo Mexico rarely considers its African ancestry in this mixture (Knight 1990).

Beyond issues of selective memory, demographic history explains the decline of Afro-Mexicans as a distinct group quite clearly. Colonial records show that, more than other ethnic groups, Afro-Mexicans married (or otherwise procreated) with others. Writing about this phenomenon in Veracruz, Patrick Carroll describes Afro-Veracruzanos as "the most socially outgoing of any of the racial groups" (Carroll 1991, xi). The Afro-Mexican trend toward racial exogamy began early, when the imbalanced sex ratio within the slave population forced males to seek (usually Indian) spouses. The resultant Afro-Mexican outmarriage had social reasons, as well. While Indians and Spaniards retained certain privileges by maintaining their racial integrity, Spanish law and custom attached no benefits to blackness. Popular stereotypes only stigmatized Afro-Mexicans. So in effect, Afro-Mexicans had nothing to lose by intermarrying. And as this paper shows, Afro-Mexicans had something to gain by assuming a place for themselves or their children within the Indian world during the colonial period.

Discussing the demise of colonial segregation policy, Magnus Mörner asserts that the ongoing process of miscegenation allowed for "the pacific absorption of the great majority of Africans in the popular strata of Hispanic American society" (Mörner 1966, 344). As a generalization, as a way to think about the great sweep of Latin American social history, this makes sense. But the phrase "pacific absorption" masks what I believe was a series of conflicts as Africans and their descendants edged their way into both Indian and Hispanic society. While Afro-Mexicans were absorbed into a larger, mixed Mexico, their acceptance by others was inevitably questioned.

Notes

I thank Herman Bennett, Sharon Holland, Tiya Miles, and Stuart Schwartz for comments on earlier drafts of this essay.

1 Tulane University Library, Viceregal and Ecclesiastical Mexican Collection (hereafter, VEMC) leg. 61, exp. 13 (San Cristobal Ecatepec).

2 I use the term "Afro-Mexican" in this chapter to describe free blacks and individuals of part-African ancestry. In the colonial era, these individuals were commonly labeled *mulatos, lobos, pardos*, or *coyotes*. Many of them were, in fact, Afro-Indian Mexicans. On the colonial usage of *mulato*, Jack Forbes (1993, 165) offers a useful summary: "*Mulato* primarily referred to American-African mixed-bloods. On the other hand, the term also embraced the rarer Spanish-African mixed-bloods. From this we can easily deduce that *mulato* meant essentially a person who was half-African and half-something-else." Afro-Mexican slaves are designated as such.

3 "*Casta*" had several meanings, but James Lockhart and Stuart Schwartz (1983, 131) summarize it as "Mestizos, mulattoes, and Blacks (in other words, everyone not considered a Spaniard or an Indian) in a sense were a single intermediary category and as such were sometimes referred to as *castas*." Laura Lewis (2003) discusses the varied and contested meanings of "*casta*" and other racial terms.

4 See also McCaa 1984; Valdés 1987, 193.

5 See also Farriss 1984, 105; Gibson 1964, 148.

6 For example, the Royal Audiencia of Nueva Galicia (northwestern Mexico) approved land tenure by a lobo married to a cacique's daughter in Xalostitlan in 1717. The cacique noted that many other lobos and mulattos had received lands there: Biblioteca Pública del Estado de Jalisco, Civil Caja 29, exp. 9.

7 Archivo General de la Nación (hereafter, AGN) Tierras, vol. 2544, exp. 15.

8 The Indians who testified needed an interpreter, evidence that they spoke little Spanish. Molina, it was noted, did not require an interpreter "*por ser de calidad moreno* (because he was black)." Molina must have communicated with his neighbors in Nahuatl.

9 The docket does not contain the outcome of the case. Archivo Judicial del Estado de México, Tenango records (hereafter, AJEM-T), unlabeled bundle, "Antonio Navarrete, pardo, contra Andrés García," March 17, 1749 (Metepec).

10 AGN Indios, exp. 43, exp. 98 (Tianguistengo, 1718).

11 AGN Tierras, vol. 2079, exp. 14 (San Lucas Tepemaxalco, 1761).

12 AGN Criminal, vol. 124, exp. 35 (Ocoyoacac, 1790); AGN Indios, vol. 59, exp. 241 (Calimaya, 1762); AGN Indios, vol. 65, exp. 46 (Calimaya, 1775); AJEM-T, unlabeled bundle, *Ana Magdalena v. Jacinto Roque* (Tenango del Valle, 1784).

13 When two mulatto cousins wanted to marry each other, their parish priest urged that the impediment of consanguinity be excused because, as mulattos, "they could not easily marry": AGN Bienes Nacionales, leg. 217, exp. 98 (Ozoloapan, 1803). In a breach-of-promise suit, a woman complained that, "rather than fulfill his promise," her suitor "just treats me as a mulata": AJEM-T, unlabeled bundle, *Pablo Antonio Gómez v. Caterina Torres* (Tenango del Valle, 1792).

14 Mexican Archbishop Lizana offers another perspective on the causes of black and casta illegitimacy. He believed that parents denied their children the chance to marry to keep their offspring's wages within the household. Since the castas "do not even know the meaning of honor," the archbishop claimed, the birth of illegitimate grandchildren did not bother them: AGN Bienes Nacionales, leg. 131, exp. 9 (1805).

15 Indian officials accused two free mulatto workers from Xalmolonga of wounding three Indians: AGN Indios, vol. 59, exp. 155 (Malinalco, 1760).

16 Xalmolonga had about 200 slaves in the 1740s (José Antonio Villaseñor y Sánchez, Theatro americano, descripción general de los reynos, y provincias de la Nueva España, y sus jurisdicciones [Mexico, 1746] *United States v. Maine*, 475 U.S. 89 [1986]); 361 slaves in 1770 (Konrad 1980, 266); and 154 slaves in 1791 (Tulane Library VEMC., leg. 70, exp. 5).

17 Tulane Library VEMC, leg. 70, exp. 5.

18 AGN Tributos, vol. 47, exp. 14 (1738).

19 AGN Criminal, vol. 124, exp. 14.

20 AGN Tierras, vol. 2079, exp. 14 (San Lucas).

21 AJEM-T, bundle "Penal y Civil 1811–18," *Don José Mariano Hernández v. Siriaco, Victoria, y Petrona* (La Concepción, 1819).

22 The relationship between contemporary Afro-Mexican communities and the past is explored in Rafael Rebollar's 2001 documentary film *Raíz olvidada* (The Forgotten Roots, Producciones Trabuco S. C., Mexico, 2001), Bobby Vaughn's Black Mexico homepage, available at www.afromexico.com.

CHAPTER NINE

Lone Wolf

and Du Bois for a New Century

Intersections of Native American and

African American Literatures

ROBERT WARRIOR

~~~~~~~

Though no intellectual monument so grand as *The Souls of Black Folk* exists to mark it, 1903 was for Native Americans and Native American nations just as desperate and disturbing as it was for African Americans. As in the case of African Americans, progressives in the United States developed education of a certain sort as a panacea to those desperate times. In this chapter, I will look at some of the features of that time that both separated and brought together Native Americans and African Americans as a way of thinking about what it means to do comparative work in Native American studies.

I will use this one-hundredth anniversary of the publication of W. E. B. Du Bois's *The Souls of Black Folk* as a focal point. In doing so, I want to provide a partial answer to this twist on the question with which Du Bois opens *Souls*: How did it feel in 1903 to be an Indian problem? And what does it mean for us today to think about the situations of African Americans and Native Americans at the same time? Since many of us have no doubt given some serious thought to the context of *Souls*, I will begin with two illustrations of Native America in 1903.

In 1903, the U.S. Supreme Court reached a disastrous decision in the case of *Lone Wolf v. Hitchcock*.[1] Lone Wolf was a prominent member of the Kiowa Nation who resisted the allotment of Kiowa lands based on a provision of the 1867 Treaty of Medicine Creek between the United States and the Kiowas, Comanches, and Apaches. The treaty stipulated that three quarters of all adult male Kiowas had to approve of any sale or forfeiture of Kiowa lands. When the United States began doling out Kiowa land without the stipulated approval, Lone Wolf brought his suit.

Treaty making had been the main form of federal engagement with Native nations between the founding of the American republic and 1870, when Congress called for an end to the treaty-making period.[2] The same U.S. Constitution that endorsed African slavery created the rationale for treaties when its Commerce Clause reserved for the federal government the right to regulate commerce between the states, foreign nations, and "the Indian tribes." That phrase, written in an era when Native people occupied the vast majority of North American territory, established the fact that Native American tribal nations had a political status separate and apart from the United States.

The simple existence of treaties between Native groups and the United States demonstrates that separate status — a nation, after all, does not make treaties with its own constituents. In 1831, Chief Justice John Marshall would call Native groups "domestic, dependent nations" that "are in a state of pupilage. Their relationship to the United States resembles that of a ward to his guardian" (Prucha 1984, 209–10). In 1870, seeking to change the flow of the stream of Indian affairs, the U.S. Congress declared an end to treatymaking even as it inherited the negotiated agreements of nearly a century of U.S. and Native American diplomacy.[3]

Eroding and erasing Native claims to political independence was the stated goal of federal Indian policy from 1870 until 1970, and Lone Wolf's Kiowas found themselves in the direct path of that policy. In 1887, the U.S. Congress passed the General Allotment Act, which made it policy to break up communally held Native lands into individual parcels. The intent of allotment was threefold: to break down tribal ways of living communally; to create the ground for the creation of individual-based ways of life in Native communities; and to open land left over after allotment to non-Native settlement.

Along with providing a pathway to white settlement, allotment was supposed to lead to the amalgamation of Native people into the citizenry of the United States, something that Thomas Jefferson had envisioned a century before. Native nations as nations would dissolve before the onward march of American civilization, disappearing through intermarriage and assimilation. It was the age of the Vanishing Indian.

Lone Wolf and his followers, though, thought differently. While not oblivious to the power of the United States, Lone Wolf still envisioned an independent destiny for the Kiowas, an independence in which the Kiowas had lived for as long as anyone could remember and that the United States recognized at Medicine Creek. In 1892, the United States sent the Jerome Commission to Indian Territory (which became the State of Oklahoma in 1907) essentially to force tribal nations to sign on to agreements through which allotment would be executed.

The Kiowas and other tribes fought bitterly against allotment and the opening of their lands to non-Native settlement. Lone Wolf took his case all the way to the Supreme Court after the United States opened non-allotted Kiowa lands to non-Native homesteaders. The court's decision against Lone Wolf was a low point in the history of Native–white relations. As the court said, "Plenary authority over the tribal relations of the Indians has been exercised by Congress from the beginning, and the power has always been deemed a political one, not subject to be controlled by the judicial department of the government" (Prucha 1984, 776).

Post–*Lone Wolf*, then, Congress was free to follow its course of doing pretty much whatever it wanted in Indian affairs. If it wanted to respect provisions of a treaty, it did. If it wanted to ignore its history of reaching agreements with tribal nations, it did. As the court said, it was strictly an issue of politics. Native people, thus, were left at the mercy of the morality of Congress as it defined its political goals for Native destiny. Federal Indian law would lie moribund for more than a generation until the advent of the reform movement that lobbied for the Indian Reorganization Act, or the Indian New Deal, of 1934. Through those years in the wilderness and beyond, though, visions of independence and self-determination like Lone Wolf's continued to exist and in places even thrive among American Indians who clung to the idea that no nation's designs superseded their own peoplehood and right to self-determination.

Breaking into the Majors

My other example from Native America in 1903 will not take as long to describe, but it is similarly instructive as we consider the intersections of Native American and African American history and experiences. In 1903, Charles Bender, an Ojibway from Minnesota, broke into Major League baseball, the best of a number of Native Americans who played in the majors in the half century before Jackie Robinson broke what we know as the "color" barrier in baseball.

Bender, who started his career playing for Connie Mack on the Philadelphia Athletics, is widely considered one of the finest pitchers in the early part of the twentieth century. He compiled a lifetime won-lost record of 212–127 and was elected to the Baseball Hall of Fame in 1953 by its veterans committee, one year before he died (Goldstein 1996, 657). Thus, Native Americans had opportunities in professional sports that their African American counterparts would not enjoy until African Americans engaged in decades of struggle against discrimination. Indeed, the professional league that became the National Football League most likely would not have succeeded without the enormous popularity of the legendary Jim Thorpe.

As Philip Deloria argues, the success of these athletes points to one of the ways American Indians at the beginning of the twentieth century "created a new Indian world, fusing diverse cultures or fitting themselves into the interstices between a core native 'tradition' and new practices introduced from the American periphery" (Deloria 1996, 325). As he goes on to say, "This new kind of athletic competition was often part of a refigured warrior tradition, but it also provided an entrée into American society — a chance to beat Whites at their own games, an opportunity to get an education, and even at its most serious, an occasion for fun and sociality" (Deloria 1996, 326).

These athletes represented many things to both Native America and to the United States. Team owners and college athletic directors could point to these athletes as evidence that they were not prejudiced. Fans and white fellow athletes, who often foregrounded the racial otherness of Native athletes — rather unimaginatively nicknaming nearly all of them "Chief" and taunting them with hand-to-the-mouth war whoops and epithets — treated it all as another chapter in the mythical Wild West. Thorpe for a time led an all-Indian team, the Oorang Indians that, like the Harlem Globetrotters, did not have a home field and always played road games and that fed fantasies through halftime displays of tomahawk throwing and, in Deloria's phrase, "playing Indian" (Deloria 1996, 333).[4]

Deloria suggests that Native participation in college and professional sports in the early part of the twentieth century was a response to that era's crisis of masculinity. He indicates that Native athletes acted almost like spirit guides (my term, not his) through that crisis, riding "the currents of modernity with calmness and equanimity," reconnecting white men with "the pre- or antimodern, 'primitive' physicality of native men" (Deloria 1996, 329). This is ironic, of course, since simultaneously the United States was seeking to dissolve the foundations of Native peoplehood that made such manhood possible.

In both of these illustrations, what is important to note is how the line between white and Native is violated or opened by whites. The Supreme Court rips down the wall the Kiowas seek to maintain between their sovereignty and that of the United States even as the Supreme Court creates new barriers to African American participation in American society. Team owners and collegiate athletic directors seek out Native athletes in an era when they maintain a color line that keeps black athletes out.

Rather than puzzling through the complex reasons for this paradoxical situation in which Natives seeking their own space are constrained to opt into American society while African Americans seeking a way in are offered only life inside the veil, I want to offer the paradox as a given as I turn to Du Bois.

Converging on Industrial Education

Where I take a dialogue between Du Bois and the Native American situation in 1903 to be most fruitful is in the realm of education. As with African Americans, Native Americans' prospects a century ago hinged mightily on going to school. African American and Native American educational history, in fact, literally came together in 1878, when Richard Henry Pratt brought a group of Native students to Samuel Chapman Armstrong's Hampton Institute in Virginia. Pratt, while in charge of a group of Native prisoners at Fort Marion in St.

Augustine, Florida, had experimented with methods of teaching Native Americans. On their release, twenty-two agreed to accompany Pratt to Hampton to continue their educational pursuits.[5]

Pratt left Hampton after a year to open a stand-alone school just for Indian students at the Carlisle Barracks in Carlisle, Pennsylvania. The Carlisle Indian Industrial School became the flagship of a network of off-reservation boarding schools that tens of thousands of Native students would attend over the next century and beyond. Its athletic programs were nationally prominent, as Carlisle football players under the tutelage of Glenn "Pop" Warner had his teams competing against Harvard, Yale, and other powers. The 1912 Olympic decathlon and pentathlon champion Jim Thorpe was a Carlisle product, as was Charles Bender.

Pratt believed that educational success for Natives was best achieved by removing students as far from their home environment as possible, cutting male students' long hair, dressing students in modern clothing, and forbidding the use of Native languages. This was all part of an ideology summed up with the phrase most often associated with Pratt: "Kill the Indian and save the man."

Carlisle's athletic success against college teams created a perception that it offered college-level work. In fact, Carlisle and the boarding schools created in its wake did not even offer high school–level courses and were more like vocational-technical schools than anything else. Typically, students spent four hours in class and most of the rest of the day growing their own food, cooking their own meals, making their own clothes, building and maintaining campus buildings, doing their own laundry and ironing, and attending to every menial task. They were learning to be domestic workers, seamstresses, tinsmiths, farmhands, store clerks, and maintenance workers. The top-of-the-line job for young men was learning to run a printing press, while young women might aspire to living temporarily with a small group of other female students in a house-like building where they would practice domestic arts such as setting a table and managing a household.

As I read and reflect on this history, I often look for a voice equivalent to Du Bois's, railing against a system that rejects the aspirations of higher education. As Du Bois said of Hampton's curriculum, it had the "manner and tone that would make Socrates an idiot and Jesus Christ a crank" (as quoted in Lewis 1993, 353). Some Native voices of critique exist, though none of them was as vociferous as Du Bois. Henry Roe

Cloud, who in 1910 became the first Native American graduate of Yale, spent a lifetime working to establish schools and programs to promote higher education for Native youth. Luther Standing Bear, about whom I will have more to say later, became a staunch critic of the low aspirations of the Pratt-inspired system. But the one chapter in his two books he devotes to articulating an alternative is nothing like the relentless assault Du Bois made on industrial education.

Pratt saw the schools as doing something similar to what Du Bois speaks of when he talks about the role of Negro schools in "rais[ing] them out of the defilement of the places where slavery had wallowed them" (Du Bois 1961 [1904], 82). Reservations were that kind of environment to Pratt and others who were part of the movement for Native educational reform. Another well-placed observer shared something of that opinion.

While teaching at Hampton, Du Bois's great rival Booker T. Washington became "house father" to Native male students who went there for industrial training (Washington 1965, 80).[6] Washington, who displays affection and admiration for his charges, refers to these Native students as being "perfectly ignorant" on their arrival at Hampton (Washington 1965, 80). Interestingly, though, the students themselves did not seem to share this point of view. As Washington notes, "The average Indian felt himself above the white man, and, of course, he felt himself far above the Negro, largely on account of the fact of the Negro having submitted to slavery—a thing which the Indian would never do" (Washington 1965, 80). Washington seems to have happened upon the same defiant spirit of independence that would take Lone Wolf to the U.S. Supreme Court two and a half decades later.

From such backgrounds of self-determined lives in the homelands of one's ancestors is where many Native people came to the nexus of education during America's Progressive era. And Natives had arrived where Du Bois says in *Souls* that African Americans had arrived, a time in which "the industrial school was the proffered answer to [the] combined educational and economic crisis, and an answer of singular wisdom and timeliness" (Du Bois 1961 [1904], 77). Du Bois, of course, goes on to ask the crucial biblical question of those advocating training for such a life of toil: "Is not life more than meat, and the body more than raiment?"

African Americans and Native Americans at the beginning of the twentieth century shared little in the way of political status. Native Americans, perhaps because of their lighter complexions or their dwindling, nonthreatening population numbers, could slide under the radar of the color barrier onto ballfields and even into the U.S. Congress, but they shared with their African American counterparts the truth that Du Bois railed against—that "we daily hear that an education that encourages aspiration, that sets the loftiest of ideals and seeks as an end culture and character rather than bread-winning, is the privilege of white men" (Du Bois 1961 [1904], 78).

Oppositional Voices?

Well, then, were there Native voices saying something against this system? The answer is a complicated one that I think demonstrates the complex ground we travel when we engage in the sort of intergroup comparative work that every so often becomes a buzzword among scholars of color. Too often, I might say, our answers to such questions lead us only to say, "Your people had industrial schools? Well, our people had industrial schools." Or, "Your people have had trouble with the Supreme Court? Our people have had trouble with the Supreme Court." And none of the benefit of a different mirror, another perspective on well-traveled but not completely considered ground, comes from it.

The complex response, perhaps, yields more. In this case, the first place to look for answers is among the Native writers who worked in the era of *The Souls of Black Folk*. The most obvious of these is Charles Alexander Eastman, the Dakota Sioux writer who published his first book, *Indian Boyhood*, in 1902 and who attended the First Universal Races Congress that Du Bois helped lead in 1911 (Eastman 1971 [1902]).[7] Eastman was a prolific author whose contributions to the development of Native programming for the Boy Scouts of Americas continue to provide the basis for thousands of merit badges every year (Wilson 1983, 150ff.).

Eastman was born in 1858 into a traditional Dakota life on the High Plains and grew up in the midst of Sioux resistance to white encroachment. His father converted to Christianity and moved his family to a settlement of Christian Indians in 1872. Eastman went to the Santee Normal Training School (a precursor to Carlisle), then went on to earn degrees at Beloit College, Dartmouth, and Boston University's medical school.

Of the published Native writers of his generation, Eastman was among the most accomplished educationally, the most cosmopolitan, and the most exposed to benefits of higher education. He was a remarkable man whose commitment to Native communities was complete. Yet rarely did he take up the mantle of dissent against the progressive agenda that dominated the era. Even when he became disillusioned with his own treatment by the U.S. government when he worked as a Bureau of Indian Affairs physician, he retained a belief in people like Pratt and their agendas for Native people, agendas that nearly everyone now critiques as paternalistic.

In *The Soul of the Indian* (Eastman 1980 [1911]), Eastman seems to strike a Du Boisian note but is really a paragon of the contemporary liberal agenda—the idea that presenting accurate portraits of traditional Native life would lead to more widespread good feeling and just behavior toward Natives by whites. Eastman's agenda for his non-Native audience hence overwhelms all but the slightest development of a Native intellectual agenda.

Others in Eastman's generation were also reticent to criticize the boarding-school system. Carlos Montezuma, who at an early age had been kidnapped from his Apache family and sold into adoption to a white family in Chicago, was, like Eastman, a close confidant of Pratt's. Montezuma, who advocated the end of all federal intervention in Native lives and Native communities because he wanted to prove the superiority of Natives, also advocated extreme solutions such as scattering Native Americans among each and every county in the United States as a way of diffusing once and for all Native communal life and influence.

Others criticized the boarding schools for specific practices even when they did not object to their overall purpose. Gertrude Simmons Bonnin became deeply dissatisfied with the boarding-school system, but the main part of her ire was reserved for the incompetence and Byzantine machinations of the Bureau of Indian Affairs. This Native reticence to criticize Pratt's ideology is, in many ways, symptomatic of just how dire the situation was at that time. Why, in other words, rail against something when no real alternative is present? The few who could aspire beyond industrial education could, on this reading, typically find a way toward higher education. Indeed, a healthy number of members of the first national American Indian organization, the Society of American Indians, had benefited from higher education, including Eastman, Bonnin, Montezuma, and Roe Cloud (not to mention associate member W. E. B. Du Bois), but very little of the organization's efforts, if any, went toward demanding more such opportunities.[8]

Opposition on the Other "Side of the Line"

What all this points toward is a dynamic that has been part of Native written intellectual discourse since the 1660s, when Samson Occom (a contemporary and correspondent of Phillis Wheatley's) began his intellectual work. That is, written discourse has featured not a back and forth between opposing points of view, but a coming together of similar voices striving toward the same goal. Staking out a position has not prompted the staking out of an oppositional position, as in the spawning of the Niagara Movement or the later emergence of Marcus Garvey as a foil to Du Bois and the National Association for the Advancement of Colored People. In Native history, opposing points of view have existed in every generation, but often they are hard to find; they are the voices of those like Lone Wolf, voices of those holding tenaciously to Native independence in discrete Native homelands, voices that value orality over literacy. Rarely, except in U.S. government proceedings, do those voices come down to us with the clarity of the Eastmans and Montezumas on the other side.

The Ojibway author Louise Erdrich describes the place of these oppositional voices in her novel *Love Medicine* (1993). Two of that novel's main characters, Nector and Eli Kashpaw, are the youngest sons of a traditional Ojibway woman, Rushes Bear. When faced with the pressure to send her boys to school in the first part of the twentieth century, Rushes Bear

> had let the government put Nector in school, but hidden Eli, the one she couldn't part with, in the root cellar dug beneath her floor. In that way she gained a son on either side of the line. Nector came home from boarding school knowing white reading and writing, while Eli knew the woods. (Erdrich 1993, 19)

This was not the line between ignorance and knowledge but between learning to meet the demands of modern society and learning those things that had been part and parcel of Ojibway tradition for countless generations. Nector comes home outfitted for life as a night watchman and a clerk. Eli retains an older knowledge in the face of the promises of modernity.

The Lakota author Luther Standing Bear managed to straddle that line. He wrote several books and was, according to his memoir *My People the Sioux* (1975 [1928]), literally the first student through the gates of Carlisle when it opened. Standing Bear was the son of a prominent Lakota chief. He did well at Carlisle — or, he did as well as anyone could. He marched in the Carlisle band that visited New York City and accompanied Pratt to Washington, D.C. In 1883, Pratt chose him to be the first participant in Carlisle's most prestigious internship to date, at Wanamaker's department store in Philadelphia.

In sending Standing Bear off in front of an assembly of other Carlisle students, Pratt indicated what sort of work he believed Carlisle had prepared the young Lakota son of a hereditary chief for. Pratt said,

> My boy, you are going away from us to work for you this school, in fact, for your whole race. Go, and do your best. The majority of white people think the Indian is a lazy good-for-nothing. They think he can neither work nor learn anything; that he is very dirty. Now you are going to prove that the red man *can* learn and work as well as the white man. If John Wanamaker gives you the job of blacking his shoes, see that you make them shine. Then he will give you a better job. If you are put into the office to clean, don't forget to sweep under the chairs and in the corners. If you do well in this, he will give you better work to do. (Standing Bear 1975 [1928], 178)

The people at Wanamakers were able to see more potential in the bright young man and put him to work at various jobs well beyond the janitorial level.

Standing Bear left Carlisle after his experience at Wanamakers and returned to the Dakotas (Standing Bear 1975 [1928], 189–90). He worked as, among other things, a teacher, a rancher, a store clerk, and a performer in Buffalo Bill's Wild West Show (Standing Bear 1975 [1928], 192, 240, 243, 248ff.). When he wrote his first book in 1928, he mostly continued the tradition that had come through Eastman of promoting the benefits of learning to live in white culture while demonstrating the capabilities of Native people who are given opportunities.

In *The Land of the Spotted Eagle* (1976 [1933]), published five years later, Standing Bear presented a critique of where Native Americans stood vis-à-vis American society:

The white man does not understand the Indian for the reason that he does not understand America. He is too far removed from its formative processes. The roots of the tree of his life have not yet grasped the rock and soil. The white man is still troubled with primitive fears; he still has in his conscious-ness the perils of this frontier continent, some of its fastnesses not yet having yielded to his questing footsteps and inquiring eyes. (Standing Bear 1976 [1933], 248)

The problem with America, according to Standing Bear, is that "the man from Europe is still a foreigner and an alien. And he still hates the man who questioned his path across the continent" (Standing Bear 1976 [1933], 248).

Sometime in those five years, Standing Bear had become much more critical. He began advocating, as strongly as anyone ever had, that American Indian students reap the benefits of having American Indian teachers. As he wrote: "Every problem that exists today in regard to the native population is due to the white man's cast of mind, which is unable, at least reluctant, to seek understanding and achieve adjust-ment in a new and significant environment into which it has so recently come" (Standing Bear 1976 [1933], 248–49). Native teachers were key to what he saw as the development of "a native school of thought" (Standing Bear 1976 [1933], 255).

Standing Bear foresaw Native teachers teaching Native students who would be "doubly educated" in creative arts and traditional religion and philosophy, on the one hand, and modern duties and professions, on the other. As he argued:

Every reservation could well be supplied with Indian doctors, nurses, engi-neers, road- and bridge-builders, draughtsmen, architects, dentists, lawyers, teachers, and instructors in tribal lore, legends, orations, song, dance, and ceremonial ritual. The Indian, by the very sense of duty, should become his own historian, giving his account of the race—fairer and fewer accounts of the wars and more of statecraft, legends, languages, oratory, and philosophi-cal conceptions. (Standing Bear 1976 [1933], 254)

Standing Bear, by then a chief himself, had traveled a long path toward this vision of education. One can only wonder how much sooner he might have articulated it if he had had access to even the minimal normal teaching training that would have given him conceptual tools for working through these philosophical and pedagogical issues.

Conclusion

Calling Native educational discourse behind the curve of American higher-education discourse at that point in time is certainly on the mark. If we measure where African American discourse on higher education had come three decades after *The Souls of Black Folk*, Native Americans were lagging. In 1932, the Cherokee educator Ruth Muskrat Bronson scoured records and searched around the country and was able to identify 52 Natives who had earned college degrees and 385 students — or fewer than one in one thousand Natives — enrolled in college. Five schools offered scholarships for Native students (Szasz 1977 [1928], 135). While scores of higher-education institutions could trace their origins to a major concern for Native education (including Harvard, William and Mary, and Dartmouth), only two, Bacone in Oklahoma and Pembroke State in North Carolina, focused on Native higher education (Carney 1999, 82ff.).

In important ways, though, Standing Bear was exactly in step with Du Bois in understanding the function of higher education in the specific situation of a tribal people coming into modernity. Du Bois, in addressing alumni of his alma mater, Fisk University, in 1933, said, "Once upon a time some four thousand miles east of this place, I saw the functioning of a perfect system of education. It was in West Africa, beside a broad river. . . . There under the Yorubas and other Sudanese and Bantu tribes, the education of the child began almost before it could walk" (Du Bois 1971, 51).

Du Bois goes on to say of African tribal education, "There could be no education that was not at once for use in earning a living and for use in living a life. Out of this education and out of the life it typified came, as perfect expressions, song and dance and sage, and ethics and religion" (Du Bois 1961 [1904], 51). This was to Du Bois at the moment an ideal even if it was all but impossible to replicate within the confines of modern education. He argued that he had seen that ideal reflected at Fisk, at Harvard, and at the University of Berlin. In each case, the institution was highly aware of its main purposes and the specific circumstances in which it operated — the approach of the universal from the context of the particular. That approach could be problematic, especially in cases like Berlin, where national superiority and others' inferiority were topics as much as human limits, but Du Bois saw no way toward larger truths than the embrace of a people by themselves where they are.

For Du Bois, no one ever merely founds a university. Instead, a university begins where it is, whether it is French, Spanish, or Negro. Like Standing Bear, he saw clearly the limiting confines of industrial education and sought instead a path that would embrace the actual conditions of people even as it would also embrace the resources, capabilities, and talents of those same people. Doing so, of course, required a belief in the capability of those people to reach toward new knowledge.

Standing Bear's and Du Bois's vision was one that has been shared, if sometimes only in bits and pieces, by thousands of leaders, such as Standing Bear's father, who looked at the present and wondered about the possibilities of the future. In Native America, perhaps the strongest results of that vision have been the tribally controlled college movement in Canada and the United States. Those colleges and universities have articulated an educational mission that seeks to support the process of someone becoming who they are as Diné, Lakota, Dakota, Ojibway, and Cheyenne at the heart of also becoming better able to participate in and to understand the contemporary world of which they are a part.

Native American higher education, then, has not so much lagged behind African American models as it has been on a different, sometimes convergent journey. From intact if embattled traditional cultures, Native people have emerged into a new century as legacies of the risks parents and leaders took along the way, risks that endangered the present in the hope that the future would provide a forum for promoting and professing that which the progressives saw only as backward detritus.

Perhaps as Native people continue to move forward in the challenge of understanding ourselves in the midst of an ever more complicated world, Du Bois and other African Americans from then and now will become crucial voices in illuminating the path behind and ahead. And perhaps Native voices will, likewise, help fill in the gaps of conversations never completed and alternative realities not yet explored. That is the great promise of comparative work in Native American studies, and the great challenge.

Perhaps such work will help us reask that question, "What does it feel like to be a problem?" Certain sorts of Native responses may sometimes be hard to find, but one hundred years after Du Bois asked the ques-

tion, I can say this: Native Americans do not appear to have any intention of stopping being a problem anytime soon.

Notes

1 187 U.S. 553, 23 S. Ct. 216, 47 L. Ed. 299 (1903).

2 For a comprehensive overview of the history of treaties and the treaty-
making process, see Deloria amd DeMallie 1999.

3 Treaties, I should say, are ambiguous documents from a Native point of
view. My tribe, the Osages, signed a series of them with the United States over
the course of the nineteenth century. For some of them, the United States
enticed decidedly marginal leaders of Osage subgroups to negotiate a treaty
supposedly on behalf of the tribe as a whole. In others, Osage needs to pay
mounting debts to white traders brought leaders to negotiations even as they
complained that the United States had failed to abide by previous treaties. All
of them were attempts to stem the tide of white settlers who were squatting on
Osage lands. In all, Osages agreed to land cessions involving 100 million acres.
In return, we received the equivalent of one penny for every six acres. However,
the treaties are proof that the United States recognizes our continued claim to
independent peoplehood, which we have recognized as ours since our emergence as a people centuries before the arrival of European settlers in our homeland.

4 For a more complete discussion of this phenomenon in American history,
see Deloria 1998.

5 Pratt and the boarding-school ideology that he was a leader in developing
has been the subject of much recent significant scholarship. Among many titles,
see Child 1998; Lomawaima 1994; Adams 1995; Archuleta et al. 2000.

6 Washington indicates that in 1879 he was in charge of the first group of male
Native students at Hampton, but more likely he was in charge of the first group
the year after Pratt left to establish Carlisle.

7 According to Eastman's biographer, Raymond Wilson, Du Bois and Eastman gave speeches at the same session of the event on July 28, 1911 (Wilson
1983, 153). David Levering Lewis mentions "a Sioux from the United States as
being among the delegates to the congress that made an impression on Du
Bois" (Lewis 1993, 442).

8 See Hertzberg 1971, 83. Hertzberg indicates that Du Bois's membership at
the associate level was mainly window-dressing. One can speculate whether Du
Bois's nominal involvement grew out of his contact with Eastman, one of the
Society of American Indians' leaders, in London in 1911.

CHAPTER TEN

Native Americans, African Americans,

and the Space That Is America

Indian Presence in the Fiction of Toni Morrison

VIRGINIA KENNEDY

~~~~~~~

In her article "Unspeakable Things Unspoken: The Afro-American Presence in American Literature," Toni Morrison states that "cultures, whether silenced or monologistic, whether repressed or repressing, seek meaning in the language and images available to them" (Morrison 1990, 208). But, she continues, "Silences are being broken" (Morrison 1990, 208). Morrison's essay, as well as the vast array of criticism by American writers who must necessarily be defined by hyphens and added adjectives, interrogates the notion of "other" and examines the context of traditionally accepted definitions of "American."[1] These writers speak from what R. Radhakrishnan (1993, 755) calls a "third space," a space where agency and determination are employed to define an authenticated self and a place in a multiethnic community rather than have it imagined by a restrictive dominant narrative. Through this literature and the criticism that examines it, the dominant ideology that defines America is made accountable to previously silenced stories.

Many emerging stories have intersecting paths, and they have in common the power to subvert a politically imposed hegemony built on the perceived superiority of Western culture. Yet intersections between these cultures are the focus of relatively few critical inquiries. In "The Hidden History of Mestizo America," Gary Nash (1995, 961) asserts that "multiculturalism" has been construed as "multiracialism" and has led to a "definitional absolutism that has unwittingly defeated egalitarian and humanitarian goals by smothering inequalities of class and fueling interethnic and interracial tensions that give more powerful groups opportunities to manipulate these divisions." It is not the purpose of this essay to argue Nash's model for hybridization, a model that advocates a "comprehensive, cosmopolitan cross-ethnic and cross-racial community" that moves beyond the cultural communities David Hollinger calls "vital sites for the formation, articulation, and sustenance of cultural values, social identities, and political power" (Nash 1995, 961). However, Nash's point about the manipulation of tensions by more powerful groups cannot be ignored. It is in the interests of the powerful to deemphasize value in cultural diversity while exploiting and racializing difference. When the powerless have embraced these imposed differences as a method of gaining agency and authenticity to the point of rigidifying "ethnoracial particularisms," diversity becomes a tool in its own destruction. Radhakrishnan (1993, 755) describes a definition of "authenticity" with enough room for "multiple-rooted-ness" in a "vibrant collection of constituencies." He alludes to Gandhi's metaphor envisioning a free India, a vision opposed to Nehru's "transgression of existing identifications," which promoted the pan-Westernization of Indian cultures (Radhakrishnan 1993, 756). Gandhi spoke of a "house with open windows all around so that breezes may blow in from every possible side, but there is a constraint: that the house itself not be blown away by the force of the winds from without" (Radhakrishnan 1993, 756).

The project of contemplating America as just such a "house" means more attention focused on the common grounds of emerging historiographies. African–Native American intersections are powerful sites for this type of examination. William Loren Katz (1986, 3–4) writes in *Black Indians* that "the relationships between Europeans and Native Americans and between Europeans and Africans have been thoroughly studied. But, one relationship has not. Conspicuous by its neglect is the relationship on this soil between red and black people." Though this omission has become more frequently addressed in historical studies, fiction is also a powerful site for exploring, as Sharon Holland (1994, 337) writes, "the dynamic between both subject positions."

The fiction of Toni Morrison engages this dynamic and explores legitimate historical connections between black and Indian peoples on American soil that have remained outside the realm of traditional historical accounts. Barbara Hill Rigney (1991, 60) describes Morrison's novels as, "in a real sense, 'historical novels,' quasi documentaries that bear historical witness. Her characters are both subjects of and subject to history, events in 'real time,' that succession of antagonistic movements that includes slavery, reconstruction, depression, and war." Because of these "origins in reality," Rigney (1991, 77) explains, Morrison's "is a voice of political conscience, making poverty, slavery, oppression immediate even to those readers who have never experienced them, even to those readers who would choose to forget." In Morrison's fiction, African Americans and Native Americans bump into each other, come across each other, and interconnect with each other. They share experiences and bloodlines, because as these fictions assert, they *are* together in the American landscape. They are present with Euro-Americans who seek to silence and remove them—literally, through domination and exploitation, and figuratively, through imagining them in objectified forms.

Jack Forbes (1993, 1) writes that "the entire Afro-Native American cultural exchange and contact experience is a fascinating and significant subject, but one largely obscured by a focus upon European activity and European colonial relations with 'peripheral' subject peoples." In addition to the Eurocentric perspective Forbes describes, the political need to maintain the separation between black and Indian cultures has deep historical roots. European and, later, Euro-American power structures feared alliances between these two groups of oppressed peoples. Katz argues that European attacks on Indians may have had as much to do with keeping them apart from enslaved blacks as with hunger for land and greed (1993, 7). He writes, "To prevent Africans and Native Americans from uniting, Europeans played skillfully on racial differences and ethnic rivalries. They kept the pot of animosity boiling" (1993, 13). The Seminole Wars in Florida, for example, demonstrate the determination of united black and Indian peoples to resist Euro-American oppression. The vehemence with which this resistance was crushed and subsequent policies toward black and Indian peoples demonstrate the determination of Euro-Americans to maintain a separation that perpetuated the use of slave labor and land occupation.

As the country formed, domination of the physical land and its resources was the base of power maintenance. Slave labor was needed to work the land, and space free of indigenous communities was needed to make room for increasing numbers of immigrants and their need for resource exploitation. For reasons that ranged in scope from logistical difficulties to the fierce resistance of black and Indian peoples and to legitimate protests of Euro-Americans who actively resisted clearly inhumane and destructive policies, attempts at literal and cultural genocide were ultimately unsuccessful. By the end of the nineteenth century, Euro-Americans did, however, gain control of the land and its resources, which meant control of food, water, and living conditions. Kevin Mulroy (1993, 151) explains that whites' attempts to classify blacks associated with and related to Native Americans during the nineteenth century were motivated by expediency and the desire to control the concentration of the material wealth of the continent. Euro-American power brokers made the rules on how resources would be doled out, and "peripheral peoples" were forced to abide by them.

In examining the nature of relationships between African Americans and Native Americans, I will focus here on three Morrison novels: *Song of Solomon*, *Beloved*, and *Paradise*. They were each written about a decade apart, and each reveals the shared experiences of Indians and blacks together in the physical space of America. These novels span more than one hundred years, from 1873 in *Beloved* to 1976 in *Paradise*. Through the ancestral stories of their characters, they reach back farther still into America's historical past. All three novels reveal a common and unerasable truth: The interactions and intersections of Africans, Indians, and Europeans were and are equally powerful components inextricably intertwined in the defining of America. In each of these books, black and Indian peoples relate to each other on American ground. Their stories interrogate literary and historical constructions that perpetuate the imposition of "whiteness" on American identity and deny blacks and Indians a powerful shared heritage. The intersection of Native Americans, African Americans, and the literal earth of America in Morrison's novels denies the hierarchy inherent in the colonial "us" and "them" constructs and critiques the European quest for dominance over land and people.

Beloved, *Song of Solomon*, and *Paradise* are three novels that expose the destructiveness of America's race–land relationship. Through the course of each novel, Morrison demonstrates the coming together of blacks and Indians and the land, suggesting a powerful resistance to the exploitation of bodies, and of the earth, for material gain. Her fiction claims the space that is the American nation for all the people who have played a part in its evolution. These stories unbalance America's Eurocentric history and demand that the stories of all of the continent's peoples be laid beside each other for honest examination. In the words of Melvin Dixon (1987, 2), Morrison's fiction inverts "assumptions about place and endow[s] language with the power to reinvent geography and identity."

Colonizing cultures write their maps over the maps of the peoples who are invaded and dispossessed. In *Mixedblood Messages*, Louis Owens (1998, 211) writes that mapping in this sense is "an intensely political enterprise, an essential step toward appropriation and possession. Maps write the conquerors' stories over the stories of the conquered." Morrison's characters resist the imposition of the dominant culture's mapped boundaries, both in the physical and in the spiritual sense. They go beyond these imposed boundaries into a wilderness that is not "wild" in the Western sense of the world but that encompasses an alternate reality. It is a space where, if people pay attention, land and the spirits of the people who have lived and died on it are not silent. In Rigney's words, writing for Morrison "is a process of undoing the work of death, of conjuring ghosts, of accounting for 'the disremembered and unaccounted for'" (Rigney 1991, 80). African American and Native American cultures in communion with the land where they have been forbidden an authentic presence stake a claim to a physical and spiritual home in America (Dixon 1987, 1).

The Indian presence in *Beloved* is both ghostly and real and cannot be separated from the physical site of indigenous communities where removal and exploitation had taken place. Renee Bergland (2000, 1) states that, "for more than three hundred years, American literature has been haunted by ghostly Indians." African Americans also haunt American fiction, Bergland says, and proves the point by stating that "Toni Morrison uses ghosts in her own fiction, and in the critical essay, 'Unspeakable Things Unspoken,' [Morrison] proposes that African Americans function as 'ghosts in the machine of nineteenth-century American letters,' describing them as 'active, but unsummoned presences that can distort the workings of the machine and can also make it work'" (Bergland 2000, 18).

The central argument of Bergland's study is to reveal the "story of a triumphant American aesthetic that repeatedly transforms horror into glory, national dishonor into national pride" (Bergland 2000, 22). While this is a powerful and accurate assessment, Bergland does not make it clear that Morrison's ghosts operate outside this "American aesthetic": Morrison's ghosts function in ways directly opposed to

Euro-American configurations of native ghosts. Bergland proposes that in *Playing in the Dark*, Morrison explores the invisibility of African Americans. However, Morrison's project is more accurately described as an exploration of the undeniable *visibility* of an Africanist presence in a literature and body of criticism that jumps through hoops to deny its powerful existence (Morrison 1992, 1990, 11–12).

Bergland's argument asserts accurately that, for Euro-Americans, spectral images of Indians allow for assuaged national guilt over a violent conquest and removal. At the same time, they provide the vehicle to create ancestors who are American rather than European. Indians are dispossessed, claimed, and reimagined in the national narrative: "In American letters, and in the American imagination, Native American ghosts function both as representations of national guilt and as triumphant agents of Americanization" (Bergland 2000, 4). The Native ghosts of Euro-American imagination haunt the landscape to suggest that an *actual* Indian presence has vanished. Constructed as phantoms of a former presence and relegated to a supernatural realm, these ghosts haunt the edges of Euro-American consciousness but are essentially powerless in the shaping of nation.

Morrison's ghosts function in a manner directly opposed to this lack of agency. They exist as a "real" presence within the physicality of American space and therefore critique the invasive and destructive behavior of the dominant culture. Morrison herself explains that "the acceptance of the supernatural and a profound rootedness in the real world at the same time, with neither taking precedence over the other . . . is indicative of the cosmology, the way in which Black people looked at the world. . . . Superstition and magic [are] another way of knowing things" (as quoted in Rigney 1991, 79). Acceptance of "manifestations beyond nature is intrinsic in *Beloved*," as it is in all of Morrison's fiction (Rigney 1991, 80). These manifestations are a way of seeing rather than of not seeing, a way of reinventing what the national narrative has attempted to erase.

Beloved is Morrison's Pulitzer Prize–winning account of slavery, the haunting force of memory, and the redemption that comes from learning how to acknowledge the past. Sethe, the young slave woman who runs from the abuse of the ironically named Sweet Home plantation, struggles for a new life in Ohio. At her house on 124 Bluestone Road, the Sweet Home men arrive to take her and her children back to slavery in Kentucky. Hiding in the woodshed, she attempts to kill her children rather than have them returned to the South. She succeeds in killing only her "crawling already" daughter before she is stopped. The child named "Beloved" becomes the ghost that is haunting 124 when Paul D., one of the former Sweet Home slaves, arrives after eighteen years, seeking Sethe. Paul D.'s story entwines with Sethe's to form a profoundly compelling narrative that unabashedly examines America's past and its implications. It is mainly Paul D.'s memories that join African slaves to dispossessed indigenous peoples in American space and history.

When Paul D. remembers, "Sixo went among trees at night. For dancing, he said, to keep his bloodlines open," the dichotomy between defining land exploited through the enforced labor of enslaved Africans and land which literally sustains the spirit of the slaves is evident (Morrison 1987, 25). Significantly, it is during one of these "night creeps" that Sixo discovers "the deserted stone structure that Redmen used way back when they thought the land was theirs," and he asks it permission to enter (Morrison 1987, 24). Once inside, "having felt what it felt like, he asked the Redman's presence if he could bring his woman there, [and] it said yes." That they "*thought* the land was theirs" does not deny indigenous people's prior claim to the land. Sixo clearly acknowledges and respects this claim by asking permission to enter a dwelling empty of everything but a special Indian presence. Neither does the supernatural presence function to ghost the original inhabitants out of actual existence. The dwelling is concrete physical evidence of a people removed by those who now enslave both Sixo's body and the land he is forced to work. Sixo's request for permission to enter and to bring his woman there overtly critiques the invasive nature of colonial conquest of Indian lands. His discovery of the lodge while dancing in the woods to keep his bloodlines open, his acknowledgement of Indian presence, and his respect for "what it felt like" connects both cultures in a common heritage of oppression and resistance to oppression. The bond between land and the sustenance of spirit reaches beyond the restraints of the plantation and supercedes the material ownership of body and earth. For Sixo, Indian presence has not been erased by physical removal, and the woods beyond the cultivated property of Sweet Home are alive with a presence he understands as real and respects. Sixo's spirit, which like the "Redmen's presence" could never be enchained or erased by legal ownership, pronounces itself in song and laughter, even when he is burned to death by those who think they have mastered him.

In another memory, Paul D. remembers that it is literally inside the

Southern earth that he and rest of the men to whom he is chained are locked down in the heinous prison of Alfred, Georgia. They are released each day, when "they chain-danced over the fields, through the woods to a trail that ended in the astonishing beauty of feldspar" (Morrison 1987, 109). To those who imprison the men, this rock of astonishing beauty must be broken for sale, for use, but for the prisoners themselves the rock is life. Hammering on the feldspar, they sing out their lives—the people, places, and moments in them—and they beat the stone until "life was dead" (Morrison 1987, 109). It is the rock, his hammer, and his fellow prisoners that get Paul D. through the eighty-six days until the rains come to Alfred. In the torrential downpours, the earth that entombs their cells turns to mud, and the fields where they chain-danced are flooded. But the rain and mud that keep the white man home lest he flood his gun soften the ground for forty-six men chained together to escape their wooden tombs: "Like the unshriven dead, zombies on the loose, holding the chains in their hands, they trusted the rain and the dark, but mostly Hi-Man and each other" (Morrison 1987, 110).

They escape through the shelter of the thick Southern woods, the rain and mud covering their tracks and their scents. "Hoping for a shack, solitary, some distance from its big house, where a slave might be making rope or heating potatoes at the grate," they find instead a camp of Cherokee resisters who have fled to the shelter of the woods rather than be forced west to "Indian Territory" in Oklahoma (Morrison 1987, 111). Morrison's description of the Cherokee is both a tribute to their pride and humanity and a critique of the "civilized" culture that imposed on blacks the atrocities of Alfred, Georgia, and betrayed Indians, forcing them into hiding on their own home land:

> Decimated but stubborn, they were among those who chose a fugitive life rather than Oklahoma. The illness that swept them now was reminiscent of the one that had killed half their number two hundred years earlier. In between that calamity and this, they had visited George III in London, published a newspaper, made baskets, led Oglethorpe through forests, helped Andrew Jackson fight Creek, been experimented on by Dartmouth, established asylums, wrote their language, resisted settlers, shot bear and translated scripture. All to no avail. The forced move to the Arkansas River, insisted upon by the same president they fought for against the Creek, destroyed another quarter of their already shattered number.

That was it, they thought, and removed themselves from those who signed the treaty, in order to retire into the forest and await the end of the world. (Morrison 1987, 111)

The Cherokee, sick themselves from the "whiteman's disease," cut the chains to free the black men, and then the Cherokee feed and shelter them. They call the Africans Buffalo men. Some stay on with the Indians, moving to a healthy camp where they are told that three Buffalo men already live. The land of the southeastern woods becomes the common ground where black and Indian meet in resistance; the Cherokee rootedness in their home and consequent refusal to move West is linked to the necessity of Paul D. to go north over the same ground, to escape those who would repossess him. The joining of the Buffalo men to the Cherokee resisters envisions the historical communion between escaped slaves and dispossessed Natives that fueled the resistance to white domination by maroon and Indian–black freedmen communities.

Unlike his fellow convicts who speak knowledgeably about rivers, streets, towns, and territories, Paul D. has no information on routes or roads to places where he would be safe. Despite the knowledge of his fellow prisoners, Paul D. asks the Cherokee, whose understanding of the land does not exist in the linear boundaries of colonial settlement, for directions to the "free North. Magical North" (Morrison 1987, 112). The Cherokee man who answers him smiles in response and looks around at how the flood rains "had turned everything to steam and blossoms" (Morrison 1987, 112). He points toward the blossoms and instructs Paul D. to follow them: "As they go, you go. You will be where you want to be when they're gone" (Morrison 1987, 112). Like the feldspar and the rains that saved him from the underground prison of Alfred, Georgia, the blossoms take Paul D. north to Ohio and Sethe.

In Ohio, Paul D., like Sixo in the woods around Sweet Home, feels Indian presence in land hijacked through treachery, massacre, and disease. Walking a route home from the riverside slaughterhouse takes him through a "cemetery as old as sky" (Morrison 1987, 155). There he senses "the agitation of the Miami no longer content to rest in the mounds that covered them" (Morrison 1987, 155). They had been awakened by roads, wells, and houses built in their "earth pillows." The Miami ghosts, far older than any European presence on the land, are literally part of the earth in which they are buried. Once woken from "eternal rest," like the Cherokees who would not go West, they do not desert their homeland. They stay and growl on the banks of the river, sigh in the trees of Catherine Street, and ride the wind above the pig yard. Paul D. acknowledges their habitation in the river and trees and the air above the pig yards because, like Sixo, he experiences "the spiritual connection to the world around [him] as a given" (Fulweiler 2000, 134). But unlike Sixo's respectful request from the Redmen's presence for entry into their dwelling, Paul D., hearing their agitation, stays on regardless. The work "poking, killing, cutting, skinning, case packing and saving [the] offal" of pigs "wasn't a bad job" (Morrison 1987, 155). Like the restless Miami "outraged by their folly in believing land was holy," he is forced to accept the reality of a material relationship to the land to survive as a "free" man in a space being usurped by Euro-American expansion across the continent (Morrison 1987, 155). To what degree are the communal structures of black and Indian communities compelled to assimilate the values of land use inherent in an imposed capitalistic system?

This question is a focal point of *Song of Solomon*. Dixon (1987, 157) writes that the conflict between family and property ties is one of the principle organizing structures of the novel. The central character of *Song of Solomon* is Milkman Dead, the son of a wealthy landlord, Macon Dead Jr., and Ruth Foster Dead, the daughter of deceased Dr. Foster, who had been the only black doctor in their Michigan town. Milkman grows up bored and privileged and believing that money will free him from his oppressive father. Through his relationship with his eccentric aunt, Pilate, and her daughter, Hagar, Milkman is provoked to undertake what he believes is a search for lost gold but that evolves into a quest for his ancestral heritage. Milkman journeys from North to South less than one hundred years after the Cherokee point Paul D. in the opposite direction. What begins as a quest for gold ends in a town in Virginia, where Milkman finds his black and Indian ancestry and an understanding of the roots he has in the roots of his ancestors' blood and in the land of their birth and suffering. In reversing the direction of Paul D.'s journey, leaving the industrialized North for the rural South and relinquishing a quest for material profit to embrace the importance of family heritage, Milkman demonstrates the priority Morrison's fiction places on communal values among people and communal ties to the land. Milkman's journey points to a reclamation of identity in the very land deserted by Paul D. and Sethe during their quest for survival and freedom.

Dixon (1987, 161) explains that land and family heritage are "the battlegrounds for the continuing struggle between Pilate and Macon" as they vie for influence on Milkman's understanding of himself and his place in the world. Macon Dead advises his son to "own things. And let the things you own own other things. Then you'll own yourself and other people too" (Morrison 1977, 55). Deborah Guth (2000, 320) writes that in Macon Dead's "all consuming pursuit of status and property . . . is the uncanny similarity between him, as he evicts poor tenants who impede the growth of his wealth, and the white landowners who 'evicted' his father (through murder) in order to increase their own." Milkman's aunt Pilate, the sister estranged from his father who has "as much to do with his future as she had with his past," offers Milkman an alternative view of the world (Morrison 1977, 36). Pilate's "harking back to her dead father's words, the bones which hang in her living room, the earring she wears, and the song she sings are all signs of a deep connectedness from which she gains both her charisma and her inner peace"(Guth 2000, 321). While Pilate remains connected to her past through her memories, songs, and the ghost of her father, she is free of the material encumbrances and desire for power and acceptance that weigh her brother down.

The sack in Pilate's shack actually contains the bones of Pilate's dead father, though she initially believes they belong to a miner her frightened brother had killed in a cave. Macon had wanted to steal the miner's gold; Pilate forced him to leave it. Milkman and his cohort Guitar are enticed by Macon to steal the sack from Pilate, since Macon convinces them that Pilate had gone back to the cave to take the gold for herself. Guitar needs money to support his work for "Seven Days," the group responsible for taking the life of a white person for every black person killed in a racial crime. Milkman needs gold to escape the tyranny of his father and the monotony of his life. But Milkman and Guitar discover that the bag contains only bones. Milkman decides the gold must still be in the cave and heads back to the land of his father's father to find it.

Milkman's trek through the land of his grandfather's farm yields the cave, but no gold. In the time he spends waiting for a ride out to his grandfather's property, the local people's stories of his grandfather, father, and Pilate yield the roots of a tradition his father had relinquished. Milkman did not recognize his father, the "stern, greedy, unloving man in the boy they talked about, but he loved the boy they described and loved that boy's father, with his hip-roofed barn, his peach trees, and Sunday break-of-dawn fishing parties on a fish pond that was two acres wide" (Morrison 1977, 234–35). More important, the stories of his grandfather's thriving farm reveal the powerful, communal relationship with the land his father rejected for the detachment of ownership. In a lyrical and powerful passage, the farmland defines itself:

> "You see?" The farm said to them. "See? See what you can do? Never mind you can't tell one letter from another, never mind you born a slave, never mind you lose your name, never mind your daddy dead, never mind nothing. Here, this here, is what a man can do if he puts his mind to it and his back in it. Stop sniveling." It said. "Stop picking around the edges of the world. Take advantage, and if you can't take advantage, take disadvantage. We live here. On this planet, in this nation, in this country right here. Nowhere else! We got a home in this rock, don't you see! Nobody starving in my home; nobody crying in my home, and if I got a home you got one too! Grab it. Grab this land! Take it, hold it, my brothers, make it, my brothers, shake it, squeeze it, turn it, twist it, beat it, kick it, kiss it, whip it, stomp it, dig it, plow it, seed it, reap it, rent it, buy it, sell it, own it, build it, multiply it, and pass it on—can you hear me? Pass it on!" (Morrison 1977, 235)

Dixon (1987, 163) writes, "This land, its voice full of the language and cadence of Negro spirituals and rich with sources of identity, should offer prosperity to any family willing to use it in the ways suggested above; not merely acquire more and more of it."

The first Macon Dead, a freed slave and, as Milkman learns eventually, married to an Indian woman named Sing, carved a home in land that had been the site of their pain. The ex-slave man and the Indian woman dispossessed of their lives and their identities find home, healing, and sustenance in relationship with the land, which provides for them and nurtures them. Though they are again destroyed through violence and greed when the first Macon Dead is murdered by whites who want his farm, the continual appearance to Pilate of her father's ghost and his repetitious utterance of her mother's name, "Sing," keep alive the values that built their farm and that have been denied by Milkman's father. Pilate explains to Milkman that it was her father's ghost who sent her back to the cave for the bones of the dead miner. She urges Milkman to believe that "a human life is precious. . . . If you take a life, then you own it. You responsible for it . . . and the dead you kill is yours. You can't take a life and walk off and leave it. Life is life. Precious. And the dead you kill is yours. They stay with you anyway, in your mind. So it's a better thing, a more better thing to have the bones right there with you where you go. That way, it frees up your mind" (Morrison 1977, 208).

Milkman finally comes to understand himself in relationship to his ancestors and the land of their struggle. In so doing, he denies the finality of the violence perpetrated on his grandparents and any perverse legitimacy that could be attached to its motivations. In a larger sense, Pilate's words address the blood of African Americans and Native Americans that cannot be removed from the soil where it has been spilled. Her words speak to the perpetrators and urge that the only real reconciliation with exploited peoples lies in remembering, in acknowledgment. It is not until then that the bones can be buried and healing can take place.

Milkman's struggle through overgrown orchards of his grandfather's farm, "stuff he could barely walk through," communicates his initial resistance to the lessons in the local people's stories (Morrison 1977, 250). "He thought of the pitiful hungry eyes of the old men, their eagerness for some word of defiant success accomplished by the son of Macon Dead, and of the white men who strutted through the orchards and ate the Georgia peaches after they shot his grandfather's head off" (Morrison 1977, 250). Macon Dead's thirst for gold began as a salve to the injustice in his father's murder. Milkman, still immersed in his father's materialistic ideals, relives it, arriving at the cave smelling money, "although it was not a smell at all. It was like candy and sex and soft twinkling lights" (Morrison 1977, 250–51). He discovers an empty cave. Still believing that Pilate took the gold, he heads for Virginia, following the path that Pilate took when she and her brother parted in anger.

In Virginia, the local people force Milkman to strip his city trappings. Everything that has monetary worth — his expensive clothes, his car, his wallet, his watch — becomes the weight that keeps him from gaining their confidence. A storefront brawl and a midnight hunting trip serve as Milkman's initiation into the culture of Shalimar, Virginia. Stripped of his father's influence and relieved of the material possessions that weigh him down, Milkman's second errand into the wilds of the South bears fruit. Lost in the dark of the Blue Ridge Mountains, knowing that

Guitar wants to kill him in the belief that Milkman has found the gold and kept it, Milkman hears the primal language of a long-forgotten relationship between humans and the natural, physical world:

> It was all language . . . No, it was not language; it was what there was before language. Before things were written down. Language in the time when men and animals did talk to one another, when man could sit down with an ape and the two converse, when a tiger and a man could share the same tree, and each understood each other; when men ran with wolves, not from or after them. And he was hearing it in the Blue Ridge Mountains under a sweet gum tree. (Morrison 1977, 278)

Guitar attempts to strangle Milkman against the sweet gum tree; Milkman fights him off, and leaves the woods, having survived more than the murder attempt. He surmounts the ultimate detachment from himself and the physical world around him. He finds himself "exhilarated by simply walking the earth. Walking it like he belonged on it; like his legs were stalks, tree trunks, a part of his body that extended down down down into the rock and soil, and were comfortable there" (Morrison 1977, 281). Having reached this understanding with the earth, Milkman's search for gold is transformed into a quest for the people who connected this land of the South to his past.

Milkman discovers through the words of a children's song, which Pilate had also sung, that his grandfather was raised by Heddy, an Indian woman, after his great-grandfather Jake had "flown" from a mountainside in Shalimar. The legend of the "flying Africans" who could literally fly back to the land of their birth is joined to the story of the Byrds, who were forced to Americanize their names. Singing Bird is Sing, the wife of Milkman's grandfather and the daughter of Heddy. Morrison makes a point through Susan Byrd, who tells Milkman the story of his people, that Indians were able to pass for white, and though black and Indians "mixed a lot . . . some Indians didn't like it," preferring to remain closer in color to whites, who doled out mistreatments based on the darkness of skin (Morrison 1977, 322). In a love that is clearly resistant to imposed racial identities that encouraged the maintenance of separation between blacks and Indians, Milkman's grandmother, who "looked white," married "Black Jake. Black as coal" (Morrison 1977, 321). Milkman, descended from "flying Africans" and "birds," becomes whole in his rootedness to the land and his heritage in the two cultures. His rootedness in the earth of the South enables his liberation from the vanities that grounded his father and allows him to take the "flight" of his great-grandfather.

Unencumbered by the immaturity and selfishness with which he first journeyed to the South, Milkman returns to the North to retrieve Pilate and bring her to the hill where his great-grandfather "flew." Morrison describes Milkman's new relationship to the land reaching from Virginia to Michigan as one that has its source in the blood and history of his ancestral identity. The land claimed by Euro-American settlement and expansion becomes alive with the agitation of silenced stories. The stories of *all* peoples whose shared experiences inextricably tie them to the land are buried within it, inseparable from it. In Milkman's musings, he asks the question that acknowledges a heritage of dispossession and survival that is shared by African Americans and Native Americans. It is also a question that resuscitates stories the dominant narrative attempts to bury alive:

> He looked out the window. Far away from Virginia, fall had already come. Ohio, Indiana, Michigan were dressed up like the Indian warriors from whom their names came. Blood red and yellow, ocher and ice blue.
>
> He read the road signs with interest now, wondering what lay beneath the names. The Algonquins had named the territory he lived in Great Water, nichi hami. How many dead lives and fading memories were buried in and beneath the names of the places in this country? (Morrison 1977, 329)

When Milkman returns with Pilate to Solomon's Leap, Guitar, who had "assumed the 'greed for gold' that Milkman has outgrown," is waiting to kill him (Dixon 1987, 159). Guitar misfires and kills Pilate instead as she and Milkman bury the bones of her father in the land of his birth. Holding Pilate in death, Milkman sings to her the song of their ancestors and discovers "why he loved her so. Without ever leaving the ground, she could fly" (Morrison 1977, 335). In a gesture that unites him to his African grandfathers and Indian grandmothers and that is made possible only by his new understanding of connection to the land, Milkman leaps toward Guitar. The novel ends with Milkman in mid-flight, like the flying Africans and the singing birds, no longer weighed down by the rootless material vanities that informed his original quest for gold.

It is these vanities that present themselves with a vengeance in the men of Ruby, Oklahoma, the day they set out to murder the women they define as threatening outsiders in *Paradise*. In *Song of Solomon*, the destructive path Macon Dead takes away from his father's farm is reversed by Milkman's return path home to the sustenance of his ancestral land and family ties. He is healed by the land and people of Shalimar, Virginia. In *Paradise*, Macon Dead's greed is multiplied in the townspeople who settle Ruby after being chased from positions of political power in the postbellum South and forced from Haven, their first refuge, where they had formed a community rooted in communal values. Brothers Deacon and Steward Morgan and the families of Ruby they govern become precisely what they feared and fled. Their climactic encounter with the eclectic community of women who populate the once brothel, once school, once convent on the outskirts of town frames the stories that join the people of Ruby to the women they seek to destroy.

The racial politics of Ruby fused with capitalistic greed are as destructive as the forces of exploitation that enslaved Paul D. and Sethe and divested the Cherokee of their land in the Southeast. *Paradise* is a scathing critique of the culture Ruby becomes when its families embrace the same model of racial isolation and land exploitation practiced by the colonizers and settlers who had enslaved their ancestors. Frequent instances through the novel refer to the trouble inside the culture of Ruby rather than on its edges, where the figurative margins of the town rub along the edges of the outside world. "Scary things not always outside," says the character Connie, the matriarch of the convent, "most scary things is inside" (Morrison 1998, 39).

The novel begins on the day Ruby's men will try to kill the women of the convent and ends with the results of the attempt. In the spaces between, the history of the novel's major characters is an opportunity for Morrison to trace a path back and forward again, examining the stories that bring the women to the convent and the men to the desire to murder them. Through the accidents and tragedies of their lives, the convent women find refuge there and cannot seem to permanently leave — either the building or Connie, the woman who had lived in the convent since being brought there by the mother superior who originally ran the school. The school, named "Christ the King School for Native Girls," was first a school "where stilled Arapaho girls once sat and learned to forget" (Morrison 1998, 223, 4). Indians are frequently intertwined with the journeys of Ruby's founders and the lives of the convent women. Most often, indigenous peoples provide aid to the midnight-black people who identify themselves as "8-rock," an allusion to the deepest, darkest level of extraction in the coal mines of the Southeast (Morrison 1998, 193). After their ejection from the Southeast, the 8-rock families leave for "Indian Territory" (Oklahoma), where they meet with a "new separation: light-skinned against black. Oh, they knew there was a difference to the minds of whites, but it had not struck them before that it was of consequence, serious consequence, to Negroes themselves" (Morrison 1998, 194). "Disallowed" by lighter-skinned blacks who do not welcome them into their community, the 8-rock families eventually bargain with "state Indians" to work in trade for land the Indians had been allotted by the government (Morrison 1998, 98). This land becomes their thriving community of Haven and the site of what they referred to as "the disallowing, part two," when "rednecks and Sons of the Confederacy" violently force them to move once again (Morrison 1998, 194).[2]

In Ruby, under the leadership of the Morgan brothers, the 8-rock families degenerate into the politics of racial isolation and land exploitation that forced the migrations of their forefathers. In Morrison's words, "isolation . . . carries the seeds of its own destruction because as times change, other things seep in, as it did with Ruby."[3] Deterioration through isolationist values begins to destroy Ruby in the span of just one generation, from the time the 8-rock families are forced from Haven to the time Ruby develops into an enclosed community fearing the convent women living on the edge of their town.

A story of the Morgan brothers' father demonstrates the essence of community the people of Ruby have exchanged for the elitist values of their oppressors. In 1929, when Haven was gripped by rocking pneumonia, Deacon and Steward's father, still able-bodied, rode out of town for supplies. Happening on a community ironically named "Pura Sangre," Big Daddy, as he was called by his sons, was stopped from entering the place by three Sac and Fox men, who warned him that entering would mean his death at the hands of racist whites (Morrison 1998, 153). A generation later, Deacon and Steward, who literally own the town of Ruby, foreclose on the house of Menus Jury when he cannot meet his mortgage more to stop him from marrying the "redbone" girl from Virginia than to claim the house (Morrison 1998, 278).

The name of the storied town Pura Sangre, or "Pure Blood," denotes on its most literal level the racist nature of the violence against blacks and Indians the Sac and Fox describe to Big Daddy to keep him from entering the town. "Pure Blood" is also an allusion to Ruby, where the blood of the convent women will be spilled ostensibly to keep the town "pure." Joining the towns "Pura Sangre" and "Ruby" in the color of blood, in the allusion to pure bloodlines, and in the act of violently shedding blood, connects the notion of a hierarchy constructed on racial purity to acts of destructiveness and violence. Outside Pura Sangre, the Sac and Fox who protect Big Daddy are different from the light-skinned blacks of the first "disallowing" and from the Indians who, because they could pass for white, would not associate with blacks in *Song of Solomon*. By aiding Big Daddy, the Sac and Fox demonstrate the communal values and resistance to colonial exploitation that saved Paul D. in the woods of Georgia, values that powerfully critique the oppressors' racial configurations practiced by the white killers in Pura Sangre and assimilated by the people of Ruby.

Ruby is gripped by growing conflicts arising from its self-imposed isolation, its stranglehold on an interpretation of the past that has no space for growth or reexamination, and a separation from the communal land values on which the original 8-rock town, Haven, was founded. Haven, after years of discrimination and denial, had been a refuge sought and worked for. Haven thrived because "families shared everything, made sure no one was short" (Morrison 1998, 109). Deacon laments the lost values of Haven as he considers that Ruby "was a far cry from the early days of Haven and his grandfather would have scoffed at the ease of it — buying property with dollars ready to hand instead of trading years of labor for it" (Morrison 1998, 111). This reflection intimates how the values extolled in the sermon of the first Macon Dead's land have been ignored by the men of Ruby, just as they had been by Milkman's father. Symbolically, with each material gain resulting from exploiting Ruby's physical land, the Morgans suffer losses that cannot be measured monetarily. Not the least of them is the death of Deacon's sons in Vietnam and of Steward's through miscarriages.

During Christmas season of 1976, the town's oldest member, Nathan Dupres, makes a speech before the yearly Christmas play and reveals a dream that defines the trouble of Ruby. Nathan describes Ruby as a place with honey in the land sweeter than any he knew of, a place where the dirt tasted like sugar (Morrison 1998, 204). But still he carries a sadness that he cannot quite name. He dreams of a Cheyenne Indian who identifies his sadness for him:

Was an Indian who come up to me in a bean row. Cheyenne, I believe. The vines were green, tender. The blossoms coming out all over. He looked at the row and shook his head, sorrow-ful like. Then he told me too bad the water was bad; said there was plenty of it but it was foul. I said, But look here, look at all the flowers. Looks like a top crop. He said, the tallest cotton don't yield the best crop; besides, those flowers the wrong color. They's red. And I looked and sure enough they was turning pink, then red. Like blood drops. Scared me some. But when I looked back he was gone. And the petals was white again. I reckon that sighting is like this here story we going to tell again this evening. It shows the strength of our crop if we understand it. But it can break us if we don't. (Morrison 1998, 205)

Morrison explains that "isolation, the separateness, is always a part of any utopia. The novel, she says, is her "meditation . . . and interrogation of the whole idea of paradise, the safe place, the place full of bounty, where no one can harm you. But, in addition to that, it's based on the notion of exclusivity. All paradises, all utopias are designed by who is not there, by the people who are not allowed in."[4] Denying kinship with the land and forbidding kinship with Menus Jury's "redbone" girl from Virginia ("redbone" is a reference to the black Indian communities of the South who form Milkman's ancestry in *Song of Solomon*) and refusing any who they defined as outsiders, the people of Ruby maintain the borders of their "paradise" with guns, with money, and with racial oppression that mirror the tragedy of their own historical experience.

The convent outside Ruby, like the town, is a community unto itself, but it is not "paradise" in the same sense. The significant difference is the permeability of its borders. No one is refused entry there, including heartsick and drunken Menus Jury, though its permanent inhabitants are women. Rigney (1991, 75) explains that when women live communally without men, as they do in all of Morrison's novels, "they operate outside of history and outside of the dominant culture, even outside of black culture." Morrison describes the convent as follows:

Well, Ruby has the characteristics, the features of the Old Testament. It's patriarchal. The men are very protective of their women, very concerned about their role as leaders. The convent, as it evolves, becomes a kind of crash pad for some women who are running away from all sorts of trauma, and they don't seek the company of men. They have been hurt profoundly by men, so that even though they quarrel and fight most of the time, they're in what they consider a free place, a place where they don't have to fear that they are the people to be preyed upon.[5]

The women of Ruby travel between the town and the convent seeking aid, refuge, and camaraderie. Unlike Ruby, which seeks to be "paradise," the convent harks back to the image of the original town, "Haven," a place where the past in all its pain can be remembered and confronted, but where the soil can be tilled for healing to take place. As Rigney (1991, 1) explains of Morrison's writing in general, the convent is a place that "disrupts traditional Western ideological confines and modifies patriarchal inscription." The convent is not "totally outside of the dominant signifying structure," connected as it is to Ruby by the road between them. It is "nonetheless an area on the periphery, a zone both chosen and allocated, which represents a way of seeing and of knowing that disconcerts and finally discounts the very structure which excludes it" (Rigney 1991, 1).

Even though the men of Ruby seek to murder the convent women, they cannot succeed. The women of Ruby who seek to prevent the massacre bear witness to the mindless and exploitive inhumanity of the act. When Lone Dupres, who taught Connie the arts of healing and of "stepping in" to reclaim a body from death, overhears the murder plot, she gathers the women against the men. After the killing is disrupted by the women, she becomes the bearer of the story that contests the one the men construct to place blame with the convent women for the violence the men chose to perpetrate. Lone's story forces the people of Ruby to lay the two versions of history beside each other and interrogate the version of the powerful men, who they would not previously question. Connie dies, but because of her protection and "stepping in," all the other women survive, each returning to the sites of their individual traumas, their lives prior to their times at the convent. They are wounded still but stronger and more capable because of their time with each other in the convent community.

Especially significant to the strength Morrison builds into the convent community structure is the ambiguity as to the race of the women. "They shoot the white girl first," is the first line of the novel, but reading the novel does not reveal with any certainty which girl is white. In addition, green-eyed Connie was taken by Mary Magda, the original Mother Superior, from the street garbage in which she sat in some unnamed city. They boarded a ship where "nobody questions Sisters devoted to Indian and Colored people paying cut-rate passage for three certainly not white urchins in their care, which stops in Panama and then returns to the states" (1998, 223). But Connie's racial background or origin is never clarified further. Morrison explains:

> Well, my point was to flag raise and then to erase it, and to have the reader believe — finally — after you know everything about these women, their interior lives, their past, their behavior, that the one piece of information you don't know, which is the race, may not, in fact, matter. And when you do know it, what do you know?[6]

Morrison's question is an essential question of the novel and one that forces the reader to acknowledge the dimensions of racially imposed identities manipulated with such power by the dominant culture throughout American history. In Ruby — in paradise — life is defined by race, but the convent is community because life is defined by shared experience. "*Paradise* is a complex story of epic proportions about becoming what you hate. The 8-rock people abused and turned away, learned to turn others away instead of making room."[7] Yet woven into the stories of *Paradise* are places of communion between cultures, the common ground that resists the damaging construction of racial hierarchies. These points of connection in the past and present, even in the darkest moments in the novel, serve to illuminate.

Sharon Holland (1994, 337) writes that, to find "a space let alone a subjectivity that embraces both African and Native identity is also an endeavor to develop an understanding of literature as a process of both emancipation and sovereignty, as we are seeking the history and lives of a people whose experience crossed both the barriers of enslaved bodies and lands." Morrison's fiction finds the space and subjectivity Holland defines. Morrison has said that in the end she writes about that which "has something to do with life and being human in the world" (Rigney 1991, 2). The stories in these three novels bear witness to the communion of African American and Native American peoples in the physical space of America. They resist the policing narrative that attempts to enact the burial of blood, bones, and stories in willfully naive images of the birth of a nation — "The land of the free and home of the brave." Pilate reveals in *Song of Solomon* that the memories of people you hurt, "they stay with you anyway" (Morrison 1977, 208). Learning the stories, as Morrison writes in *Beloved*, of "the disremembered and unaccounted for" (Morrison 1987, 275) provokes healing and a way forward; they are a means to first face and then eventually heal the divisiveness that racial hierarchies continue to perpetuate in America. Morrison's fiction pushes open more windows in America's house, and the breezes that blow through them are at once invigorating and life-sustaining.

Notes

1   The word "American," as I use it throughout this essay, applies specifically to the geographical space encompassing the United States, since, as one of my Ecuadoran students pointed out to a classmate who told him he was not American, "You guys don't live in the only 'America' on the planet."

2   Although I did not have space for it within this essay, the travels of the 8-rock families, their genealogies, and their Native connections in conjunction with the specific dates Morrison uses in explaining their migrations bear in-depth analysis in terms of underexplored Native–freedmen history.

3   Toni Morrison, interview with Elizabeth Farnsworth, *Newshour with Jim Lehrer*, 1998, online transcript, available at www.pbs.org/newshour/bb/entertainment/jan-june98/morrison_3-9.html.

4   Ibid.

5   Ibid.

6   Ibid.

7   Mick McAllister, personal conversation. I am indebted to Professor McAllister for engaging in in-depth discussion regarding my disagreement with the negative interpretation of Native presence in Morrison's *Playing in the Dark* expressed by Louis Owens in sections of *Mixedblood Messages* (1998) and *I Hear the Train* (2001). It was my initial discomfort with Owens's perceptions that led to the line of inquiry in this essay.

CHAPTER ELEVEN

Knowing All of My Names

TAMARA BUFFALO

~~~~~~~~

The Minneapolis artist Tamara Buffalo discovered that she had African ances-try when she was thirty-six. Here she recounts the discovery, the circumstances of her early life, and how these experiences influence her art. This article is re-printed with permission from International Review of African American Art *17, no. 1: 2000, 41–44.*

The common mistake most people made about me as I grew up was that I was black. Correcting everyone about my race was a constant chore for my adoptive parents. I was introduced as their adopted daughter. That was the immediate and necessary explanation for my dark skin and nappy hair. The fact that most white folks demanded more information irritated them. The words "adopted daughter" hung like a sign above my head with an asterisk next to it that said, "See parents for more information." I was a prize for my parents—well behaved, pretty, shy but smart—and that dark skin could be explained away. I was Mexican and Indian.

When my mother corrected those folks who thought I was black and told them, "No—Mexican and Indian," they often looked disap-pointed. The mixture of Mexican and Indian was not as captivating as African American, as having a "Negro" in room. Indians, at least in the Minnesota suburb that I grew up in, meant Western movies, buckskin, a vanishing culture, a dying race, maybe a public television special on Sunday afternoon. I didn't look anything like the light-skinned, straight-haired Pocahontas everyone pictured when the word Indian came to mind. I was too dark and my hair too bushy with tight curls.

Since I was mixed, I had no pure exotic blood to call forth, to conjure up. I was a disappointment for those curious white women standing in front of, or behind, my mother and me in line at the grocery store. Some would ask what tribe I was from and, my mother would tell them Minnesota Chippewa. Then she would launch into my arrival story.

I began to realize the importance my arrival story had in my family. It was told over and over to reaffirm the place of specialness that I held in my adoptive family as well as to prove how special they were to adopt me.

Like most adoptive children, I was not born, I arrived. I arrived fully formed and three weeks old. Sprung from the arms of a social worker. Better than left at a doorstep, better than found in a cabbage patch. Better than sold on the street. My arrival marked the beginning of my life with my foster family, and for them it was the beginning of my life. They controlled the story. They manufactured it and relayed it to anyone who asked.

Even now when I say I am adopted, people have no qualms about asking very personal questions. I've thought of just handing our cards that read:

> Yes I have found my birth family.
> Yes it was hard growing up.
> Yes I am angry.
> Yes I am lucky.
> Yes I am still searching for meanings and reasons.
> Yes I am still here still standing, and yes I know who I am.
> Yes I have many names.
> One of my names is adopted.
> One of my names is abandoned.
> One of my names is rescued.
> One of my names is discovered.
> One of my names is owned.
> One of my names is Ojibwa.
> One of my names is Mexico.
> One of my names is Africa.

The Arrival Story

Everyone wants to hear it. It's normal to be curious about such a life-changing moment, you can argue. No one can blame you for wanting to know, for maybe even wanting to be there when I arrive. You want to stand next to the car when the social worker gets out. She is holding me, a tiny, prematurely born, dark brown baby. You want to see how she walks so carefully up to the house of my new foster parents, who will eventually adopt me.

You want to hold the door as she and I walk into the house. She shakes the blanket to make sure I am in there and laughs. You stand next to the couch as my twelve-year-old foster sister sits down and smoothes out the skirt of her dress. She's handed the small squirming bundle of unruly black hair and tiny brown limbs. I lie in her arms, quiet, my almond-shaped eyes wide, watching.

My foster mother cries; my foster father signs all the necessary papers, and the world is a bright, happy place. There you are, watching my new family embrace me and I am safe and instantly loved and you rush to open the door for the social worker as she leaves and as your hand reaches the doorknob the social worker turns to tell my foster parents:

"I know she's dark, but we've done the blood test, and she doesn't have a drop of Negro blood in her. She should be very adoptable." She waves.

Thirty-six years later, my Ojibwa uncle tells me that I am related to a black man named George Bonga. He gets up from his chair and finds a book and shows me the picture of that famous black Indian.

My brother gives me a family tree, and there are over fifty people named Bonga in my list of relatives. My great-grandmother was a Bonga.

I grew up listening to the story of my arrival in the new land called no history. I grew up listening to the story of my arrival to a house on the street called adoption.

I grew up listening to my various names: Adopted, Mexican, Chippewa, Brown, Nappy, Outside, Motherless, Nigger.

Maybe the social worker was told to lie; maybe she believed there was a blood test. My parents believed it and repeated the story to me. I told it to my young friends who made that common mistake of thinking I was a Negro. I stayed out of the sun and straightened my hair. I

A Blind I Can C. Mixed media collage by Tamara Buffalo confronts stereotypes about Native Americans and African Americans. *Used by permission of The International Review of African American Art, Hampton University Museum.*

The Singer. Painting by Tamara Buffalo engages ceremonial meanings of the mask. *Used by permission of The International Review of African American Art, Hampton University Museum.*

avoided rain and anything else that would make my hair go back to that huge mass of tight stubborn curls.

One of my earliest lessons in life was growing up in a white family, being a part of a white family and yet not being part of them at all. I was both inside and outside at the same time. So I think that I was primed from an early age to understand how two or more things can be true at the same time.

Up until I was eighteen, I had never met another Indian person. I knew nothing about Native people. But I had a piece of paper as an enrolled member of the Minnesota Chippewa tribe, and I felt responsible to someone somewhere who had come before me. The piece of paper was a clue to an eighteen-year-old mystery. The mystery of my brown skin. A door opened up inside of me. I knew I was more than a piece of paper.

My uncle Larry once told me that Indians did not believe that adopted children had to give up one family to belong to another. The children simply became a part of both families. Not either–or but both. And when I arrived on the doorstep of my Indian family, already grown, they embraced me as a lost child that had returned.

My journey was not unique but typical. So many of us had been stolen from our home places and raised to hate the skin we wore. So many of us had fought back to love ourselves and each other.

I was raised by a white family who said they loved me. They told me that I was just like them. Then when I was five we moved out of our North Minneapolis neighborhood because too many Negroes were moving in. We moved to the all-white suburbs. My parents told me our old neighborhood was no longer safe and that this all-white suburb was the best place to grow up.

My parents continued to reassure me and anyone else who cared to know that I was not colored, not Negro. They had been told there was a blood test to check for Negro blood and that I had passed it. I was theirs, their adopted daughter, and if there was a question of race, they had proof: the mythical blood test. I knew they loved me and that they were afraid of all dark-skinned people, and the mirror said I was dark-skinned. So I knew that I was loved and not loved at the same time.

I noticed something whenever my family and I went to a place where there were non-white people. The brown folks looked at me, and sometimes they would even try to claim me. One East Indian man said, "Is she from India?" An Asian woman asked if I was one of those "Korean

War orphans." Mexican folks claimed to see my Mexican nose or eyes. Black people looked at me, too. But they didn't lay claim to me; they rarely even came up to my parents. Mostly they just took notice of me. Not like white people who stared and gawked. Black people stopped what they were doing and took notice. They looked me straight in the eye, and usually they nodded hello. Just one quick nod. It always happened. Sometimes I saw concern or sorrow in their eyes when my mother dragged me away from them. Sometimes they would try to talk directly to me. Catch my attention. Their smiles, their nods meant: We see you. You are dark like us. It meant: We know you. It meant family. In that sea of white faces that I lived in every day, every so often a brown or black face looked at me and saw me and said with a nod or a glance that I was known. It was an acknowledgment of my humanity.

Throughout my life, I got that small nod, slip of a smile that said I see you, you are human. They saw my skin and my humanity at the same time. All those small nods and tiny smiles, often behind my parents' back, was like food to a starving person, but I did not know I was starving. All I knew was that I was suffering in my wrong skin with my wrong hair.

I didn't look like an Indian. I was wrong as an Indian. Even though my parents told me I got my curly hair and dark skin from some mysterious Mexican father, all I knew was that I was wrong, no matter what explanation was given.

But I believe, with all my heart, those slight nods and small smiles and deliberate glances were love. Somehow it was love. And it was that love, combined with a hundred other kinds of love, that saved me. Every smile, look, glance that loved my small brown face saved me from utter oblivion. It made me real. Their smiles told me I did not have to be white to be human. Their nods told me I did not have to "look" more Indian to be human. Their acknowledgments said, "Just as you are, just as you are."

The second experience that brought me here to this place of love and celebration was working with a group of Indian women. These women were from many different tribes. They were from all walks of life; some of them, like me, had been raised as adopted or foster children. Some had grown up on reservations; others had always been in the city. They were all shapes and sizes, and they were all colors.

Every day I went to work and saw every kind of beautiful brown skin that you could imagine. I watched them smile and weep. I watched

Artist and writer Tamara Buffalo at her desk. *Used by permission of The International Review of African American Art, Hampton University Museum.*

them struggle and overcome or sometimes succumb. I watched them and in them I saw my own nose, my own mouth, my own almond-shaped eyes, my own brown skin, my own curly hair, my own broad shoulders and wide hips, my own gestures and facial expressions.

I saw my own beauty in them, and it was very important that it was a daily experience. No book, no conference, no special camp, no twelve-week support group, no college course could have given me the same daily, hourly experience of breathing the same air as these women. I was home. I was family. And I saw in them how beautiful Native women could be, no matter what their color, what their tribe, what their history. From that wonderful daily experience of being around Native women, maybe I know how it might have been to live with my mother, my grandmother, my sisters, my aunts. Maybe I could have breathed in the air of their being and, having loved their brown skin, known how to love my own. But I know now.

My art has grown out of a need to express myself outside of the world of words. I saw a mask by the wonderful Native artist Lillian Pitt called "The Singer," and I felt a connection to the idea of the mask as a ceremonial object rather than just a metaphor or a disguise. The singer's mask that I painted came out of my desire to show my own mask of creativity; my mask serves the ceremonial need to express beyond words my multiple selves.

A Blind I Can C is a work about the stereotypes of African and American indigenous people. It's my attempt to again escape the boundaries of words and meanings and provoke discussion. Stereotypes surround us. We breathe them in on a daily basis. I tried to pick images that were not necessarily offensive but nonetheless based on stereotypes.

Now I can tell you these stories and show you this artwork and know that I am not different, not something less. I am not a specimen, not an oddity, but at home among family.

CHAPTER TWELVE

After the Death of the Last

Performance as History in Monique Mojica's

Princess Pocahontas and the Blue Spots

WENDY S. WALTERS

~~~~~~

Performance and human silence are strategies of survivance.
— GERALD VIZENOR (1994, 16)

When I die / I won't stay / Dead. — BOB KAUFMAN (1965, 31)

Performances of History

The concept of diaspora inherently contradicts the idea of the native
"breaking" ties with the homeland — geographically, spiritually, or culturally. Where assimilation and extinction have been predictable outcomes for Native American and African American historical figures, the
opportunity arises to consider how such colonial narratives affect the
concept of diaspora. Colonial narratives have largely ignored the concept of diaspora, choosing instead to depict an inevitable teleology —
belief in the purposeful movement of a narrative toward a certain end
— of colonial dominance to valorize the colonial project through the
retelling of history. These teleologies of assimilation and extinction do
not account for a colonial subject's ability to maintain connections with
her indigenous culture, spirituality, cosmology, or nation. They also
fail to acknowledge the power of the colonial subject to invent other
histories, including ones in which the colonial power is defeated

through sustained resistance. This essay, while not overtly about the African experience, extends the discussion of the African diaspora into Native American spaces to encourage a reconsideration of the ways in which the invention and performance of narrative can contribute to a people's cultural survival. By juxtaposing African American and Native Canadian narratives of cultural survival within a discussion of performative identities, we can start to see how distinct colonial narratives overlap and inform each other. Such a comparison also shows us how deeply rooted the supposition of white superiority is in those narratives that justify assimilation and extinction as inevitable outcomes of cultural progress.

When dramatic narrative is conveyed discordantly with known and accepted narratives of colonial history, the opportunity to recognize powerful moments of political and cultural resistance arises in the act of performance. These moments, however, must be measured against a history of performance in which race or culture serves as the primary signifier of identity. In performance and essays, Coco Fusco has documented centuries of ethnographic "performances" that falsely represented the cultural history of black, Native, and Asian peoples;[1] testify to their limited intellectual capacity; and assume an inability to adapt to changes borne of modernity:

> Since the early days of European "conquest," "aboriginal samples" of people from Africa, Asia, and the Americas were brought to Europe for aesthetic contemplation, scientific analysis, and entertainment. Those people from other parts of the world were forced to first take the place that Europeans had already created for the savages of their own Medieval mythology; later with the emergence of scientific rationalism, the "aborigines" on display served as proof of the natural superiority of European civilization, of its ability to exert control over and extract knowledge from the "primitive" world, and ultimately, of the genetic inferiority of non-European races. (Fusco 1995, 41)

Because so many of these images of racial or cultural inferiority evolved out of anthropological spectacles of race or reenactments of colonial history, stalwart alternatives have seldom been incorporated into mainstream performance culture. Perhaps the discourse of racial inferiority often goes unchallenged in performances about history because the known history does not offer opportunities for resistance beyond assimilation, psychosis, spiritual dissolution, or death.

In Monique Mojica's (Kuna/Rappahanock) play *Princess Pocahontas and the Blue Spots* (1991), Pocahontas must first relive the colonial historical accounts through which she is more commonly known. However, after acting out her own ultimately tragic role in colonial history, she evolves into another, more highly politicized self who defies the narratives that have defined her only through her relationship with the European colonists.[2] To better understand the significance of the play's reinvention of history, we first need to consider the means by which the politics of representation may be negotiated, debated, and ultimately revised in performance.

According to Ngugi wa Thiong'o, performance is the "representation of being—the coming to be and the ceasing to be of processes in nature, human society, and thought" (Ngugi 1997, 11). If performance can be a representation of being, as Ngugi suggests, subject to the unexpected designs of nature, humanity, and thought, then it has the potential to be made anew despite the history that may previously have defined it. Elin Diamond (1997, 1) describes performance as "embodied acts, in specific sites, witnessed by others (and/or the watching self)" and "the completed event framed in time and space and remembered, misremembered, interpreted and passionately revisited across a pre-existing discursive field." Both acknowledge an ebb-and-flow quality to performance—a kind of discourse, though not entirely verbal—that is both created and erased, made and unmade.

Ngugi and Diamond also recognize the presence of history in any performance, which cannot be eliminated in this movement between action and reflection on that action. Performance is implicated with the history that helps to define its place, identity, and politics, as well as the history of performance itself. Diamond (1997, 1) asserts: "Every performance, if it is intelligible as such, embeds features of previous performances: gender conventions, racial histories, aesthetic traditions—political and cultural pressures that are consciously and unconsciously acknowledged." If, as Diamond suggests, a performance embodies qualities of previous performances, then it is unlikely that it could bring forth a history wholly unscripted, nascent, or unknown. But if a performance is indelibly tied to a legacy or ancestry of discourse and performance, it is possible that it may also possess the quality of being first, inchoate, or initial. A performance that demonstrates this duality will be called, from here on, a *performance of history*.

Performances of history are didactic representations of past public events and human affairs that address the intricacies of the human experience typically not accounted for in written history or folklore. Through a depiction of an individual or collective character's emotional journey through a historic event or circumstance, a performance of history teaches about the past without catering to a limited perception of that character's humanity that has been circumscribed primarily by the distinction of race. To this point, Kimberly Benston (2000, 10) attests that blackness, for example, "establishes and yet also destabilizes the very ground of its own figuration, thus simultaneously asserting and dislocating its own privileged status as arch-signifier of African American expression." When a character in a performance demonstrates the ability to create an alternative history to that which is commonly known, a new chronicle of the past is invented through a visual actualization of authorship. The performance also provides a unique opportunity for a character to create a new identity, one that is not defined by the colonial imagination. Within this framework, the colonial imagination is that which prescripts Native or black characters with expectations of behavior, physicality, and intellect, all of which are used to devalue their humanity.[3]

In a performance of history, a character is only tied to expectations legitimated by the colonial imagination insofar as they can be revised or dismissed. In her analysis of Spiderwoman Theatre's *Reverb-ber-ber-rations*, Rebecca Schneider (1997, 169–70) calls this phenomenon "counter-mimicry" or a "turn upon the historical representation of the native, upon colonial mimicry of native identity." Beyond providing an occasion to define a "cultural self" as a counterpoint to the colonial self, a performance of history also grants a colonized character the opportunity to create her own image outside of that known history. This is a symbolic assertion of her (and metonymically all those she represents in the colonial narrative) right to self-determination. If a character is endowed with the autonomy to create an image of herself within the time and space of a performance, that image has the potential to become material in the imagination of the audience. A character can evolve out of colonial subjecthood through the kind of invention that is performed as authorship.

Authorship allows a historical character the opportunity to refute subjecthood, but only after first acknowledging the defining qualities and characteristics that make her knowable.[4] This is true for not only for a performed black identity but also for Native, Asian, and Latina/o characters whose race significantly informs the range of experience and action available to them. When a character's actions are limited by prescriptive traits used for racial identification, she often develops no further than stereotype allows. If we consider the negative implications with which a stereotype in general might inform a performance, perhaps we can begin to unpack the complicated ways in which the racial stereotype restricts a character's experience and action. Emily Apter's work on the status of Orientalism in late-nineteenth-century French gay and lesbian theater takes up this issue of the stereotype in broad terms. Apter addresses the innuendo it brings: "The notion of *imprinting*, whether visual or discursive, remains a key to understanding the negative reputation of the stereotype as that which stamps the complex subject with the seal of reductive caricature and/or bad habit" (Apter 1996, 17). This "imprinting" functions as the ontological prescript by which the legitimacy of a performed identity is judged. For a character that is primarily identified by race, the reductive caricature or bad habit appears as a lack of humanity. Inherent in this prescript is the certitude that the stereotypical identity is fixed, recognizable, and consumable for the spectator who has identified her. Apter reminds us that the "association of the stereotype with 'permanence' and 'fatality' implies that the stereotyped character is flawed, even deviant, insofar as it contains a groove of moral decadence veering towards the death drive" (Apter 1996, 18). The imminent destruction of the stereotype, whether through death, spiritual dissolution, assimilation, or psychological illness has become a common trope in the spectacle that is the performance of racial identity.

To this point, Ward Churchill notes how the racial stereotype fits into a larger discourse of colonialism. He cites the saturation of specific and repetitive representations of Indian identity. For example, the repeated portrayal in movies and plays of the Plains peoples' battles with soldiers and settlers in the years between 1850 and 1880 has resulted in characterizations that have been "carefully contrived to serve certain ends" (Churchill 1998, 167). Such stereotypes are replayed to reify and legitimate a violent and repressive colonial history that has not yet been accurately represented in performance. Churchill argues that it is important, in order to combat these stereotypes, to represent Native peoples outside of a colonial history. The most damaging stereotypes are the ones that suggest that there is no Native identity or history beyond the agonisms of Indian–European interaction: "Cinematic Indians have no history before Euroamericans come along, and then, mysteriously, they seem to pass out of existence all together" (Churchill 1998, 168). The infrequency with which Native characters are portrayed outside a context of colonialism brings us back to Apter's notion of the visual or discursive imprinting that is implicit in the stereotype. But while Apter celebrates the subject "that makes itself *be* through the enactment of objectification" (Apter 1996, 18), Churchill calls for the transformation of Native stereotypes "from reel to real in the popular imagination" (Churchill 1998, 206). It is the latter effort that most closely relates to this study of the performance of history.

The challenge of representing "the real" in a performance of history lies in uncovering the limitations placed on a character's experience and actions according to racial classification. To meet this challenge, it must be acknowledged that the conflicts over a person's "right to define his or her culture and icons" are also relevant to a character who aims to move beyond colonial subjecthood (Fusco 1995, 31). Fusco notes that "symbolic representation is a key site of political struggle," and as it refers to the depiction of "the real," there is no fixed concept of race that can sufficiently represent a character's identity (Fusco 1995, 31). As the conceptual artist Adrian Piper's work on "passing" has pointed out, there are too many points of signification that can be deemed "unacceptable" or "inappropriate" if a character's experiences or actions veer from the teleology prescribed for her in the colonial imagination. If a character invents her identity and history instead of performing the teleologies that have previously defined each, then perhaps we can consider the performance of history to be a new strategy for cultural survival.

Challenging Stereotype

In recent years, there have been many groundbreaking works that challenge commonly known stereotypes and colonial histories of African American and Native Canadian characters.[5] The work of Suzan-Lori Parks is particularly noteworthy in its ability to deliver reinvented history without relying on or formally acknowledging the history it casts aside. She explains,

> The mission of many plays is to tell a *known history*. But there are a lot of things black people have done that haven't been written down — haven't been chronicled, are not remembered. There is a lot of history that has fallen

through the gaps, the cracks; we read these events as having never happened. Those unchronicled events are what I am interested in writing about. (Parks 1994, 242)

Parks's strategy is akin to Mojica's in her displacement of a fixed and known history for the kind of indeterminate and emended history that can be invented through performance:

> Parks challenges the supremacy of the actual as an index of truth by privileg- ing iteration over explanation. . . . Riffing on particular lines and phrases allows Parks not only to connect characters but to evoke the historicity of metaphor, the way in which metaphors stored in the cultural image bank are borrowed and resisted at different points in time — sometimes deliberately, sometimes less so. Each iteration surveys the distance that has been traveled since the last iteration in terms of both time and consciousness. Parks mines the gap between what has happened and what has not happened, what is lost in memory and what is over-familiar. (Frieze 1998, 528)

Crossing that "gap" between lost memories and the "over-familiar" can then be an exercise in revision, reinvention, and reimprinting that al- lows a stereotype to demonstrate new strategies for cultural survival. We might also consider such a performance of history to be praxis, as Françoise Lionnet defines *métissage*, or the inter-referential reading on the nature of a particular set of texts that "cannot be subsumed under a fully elaborated theoretical system" (Lionnet 1989, 8). The praxes of authoring identity and history are informed by the discourses of perfor- mance, postcolonial studies, history, and literary studies, and are like- wise replete with contradictions in how a character's identity is per- ceived by an audience as well as how she imagines it.

A character's invention of identity during a performance of history is an extremely effective method of claiming authority because it chal- lenges the implied passivity that constitutes her subjecthood. It re- affirms her right, and that of those she represents, to transform identity and history.[6] It is rare, however, to find a character that possesses the kind of inventive vision that allows her to assume authority over her subjecthood. But a character who does own such a vision and creates a new history or identity during a performance of history achieves the authority of a writer, which I will term *initial authorship*. If a character uses this power to create history, she can rewrite her fate as well as that of the colonial history of the people or community she represents. If she employs it to invent identity, her self-autonomy is momentarily ensured by the contingency of her own authorship. The act of writing history, then, becomes a testament to a character's humanity and survivability in these performances of history, especially those that challenge accounts of Native people's and black people's participation in their own oppression and degradation.

Spiderwoman Theatre's 1997 production of *Sun Moon and Feather* at the American Indian Community House in New York showed me how a character's reinvention of history can have significant and profound implications on the way that history is experienced by an audience when the "natural" course of history is no longer satisfactory.[7] The play deeply influenced my understanding of how a character's self-conscious demonstration of remembering could result in a reinvention of history. The main characters are the three women playing themselves as younger sisters — Lisa Mayo, Gloria Miguel, and Muriel Miguel — whose memories are performed on three different levels: acted out on stage, projected in home movies against a backdrop on stage, and played in audio recordings of a discussion about poverty. These memories chronicle the experiences of three sisters growing up poor and often hungry in Brooklyn and address the challenges of being Kuna in a community that did not understand the culture. At one point, Gloria and Muriel recount their feelings of isolation:

> *Gloria*: (Sings) We three were all alone
> *Muriel*: (Talks) We were all alone
> *Gloria*: (Sings) Living in a memory
> *Muriel*: (Talks) Ah memories
> *Gloria*: (Sings) My echo, my shadow and me
> (Spiderwoman Theatre 1996 [1981], 303)

Since I saw this performance, I have been intrigued by the idea of three sisters living together in a memory, as if they shared the same vision of the past. I was also affected by the idea of a memory being made up of an echo, a shadow, and each of the character's recollection of herself. The three sisters, by remembering collectively — or, perhaps, by imagining that they do — assert authority over how history defines their collective character. The home movies and tape recordings suggest that their "imagined memories" are made up of projections of the self thrown out to the world, aurally and visually. They also suggest that each character's demonstration of imagination could similarly affect the way that history is portrayed. In *Sun Moon and Feather*, the power of imagination provides the sisters with an opportunity to assume roles that, in the colonial imagination, have not been designated as appropriate for them with regard to race, gender, or body type.[8] But most important, the sisters wield authority over their relationship with the past.

As in *Sun Moon and Feather*, the characters of *Princess Pocahontas and the Blue Spots* acquire intuition by listening to each of their own genealogical, cultural, and spiritual ancestors, who in turn provide them with a more seamless vision of an "imagined memory" than they could muster out of their own experience.[9] With regard to this strategy of visualizing the past, Edouard Glissant (1989, 64) offers the colonized writers of the Caribbean as a case in point: "Because the collective memory was too often wiped out, the Caribbean writer must 'dig deep' into this memory, following the latent signs he has picked up in the everyday world." Such a collective memory, much like the one the sisters share in *Sun Moon and Feather*, becomes a formidable vision of the past that is invented and realized though the performance. But to achieve this revisioning, a character must have a clear sense of those teleologies of history and identity that in the present delimit her past:

> Although American society has defined progress as a focus on the future, we must now return to the past in order to place ourselves in that history and understand how we got where we are. As we try to grasp at crucial parallels and tease new stories out of them, *new alternative chronicles surface* ; these are the latest examples of how collective memories, those storehouses of identity, once activated, become powerful sites of cultural resistance. (Fusco 1995, 36; emphasis added)

A performance of history "situates" a character in "the past" while making new strategies of cultural resistance available. As articulations of history that are not overdetermined by the agonisms endemic to colonization, these new alternative chronicles demonstrate cultural resistance by declining to comply with the presumptions of the colonial imagination. This kind of progress is the result of a black or Native character's refusal to be defined by only her responses to colonialism. Perhaps the connection between a character's embrace of new alternative chronicles and cultural resistance, as Fusco has articulated it, is not yet completely obvious to the reader, but, as Fanon once requested, "Here the reader is asked to concede certain points that, however unacceptable they may seem in the beginning, will find the measure of their validity in the facts" to surface in the forthcoming pages (Fanon 1967, 18).[10]

Rejecting a Bipolar Dialectic

When the relationship between non-white and white characters is considered too simply, in terms of dynamic oppositions, the ontological possibilities available to those characters are severely limited. This *bipolar dialectic* situates and defines classifications of racial identity by the fact that they are impossibly linked. As racial categories are not located in a specific culture, the dichotomy is constituted of color categories that appear to be fundamentally opposite, generally positioned as other versus white. Although there are ways in which culture can be defined within these racial groupings, an underlying assumption is the incompatibility of a white identity with any other color-defined category — red, yellow, brown, or black.[11] From within this dialectic, it is difficult to locate a tenable position between the two categories.[12] Perhaps this is because, as Benston (2000, 9) has shown us, race is better conceived of as "a mediated, socially constructed practice, a process and not a product of discursive conditions of struggle."

Implicit in this bipolar dialectic is an assumption of Native/black inferiority and white superiority. Nativeness and blackness are defined in opposition to whiteness; the resulting co-dependence creates categories of identification that give credence to a hierarchy of white superiority and Native/black inferiority. Identities within each respective category of racial classification must respond to the assumptions endemic in such a hierarchy. Any acknowledgment of these assumptions, even to the contrary, has the effect of reinforcing them. This position is best articulated by Glissant, who assures us that "one cannot transcend in one's consciousness (even if it is only to take the opposite view) what is nothing but the expression of a deficiency, of an experienced inadequacy" (Glissant 1989, 202–3).

To invalidate this perceived inadequacy, an inevitable result of a bipolar dialectic, a character must provide a new teleology of cultural survivance and self-determination beyond the colonial narrative for the racial/cultural group whose history is being represented. Such a demonstration of sovereignty in a performance of history is a strategic proclamation of the eternal end of colonial subjecthood.[13] It is an articulation of initial authorship through performance that both embodies qualities of previous performances through the dismantling of established narratives and initiates a discourse about the representation of being beyond teleologies of death, psychosis, spiritual dissolution, and assimilation. Vizenor calls such demonstrations "postmodern simulations" of the "postindian warrior," which "undermine and surmount, with imagination and the performance of new stories, the manifest manners of scriptural simulations and 'authentic' representations of tribes in the literature of dominance" (Vizenor 1994, 17). This discourse begins with a character's enactment of authorship.

Unbecoming a Princess in
Princess Pocahontas and the Blue Spots

Pocahontas is largely revered for her gallant intervention in the execution of Captain John Smith, an English colonist of the first Jamestown settlement. The legend of Pocahontas has appeared in storybooks, plays, films, and pageants by non-natives who laud her compassion and empathy for the colonialist project of the English.[14] She is also known as one of the first Indian women to convert to Christianity and marry an Englishman. For those who believe Native people are tragically fated to disappear from existence or become a part of white society to survive, Pocahontas's legend provides an optimistic model for integration and cultural assimilation.

The legend of Pocahontas is derived from an account in John Smith's *The Generall Historie of Virginia, New-England, and the Summer Isles* (1624). According to Smith, he was captured by the Powhatan Indians on the coast of what is now known as Virginia, and his execution was ordered:

> Having feasted him after their best barbarous manner they could, a long consultation was held, but the conclusion was, two great stones were brought before Powhatan: then as many as could layd hands on him, dragged him to them, and thereon laid his head, and being ready with their clubs, to beate out his braines, Pocahontas the King's dearest daughter, when no intreaty could prevaile, got his head in her armes, and laid her owne upon his to save him from death: whereat the Emperour was contented he should live to make him hatchets, and her bells, beads, and copper; for they thought him as well of all occupations as themselves. (Smith 1624, 49)

The valiance with which Pocahontas saves the life of Smith and the intimate gesture that is his rescue have inspired many romantic interpretations of Smith's story. Pocahontas's embrace of Smith suggests that they are close as lovers, even if Smith's account does not directly state that idea. For centuries, the story of Pocahontas's selfless sacrifice has made her an object of desire in the colonial imagination (thus also setting her up as an attractive character for Englishwomen to play, even though as a Native woman she was considered to be of a "wild" nature). Her surprising loyalty to Smith, who she chooses over her own father, makes her assimilation all the more valuable in a colonialist plan of integration. That she was willing to sacrifice her own life to preserve Smith's is perceived as the most remarkable aspect of her character. It is implied that even an "uncivilized" Pocahontas recognized that she should shield Smith with her less valuable brown skin. These messages underpin the legend of Pocahontas, and as Rayna Green (1975, 700) reminds us, "Whether or not we believe Smith's tale — and there are many reasons not to — we cannot ignore the impact the story has had on the American imagination."[15]

While Pocahontas represents a non-native ideal of Native womanhood, much of her personal history has been elided in the legend, including her true name, Matoaka. "Pocahontas" was a nickname meaning "playful little girl," and she was the daughter of Powhatan, the chief of the Powhatan Confederacy, one of the largest coastal organizations of Native Americans prior to the Revolutionary War. In 1613, while she was still a teenager, Pocahontas's husband, Kocoum, was killed. Shortly thereafter, while visiting with a neighboring tribe, she was kidnapped by the English. Accounts of her kidnapping are generally left out of the legend of Pocahontas, although it is briefly noted in Smith's narrative (Smith 1624, 112). Smith suggests that she was taken because it was known that she was her father's favorite, and the colonists felt that such an action would elicit Powhatan's compliance with their demands for corn and supplies; Captain Samuel Argall of the Jamestown colony had offered a copper kettle to anyone who could capture her (Smith 1624, 112). Kidnapping was a method commonly used by the English to force negotiations for the tools, weapons, and food they were not able to provide for themselves. When Powhatan refused to pay the ransom, the eighteen-year-old Pocahontas was left to remain in the Jamestown colony for many months. And even though she did help to save the life of Smith, there is no evidence that she fell in love with him or wanted to marry him (Sharpes 1995, 231). But while waiting for rescue or an opportunity to escape, she learned English and other customs of the colonizers. Eventually Pocahontas was baptized with the name Rebecca after converting to Christianity, and on April 5, 1614, she married John Rolfe, a tobacco grower, who eventually became the secretary of Jamestown (Sharpes 1995, 234). In 1616, the Rolfes and their young son moved to England. Lady Rebecca met with many dignitaries there, including King James I and the bishop of London. Because of her widely known acquaintances with royalty, she earned the title "Princess," but soon after her arrival in England, she became ill and died. Lady Rebecca was buried in March 1617, just off the Thames at Gravesend, a few miles outside London.[16] The garden at the parish church of St. George is named for her.

While Pocahontas's real life was complicated with personal losses and betrayals, the legend of Pocahontas represents a "peaceful" and "appropriate" union of opposing racial and cultural identities as an unanticipated benefit of the colonial project. The legend also allegorizes the conquest of the Americas, with Pocahontas's body representing the lush and uncultivated landscapes, bountiful natural resources, and fecund soil that eventually submitted to the masculine, coercive power of the British colonists.[17] Her marriage to Rolfe and self-sacrifice on behalf of Smith thus may be read as testaments to the righteousness and justness of the English invasion.

Pocahontas epitomizes the ideal of the Indian princess, a dehumanizing portrait of a Native woman's identity that requires her to betray the customs and values of her own culture: "To be 'good,' she must defy her own people, exile herself from them, become white, and perhaps suffer death" (Green 1975, 704). As in the virgin–whore dichotomy, the often light-skinned princess is posed in opposition to the stereotype of the brown-skinned "squaw" who refuses to assimilate and is incapable of doing so. In spite of her demonstrated resistance to colonization, the squaw is not necessarily free from a dehumanizing portrait. Green asserts that "as the Squaw, a depersonalized object of scornful convenience, she is powerless. Like her male relatives she may be easily destroyed without reference to her humanity" (Green 1975, 713). And just like the princess stereotype, the squaw is a passive subject in her own history. *Princess Pocahontas and the Blue Spots* focuses on several characters that embody the princess stereotype, including the mothers of the Métis and La Malinche. The different characters of Pocahontas are also performed as separate selves—Storybook Pocahontas, Lady Rebecca, and Matoaka. Each retells a part of the legend and reveals that in the struggle for Native survival, the participation of all Native women, including the princesses, is essential.

There are thirteen transformations in *Princess Pocahontas and the Blue Spots*, which also function as scenes in the play.[18] Each reveals a stage in the evolution of the princess stereotype and operates as a separate vignette. The play opens with a contestant from the 498th Miss North American Indian Beauty Pageant, Princess Buttered-on-Both-Sides. In the program notes, she is described as "one of the many faces of the Trickster, Coyote," but her mutability is not instantly apparent (Mojica 1991, 14). Mojica explains the trickster as one who moves

> between here and the spirit world, for the benefit of mankind. It represents constant change, transformation, moving on; Trickster becomes a shit-disturber when things become too static and can use sexuality, profanity and lewdness to achieve this. It mirrors us so we can see our follies—pushes us past them, pushes us on. Trickster is neither human nor animal, male nor female, good or bad; Trickster can be Coyote, or Weesagetchak, or Nana-bush—different mythic characters of its aspects. (Cashman 1991, 23)

It is the trickster who introduces us to the multiple incarnations of Pocahontas and helps direct our attention to each of their "follies."

Each scene in the play features the evolution of a princess character, generally from a Native stereotype to a more self-determined identity. At the onset of the play, Princess Buttered-on-Both-Sides demonstrates her many talents by dancing to the song "Sacrificial Corn Maiden," the theme from the film *The Good, the Bad and the Ugly*, and the Mazola Corn Oil jingle; she also sings the song "Indian Love Call." Each tune draws attention to popular, demeaning, and commercialized stereotypes of Native women. In addition, Princess Buttered-on-Both-Sides performs a dance of the "Hollywod Injun" variety. She also proclaims her love for an unseen Captain John Whiteman, who has loved and left her behind: "For the talent segment of the Miss North American Indian Beauty Pageant, I shall dance for you, in savage splendour, the 'Dance of the Sacrificial Corn Maiden,' and proceed to hurl myself over the precipice, all for the loss of my one true love, CAPTAIN JOHN WHITEMAN (*swoons*)" (Mojica 1991, 19). At the end of the dance, she throws herself off Niagara Falls, while shouting the punch line "GERONIMOOOOOOOOOO!!!!!" (Mojica 1991, 19). Her suicide parodies the romantic and tragic portrait of the Native woman. It is a "show" of ardent loyalty to the colonists and an inherent lack of self-identity. Princess Buttered-on-Both-Sides's performance demonstrates the pervasiveness of commercialized stereotypes of Native women and a need to create an identity that exists outside of a colonial context. Her "act" also foreshadows the inevitable death/extinction of that kind of Native female identity. The struggle for the survival of other Native women is foreground by her suicide, and the issue of their contributions to sovereignty is broached but not named as such.

This initial encounter with Princess Buttered-on-Both-Sides highlights the dilemma Native women faced while engaging with the colonizers and attempting to stay loyal to their own people. The melodramatic suicide, a result of her inability to choose one set of cultural kin, is an all too familiar trope that is also deeply ingrained in the legend of Pocahontas.[19] As the trickster, Princess Buttered-on-Both-Sides introduces this melodrama to contrast with the real, untold histories of the various princesses. Thus, *Princess Pocahontas and the Blue Spots* is a performance of history that chronicles the evolution of tragic princesses who die — culturally, spiritually, or physically — into women who live.

The second scene/transformation features Contemporary Woman No. 1, who, like Princess Buttered-on-Both-Sides, is standing "on the precipice" between death and survival. To Contemporary Woman No. 2, Contemporary Woman No. 1 says that there is "no map, no trail, no footprint home" suggesting there is no easy path back to the past (Mojica 1991, 19). She then quotes a man who once said to her, "It is time for the woman [*sic*] to pick up their medicine in order for the people to continue." She asked him what that medicine was, and he responded: "The women are the medicine, so we must heal the women" (Mojica 1991, 20).[20] But what does it mean to heal the women, and how are they the medicine? Where previously the identity of Native women has been co-opted through commercialization, assimilation, and religious conversion (so aptly demonstrated by Princess Buttered-on-Both-Sides), healing means restoring the authority of Native women so that they might be able to define their identity, history, and participation in the future of Native survival. But before this healing can take place, some of the roles women have played in Native history must be reconsidered. Only then can the true value of women as the "medicine" be realized.

Thus, we are introduced to the complexities of Native women's history by characters from the present day. Contemporary Woman No. 1 washes herself with water she has been carrying in a bucket. She then stoops down to give birth. As she cradles her newborn child, she explains the significance of the "blue spots" named in the title of the play:

> When I was born, the umbilical cord was wrapped
> around my neck and my face was blue.
> When I was born, my mother turned me over to
> check for the blue spot at the base of the spine —
> the sign of Indian blood.
> When my child was born, after counting the fingers
> and the toes, I turned it over to check for the blue
> spot at the base of the spine.
> Even among the half-breeds, it's one of the last
> things to go. (Mojica 1991, 20)

In this description, the umbilical cord acts as a physical connection to the mother, one that supports the child's life through the transition that is birth. Likewise, the blue spot has the power to connect a child to the generations before her and thus imbue her with the power of her ancestors. The blue spot is an essential marker of identity, history, and community.[21] Its presence demonstrates the continuity of Indian identity especially in the face of integration, assimilation, and shifting national borders.

Contemporary Woman No. 2 refers to the transformation of the Native woman into a princess, all of which occurs through the colonial gaze:

> Princess, Princess, calendar girl,
> Redskin temptress, Indian pearl.
> Waiting by the water
> for a white man to save.
> She's a savage now remember —
> Can't behave! (Mojica 1991, 21)

In syncopation, Contemporary Woman No. 1 quotes Cherríe Moraga: "The concept of betraying one's race through sex and sexual politics is as common as corn" (Mojica 1991, 21). This idea relates specifically to the mothers of Native–European children and is developed through subsequent princess characters in the play. From Pocahontas to La Malinche to the Mothers of the Métis, the idea of forsaking one's people for a romantic union with a European colonist underpins each story.[22]

The idea of women betraying their race through sex is further explored in the third transformation. La Malinche is called forth, and Contemporary Woman No. 1 curses her for her disloyalty. The harsh words hurt La Malinche deeply, and she retorts, "They say it was me betrayed my people. It was they betrayed me!" (Mojica 1991, 22) She reveals that her name is Malinali, not "La Chingada" or "the fucked one," as she is often called. Malinali speaks to her children, whose bodies bear physical traces of their Mayan ancestry — black hair, eyes set wide apart, broad feet, and the telling blue spot on their posterior (Mojica 1991, 22):

> You are the child planted in me by Hernán Cortez who begins the bastard race, born from La Chingada! You deny me? (*whips volcano, throws it over her head, emerges from under it, downstage right*) I was the face of Malinali Tenepat. I see this face reflected in the mirror. Mirror my eyes reflecting back at me. Reflecting words. It is my words he wants you to see. . . . I am the only one who can speak to the Maya, to the Mexica. It is my words that are of value. (Mojica 1991, 23)

Traditional accounts of Malinali's life suggest that as Cortez's wife and translator of his false intentions to the Mayans, she helped to lead her people to slaughter and conquest. But there is another way to interpret the significance of her words: They reflect who she sees in the mirror. Her words define who she is, despite all that is said about her by others — including those who renamed her La Chingada. She goes on to explain how it is her ability to "translate" that gives her words power: "I can change the words. I have power. . . . Smart woman. I am a strategist. Dangerous woman" (Mojica 1991, 23). The power to change the words and the history that is made of them is the same that Mojica exercises in rewriting the history of Pocahontas. This is initial authorship, and it constitutes La Malinche's first step toward asserting a strategy for the survival of herself and her descendants.

Christened by the Spanish Doña Maria, La Malinche is also called "princess." She recounts the legend of betrayal that follows her name — that she was easily seduced by Cortez and thus became an accomplice in the death of her father, Moctezuma, and her people. She reacts to that history by offering a slightly different version: "I was a gift. Passed on. Handed on. Like so many pounds of gold bullion, dragged out of the earth, dragged out of the treasure rooms of Moctezuma. Stolen! Bound! Caught! Trapped!" (Mojica 1991, 24). Malinali's perceived betrayal of her people, for what has been called love, is challenged by the fact that she did not choose her union with Cortez. She also reveals how profoundly the massacre of her people changes her. After witnessing their slaughter by her husband's army, a fiery vengeance grows within her, and she becomes a volcano:

> I spit, burn and char this earth. A net of veins binding me to you as I am bound to this piece of earth. So bound. A volcano, this woman. . . . I turn to tree whose branches drip bleeding flowers. Bleed into this piece of earth where I grow, mix with volcanic ash and produce fertile soil. *Born from the earth, fed with my blood, anything alive is here alive because I stayed alive!* (Mojica 1991, 24–25; emphasis added)

In her fury, Malinali asserts the importance of transformation and the value of the cycles of death and rebirth in sustaining life. She reminds us of the value of her life in the survival of her descendants and, accordingly, the value of Native women to the continued survival of Native people.

In the next transformation, a Musician and a Sacrificial Virgin appear out of the volcano that was La Malinche. The musician implores the Virgin to "JUMP NOW!" She replies, "Have you got the wrong Virgin!" and exits for something she has left on the stove (Mojica 1991, 25). Princess Buttered-on-Both-Sides returns in her place. She introduces herself as Pocahontas and sings a doo-wop love song to the aforementioned Captain John Whiteman. With this song, she demonstrates her willingness to choose a white man as her lover, to adapt to the customs of the colonizers, and to forgo her spiritual beliefs for Christianity:

> Captain Whiteman for you, I will convert,
> Captain Whiteman, all my pagan gods are dirt.[23]
> If I'm a savage don't despise me,
> 'cause I'll let you civilize me.
> Oh Captain Whiteman, I'm your buckskin-clad dessert. (Mojica 1991, 26)

The song suggests that Pocahontas is something to be consumed, a sweet treat literally to be eaten after a hard day's colonizing. At the end of her song, Princess Buttered-on-Both-Sides reveals that, like La Malinche, she calls herself by other names: Storybook Pocahontas, Lady

Rebecca, and Matoaka. Each appears as a separate incarnation of Pocahontas and characterizes a stage in her evolution from subject of legend
to an initial author.

The first Pocahontas encountered, Storybook Pocahontas, is described as "the little Indian Princess from the picture books, friend of
the settlers, in love with the Captain, comes complete with her savage-
Indian-Chief father" (Mojica 1991, 14). Her four proclamations reveal
the entirety of the Pocahontas legend:

> 1) NO! (*hands overhead, on knees*) He's so brave his eyes are so blue, his
> hair so blond and I like the way he walks.
>
> 2) DON'T! (*arms cradling Captain's head*) Mash his brains out! I don't
> want to see his brains all running down the side of this stone.
>
> 3) STOP! (*in the name of love*) I think I love him.
>
> 4) Oooh (*swooning, hands at cheeks*) He's so cute. (Mojica 1991, 27–28)

Storybook Pocahontas appears simple-minded, which is shown in her
repeated use of imperatives. But if her initial statements are read without the subsequent explanation of what she means, she appears to be
saying "No, don't, stop, oooh —" Indeed, she willingly participates in
her seduction and exploitation. Storybook Pocahontas is a characterization of *only* the familiar legend of Pocahontas and offers very little
insight into what it really means to be a princess. But the following
characters of Pocahontas articulate what difficulties are incurred while
they attempt to survive as such.

The next character of Princess Pocahontas enters with a Troubadour
who is singing a ballad based on her legend. The Troubadour reveals
John Rolfe's growing affection for her and his desire to marry. At that
moment, Pocahontas becomes Lady Rebecca and puts on the lace cuffs
and collars worn by the wife of a nobleman. She recites the Apostle's
Creed and explains her relationship with her husband: "I provided
John Rolfe with seed to create his hybrid tobacco plants and I provided
him with a son, and created a hybrid people" (Mojica 1991, 31). However, like La Malinche, Lady Rebecca also tells a story of being given
away: "What I owe to my father? Waited I not one year in Jamestown, a
prisoner? One year before he sent my brothers to seek me. 'If my father
had loved me, he would not have valued me less than old swords, guns,
or axes: therefore I shall dwell with the Englishmen who love me'"
(Mojica 1991, 31). These lines reveal the pain, disappointment, and

anger that may have affected Pocahontas's decision to marry Rolfe. The fact that she was exchanged for common goods discounts a history that says she betrayed her race for romance alone.

Rebecca Rolfe is quite aware that her becoming an Englishwoman was instigated, in part, by a criminal act: "Now see you here, I wear the clothes of an Englishwoman and will disturb you less when I walk. Here, I am Princess and Non Pareil of Virginia. I am Lady Rebecca. For me the Queen holds audience. Treachery, Captain, I was kidnapped" (Mojica 1991, 30). As has already been mentioned, Pocahontas's kidnapping is often left out of her legend, and as a result she appears to be complicit in her own colonization. Throughout the scene, Lady Rebecca speaks with great devotion about her conversion to Christianity, Jesus Christ, and the Holy Ghost. She says she does not remember how to plant corn, one of the things for which she was originally stolen, and she wishes never to return to the place where she was once known as Matoaka. Perhaps she believes that a new name and religion will confirm her value to the Europeans and that they will not forsake her because she so evidently belongs with them. It is quickly apparent, however, that Lady Rebecca's concerns for her own life are minimal. When she speaks about her imminent death, she says, "It is enough that the child liveth!" referring to her only child, Thomas (Mojica 1991, 31).

What he *liveth* to do, however, is to betray Powhatan's legacy by helping the English to acquire the lands surrounding the Jamestown colony. Rebecca Rolfe's own life is cut short by illnesses she acquires in Europe, and in her weakened state she sees that there is no mark, no trail, no footprint home. Unlike the suicide performed at the beginning of the play by Princess Buttered-on-Both-Sides, Rebecca Rolfe has an actual death, not a symbolic one. This is significant because it is Lady Rebecca that is enshrined at St. George's Cathedral, the Pocahontas whose transformation into a European "Lady" made her worthy, in the minds of the English, of the title "Princess."

Lady Rebecca's story of being given away, like La Malinche's, can be compared with the story of the Indian Mothers of the Métis, portrayed in their transformation as a collective character. These Cree women recount their relationship to the French and British settlers of Canada's northwestern provinces during the mid-eighteenth century.[24] They teach their European husbands how to hunt, fish, trap, make canoes, and string snowshoes to survive the long northwestern winters:

Among my sisters I am the best moccasin maker. I have three sisters, one older and two younger — but I'm the best moccasin maker. That's why I am here. They came, mistegoosoowuk, they came and told my father they had no one to help them. They had no one to make moccasins, to cook for them to show them where to pick berries, to make canoes. . . . No one to help them. No one to help them. . . . Among my sisters I am the best moccasin maker, so my father sent me. (Mojica 1991, 41)

That this woman's claims to be "the best" moccasin maker suggests that she recognizes her own value. Perhaps, then, she wonders why she was given away to a European man who could not possibly know how important she was. Once again, there is the sense that she has been betrayed and denied the opportunity to contribute to the survival of her people.

Meanwhile, the Métis women suffer through the long winters with men who do not know how to provide even for themselves. They catch diseases that go untreated:

> We die from,
> smallpox, syphilis, tuberculosis, childbirth.
> We claw at the gate of the fort or we starve and
> freeze to death outside.
> We birth the Métis.
> When there is no more to trade, our men trade us.
> Fathers, uncles, brothers, husbands, trade us for
> knives, axes, muskets, liquor
> My husband didn't have a good hunt this season. (Mojica 1991, 46)

Just as Lady Rebecca was traded for "old swords, guns, or axes," the Métis women become commodities when resources are scarce (Mojica 1991, 31).[25] The women tell us that many Métis marriages dissolve when European women come to the outpost settlements and claim the white men for their husbands; the Indian women lose their status as wives and, along with their children, are discarded by the men for whom they worked and cared (Mojica 1991, 46). Because the children of the Métis women are not recognized as Indian or European, they must become a new people.[26]

While the Mothers of the Métis and La Malinche have shown the continuance of Native identity through their children, it appears that Pocahontas's story ends with the death of Lady Rebecca. But the Troubadour offers the audience an opportunity to prolong the story of Pocahontas:

> And so here ends the legend
>   of the Princess Pocahontas —
> Fa la la la lay, fa la la la la LELF —
> if you want any more, make it up yourself.
>   (Mojica 1991, 31)

That the audience is invited to make up an end to the story suggests that Pocahontas's legend is unfinished as it has been told. When a young Matoaka suddenly runs across the stage and climbs into a tree, it appears that Pocahontas has decided to make up an alternative ending where a younger, more spirited version of herself gives life to her character after Lady Rebecca's demise. As she imagines herself before marriage, before being kidnapped, and before sailing to England, the possibility of finding a mark, a trail, or a footprint in the direction of home *becomes* possible. By imagining Matoaka as the final actor in this performance of history, Pocahontas achieves a life that exists beyond colonialism and death.

Matoaka's presence at the end of the sequence of Pocahontas characters becomes more important when she reveals that she is on the verge of her own transformation. She describes her forthcoming participation in the girls' portion of the deer clan dance. Matoaka explains that it is an event of great significance, especially the painting of her face. With this, she has the power to change her visage and embodies the power of both the trickster and a woman: "I have to find my own colours and mix my own paint. My mother says I have to wait until I know and I'm really sure that that's how I want my face paint to be. Because that will be my paint and my face and forever. It's very important" (Mojica 1991, 32). The mask Matoaka creates represents a fixed portrait of identity, but unlike the princess or the squaw, it is not synecdoche; it comes with authorial power that extends beyond the image of the self it provides. Choosing the appropriate colors of paint for the mask is an exercise in initial authorship, an act of sovereignty over her person — but it is also a restorative gesture to Pocahontas's legacy. Through the character of Matoaka, Pocahontas is reconnected to the possibility of her own physical and spiritual growth. Once again, she experiences transformation, something that is impossible to do in the unchanging state in which the storybooks kept her. The ritual of maturation is left to the audience's imagination and is not performed on stage.[27] It is personified, instead, by the character Ceremony, who is "the instructions of the Grandmothers, she is the fast, she is the songs, she is the paint, she is the sacred blood, she is the initiation" (Mojica 1991, 16). Matoaka paints the top of her feet and her arms while facing toward each of the four directions Ceremony dances. Moving toward her first, and then by growing still, Matoaka completes her transformation.

Matoaka is arguably the farthest evolved incarnation of Pocahontas in spite of the fact that she is also the youngest. She has a keen awareness of her connection to the world she lives in and is able to articulate her connection to it:

> Becoming woman / child — open up / Look!
> All around your world, everything's alive
> everything is growing, everything has a spirit,
> everything is breathing,
> everything needs water, everything needs sunlight,
> everything needs rest. (Mojica 1991, 34).

Of all that is alive, Matoaka is a part. And as the living world receives nourishment from the water and sunlight, so will Matoaka. She is connected more deeply than the Pocahontas characters before her; thus, it is fitting that she is the last one to appear. Unlike the other characters of Pocahontas, Matoaka is instinctually compelled to grow, develop, and change. And as she evolves, she undoes the legend of Pocahontas by releasing all of her characters from the prison of their passivity. Matoaka returns to them their natural powers for transformation, reinvention, and growth.

When the Beauty Pageant Host returns to crown Princess Buttered-on-Both-Sides the winner of the 498th Miss North American Indian Beauty Pageant, it is now clear that what it means to be an Indian Princess is to survive abandonment, assimilation, and violent attacks on one's people. The Mothers of the Métis, La Malinche, and Pocahontas have shown how their "betrayals of race through sex" with European colonists were not only a result of their choices. Their value as Native women was determined, at times, by the exchange of tools, food, and weapons in the struggle for control of the North American lands. In these exchanges of women for goods, the women's power, humanity, and contributions to their people were forgotten. The final transformation of the play calls for the recognition of the importance of Native women in past and contemporary struggles for survival. This sentiment echoes in the Cheyenne maxim that closes this performance of history: "A nation is not defeated until the hearts of its women are on the ground — then it is done, no matter how brave its warriors, nor how strong its weapons."[28]

Princess Pocahontas and the Blue Spots offers a critique of the princess's relationship to geographical, cultural, sexual, and spiritual colonization. It revives the humanity of several princess characters of legend who, like Pocahontas, have been denied a history outside of or apart from their relationship with the European colonizers. Mojica accomplishes this resurrection without attempting to legitimate Pocahontas's humanity; it is offered as a given. *Princess Pocahontas and the Blue Spots* exposes a history of complex gender relationships within Native communities through the legends of Pocahontas, La Malinche, and the Mothers of the Métis. It emphasizes the importance of restoring agency to those women whose representation in colonial history has stripped them of power and focuses on the inimitable value of female characters in the continuing struggle for Native sovereignty.

After the Death of the Last

Lady Rebecca also might be considered the last figure of the original Pocahontas legend, who in death becomes extinct. There is no other woman after her who represents the gross assimilation of Native identity into European culture as well as Princess Pocahontas, no other woman whose skin is appropriated so readily by those who want momentarily to "act" Indian, whether in the present or in performances about history.[29] The death of the last means that there are no more to be killed, no others to interfere with the project of constructing history around the "defensible necessity" of colonialism. While colonial history survives after the death of the last, the character that had once been extinguished gains a kind of authorial autonomy that was otherwise denied. As we see in *Princess Pocahontas and the Blue Spots*, extinction then becomes liberation from teleology. Once Pocahontas's demise is incontrovertible, once she has no more deaths to act out, Matoaka is freed from worry over death. Instead, she may focus on the invention of her life. Thus, we might consider the death of the last to be another kind of extinction: the extinguishing of the conflagration fire that has forged the idealized character of Pocahontas. In the aftermath of ash, cinder, and smoke, a new identity is springing forth.

As I explained at the beginning of this chapter, my primary objective is to extend the discussion of the African diaspora into Native American spaces to encourage a reconsideration of the ways in which the invention and performance of narrative can contribute to a people's cultural survivance. But to make the intersection between these cultural contexts more apparent, it is important to consider how teleologies of death and extinction have also been reauthored within an African American context. Suzan-Lori Parks's plays provide a context. They are "both about and NOT about the 'black experience'; [they are] concerned with the stories her figures tell to inhabit their experience as they speak their way into history. In the telling, identities (including, but not limited to, racial) are performed, reinhabited, reimprinted . . . but never for the first time" (Drunkman 1995, 57). Parks's 1990 play *The Death of the Last Black Man in the Whole Entire World* focuses on the extinction of the African American man through various acts of demise. Like many of Parks's other works, including *The America Play* (1993), *In the Blood* (1999), and *Topdog/Underdog* (2001), *The Death of the Last Black Man* shows that "historical events and personages happen first as tragedy, second as farce, and thereafter as Theatre of the Absurd" (Drunkman 1995, 57). History becomes the "discursive whirl/world of the 'worl,'" and it provides a context for her characters to evolve out of history through their own efforts to invent, imagine, rewrite, and speak themselves into being:

> Slowly, barely perceptibly, Parks characters shed their ingrained ways of knowing: they begin to unlearn. Analysis of their own failure causes the characters to question ways of seeing, including their own. The retrospective questioning comes to a head in veiled epiphanies — critical visions which, for character and spectator alike, are revelatory but muffled. These fragmented visions do not burst in from outside the machine of the narrative; they are precipitated by its breakdown. (Frieze 1998, 529)

This breakdown of teleology promotes a vision of what exists outside of history, including that which may never have been spoken or written.

In *The Death of the Last Black Man*, we are introduced to characters whose names are deeply enmeshed in stereotype and caricature — for example, Black Man with Watermelon, Lots of Grease and Lots of Pork, Queen-then-Pharaoh Hatshepsut, and Old Man River Jordan.

Right away we learn that Black Man with Watermelon has just come to his death "yesterday today next summer tomorrow just uh moment uhgoh in 1317 dieded" (Parks 1994, 250). Already, time is set outside of chronological history, for it is not clear whether this death is foretold or in retrospect. Throughout the performance, Black Man with Watermelon continues to experience death in very different ways. His first death, death by descent, occurs when he falls twenty-three stories out of a "space ship." While the audience may not yet be aware of the scope of Parks's skill with challenging dialect or language play, it quickly become obvious that this space ship might also be signifying on the idea of being abducted by "aliens" via a slave ship. The second death occurs by the electric chair. Black Man with Watermelon says of the method of execution, "Uh extender cord 49 foot in length. Turned on thuh switch in I started runnin. First 49 foot I was runnin and they was still juicing" (Parks 1994, 256). And then, "First just runnin then runnin towards home. Couldn't find us. Think I got lost. Saw us on uphhead but I flew over thuh yard. Couldn't stop. Think I overshot" (Parks 1994, 257). In the third and final death act, Black Man with Watermelon thinks he is waiting for a train when in fact he is standing at the gallows:

> Put me on a platform tuh wait for a train. Uh who who uh whouh where ya gonna go now — Platform hitched with horses/steeds. Steeds runned off in left me swingin. It had begun tuh rain. Hands behind my back. This time tied. I had heard one of uh word called scaffold and thought that perhaps they just might build me one of um but uh uhn naw just outa my vocabulary but uh uhn naw trees come cheaply. (Parks 1994, 266)

While Black Man with Watermelon appears to escape his execution, we discover that he did not in fact at all escape death. Instead, it is the fact of his meeting death repeatedly throughout the play that allows him to be free. "When I dieded they cut me down. Didn't have no need for me no more. They let me go. . . . They tired of me. Pulled me out of thuh trees and then treed me then tired of me. That's how it has gone. Thats how it be wentin" (Parks 1994, 267). As "they" grow tired of watching the black man's body hanging from the tree, so also do they lose a fixation with killing him.

Black Man with Watermelon's ability to endure these attacks on his body, spirit, and humanity is tantamount to the kind of fortitude demonstrated by the women in *Princess Pocahontas and the Blue Spots*. It is significant that neither of these works makes a spectacle out of the death/murder of their principal characters. Such a demonstration would only serve to reaffirm the existing history and leave the kind of images that would not be easily undone by whatever resurrection of identity came next. Telling death repeatedly as opposed to performing death also nods to a history, oral or written, that must be authored if the characters will have any access to the future. The future, after all, is the only thing really at stake: Changing history is only significant for the effect that it has on what can be perceived as possibility in the future. At the end of *The Death of the Last Black Man*, Yes and Greens and Black-Eyed Peas Cornbread, one of Black Man with Watermelon's spiritual kin, makes this point:

> *Yes and Greens and Black-Eyed Peas Cornbread* : You will write it down because if you don't write it down then we will come along and tell the future that we did not exist. You will write it down and you will carve it out of a rock.
> (*Pause*)
> You will write down thuh past and you will write down thuh present and in what thuh future. You will write it down.
> (*Pause*)
> It will be of us but you will mention them from time to time so that in the future when they come along theyll know why they exist.
> (*Pause*)
> You will carve it all out of a rock so that in the future when they come along we will know that the rock did yes exist. (Parks 1994, 278–79)

It is not entirely clear whether "you" refers to the black man or to the audience. In either case, the implication is that the question of the ancestors'/spirits' existence in the future is dependent on the past; in writing "it down," there is the presumption of existence. The fact that this written record "will be of us" suggests that its essence emanates from a "whorl" of energy that justifies the "why" of the others who exist. Carved in stone, this history will attend to the fact of existence above all else, and the rock, like the words engraved in it, will matter because they are a part of this story. History survives through the foretold enactment of its materiality, all of which is now possible after the last death of the last black man in the whole entire world.

Where death historically has punctuated a character's attempts to resist colonial coercion, death does not erase Pocahontas or the Black Man from contemporary discussions in which their absence has served as justification for their assimilation. Without the dramatic trajectory of tragedy, Pocahontas and the Black Man are defined by internal, unknown, and continuously changing attributes that materialize during the performance. Their characters are not discernable loci of sentiment, romance, or disgust and thus cannot be occupied or inhabited by those who want to "perform" or "write" Nativeness or blackness.[30] A "dead" Pocahontas and Black Man reject ontological stasis because death is merely one moment in their enactment of identity.[31] In *Princess Pocahontas and the Blue Spots* and *The Last Black Man*, the characters refute tragedy with their confrontation of colonialism and reassert the power in performing history. Their invocation of examples of racialized identity that survive physical death and assimilation makes a new teleology of sovereignty inevitable.

Notes

1 In this chapter I use the term "Native" to reflect both Native American and Native Canadian peoples.

2 Monique Mojica was raised in New York City. Originally attracted to Toronto because of its reputation for having work for Native actors, writers, and directors, she has performed in numerous plays and written for Ontario television. *Princess Pocahontas and the Blue Spots* was developed through grants from the Canada Council, the Ontario Arts Council, and the Toronto Arts Council. Mojica is the author of the radio play *Birdwoman and the Suffragettes: A Story of Sacajewea* and is currently developing new work for solo performance. *Princess Pocahontas and the Blue Spots* premiered as a work in progress at the Groundswell Festival of New Work by Women in 1989 and was performed at Theatre Passe Muraille in 1990.

3 Instilling such a perception is an essential part of the colonial process, and when successfully enacted it is ultimately accepted and acted out by the colonial subject. "Recent work of some scholars and theorists, especially of the so-called 'invented traditions' school, has convincingly shown, if any demonstration or proof of the matter was required, that the political regime of colonialism in Africa and Asia *needed* to exercise hegemony by winning the 'hearts and minds' of 'native' populations who were not only numerically superior but also racially and culturally 'different'" (Jeyifo 1997, 112).

4 Before a character can move beyond the subjecthood ascribed to her by the colonial imagination, she must first realize how it reveals her. Often, the process of gaining this knowledge comes at the expense of her dignity, her humanity, and even, on occasion, her life. Adrian Piper recounts an experience about the discovery of her own subjecthood while attending the new graduate stu-

dent reception for her class in 1967. Piper was full of pride and arrogance for having the opportunity to pursue her intellectual interests in philosophy at one of the world's most elite universities. These feelings were mixed with a sense of awe about being in the company of those scholars whose work she had so greatly admired:

> To be in the presence of these men and attach faces to names was delirium enough. But actually to enter into casual social conversation with them took every bit of poise I had. As often happens in such situations, I went on automatic pilot. I don't remember what I said; I suppose I managed not to make a fool of myself. The most famous and highly respected member of the faculty observed me for awhile from a distance and then came forward. Without introduction or preamble he said to me with a triumphant smirk, "Miss Piper, you're about as black as I am." (Piper 1996, 235)

While Piper's looks did not meet the professor's expectations of blackness, it also appears that she did not perform her "blackness" in a manner that was recognizable to him. Many years later, another professor demanded that Piper explain why she identified as African American while on the job market. The professor asked Piper "what fraction of African ancestry [she] had" (Piper 1996, 238). This inquisition into Piper's blackness reflected the professor's disbelief that a legitimately black person could look and act as Piper did: "The implicit accusation behind both of my professor's remarks was, of course, that I had fraudulently posed in order to take advantage of the department's commitment to affirmative action" (Piper 1996, 238). Piper's experiences draw attention to the unstated preconceptions and expectations that confront a racialized identity in real life and that a "true" identity could be rendered false by a gaze blinded by speculation. Most notably, the invalidation of ontology by Piper's professor is a gesture of negation, conceptual obliteration for the sake of maintaining a hierarchical model of codependence. It is reasonable to assume that such presumptions are exacerbated in a performance where a character's racial identity constitutes the essence of her "character."

5 Strongest among these works are the plays *Almighty Voice and His Wife* and *The Indian Medicine Shows*, by Daniel David Moses; *Toronto at Dreamer's Rock* and *Someday*, by Drew Hayden Taylor; *Moonlodge*, by Margo Kane; *Sally's Rape*, by Robbie McCauley; *Toussaint*, by Lorraine Hansberry; *I Am a Man*, by OyamO; *X*, by Thulani and Anthony Davis; *Jelly's Last Jam*, by George C. Wolfe; *Remembering Aunt Jemima: A Menstrual Show*, by Breena Clarke and Glenda Dickerson; *I Ain't Yo Uncle*, by Robert Alexander; *Twilight* by Anna Deveare Smith; and *Death of the Last Black Man in the Whole Entire World*, by Suzan-Lori Parks. Each of these works offers a response to a known characterization of a black or Native stereotype or historical figure.

6 The theater and performance studies scholar Tejumola Olaniyan explains how invention in performance functions on at least two levels: "'Invention' is simultaneously a key category of dramatic / theatrical production and a sugges-

tive epistemological foothold into certain social processes. Thus 'inventing cultural identities' does not refer simply to the *cultural self*-definitions evident in black dramatic practice but also to the fact that subjectivity as such is inaccessible to us except through staging, representation, performance, invention, *work* — self-autonomy is never absolute and the space of the subject is always a contingent one" (Olaniyan 1995, 7; emphasis in original).

7 *Sun Moon and Feather* was Spiderwoman Theatre's original production at the company's inception in 1981. The title is taken from parts of the Native names of each of the three sisters (Spiderwoman Theatre 1996 [1981], 299). The hearts and minds of Spiderwoman Theatre are its three Kuna/Rappahannock sisters, Lisa Mayo, Gloria Miguel, and Muriel Miguel, whose plays explore history and identity. "The differences they explore, like the realities they explore, are rarely limited to the strictly visible ones" (Schneider 1997, 168). Spiderwoman takes its name from the Hopi goddess who taught the people to weave and said, "You must make a mistake in every tapestry so that my spirit may come and go at will" (Spiderwoman Theatre 1996 [1981], 297).

8 Throughout most of *Sun Moon and Feather*, the women that comprise Spiderwoman, Lisa Mayo, Gloria Miguel, and Muriel Miguel play little girls. Yet "these are big strong women. These are grandmothers, dressed in outrageous filigree and wielding a sharp reflexivity. There may be a feather in someone's hair, but there is also loud lamé, glitter, and especially in *Winnetou*, a purposeful polyester sheen. Working against the expectations that surround 'native performance,' Spiderwoman's actors enter the stage fully aware of the complexities in the identifications they are weaving" (Schneider 1997, 163).

9 A similar type of "ancestral ghosting" appears in Robbie McCauley's performance *Indian Blood*. In this "unrighteous fantasy," the cries of ancestors are heard as "the interior phantom voices, which seemingly call for revenge of an evil yet to be acknowledged" (Murray 1994, 38).

10 Thinking about how imagination affects a character's demonstration of initial authorship in a performance of history posed some fortuitous conceptual challenges for me. First, a character's implementation of imagination is a hard thing to quantify. Defining a character's use (or, sometimes, lack of use) of imagination seemed at times to be a daunting prospect, while other actions such as declaring identity, claiming territory — physical or cultural — or countering existing narratives seemed more easily recognizable and interpretable. Exploring how a character imagines an alternative chronicle of history required me to think about whether or not a given work effectively demonstrates that character's self-determination. Admittedly, this kind of speculation is dangerously close to a study of the artist's intentions. And on occasion, I have had to make some presumptions about the artist's vision, including whether or not it was fully realized. But I feel justified in this approach for one simple reason: The text provides the best residual information as to what is the artist's vision of cultural resistance.

11 The category of "black" implies color, not more specific details of geographical origin, urban or rural culture, mixed ancestry, lingering connections to specific peoples in Africa, and so on. Of course, a playwright may give a character a subcategory of identification, but when the agonism between black and white characters is a result of white racist aggression, black is posed in opposition to white.

12 The challenge of being "in the middle" of a bipolar dialectic is demonstrated by Adrienne Kennedy's *Funnyhouse of a Negro* (1964) and *The Owl Answers* (1965). Such an experience is also noted in Langston Hughes's play *Mulatto* (1960) and in Lisa Jones's *Combination Skin* (1986).

13 For the sake of this discussion, a performance of history that promotes self-autonomy is successful because it challenges characterizations that have been long dominant in the colonial imagination. This is not to say that all dramatic depictions of history should accomplish this precept.

14 James Barker's and John Bray's operatic melodrama *The Indian Princess, or La Belle Sauvage* (1808) focuses on the assimilation of Pocahontas and the transposition of her actual family with the family she finds in the English colonists. With John Smith acting as her brother, she is given sanction to choose a lover, John Rolfe, whose relationship with her, albeit romantic, is also undoubtedly patriarchal. George Washington Custis's play *The Settlers of Virginia* (1827), Robert Dale Owen's *Pocahontas: A Historical Drama in Five Acts* (1837), John Brougham's *Po-ca-hon-tas: or the Gentle Savage* (186?), and Elliot Carter's ballet *Pocahontas* (1969) also represent the meeting between Pocahontas and John Smith as the defining moment of her character.

15 Green's analysis of the Pocahontas legend finds many similarities between it and older European tales that romanticize an English adventurer in a strange, foreign land. She cites the ballads "Young Beichan" or "Lord Bateman" and the "Turkish King's Daughter": "The natives are of a darker color than he, and they practice a pagan religion. The man is captured by the King (Pasha, Moor, Sultan) and thrown in a dungeon to await death. Before he is executed, however, the Pasha's beautiful daughter—smitten with the elegant and wealthy visitor—rescues him and sends him homeward. But she pines away for the love of the now remote stranger who has gone home, apparently forgotten her, and contracted a marriage with a 'noble' 'lady' of his own kind. In all the versions, she follows him to his own land, and in most, she arrives on his wedding day whereupon he throws over his bride-to-be for the darker but more beautiful Princess. In most versions, she becomes a Christian, and she and Lord Beichan live happily ever after" (Green 1975, 699).

16 According to Sharpes (1995, 235), the Cherokee Nation brought soil from Virginia in 1984 and placed it over Pocahontas's grave so that she would always lie beneath the soil of her own people.

17 Disney's animated film *Pocahontas* employs the discourses of environmentalism, feminism, and multiculturalism to recuperate the colonial story. Pocahontas's story is an easy metaphor for the European conquest of land, which does not threaten the dominant culture's perception of their right to that land (Buescher and Ono 1996, 151).

18 The thirteen transformations also represent the number of moons in a calendar year.

19 Rayna Green elaborates on this phenomenon: "If unable to make the grand gesture of saving her captive lover or if thwarted from marrying him by her cruel father, the Chieftain, the Princess is allowed the even grander gesture of committing suicide when her lover is slain or fails to return to her after she rescues him. In the hundreds of 'Lovers Leap' legends, which abound throughout the country, and in traditional songs like 'Indian Bride's Lament,' our heroine leaps over a precipice, unable to live without her loved one. In this moment of political symbolism (where the Indian woman defends America) to psychosexual symbolism (where she defends or dies for white lovers), we can see part of the Indian woman's dilemma" (Green 1975, 704).

20 Mojica credits this statement to a speech Art Solomon gave at the Native Canadian Centre of Toronto in fall 1989.

21 The blue spot brings up the question of what physical sign demonstrates the continuance of Native identity. And how do those signs survive a Native woman's purported betrayals of her people? The blue spot immediately counters the assumption that the identity passed down by a Native mother could be erased by the European, colonial masculinity of the father. Where it has been assumed that the descendant of such a relationship would fully assimilate into the father's culture, another question arises: What did the mixed-blood children of the early North American colonies inherit from their Indian mothers?

22 In this context, the Métis represent a people of mixed Amerindian, French, and Scottish heritage.

23 Green reminds us of the importance of Christianity in designating a princess: "Nearly all the 'good' Princess figures are converts, and they cannot bear to see their fellow Christians slain by 'savages'" (Green 1975, 704).

24 "The Métis way of life had developed under the economic umbrella of the fur trade and in the isolation of the Northwest. . . . At Red River, in the District of Assiniboia, a Métis sense of identity crystallized with the troubles that developed after the coming of the Selkirk settlers in 1812 — in the clash of cultures but above all in the rivalries of opposing fur-trading interests" (Dickason 1997, 236). In 1845, a group of French-speaking Métis asked the governor of Red River to define their status as Natives as they were being treated as such with regard to the quality of their schools and impending economic hardships. The status of the Métis was debated in the British Parliament for years. In 1869, Louis Riel staged a blockade at the border to Assiniboia as a demonstration against the transfer of lands from Britain to Canada. It was a peaceful demonstration that forced the new dominion "to come face to face with the new nation whose existence it had steadily refused to acknowledge" (Dickason 1997, 43).

25 We are reminded of Princess Buttered-on-Both-Sides's earlier appropriation of the Mazola Corn Oil song, which now appears to signify *centuries* of the commodification of Native women.

26 According to Olive Dickason, in 1934 the Ewing Commission took into consideration the extreme poverty of the Métis. Many of the Métis were descendants of Indians who had entered treaties with Canada's national government but were not receiving treaty benefits. The Métis Association of Alberta described it members as "anyone with any degree of Indian ancestry who lives the life ordinarily associated with the Métis," which was the accepted definition until Alberta amended its Métis Population Betterment Act in 1940. At that time, the Métis became known as "a person of mixed white and Indian ancestry having not less than one-quarter Indian blood" (Dickason 1997, 335).

27 The director Floyd Favel Starr has discussed the importance of protecting the value of rituals in performance. He says that Native performance culture is the "upstream journey to the source of the river of our culture, country and ourselves" (Starr 1997, 85) and that the co-optation of Native customs by nonnatives is an act disrespectful to a "living" culture, as "revealing naturally weakens the sacred things" (Starr 1993, 140). To avoid this, he suggests reducing sacred dance or drumming to its most essential elements and using that essence in the performance instead. By avoiding the explicit demonstration of rituals, the enacted culture retains an elasticity and ability to critique mortified images that are incapable of conveying the full humanity of a character.

28 Monique Mojica, *Princess Pocahontas and the Blue Spots* (Toronto: Women's Press, 1991), 60.

29 A Washington's Birthday celebration in Laredo, Texas — the Princess Pocahontas Council, founded in 1980 — aims "to revise and promote interest in the customs and legends of the American Indian culture [and] . . . to enhance the role of Pocahontas and her court on the celebration" (Young 1998, 81–82). There is a special connection to the legend of Pocahontas for the people of Laredo, writes Elliot Young, because Pocahontas's marriage "to the white colonist John Rolfe echoed the friendly and benign model of miscegenation that characterized relations between Anglo men and Texas Mexican women. In the mid-eighteenth century, Rev. Peter Fontaine of Virginia suggested that intermarriage with Indians would solve the problem of the degenerating white racial stock caused by mixing with blacks. Fontaine's argument prefigured the racial logic that would unite Anglos and Mexicans in Laredo a century later: 'Now if instead of this abominable practice [mixing with blacks] which hath polluted the blood of many amongst us, we had taken Indian wives in the first place, it would have made them some compensation for their lands'" (Young 1998, 82–83). Although Indian participation in Laredo's politics and economy was aggressively discouraged, Indian women were considered a worthy acquisition for Anglo and Mexican men. Fontaine's racist and chauvinistic idea about "compensating" Native people for the violent confiscation of land also implies that such marriages would benefit Native peoples and that a Native woman's "value" would be increased by her relationship with white and Mexican men. Thus, the assimilation, consumption, and eradication of Indian women's identity were presented as a means of achieving local peace.

30 Ward Churchill cites three examples of how a "wannabee" desire can inhibit performances of Native identity, especially in works about history by non-natives. First, Indians are seldom invited to play themselves, and non-native actors often rely on dehumanizing stereotypes for information about how Indians look, speak, and act. Second, many roles are designed with no attention to cultural specificity and thus represent inaccurate, composite, or generic "Indians" in place of those whose history is supposedly being told. A lack of cultural specificity also allows for the interchangeability of whites and Indians in both the actual performance and the imagination of the audience. Whites and Indians "become indistinguishable in the end, following as they do a mutual trajectory to the same destination within the master narrative of an overarching 'American story'" (Churchill 1998, 186). An Indian character comes to represent the underdog position desired by non-natives or an incarnation of the natural "wildness" of the North American landscape. Neither of these characterizations sufficiently represents a legitimate humanity.

31 In *Princess Pocahontas and the Blue Spots*, there seems to be a conscious effort to avoid a fixed portrait of Native identity. Mojica avoids tragedy as the means for concluding the narrative. Where dramatic tragedy connotes the portrayal of serious events of great magnitude that are complete in and of themselves, the conflicts portrayed in these performances of history are not resolved. Though deaths do occur, and the outcome of the characters does not always meet their expected ideal, transformation is the predominant means for resolving the tension between opposing ideologies. The tragic form has hollowed out Native identity in performance. Perhaps it is the perceived expendability of a character's humanity that has allowed this to happen, or maybe it is the frequent portrayals of the death of Native characters that do not allow for a sufficient representation of life.

CHAPTER THIRTEEN

Katimih o Sa Chata Kiyou (Why Am I Not Choctaw)?

Race in the Lived Experiences of Two Black

Choctaw Mixed-Bloods

ROBERT KEITH COLLINS

~~~~~~~~~

Back then, they used to say, people looked at them all the time. Here you got this big beautiful black man and this stunning Indian woman. Now, I see the same problem. Kids telling my kids and grandkids that they are not Indian because I married a black man. He is also Choctaw. I guess if you are blind you can't see it. His mother was Choctaw and spoke the language. He speaks the language. It hurts to see my kids going through the same thing my folks went through. The only people who can tell you who you are are the ones that gave birth to you.

— MS. BEA, Foi tamaha elder, interview 1999

In the United States, people talk about Native American identities as if they were homogenous and synonymous with appearance. Most Native Americans, by the time they develop a "real" understanding of self, rely on these tropes as adequate signifiers of their indigenous ancestry. To the observer who assumes Native American identity from appearance, there may be considerable irony in individuals' claiming tribal-specific Native American heritages while their appearance is inconsistent with commonly held stereotypes about what a "real" Native American looks like. Consequently, such individuals are labeled "Wannabes." However, for the individuals involved, understanding self is anything but ironic. Confronting and coping with such stereotypes is but a basic attempt to navigate conflicting cultural systems of identification through the assertion of a self indelibly linked to family and how one was raised (Holland 1992).

The statement from Ms. Bea, a local elder, alludes to a much less discussed notion, particularly that of clashing systems of identification (i.e., the potential conflict that may arise between formulations of self inherited from family and culture and local American systems of recognizing race and belonging). Inspired by Russell Thornton's "The Demography of Colonialism and 'Old' and 'New'; Native Americans" (1998) and Raymond D. Fogelson's "Perspectives on Native American Identity" (1998), this chapter addresses the notion that identities, or understandings of self, are derived from two major practices in the process of identity formation: recognition and identification. Further, the motivating force behind an individual's assertion of a particular identity — even if it is inconsistent with his or her own skin color — may not be a desire to escape a feared identity but, rather, a basic assertion of an understanding of self formulated from understanding the lack of consistency that exists between these two practices.[1]

This chapter examines the lived experiences of Ms. Bea and Tuchina, two individuals of mixed black and Choctaw ancestry, as discernable from their life-history interviews. This study, conducted from 1998 to 2000, was designed to investigate Choctaw lived experiences in Foi tamaha (a fictitious name), a tranquil town along the Red River in southeastern Oklahoma on the northeastern Texas border.

The community is composed of about 1,500 individuals from various walks of life. Most individuals in the community are descendants of Choctaw families removed to the present-day states of Oklahoma and Texas from the territory encompassed by the states of Louisiana and Mississippi in 1838. Over half are unmixed Choctaws (full bloods) and *Chatalusa* (black Choctaws), or Choctaws of African American admixture. The remaining population consists of *Chatatohbi* (white Choctaws), or Choctaw individuals of Caucasian admixture, and unmixed African Americans, Caucasians, and Mexican Americans.

Local elders suggest that the community was largely segregated until the 1970s. Despite desegregation, whites and white Choctaws still largely live on one side of the Pacific Railroad tracks that separated the town. Full-blood Choctaws, black Choctaws, blacks, and "Mexicans" (Mexican Americans) live on the other. There are two churches in the community. One is Pentecostal on the "black" side of town that also provides Choctaw services; the other is an Evangelical Baptist church on the "white" side of town. There is also an elementary school, a high school, and a general store on the "white" side of town; they are used by all.

While Foi tamaha was unique on the surface in the number and diversity of residents asserting a Choctaw identity, it was not that different from other, non-Choctaw communities of the area. Families and extended families live close to one another. Elders are respected and often consulted for advice. Sunday is the day when individuals come together for community activities, after church. Adults work at various trades. Some are seasonal laborers, while others are local factory workers, waiters, maids, teachers, secretaries, office workers, lawyers, doctors, and so on. Children attend the local elementary school or high school.

One theme found in the interviews, particularly those with black Choctaws, dealt with experiences in which people negated the respondent's Choctaw ancestry because of their skin color. I used a person-centered ethnographic approach in which each respondent participated in at least fifteen open-ended interviews. This interview strategy differs from other life-history investigations methodologically because it enables respondents to reflect on and evaluate their life experiences over many sessions rather than recount a series of lived experiences according to conventional cultural practice in one sitting (Crapanzano 1977; Levy and Hollan 1998). This approach made it possible to follow their developing understandings of self and skills for resisting the negation of their Choctaw ancestry.

Nested at key moments in their life histories were references to the formative influences that interpersonal interactions had on understandings of self and decisions whether or not to assert themselves as Choctaws. Participation in their everyday lives enabled me to witness similar situations to those described in the interviews in which the respondents' skin color shaped how they were dealt with by others (Barth 1969).

Race and the Subjectivities of Native American Identity

The larger issue of this chapter is a perennial one for scholars of identity, particularly Native American identity: What motivates people in the United States to claim identities that are inconsistent with their skin color? This question is important because it lies at the intersection between social recognition and self-identification practices — or, more specifically, racial and cultural understandings of self — and is frequently discussed in social-science and anthropological studies of race, culture, and identity. Thornton alluded to the importance of understanding this intersection for Native Americans in his 1988 essay. Today, over 60 percent of all Native Americans are married to non-Native Americans. It is projected that within the next century, the percentage of Native Americans of one-half or more blood quantum will decline to only 8 percent of the total Native American population. Moreover, these individuals will likely reflect the intermarriages that produced them. Thornton's work further suggests that with the ever changing requirements of culture, blood quantum, collective names for recognizing Native Americans, and social and political criteria for establishing and maintaining legitimacy as a Native American, the appearance and heritage of such individuals will indelibly preclude them from ever living up to common images of Indianness (Thornton 1998).

In a similar vein, Fogelson's essay recognizes that such individuals may develop "an ideal identity, an image of oneself that one wishes to realize; a feared identity, which an individual thinks closely approximates an accurate representation of the self or reference group; and a claimed identity that is presented to others for confirmation, challenge, or negotiation in an effort to move the 'real' identity closer to the ideal and further from the feared identity" (Fogelson 1998, 41). This means, for example, that in a particular situation a Native American may have an ideal identity as a part-black traditional Indian, a feared identity as being seen only as black, a real identity of one-quarter Indian blood and raised away from tribal-specific culture, and a claimed identity as a person of one-half Indian blood who was raised "traditional."

Despite Fogelson's illumination of such components of identity, serious dissention continues in both the social sciences and anthropology as to the proper conceptualization of the relationship between race and understandings of self. In the social sciences and anthropology, both are discussed in terms of identity. To what extent does race determine identity? Is race — defined as knowledge of individuals based on skin color — intrinsic to the point that it defines and illuminates all American understandings of self? Or is race a secondary color-coded schema of convenience for recognizing human variation socially? How these questions have been answered has profoundly shaped how identity — especially Native American identities — has been investigated.

Where race is assumed to define and determine individual American identities as understandings of self, the focus is on individuals as members of particular racial groups. Most scholars interested in the relationship between race and identity take this approach (Omi and Winant 1994; Sanjek 1994). Its strength lies in its ability to illuminate the reality that many Americans have internalized racial identities to the point that their own understandings of self are oriented toward them. From these orientations of self, common experiences with racism, prejudice, and so on can be examined (Barth 1969; Roosens 1989; Smedley 1993).

However, where race is examined as a socially ascribed labeling based on skin color, the focus of analysis is on the salience of race to individual understandings of cultural selves. This approach can be found in much of the same literature, as well as in literature addressing issues related to mixed-race and Latino experiences with race in the United States (Rodriguez 1994; Zack 1995) A third approach — person-centered investigations of the motivational forces behind self-understanding and assertion during the life cycle — is far less common in the social-science and anthropological literature and is taken here (Holland 2001; Levy and Hollan 1998).

In the person-centered ethnographic approach that informs this case study, identity is taken as an understanding of self as an actor within culturally constructed systems of identification. Further, the assertion of a particular identity marks the point where the identification system(s) that one has been interacting with or ascribed becomes a context-dependent method for self-presentation (Holland 1992, 83). In the context of interpersonal interactions, the individual comes to understand and internalize the meanings behind identification systems. Internalized systems of identification enable a person to navigate the differences between what they represent to themselves and others. F. C. Wallace's and Raymond D. Fogelson's "The Identity Struggle" (1965) provides an example of the kind of study and perspective implied by the person-centered approach. Although Wallace and Fogelson do not discuss person-centered ethnography, their work illuminates how individuals acquire skills for resisting ascribed identities during the identity struggles. Wallace's and Fogelson's work challenges prevalent ideas then and now that people always understand self in accordance with social practice.

Furthermore, their work shows how understandings of self are negotiated through interpersonal interactions. Wallace's and Fogelson's work encourages attention to the meaning-making components of identity and the different images of self they can produce. These images comprise those of oneself in relationship to images of one's group, and vice versa. Also involved is the understanding of self or one's group intrapsychically to oneself or asserted to others. They found that while many Native Americans simultaneously live within racial and cultural systems of identification, the meanings and significance that these systems hold for them are actively negotiated and navigated by the individual during interactions with others, not passively and uniformly accepted. Thus, Native Americans not only learn what they represent to others collectively and individually as "Indians"; they also formulate understandings of self that are distinctly their own and relative to their tribal-specific heritage and family (both blood-related and fictive kin).

Case Studies

The lived experiences of these two black Choctaws illuminate why, when, and in what context they continue to assert themselves as Choctaws. Such practices can be seen in the lived experiences of other Americans, as well (Brodkin 1999; Rodriguez 1994). Examining the lived histories of individual black Choctaws within this community provides insight into how people navigate the opinions of others. The following case studies are excerpted from my dissertation fieldwork and are part of a larger, ongoing life-history project on black Choctaws. The major question probed in these life histories is: Why do they maintain an identity that is inconsistent with their appearance? These case studies will illuminate generational differences in how two black Choctaws formulate understanding of self and differences in lived experience according to skin color.

"*Sapokni Anumpa Tuk, Sa Chatah* (My Grandmother Told Me I Was Choctaw)"

Ms. Bea looks like a fair-skinned African American, despite her three-quarter-degree of Indian blood. She remembers being recognized throughout her life as everything from French to Mexican. Born and raised in Foi tamaha in 1920, she grew up speaking Choctaw as her first language and hearing the stories of hardship endured and life strategies developed by her grandparents. They had been removed by steamboat and then by foot from their homes in what is now Louisiana to Oklahoma. Her grandparents and parents chopped cotton to buy the land their home and small farm rests on. From this labor they were able to help their kin purchase tracts of land and make a living. She remembers her parents' home as loving, proud, and dignified. At home and in school she learned to speak English but dislikes speaking it to her children. This, she explains, is "why our children are calling one another black or white, etc., and forgetting about being Choctaw."

Interviewer: Throughout your life, who or whom do you remember as having had the biggest influence on who you are today?

Ms. Bea: Well, let's see. Before I left to work for this white family, my grandmother told me that even if some people see me as Indian and others see me as black, I ain't going to be nothing but Choctaw. I laughed when she said that, but I got hit. Back then you listened to your elders. Life answered your questions.

Interviewer: What did that teach you?

Ms. Bea: What do you think? Even after I went to work, I still came back home. And when I did, I spoke my language and did not act foolish. I kept on learning from that old lady—learning about our family, how my grandmother's brothers had died on the walk [Choctaw Trail of Tears] and from consumption [alcoholism], and how her sisters almost got raped and didn't because they learned to fight like men, what they went through because they were so tough, and to remember it so that it never happens again. Me and my grandmother sat over many meals and coffee speaking in Choctaw, worked the land together, told the stories, sang our songs—not Choctaw songs like these fools say today—the ones we made up. Some of them were old that we sang, don't get me wrong. I went to stomp dances, tick dances, dinners, and pow wows. Now, a pow wow—that is what Indians did, or Native Americans, like my grandbaby say today (laugh). I learned that I was never too grown to be without family, and to never give up or be ashamed of them, to forgive them when they messed up, and how to do this for my own kids so that they can handle being in this world and still be proud to be a member of their family, the way they look, and why they ain't like everybody else. . . .

The last White family I worked for did not know what I was. I would get ready to go to pow wows, and it was like I did something wrong. They would ask me why I was dressing like that. They looked at me sideways. Their father even said colored folk should not pretend to be something that they are not. That is, I should be proud to be what he thought I was—a nigger. Now, I am as close to full blood as you can get in these parts. That is even what it says on that stupid card (laugh). However, I do have African roots (laugh). His wife didn't know what to do. The worst, though, is I got the same thing at the pow wows, especially from folks trying to be more Indian than everybody else, or worst, these white Indians lookin' to see if you got some black blood in you. I wish they would learn that we aren't the same. *Pisa!* [See!] That is how you know who has been raised right. They won't tell you how to act. How can, say, a Lakota tell a Choctaw how to live? That is foolish. They ain't us.

Ms. Bea's words show that race became a part of her life through her interactions with the individuals she encountered. From her grandmother's words, she learned how to cope with these situations and how to understand her family and her responsibilities within it. That meant, in turn, that she learned how to raise children who could cope with the rigors of life, particularly those created by the various ways others would look at them and the potential judgments passed, not from hypothetical situations but situations that had already come to pass.

Later in the interview, Ms. Bea explained how these lived experiences affected the way that she raises her children and grandchildren today.

Ms. Bea: This is what I teach my grandkids, great-grand, and the great-greats. To them, I am *Hvshki chito* [Big mama]. They can't get these stories in school, because the teachers just care about their minds; I care about their soul. I have gone from Indian to Native American and from Negro to colored to African American. And still nothing has changed; it is still somebody else's opinion about what I should be and [be] called, and always it is different from who I am. Ain't nothing changed. When my mom was alive, you could be shot on sight if you were Chata [Choctaw] or black and did not have a place to be going. But back then, folks — like today — couldn't tell Choctaw from black, so they shot you anyway. You can sit and look at me and think that this old lady is crazy. But let me tell you about crazy: My grandson came home the other day talking about school. He says his teacher made him write about his family. He wrote that his family was Choctaw and put down the different people in his family. So I guess when she saw the paper, she took it and told him to stop making stuff up. She says that even though some of his family was Choctaw, he wasn't. He was black. My grandson says, I know I am black. But my grandmother tells me I am Choctaw, too, and to be proud. This made me happy, because I know he is coming up right. But, you see, this should teach him that blood doesn't divide itself; people divide it — in this case, people who have nothing to do with how he was brought into the world. But what is so terrible is that I went through the same thing. All I know is that the only people who can tell you who you are are the ones who gave birth to you.

Interviewer: *Akostininchi li* [I understand].

Ms. Bea: This is why I speak Choctaw to my grandchildren. I don't want them to forget. I see some of these kids my grandsons' age crying because their cousin, or some boy down the street, called them black dirt or something stupid like that. Choctaws have always been dark. So I bring them up the way I was brought up and hit them just like my grandmother did me so later on they won't cry and they won't try and be what other people want them to be! They will just be. They will know that who they are is determined by family, not somebody's opinion about how they look.

"*Katiomih osh Sa Chata Kiyou* (In What Manner Am I Not Choctaw)?"

The second respondent is a young woman whom I will call Tuchina ("three" in Choctaw). On appearance, she is a dark-skinned eighteen-year-old African American who just finished high school and is working as a clerk in a neighboring town. Tuchina's lived experiences illuminate the types of problems experienced by darker-skinned individuals in the community who assert a Choctaw identity. Despite her dark skin, Tuchina's blood quantum, if her family allowed her to enroll, probably would be a little more than half, because her mother is three quarters Choctaw and one quarter African American. Her father is one quarter Choctaw. She remembers being constantly confused while growing up because her family raised her to be Choctaw, and the people she interacted with told her that she was black and expected her to behave accordingly.

Interviewer: What was most confusing about growing up here?

Tuchina: Most people never look at me and think Indian, let alone Choctaw. Maybe it is because I am dark, my hair nappy, and my face is round. But I look like my grandmother, whose mother is the only enrolled member of our family. My mom does not think that enrollment is right and wants me to wait and decide. It seems that every time my friends, and now [my] co-workers, ask me about my family, I get into an argument. I work with whites, blacks, and Indians from up north and down here. But it seems every time I mention anything about being Choctaw, they say, "Here we go with the Indian stuff again." Even the Indians ask where is my card. When I tell them that my family does not want to enroll, they tell me: Then they are not Indian. Maybe this is a good thing. One lady making a comment says, "Why can't you people just be black?" You people? I almost got fired that day. I got too much of my grandmother in me.

Interviewer: What do you mean?

Tuchina: When I was little, I went with my grandmother to the store. While there, we ran into this sista [African American woman] who said, "Oh, what a cute little gal you have there." My grandmother said proudly, "*A* [Yes], she is my granddaughter." The lady looked at her funny and said when she grows up ain't nobody going to believe she your granddaughter. That was the first time I saw my grandmother hit another woman. After that, she told me never let anybody put me down. To this day I don't.

Another time, not too long ago, I went to the big pow wow up by Oklahoma City to dance. I didn't know what was going on, but this lady told me that I was disrespecting her circle. I have been dancing since I was ten. How was it her circle all of a sudden? She said that I was not Indian and needed to go home. I looked at her and told her to get out my face. I wanted to knock her out, but that would be disrespectful—to the circle, that is. But this isn't the first time this has happened or the second. It has happened all my life. Sometimes I wonder why I even bother to go. A lot of my folks don't go anymore, either. They say there is too many people not raised right at those places. So our cousins throw one every now and then. Not that how we are raised is the best way, but at least we tolerate people and don't put them down.

Tuchina further explained how her skin color is a problem for people not only outside of her family but also inside it.

Tuchina: Not too long ago, my little brother and I got into a fight because he called me cotton. Now, you know, that ain't right. Even though his daddy is light—half Ponca, I think—that man has got as much black blood as I do, if not more. I knocked his block off. Afterwards, I ask him why can't he stop being like these folks that go around telling other folks how to act. That ain't right. Mama [grandmother] did not raise us like that. But he hangs out with these so-called Indians. And they ain't all from around here. Some are Cherokee and others from around Montana or something. They don't like me. Maybe that is a good thing, but they can't make me into what they want from what they say.

During the interview, Tuchina explained that she thinks that having to convince people of her Choctaw heritage is making her a mean person. In a follow-up interview, she summed up how she copes with this situation. "I keep it to myself and my own—family, that is. I know who I am, and so do they." She points out that when you have dark skin, everyone sees black. Consequently, she goes along with just being black as long as she is treated fairly. But, she says, she has no friends at work because everyday is a reminder that they are not looking at her—Tuchina—but at her black skin. This has caused her to believe that when they ask about her family, they want to know not about all her relatives, just about those who are African American. To solve the problem, she says: "So I tell them about them all; I just keep the Choctaw part out."

Many other respondents not presented in this paper—including Choctaws of white admixtures—discussed how they were often assumed to be of an identity that was consistent with their appearance. For all Choctaws in the study, especially these two black Choctaws, their racial appearance seems to take precedence over their total heritage more for others than for themselves.

Interpretation

We now come back to the question asked at the beginning of this chapter: Why might an individual hang on to an identity that is inconsistent with skin color? By now, the answer to this question should be apparent, because it is basic understandings of self inherited from family and associated life strategies that have become—in each case—part of these individuals' repertoire of strategies for asserting self. Asserting a Choctaw identity asserts their understandings of self as it relates to culturally specific upbringing, heritage, and family and how this family interprets ways of thinking and comporting oneself that are not just Choctaw, but also reflective of the everyday racial encounters they have had (Cialdini 1984; DeMallie 1998).

The narratives of Ms. Bea and Tuchina illuminate the ways that family members and the life strategies they passed down have influenced their understandings of self as Choctaw. Their lived experiences also illuminate the contexts that have caused them to share in a growing American belief that skin color is an inadequate indicator of identity and heritage (Root 2000). From these concerns come Ms. Bea's desire —one that she also holds for her children—to be recognized in the exact same manner in which she identifies herself and Tuchina's hope that her co-workers will stop doubting her Choctaw ancestry because she appears to be only black and does not resemble common images of who is Native American. Each individual represents a locus of culture and identity to which the various dynamics of race have become only partially salient because of the beliefs of others (Kelly 1983; Miner-brook 1996; Rodriguez 1994).

These individuals' identities are related to race but are not completely shaped by it, despite their experiences. Although Ms. Bea and Tuchina were of different skin colors, and generations, there is little variation in the degree to which they have allowed race to supplant the totality of their identities. Neither found race compelling in understanding self or salient to being Choctaw. Instead, their familial practices were more compelling—particularly the life strategies they gave for resisting and handling the misplaced assumptions of others: that they were only black (Moses 1998; Nagel 1996).

Further, they also varied in their identification with the socially and culturally constructed worlds of local race-making practices. Tuchina seemed to follow her grandmother's habits. She also seemed to have less experience in navigating the responses that her assertion of self as a Choctaw seemed to evoke (Holland 2001; Jackson and Chapelski 2000). We later see her experience much sadness when her co-workers, as well as fellow non-Choctaw pow wow participants, refuse to accept her Choctaw heritage because of her appearance. Ms. Bea, by contrast, was more capable of coping with such situations. Perhaps time and the repetition of past action by individuals in the present has taught Ms. Bea to rely on the life strategies given by her family as a resource rather than merely to follow them. Thus, she seems to have developed enough competence in avoiding, resisting, and ignoring the racial-ascription practices to pass these strategies on to her grandchildren. They are strategies that will, according to Ms. Bea, enable the children to under-stand that "who they are is determined by family, not somebody's opinion about how they look."

If the language Ms. Bea and Tuchina used in their rationale for assert-ing Choctaw identity reflects any moral assumptions, those assump-tions concern the rights of all individuals in the United States to be understood in the same manner that they understand themselves. These two women's concerns reflect another imperative for understanding identities in the United States: that people are not always going to honor socially assigned identities and associated assumptions about their heritage (Fogelson 1982; Thornton and Nardi 1975). Both appear to share unquestioned conviction formulated from the resources provided by family that, as human beings and individuals, they have a right to be recognized in accordance with how they see themselves (Yellowbird 1999). It is natural that these individuals feel the need to assert themselves as Choctaws. After all, are they not who they say they are? And if they are not, then who — other than those that gave birth to them — has the right to truly determine who they are?

Note

1   See Erikson 1967; Fogelson 1998; Hollan and Wellenkamp 1994; Quinn 1992; Thornton and Nardi 1975.

CHAPTER FOURTEEN

From Ocean to O-shen

Reggae, Rap, and Hip Hop in Hawai'i

KU 'UALOHA HO 'OMANAWANUI

~~~~~~~~

> Are the[re] traditional musics left that have never heard a modern musical
> transcription? Are there any musics left that have not been influenced by
> some other music? All the most explosive modern musics are crossovers.
> The aesthetics of modern popular music is the aesthetics of the hybrid, the
> aesthetics of the crossover, the aesthetics of the diaspora, the aesthetics of
> creolization.
> — STUART HALL (1991, 38–39)

Like contemporary Hawaiian poetry, contemporary Hawaiian music
draws its imagery, style, and power from two distinct sources: *Kanaka*
Maoli (Native Hawaiian) traditions reaching back to ancient times
prior to contact with the colonizing West (1778) and a range of post-
contact sources (ho'omanawanui 2005). From first contact, Native
Hawaiians were exposed to Western music through the crude songs and
instruments brought by Western sailors and explorers. In the 1820s,
efforts to teach Hawaiians a foreign style — choral singing (*hīmeni*) —
began with the arrival of the American Calvinist missionaries from New
England. From that point forward, different musical styles were introduced to Kanaka Maoli, who adapted foreign techniques, instruments,
and styles to fit their own form of musical expression.[1]

Like other vibrant musics, contemporary Hawaiian music is constantly evolving. Over the past three decades, the primary impetus for
these changes is the influence of African-diasporic musics — namely,

reggae, rap, and hip hop—which has resulted in the creation of a dynamic new hybrid sound unlike any previously heard in Hawai'i. But what are the repercussions musically, culturally, and otherwise of this increasingly popular new sound? In this chapter, I will explore the influences of reggae and rap on Hawaiian music, highlighting Hawaiian, local, and Pacific musicians who have shaped and indigenized the diverse characteristics of these different musical forms and created a new, hybrid sound. In some ways, Hawaiian and African-diasporic elements have merged. In other ways, they have retained their distinct characteristics. This has led to the creation of a new music that draws from these different traditions, a music dubbed "Jawaiian" in the 1980s (a combination of *Ja*maican and Ha*waiian*) in an attempt to describe the sound. The greater historical, cultural, political, and musical context that frames the formation of Jawaiian music describes Hall's "aesthetics of the diaspora." Moreover, the mapping out of the hybridizing of contemporary Hawaiian music with African-diasporic musics can be read in multiple ways. On one hand, while global hip hop is sometimes dismissed as a weak or appropriated imitation of the sounds generated from African American musical roots, many Hawaiian musicians instead re-situate their "artistic approach within a Hawaiian context," creating a music as strongly rooted in a Native Hawaiian context as it is in the African-diasporic (Osumare 1999). Although celebrated as dynamic, the hybridization of musics is also a site of contestation. By examining the context that has informed the creation of Jawaiian music, it is possible to offer a critique of what is at stake in the creation and dissemination of the Jawaiian sound and its displacement and re-inscription of Native Hawaiian identity.

"The Music"

One of the most visible aspects of Hawaiian culture is demonstrated in the interconnection of 'ōlelo Hawai'i (Hawaiian language), music, and dance, most notably through the traditional Hawaiian dance form known as hula. While music is still produced within a cultural context, it is also exported to support tourism at the expense of cultural integrity. For many decades, representations of Hawaiian music and hula have garnered the attention of international audiences through insipid nonindigenous and colonial venues such as Hollywood movies. Fortunately, Hawaiian hula and music have also been exported through more culturally sponsored events such as tours of Hawaiian musical groups across the continental United States and abroad, as well as Hawai'i-based dance exhibitions and competitions such as the annual Merrie Monarch Hula Festival. The Native Hawaiian ethnomusicologist Amy Ku'uleialoha Stillman writes about Hawai'i's stereotyped image to the outside world, saying:

> Outside Hawai'i, the mention of "Hawaiian music" still conjures up stereotyped images of lei-bedecked musicians in colorful floral attire serenading at hotel poolsides during the sunset cocktail hour . . . [with] sounds [that] invariably include the soft strumming of guitars and ukulele, the languid sighing of the steel guitar and the mellifluous gymnastics of falsetto singers yodeling between vocal registers. . . . [T]hese images still shape what ageing tourists expect to see and hear on their arrival in the islands. (Stillman 1998, 89)

Today, modern technology such as Internet radio, podcasts, Web-based programming, and online shopping has broadened international access to Hawaiian culture and music. These media, however, mostly promote the more traditional hula, music, and images Stillman describes. Yet this stereotyped image is no longer indicative of the range of globalized sounds represented in contemporary Hawaiian music.

While Hawaiian hula and music continue to be produced by some Hawaiian artists and appreciated by a large and diverse audience, in recent years their commercial perpetuation has been eclipsed by the tsunami-like surge of music influenced by the African-diasporic forms of reggae and rap. The popularity of reggae music in Hawai'i has dramatically increased since its introduction here in the 1970s.

In contrast to the drastic change in rhythm and instrumentation that have resulted from these influences, contemporary Hawaiian song-text genres remain remarkably similar to those found in our traditional music. Samuel H. Elbert and Noelani Mahoe's *Nā Mele o Hawai'i Nei, 101 Hawaiian Songs* lists sixteen types of contemporary Hawaiian *mele* (songs), which are categorized by dominant motif (Elbert and Mahoe 1972). Of these, at least ten types are identifiable as pre-contact genres, including *mele aloha* (love songs), *mele pana* (songs honoring places), and *mele aloha 'āina* (patriotic songs).

Thematically, Jawaiian and rap song texts continue to express key cultural themes such as *aloha 'āina* — love and caring for the land and honoring ancestors and important people. They also continue to celebrate aspects of culture, such as surfing and the gathering and eating of food. The *sound* of contemporary Hawaiian music, however, has changed from songs featuring mostly a hula or pop-rock tempo to songs that include a strong and steady percussion-based reggae beat. Over the past decade, this sound has steadily grown and now dominates local radio airwaves and concert venues. With the explosion of edgy urban rap and hip-hop music in mainstream American popular culture, it is no surprise that these sounds have also influenced the production of Jawaiian music.

While contemporary Hawaiian music is rooted in the genres, styles, and traditions of Native Hawaiians, in the post-contact period this music has been influenced by foreign sounds. Some of these innovations — the accidental discovery of *kī hōʻalu* (slack-key guitar) and steel guitar, the adaptation of the Portuguese *braguinha* into the Hawaiian *ʻukulele*, and the development of *leo kiʻekiʻe* (falsetto singing) have become hallmarks of some genres of contemporary Hawaiian music. More important, however, these are changes made within a Hawaiian cultural context that occurred over a long period of time and at a time when Kanaka Maoli people and culture were not under constant attack from powerful colonial forces.

As noted earlier, what sets Jawaiian music apart from previous forms of post-contact influences is the rapidity with which the sound has developed and its exclusive association with African-diasporic musics. With the introduction of the reggae and hip-hop beats to genres of contemporary Hawaiian music, for the first time "danceable" contemporary Hawaiian music is noticeably disassociated from the Hawaiian hula.

Despite these arguments, it seems unfair to more traditional Hawaiian, other forms of contemporary Hawaiian, and even reggae music to call it "Hawaiian" or "reggae." "Hawaiian reggae," "Island reggae," "Pacific Beat," "Pacific (Island) Roots," and "Urban (Contemporary) Pacific" are all terms that artists, reviewers, and critics have used to describe this sound. Some have tried a more generic approach and employed encompassing terms such as "Island Music" or "Island Rhythms," as the Honolulu FM station 98.5 KDNN bills itself. But even these labels are problematic and do not adequately capture the essential sound or style of this musical hybrid. In my opinion, contemporary Hawaiian music, with the increased inclusion of rap and hip hop, is moving beyond a definable Jawaiian sound, as we are at the beginning of what I call the post-Jawaiian era of contemporary Hawaiian music, which is identifiable by the fusion and layering of Jawaiian and rap. However, while I have my own reservations about all of these terms, I will use the terms "Jawaiian" and "post-Jawaiian" to describe this unique genre of music.

Everybody Loves Bob Marley: The Reggae Roots of Jawaiian Music

> Ev'rybody loves Bob Marley
> Ev'ry where I go it's the same ol' story
> People of all nations
> They love the Rastaman vibrations.
>
> — MACKA B[2]

When Bob Marley and the Wailers signed with Chris Blackwell's Island records in 1971, no one knew what the international impact of reggae would be. Since then, reggae has become a global phenomenon. In Hawai'i, its popularity has been tremendous and its influence long-lasting. Reggae is included in the regular rotation of Hawai'i radio stations that feature "Island Music." In addition, some stations have special reggae programs. Island Rhythms 98.5 FM has regulary featured locally hosted reggae shows such as "Mr. Marley's Neighborhood," "Planet Reggae," and "Dr. Roots Reggae Hour." Even stations dedicated to other musical genres such as rock occasionally play reggae. The hard-core rock station LAVA Rock FM 105.9 features "Mandatory Marley" reggae tracks periodically throughout the day, while the alternative-rock station STAR 101.9 FM features the weekday "420 Joint of the Day," the only reggae song it plays in regular rotation.

Since its introduction to Hawai'i in the 1970s, reggae has been popularized in several ways: through internationally known acts (many whom have performed in Hawai'i); locally established reggae acts (some of which include at least one member of Jamaican ancestry); and local Jawaiian groups (some of whom play a combination of Jawaiian and other types of contemporary Hawaiian music).[3] Some of these musical groups have split up, with individual members continuing with Jawaiian–based musical projects.[4] Artists such as Robie Kahaka-lau and Israel Kamakawiwo'ole are "crossover" artists who perform both Hawaiian and Jawaiian music, while groups like Hō'aikane and Mana'o Company switched genres from traditional Hawaiian to Jawaiian music.[5] As Jawaiian popularity extended to the national and inter-national level, collaboration between local and international acts in-creased, resulting in a number of hit songs.[6]

But just what is "Jawaiian music"? Jawaiian is generally described as "a style of music that infuses Jah, or reggae, with Hawaiian," pertains to Hawaiian youth, and "makes you feel good."[7] Stillman distinguishes genres of contemporary Hawaiian music based on musical criteria such as *song form* (the structure of the poetic text) and *song text* (the themes or subject matter). One example Stillman gives that demonstrates the difference is the *hapa haole* (half or part Caucasian or Western) song of the early twentieth century. Hapa haole describes another hybrid form of contemporary Hawaiian music, which typically combines Hawaiian and English words and Hawaiian and other musical instruments, such as ʻukulele, bass, and steel guitar. Stillman says:

> The Hapa Haole songs of the early 20th century were somewhat amorphous at first, but quickly settled into one format that reigned for decades. Specifi-cally this is a 32-bar form used widely in popular music [such as] "Little Grass Shack." . . . This song form prevails through all of the New York-based Tin Pan Alley composers, but also in the songs of local hapa haole composers like Alex Anderson (Lovely Hula Hands) [and] Jack Pitman (Beyond the Reef). . . . The term "hapa haole song" then not only refers to the language of the lyrics, but also comes to be associated with songs that use this format. In contrast, the new songs that emerge out of the Hawaiian renaissance distance themselves from the 32-bar song form.[8]

Stillman believes that one reason Hawaiian composers distanced them-selves from the thirty-two-bar song form during the Hawaiian renais-sance period in the 1970s is that it is associated with colonial haole culture.[9] This period is viewed as a time when "young adult musicians, previously attracted to American rock and roll music in the 1960s, turned back to Hawaiian music in a quest to affirm a Hawaiian cultural identity" (Stillman 1998). The lack of "any one pattern" that Stillman described can be ascribed to Jawaiian music. Jawaiian songs lack the rigid structure of the thirty-two-bar hapa haole tunes but can be identi-fied by their rhythm, instrumentation, and language. For example, many Jawaiian songs have a strong bass beat and typically include in-struments associated with reggae music such as keyboards, trumpets, and timpani drums, yet they also feature Hawaiian instruments like the 'ukulele. Synthesizers have also added a new dimension of experimental sounds, which have been incorporated into Jawaiian and rap.

While English is the predominant language in Jawaiian (as it is in reggae), it also incorporates Hawaiian lyrics. Or, in the case of songs like Robie Kahakalau's "Pi'i Mai ka Nalu (Surf's Up)," the lyrics can be exclusively Hawaiian:

> *hui*:
> Pi'i mai ka nalu, pi'i mai ka nalu
> Kai lohe 'ia mai 'ō a 'ō
> Pi'i mai ka nalu, pi'i mai ka nalu
> E he'enalu kākou.
>
> Aia ma ka po'ina kai
> Nā nalu nui mai Kahiki mai
>
> Pae ana 'oe i ka nalu nui
> Kīpapa, kū, a he'e mai
>
> He'e ana i ka lala
> Ho'i ana i ka muku lā
>
> *chorus*:
> Surf's up, surf's up,
> You can hear everywhere
> Surf's up, surf's up,
>
> Let's [all] go surfing!
> The giant waves that come
> From far away are breaking
> Catch one of those huge waves
> Paddle, stand up, and go for it.
> Surf out on the diagonal,
> Come back on the crest. (Kahakalau 1995)

The only feature that distinguished "Pi'i Mai ka Nalu" from more traditional Hawaiian music is its Jawaiian beat. Set to hula tempo, this song could easily be danced as a hula. The song text is comparable to that of traditional songs such as "He'eia," a *mele* composed in honor of Hawaiian King David Kalākaua that uses surfing as a metaphor:

Aia i Heʻeia lā
I ka nalu e heʻe ana
Heʻe ana i ka muku lā
Hoʻi ana i ka lālā

There at Heʻeia
We go surfing on the waves
Surfing out on the crest
Returning on the diagonal.[10]

From Old School to New School: Mapping Jawaiian Music

As of this writing, no formal study of Jawaiian music has yet been undertaken. The American studies scholar Halifu Osumare, who has studied hip hop in Hawaiʻi, interviewing groundbreaking groups such as Sudden Rush, categorizes different periods of rap music as "Old School," "New School," and the "Next School" (Osumare 1999). Here, I divide the changes in the short history of the "Jawaiian movement" into similar categories. "Old School Jawaiian" began in the early 1980s and lasted until the early 1990s. Old School artists include both those who were the first to introduce the reggae sound to Hawaiian music and those who developed the Jawaiian sound, such as Butch Helemano and the Players of Instruments, Bruddah Walter Aipolani and Island Afternoon, Hōʻaikane, Kapena, Manaʻo Company, and Nā Wai Hoʻoluʻu o ke Ānuenue.[11]

"New School Jawaiian" emerged in the early 1990s and is distinguishable from the Old School by a change in sound through rhythm and instrumentation. New School Jawaiian is currently on the decline, being slowly replaced by the "Next School Jawaiian," which is marked by an increased use of rap music and hip-hop rhythms.[12] While most Old School and New School artists are Hawaiian and from Hawaiʻi, the Next School includes artists from the Oceanic diaspora such as O-shen, Fiji, Pati, and Kalei Cateres.

Kapena was the first group to popularize the Jawaiian sound with its commercially successful CDs *Satisfaction Guaranteed* (1986) and *Kapena* (1987). Kapena was soon followed by Butch Helemano's *Reggae Fevah* (1989) and Nā Wai Hoʻoluʻu o ke Ānuenue's *Colors of the Rainbow* (1989). The year 1990 was a prolific one for Jawaiian music, with successful releases by Butch Helemano (*Licking Stick* and *Block Party*),

Hōʻaikane (*Island Irie*), Bruddah Walter Aipolani and Island Afternoon (*Hawaiian Reggae*), Kapena (*New Horizons* and *Stylin'*), and Nā Wai Hoʻoluʻu o ke Ānuenue (*Jawaiian Rainbow*). During this period, other artists began to include Jawaiian songs on their otherwise traditional Hawaiian albums, such as Brother Nolan's rendition of Dennis Brown's "Big Ship" (*Native News*, 1986) and 3 Scoops of Aloha's "Sweet Lady of Waiahole" (*That Was Then, This Is Now*, 1990).

The New School Jawaiian period is characterized by a change in style that began with the Kaʻau Crater Boys' release of *Tropical Hawaiian Day* (1991). The Kaʻau Crater Boys introduced a whole new generation to the ʻukulele, an instrument that had lost favor over the previous decades among all but the most traditional Hawaiian musicians. The Jawaiianized combination of traditional "cha-lang-a-lang" strumming and "picking" stylings of Kaʻau Craters Boys member Troy Fernandez revitalized the sound of the ʻukulele, making it exciting and fresh to a young audience.[13]

Tropical Hawaiian Day took the islands by storm in 1991, highlighting the new sound that defined Jawaiian music of the 1990s. The success of this inaugural Kaʻau Crater Boys CD was followed by *Valley Style* (1993), *On Fire* (1994), and *Making Waves* (1996). As originators of New School Jawaiian, the Kaʻau Crater Boys were immensely popular and often imitated. When they began, their style of playing the ʻukulele was unique and innovative; today, this style of strumming has become so common that the Jawaiian song that does not incorporate it is a rarity. New School artists who rely heavily on the ʻukulele and the new style of playing include Hoʻonuʻa, Baba B, ʻEkolu, and Three Plus.

With the emergence of hip hop as a global music phenomenon in the 1990s, it is not surprising that it also influenced contemporary Hawaiian music. Next School Jawaiian artists have emerged over the past few years to make their own mark on the Jawaiian sound with an increased use of rap and hip-hop rhythms in their music. Some Old School artists, such as Kapena, have continued to evolve over the years by experimenting with the new sound. Kapena is the first Jawaiian group to incorporate rap into its music. "Island Stylin'" (*Wild Orchid*, 1992) "culminates in a rap that is self-promotional" (Stillman 1998, 97). Kapena's 1998 hit "Gin Gan Goolie" continues this trend. Other examples of Jawaiian songs that feature rap overdubs include "We Are Only Human" (Sunland), "Punani Patrol" (Sean Naʻauao), and "Early Morning Surf Session" (Typical Hawaiians). Thus far, the only Hawaiian group to promote itself as a rap artist rather than a Jawaiian artist is Sudden Rush.

Say What? Hawaiian Chant or Indigenized Rap: The Case of Sudden Rush

Both [Rap and reggae] . . . represent an extension of the African oral tradition of the *griot*, or storyteller, who recited the history of his tribal community — sometimes to the accompaniment of talking drums. The Jamaican tradition of "toasting" (or deejaying), which involves speaking over recorded music, in fact preceded today's rap, and as rap embraces reggae, it also acknowledges its roots.

— S. H. FERNANDO (1994, 32)

Some music scholars claim that the "fairly recent hybrid of rap and reggae" is only natural, as it "represents the latest stage of an ongoing relationship between these two musical cultures. Now there is almost a free mixing of mediums on any given rap or reggae release" (Fernando 1994, 32). Since this is the trend in mainstream reggae and hip hop, it will most certainly continue in its Jawaiianized form as the Next School of Jawaiian music takes root.

Besides the mixing of genres, there is a mixing of languages and cultures, which David Toop aptly describes as the global and polyglot metamorphosis of rap. He explains that, "by the beginning of the '90s, there were Samoan, Cuban, Mexican, Korean, Haitian, Dominican, Jamaican, Vietnamese, Puerto Rican, Ecuadorian, Chinese, Indian and British rappers in America" (Toop 1992, 187). Native Hawaiians should be added to his multicultural list. Thus far, only one group dedicates itself to a Hawaiianized rap style: the Big Island–based Sudden Rush. The trio currently has three CDs on the market: *Nation on the Rise* (1995), *Kūʻē* (Resistance; 1997), and *ʻEa* (Sovereignty; 2002). Sudden Rush raps in Hawaiian, English, and Pidgin in a manner similar to Toop's description of the Chicano rapper Kid Frost "slipping in and out of Spanish and English" (Toop 1992, 187). The Hawaiian language is so integral to Sudden Rush's identity and the sound of its music that the group promotes itself, in the words of member Keala Kawaʻahau, as "the true originators of *nā mele pāleoleo* (Hawaiian rap music).[14]

Sudden Rush is composed of three Hilo natives: Keʻala Kawa ʻauhau Jr. (King Don 1), Shane Veincent (Kid Dynomite), and Caleb Richards (Pakalō). Like other poets whose lyrics reflect their environment, Sudden Rush also employs subsets of localized lingo such as surfing slang, Big Island expressions, and reggae colloquialisms. In the tradition of its Hawaiian musical predecessors, Sudden Rush writes and performs music that focuses on Hawaiian themes and culture. Its blend of Hawaiian and African-diasporic styles is significant because the environment plays a vital role in the shaping of the music in both cultures.

Even though Sudden Rush promotes itself as a Hawaiian rap artist, the group also has been influenced by reggae and Jawaiian music. Its latest release, ʻEā, features several tracks that show reggae, Jawaiian, and Hawaiian influences, such as its version of Jimmy Cliff's "Root's Radical" and its original composition "Irie Eyes." The track "Hawaiian Iʻz" takes the intersection between Hawaiian, rap, and reggae further not only by featuring a Jawaiian-inspired beat, but also by referring to Hawaiian artists such as Israel Kamakawiwoʻole and the Jamaican artist Bob Marley (Sudden Rush 2002). Aside from its smooth melding of Hawaiian, reggae, and rap sounds, Sudden Rush is noted for the strong pro-Hawaiian rights, pro-sovereignty message in its lyrics, which are reminiscent of early socially conscious African American rappers such as KRS-1. While many indigenous Pacific hip hop performers such as King Kapisi, Nesian Mystic, Scribe, and Ill Semantics, all of whom are based in New Zealand, are expanding the movement of socially conscious and politically aware messages in their Pacific-based "flavah" of hip hop, Sudden Rush is the only Hawaiian-based hip-hop group to garner any recognition and celebrity status. Perhaps one reason is the different socioeconomic positioning of being "Local" versus "Native" in Hawaiʻi.

Are You Native? Being "Local" in Hawaiʻi

The idea of "Local" in Hawaiʻi is a contested site of negotiation between multiple ethnicities and cultures.[15] Because the "Local" label is multiethnic, it is often presumed to be inclusive, a specific counterpoint to mainstream American identity. But, again, the conflux of ethnic identities and cultures reveals itself as disputed territory, one in which Kanaka Maoli identity is often appropriated and displaced. The politics of what "Local" means in Hawai'i has been addressed by everyone from comedians (i.e., "You know you're local if . . .") to scholars.[16] In Hawai'i, Local is often viewed as "a category that cross-cuts narrow boundaries between native Hawaiians and Hawai'i residents of other ethnicities . . . [and] denotes a common culture that is shared among Hawai'i residents" (Stillman 1998, 89). Likewise, local music — an ambiguous category of contemporary Hawaiian music into which the Jawaiian sound falls, "refers to a repertoire that specifically explores local perspectives on issues of shared concern, as well as common sentiments and aspirations that unify Hawai'i's ethnically diverse population" (Stillman 1998, 90). On this point, the ethnomusicologist Andrew Weintraub concurs, stating, "Jawaiian, now synonymous with 'island-style' and 'local-style,' is less exclusive than other distinctively Hawaiian arts. Its appeal lies in its ability to 'cross over' geographic, class and racial boundaries" (Weintraub 1998, 85–86).

Yet Hawai'i's image of being an ethnic "melting pot," where the tensions that rupture between ethnic groups — and against Native Hawaiians in particular, the only non-immigrant population — are smoothly erased, melted away in a newly melded hybrid form, is a misleading representation. Native Hawaiian musicians who experiment with reggae and rap rhythms and influences in Jawaiian and post-Jawaiian rap music struggle to do so within a cultural context that relies on Hawaiian traditions and metaphors as much as the African-diasporic sound. By remaining rooted in Hawaiian culture, Jawaiian and post-Jawaiian rap resists corruption and misappropriation by haole-controlled and Asian-controlled corporations that export Hawaiian music through Western tourism for popular consumption.

Keepin' It Real: *Aloha 'Āina, Mele Inoa,* and other Hawaiian Cultural Themes

> There's a code in rap that you're supposed to rap about what you know, keep it real, so if we were to rap about being in gangs we'd be lying. We talk about what we're familiar with.
> — SUDDEN RUSH[17]

It is important to make the distinction between Native Hawaiian themes and themes expressed in other hip hop and rap music, as Hawaiian rap goes against the "values that underpin so much of hip hop," which the hip-hop writer Nelson George describes as "materialism, brand consciousness, gun iconography, anti-intellectualism . . . [which] are very much by-products of the larger American culture. Despite the 'dangerous' edge of so much hip hop culture, all of its most disturbing themes are rooted in this country's dysfunctional values" (1998, xiii).

The values which underpin mainstream American hip hop culture that George describes do not apply to Hawaiian rap, mainly because Hawaiian rap reflects the influences of the Hawaiian culture and is a product of environment. Language is one of the important elements that influence this difference. Sudden Rush, for example, is as strongly connected by the Hawaiian environment, its Hawaiian roots, and the Hawaiian language as the Chicano rappers Toop describes in Miami, who are "strongly influenced by the closeness of Cuba and Jamaica" (Toop 1992, 187). Melding Hawaiian lyrics, chant stylings, and culturally relevant themes with English lyrics and hip-hop beats has resulted in a culturally centered yet edgy urban and contemporary sound.

Because authenticity is the key to reputation in the hip-hop realm, the connection Chicano rappers in Miami or Hawaiian rappers in Hawai'i have to their environments, which are reflected in their lyrics, is important. The epigraph that opened this section explains the importance of "keepin' it real," a concept exemplified by the group in its lyrics as its members write about their experiences and their environment—or, as Kawa'auhau says, "If we were to rap about being in gangs we'd be lying." The code to "keep it real" is demonstrated in "Message to the Wannabes (Be Hawaiian)" (Sudden Rush 1997), in which the group reminds its Hawaiian audience of the importance of adhering to their cultural roots:

1. Well I remember when you used to talk with a pidgin slang
2. but now you only walk like you're only in a gang
3. Fella, is something wrong with your spine?
4. What happened—did you break your leg crossing that line?
5. I think you're lost and confused in your personality,
6. You're living a dream bro in your reality
7. So Hawaiian now have a little pride
8. Don't be a victim of cultural suicide
9. Forgettin' your roots, your past and your history
10. Why you wanna do those things to me is still a mystery
11. So wake up and get your ass out of bed

12. Wake up and take that rag off your head
13. Wake up before you get a slap in your face
14. Be proud of your blood and be proud of your race
15. Playing reggae music doesn't make you a Jamaican
16. Country music won't make you a cowboy so stop fakin'
17. Rap don't make you black so stop tryin'
18. No matter what you do you'll always be Hawaiian.

19. The black man was taken from his homeland
20. Taken to another land, forced to work for another man
21. But they survived, they overcame
22. To the Hawaiian people it is somewhat the same
23. Not to say that we were slaves, don't get me mistaken
24. To us its not the people but the land that was taken
25. So if you got the knowledge be sure to use it, don't abuse it
26. Because you sing a certain kind of music
27. if you dress hip hop and drink the big 4-0
28. Be sure you do it cuz you want to
29. Not because you saw it on a video
30. I'm the Don 1 that's me, but then I always use my last name
31. So people can see that I am Hawaiian, and that I am a winner
32. K-A-W-A-A-U-H-A-U with an 'okina
33. So if you're black, be proud and be black
34. and if you're white be proud you look like that
35. E kōkua kākou i kou mākou mau hoa aloha [Help your friends]
36. 'onipa'a, 'onipa'a, ma kēia puali koa. [Be steadfast, steadfast, like us soldiers]

37. From Miloli'i I'm Hawaiian (Hawaiian)
38. Straight from Ka'ū I'm Hawaiian (Hawaiian)
39. Coming out of Puna I'm Hawaiian (Hawaiian)
40. From Wai'anae I'm Hawaiian (Hawaiian)
41. From Nānākuli I'm Hawaiian (Hawaiian)
42. From Waimānalo I'm Hawaiian (Hawaiian)
43. When I'm rapping to the people I'm Hawaiian (Hawaiian)
44. Not a Blood or a Crip — I'm Hawaiian. (Sudden Rush 1997)

While this rap encourages Hawaiians to have cultural pride, it is not at the expense of being educated about other people's history; there is a clever intertextuality embedded in the song text, which is one of the admirable qualities of rap music. The middle "chorus" (which lists different Hawaiian locations between "verses") alludes to N.W.A.'s groundbreaking CD *Straight Outta Compton* (1988), demonstrating a knowledge of mainstream African American rap music and artists. The history of slavery in America is touched on, and this segment culminates with the evocation of the Civil Rights Movement's rally cry, "We Shall Overcome." The rap then neatly segues into lines that draw a parallel between African American and Hawaiian history. The terrible crimes committed against African Americans by Euro-Americans is similar to the Native Hawaiian experience with the same colonial powers, except in Hawai'i, "it's not the people, but the land that was taken" (line 24). Like political or "message" raps more common in the Old School rap (performed by such rappers as Public Enemy), Sudden Rush gets the point across that Hawaiians need to pay attention to the abuses committed against us by the American empire throughout history and have pride in our own culture. Furthermore, the message reaffirms that it is alright to admire African American culture and emulate it if you are doing it with forethought and respect, acknowledging that its people are experiencing a struggle that parallels Kanaka Maoli history, not "just because you saw it on a video" (line 29). This message evokes other classic raps, such as Public Enemy's "Don't Believe the Hype" (*It Takes a Nation of Millions to Hold Us Back,* 1988) and "Fight the Powers That Be" (*Fear of a Black Planet,* 1990).

What Sudden Rush has done with rap is similar to what other contemporary Hawaiian artists have achieved: the merging of aspects of Native Hawaiian culture and music with new sounds. This has been the strength of Native Hawaiian compositions. It does what poets are "supposed" to do, which the Hawaiian composer and musician Jon Osorio says is to "reflect their environment, and comment on the times they are living in."[18] As such, they are storytellers, *haku mo'olelo* of the twenty-first century following in the tradition of their Kanaka Maoli ancestors, a practice that is also central to rap music — not surprisingly, as both originate in oral cultures. *Ha'i 'ōlelo,* or storytelling, is an important influence on Hawaiian chant. Like rap, there are many genres of traditional chant. One, *kepakepa,* a style in which lines are delivered in a very rapid, conversational style, is the heart of what Sudden Rush does with its rap. In "'Ōnipa'a (Stand Firm)," Sudden Rush demonstrates the same commitment to Hawaiian issues as other raps, but part of the rap is performed in Hawaiian:

'O kēia mo'olelo e pili ana i ka 'āina
He mo'olelo kēia mai ke kanaka kama'āina.
Hāpuna, makemake au e hele
Akā, ua 'ike (au) i kekahi wahi hōkele.
'Aole au makemake i kēia mau pilikia.
Hakakā 'oe ma hope o kou inu 'ana i ka pia.
Pono 'oe e no'ono'o, mai hana pupule
E hele i ke kula a me ka halepule.
Ho'ohui, ho'ohui mai ho'olohe i ka aupuni

Makemake lākou i kekahi alanui.
I hea? Ma O'ahu, ua lohe au.
Ma hope o ka wawahi 'ia 'ana o ka heiau.
Hewa loa kēlā. E ho'olohe iā mākou.
Mālama i ka 'āina, mālama i ka po'e,
Mālama iā kākou.
Mai namunamu wale no ka mea, 'eha (ka pepeiao).
E hana e like me
Ke ali'i 'o Kamehameha.
E ha'i a ma'a, e ha'i a pa'a.
E ha'i i ka hua'ōlelo, 'Onipa'a.
'Onipa'a.

This is a story about the land.
This is a story from a Hawaiian man
Hāpuna beach, I like to go there
But I saw them building a hotel
I don't like all these problems
Every time you drink beer you end up fighting
You gotta think, no act stupid
Go school and go church
Unite, unite! Don't listen to the government
They like build another road
Where? On O'ahu, that's what I heard
After they destroy a heiau [traditional Hawaiian religious site]
Listen, that's what's wrong
Take care of the land, take care of the people,
Take care of each other.
Don't just complain, because sore (my ears)
We have to do

Like the great chief Kamehameha
Say it 'till it's stuck in your head, 'till it's stuck
In your gut. Say the word, 'Ōnipa'a (Be Steadfast). (Sudden Rush 1995)

"'Ōnipa'a" fluidly blends English and Hawaiian lyrics in a storytelling rap that speaks to the problems of modernization and displacement Native Hawaiians continually face. Yet despite the immense obstacles, the rap encourages Hawaiian to "'Ōnipa'a," be steadfast in our culture, our language, and our fight against colonial oppression.

Sudden Rush's second release, Kū'ē (Resistance; 1997), further promotes a message of cultural pride, unity, and education. On this point, Kawa'ahau states, "With songs like 'think about It,' 'Kū'ē,' and 'true Hawaiians' we continue our mission to educate the world about what really is going on and what really went on in history. Self determination and a true Hawaiian Nation is what our goal, as a people, should be" (Sudden Rush 1997).

Other examples of how Jawaiian and post-Jawaiian rap music are thematically rooted in Native Hawaiian traditions are the songs that celebrate food and surfing. Hawaiians have always celebrated the gathering and eating of food in song. As Hawaiians traditionally trace our genealogy back to Papahānaumoku, the "Earth Mother"; Wākea, the "Sky Father"; and their progeny Hāloa, the first kalo (taro) plant from whom the lāhui Hawai'i (Hawaiian Nation) descends, the 'āina (land) and the food items that are gathered from it are revered, with sacred connections to Hawaiian akua (gods).[19] There are a number of chants and traditional songs which attest to this: "Ka Uluwehi o ke Kai" is a song celebrating limu, or seaweed, to which Hawaiian historian Lilikalā Kame'eleihiwa once remarked, "Hawaiians are the only people who write celebratory songs about seaweed!"[20] Other songs glorify the eating of fish: "'Ama'ama (Black Crab)," "Aloha ka Manini (Love for the Manini fish)," and "Nā I'a 'Ono o ke Kai (The Delicious Fish of the Sea)" are but a few examples. Bina Mossman's "He 'Ono (How Delicious)" was remade as a Jawaiian song by the Ka'au Crater Boys, who brought to it a new level of popularity:

Keu a ka 'ono ma ke alopiko la
Kahi momona piko ka nenue la
Lihaliha wale ke momoni akula
'O ka 'ō'io halale ke kai la
'O ka 'ōpelu e pepenu ana la

He ʻono tomito hoʻi tau i
To puʻu te momoni aku

Oh, how delicious is the belly
The fattest part of the nenue (pilot) fish
So rich when swallowed
The ʻōʻio (bone fish) with thick gravy
The ʻōpelu (mackerel), dunked in sauce
Very delicious
A delight to the throat to swallow.

hui:
He ʻono a he ʻono a he ʻono ʻo nō
A he ʻono nō.

chorus:
Delicious, delicious, delicious indeed
Truly delicious! (Kaʻau Crater Boys 1996)

Likewise, Sean Naʻauao's hit "Fish and Poi" celebrates the eating of delicacies of the modern Hawaiian diet. The song begins, "I've been many places, I've tasted all the flavors" but nothing beats the local food in Hawaiʻi. The chorus states:

I like fish and poi
I'm a big boy
lomi salmon, pipikaula,
extra large lilikoi
squid or chicken lūʻau,
don't forget the laulau
beef or tripe stew
just to name a few, oh yeah! (Naʻauao 1997)

Besides the more commonly recognized Hawaiian staple foods fish and poi, Naʻauao mentions other island favorites: lomi salmon (a dish similar to ceviche), pipikaula (smoked meat), lūʻau (taro leaves), laulau (meat or fish wrapped in taro leaves and steamed), and lilikoi juice. The abundance of delicious food is similarly remarked on in Robert Kekaula's whimsically titled song "Kanak Attack" (1994), which alludes to what is known in Hawaiʻi as "Polynesian paralysis" — eating until one is so sated that one is "attacked" by sleepiness.[21]

Another theme popular in local Jawaiian and rap music is surfing.

Jawaiian tunes such as Butch Helemano's "Wave Rider," Sean Naʻauao's "Surf Pāʻina (Surf Party)," Hōʻaikane's "Big Island Surfing," and Bruddah Walter Aipolani's "Little Surfer Girl" are Jawaiian classics, and Sudden Rush has written an energetic surfing rap titled, "Sudden Session."[22] I have catalogued at least twenty-five songs related to surfing, many of which are done in a Jawaiian style.

Songs about food, surfing, and love of the land that reflect traditional Hawaiian themes will continue to be popular in all genres of contemporary Hawaiian music because of the cultural relationship between the Hawaiian people and their environment. Thus, while some rap critics spurn the rap and hip hop coming out of non–African American communities (for some purists, anything that cannot be traced directly to the Bronx is an "imitation"), Jawaiian and post-Jawaiian music are demonstrating how these sounds are being mixed to form geographically specific sounds that are rooted to the places and cultures from which they are derived. For these artists, themes of surfing, food, and aloha ʻāina are as reflective of the conditions of the Hawaiian environment as the themes in Jamaican reggae or American rap reflect their own sites of origin.

Another important theme in traditional Hawaiian music that has been successfully incorporated in the Jawaiian and rap genre is *mele inoa*, songs that honor people. One example is Hoʻonuaʻa's "Feel Good Island Music":

> Let me tell you a little story about how our music came to be
> It took two minds, two ʻukuleles and the feel good harmony
> something else helped to inspire us to play the way we play
> the musicians that came before us at home in Hawaiʻi nei
> C and K and Kalapana started the feel good island strum
> So don't put "The Hurt" on me baby,
> "Good Times Together" are here to come
> Peter Moon's "Cane Fire" music made you feel nice and warm
> and we thank him for our feel good sound
> that took the islands by a "Tropical Storm."
>
> When Kapena play live at the party,
> just have to "Jump on the Reggae Train"
> and if you ever get to see these guys play live
> Your life will never be the same
> Bruddah Iz has got the feeling

Natural Vibes bring the irie feeling
So "In This Life" you must have a nice day
Feel good music is here to stay

chorus:
Jammin' feel good island music, sitting under the sun
Feel good island music, skankin' til the song is done
Feel good island music, flowing through my veins
Feel good island music, takes away all my pain. (Ho'onu'a 1998)[23]

This song draws on Hawaiian cultural traditions not only because it incorporates the language, but also because it evokes the names of earlier musical artists (C and K, Kalapana, Peter Moon, Kapena, "Bruddah Iz" Israel Kamakawiwo'ole, and Natural Vibrations). While Israel Kamakawiwo'ole has passed on, all of those mentioned have influenced and inspired the members of this young group (and, by extension, other young musicians). This is a modern interpretation of a traditional form called *mele inoa* (name song). Mele inoa are originally chants or songs of praise composed to honor an individual or sometimes a family. They were a common genre in traditional Hawai'i and have remained important in the post-contact era. Here, not only are the composers and performers honored, but the song cleverly includes references to song titles of some of the hits that have made them island stars.

This technique is used in other songs. Other artists — Baba B's "West Side Pride" and Sudden Rush's "Hawaiian I'z," for example — both pay homage to Hawaiian artists. One composition dedicated to reggae artists who have a strong following and influence in Hawai'i is Shiloh Pa's "Sweet Reggae." The chorus states, "Sweet reggae, that's the music for me/There's a lot of different kinds but my favorite one is Bob Marley's" (Pa 2002). The second verse is made up of Marley song titles, while the third lists international reggae stars who are popular in Hawai'i:

1. From "Stir It Up," to "Guava Jelly,"
2. We're "Chanting Down to Babylon,"
3. "One Love," and "People Get Ready"
4. "Satisfy My Soul" and "Natural Mystic" flow
5. "Redemption Song" now baby, "Turn Your Lights Down Low,"

6. Eek a Mouse, Shabba Ranks and a Yellowman
7. Steel Pulse and UB40, and the African Bush Band

8. Jimmy Cliff, Joe Higgs and Eddie Grant

9. Respects to Gregory Isaacs and all the Rastaman. (Pa 2002)

What these original Jawaiian and rap compositions show is the continued Hawaiian cultural practice of acknowledging ancestors or important people. They are also another example of how Hawaiian musicians have successfully mixed the two cultures by using the sound of reggae and rap to exemplify Hawaiians themes.

Mele Aloha ʻĀina and Mele Kūʻē (Anthems of Protest Then and Now): The Jawaiian Context

In Hawaiʻi, there are four recognizable categories of reggae-rooted Jawaiian songs: local covers of established reggae tunes; covers of non-reggae songs in a Jawaiian style; remakes of traditional Hawaiian songs in a Jawaiian style; and original Jawaiian songs.[24] Despite — or because of? — the popularity of international reggae stars in Hawaiʻi, local Jawaiian covers of previously recorded reggae hits are very successful. Perhaps one reason these remakes are so well received lies in the way the songs have been adapted for Hawaiʻi. One example is Bruddah Walter Aipolani's resituated and Jawaiianized version of Bob Marley's "No Woman No Cry":

> 'Cause I remember when we used to sit
> In a government yard in Trenchtown
> Observing the hypocrites
> Mingle with the good people we meet
> (Marley)

> I remember when we used to swim
> In a little place in the country
> From the hills down to the sea (Hawaiʻi!)
> We would go fishin' a plenty.
> (Aipolani)[25]

By relocating Marley's smash hit to Hawaiʻi, Aipolani's lyrics reverberate strongly with Native Hawaiians; by using Marley's song and identity, Aipolani links the conditions of poverty and oppression experienced by Native Hawaiians to those experienced by Jamaicans. After Bruddah Walter popularized this song, which appears on the same CD as an original Jawaiian song, "Keep Hawaiian Lands in Hawaiian Hands," it was later paired with Marley's "Waiting in Vain" by both Hōʻaikane (*A New Beginning*, 1990) and Simplicity (*Simplicity*, 1990).

Although the original "Waiting in Vain" was written by Marley as a love song, and the Jawaiian version does not change the lyrics, its relationship with "Keep Hawaiian Lands" turns it into a patriotic song demonstrating love for the land, an anthem of protest against development, colonial dispossession, and Western encroachment. The chorus, *"Ua mau ke ea o ka ʻāina i ka pono* (the life of the Land is perpetuated in righteousness)" is often recognized as the government motto for the state of Hawaiʻi. With the exception of students of Hawaiian history, few know that this motto was first uttered in 1843 by Hawaiian *Aliʻi* (King) Kauikeaouli Kamehameha III upon the restoration of Hawaiian sovereignty after Hawaiʻi was seized for Britain by Captain George Paulet. When emissaries were sent to England to plead Hawaiʻi's case, King George sided with the Hawaiian government and restored Hawaiian sovereignty.[26]

Aipolani's composition precedes Henry Kapono Kaʻaihue's song protesting the Department of Hawaiian Home Lands' (DHHL) notoriously long waitlist, "Broken Promise," which features the refrain, "Sonny's been waiting" (Kaʻaihue 1992).[27] This line, in turn, recalls the line from "Waiting in Vain" (for Hawaiian land). The connectivity of the reggae lyrics demonstrates the power of music as a social force and as a potentially strong instrument of social and political change.

In many instances, it is the *mele aloha ʻāina*, the songs of political protest, that have given hope and encouragement to the Native Hawaiian political movement seeing justice for historical and political injustices such as the banning of our indigenous language, illegal overthrow of our sovereign government in 1893, and theft of native lands. While Hawaiians are still rallying behind the push for sovereignty, the songs of protest dovetail with an intense political movement in the early 1990s that culminated in 1993, the one-hundred-year commemoration of the overthrow of the Hawaiian monarchy.[28] In 1993, Israel Kamakawiwoʻole re-released Skippy Ioane's "Hawaiʻi '78," a poignant tune of Hawaiian protest again colonialism, loss of Hawaiian sovereignty, and cultural disruption. The song states, in part,

> If just for a day our king and queen
> could visit all these islands and see everything

how would they feel about the changes of our land?
Could you just imagine if they were around
and saw highways on their sacred grounds
how would they feel about this modern city life?

Tears would come from each others eyes
as they would stop to realize
that our people are in great great danger now

How would they feel?
Would they smile, be content, or cry
cry for the gods, cry for the people,
cry for the land that was taken away
and then yet you'll find Hawai'i. (Kamakawiwo'ole 1993)

In 1995, Kamakawiwo'ole released the CD *E Ala ē* (Rise Up). The title track, which takes its opening line from a traditional rallying chant, includes actual soundbites from the 1993 overthrow commemoration in which the unifying calls of "*Imua!* (Go forward!)" and "*Ea!* (Sovereignty!)" are clearly heard. Likewise, Sudden Rush's 1995 *Kū'ē* (Resistance) featured sound bites from a rousing commemoration speech given on the grounds of 'Iolani Palace by the prominent political activist Haunani Kay Trask, in which she stridently stated, "We are not American! We are not American! We will die as Hawaiians, we will never be American!" (Trask, January 17, 1993).

In 1993, Hawaiian sovereignty — in any form — was considered a radical impossibility. Ten years later, the potential merits and forms of Hawaiian sovereignty and federal "recognition" are being seriously debated on Capitol Hill. Many, many people have given their time, talent, and energy to making this radical sociopolitical transformation a possibility, and Jawaiian *mele aloha 'āina* (songs demonstrating Hawaiian patriotism) have certainly assisted in sustaining the movement.

"From Pop to Jawaiian": In the Mix

One of the more intriguing aspects of the Jawaiian movement is the covering of non-reggae songs in the Jawaiian style.[29] Many of these songs come from the 1950s to the 1970s, a time period in which these artists or their parents were growing up. As such, they can be consid-

ered "nostalgic" songs. Their popularity also demonstrates the influence of American music on Hawaiian artists. As with covers of reggae
tunes, sometimes lyrics are changed, relocating them to a Hawaiian
environment. In other instances, it is the repositioning of the songs in
the Jawaiian sound that localizes them, anchoring them to an island
versus a continental view. One example is Fiji's 1999 rendition of Otis
Redding's 1968 "Sitting on the Dock of the Bay":

> I left my home in Georgia
> And headed for Frisco Bay
> 'Cause I have nothing to live for
> And look's like nothing will come my way
> Sitting here restin' my bones
> And this loneliness won't leave me alone
> Two thousand miles I roll
> Just to make this dock my home.
> (Redding)

> I left my home back in Fiji
> Headin' for the Turtle Bay
> I had nothing to live for
> Look like nothing's gonna come my way
> Just sittin here restin my bones
> And this loneliness won't leave me alone
> Six thousand miles I've flown
> Just to make this rock my home.
> (Fiji)[30]

As in Aipolani's "No Woman No Cry," the changes made to the song
resituate it in a Pacific context. This recontextualization politically
charges the lyrics, which now speak to the displacement of Pacific
natives in the diaspora, a direct result of European and American
colonization of the Pacific throughout the nineteenth century and
twentieth.

From Pop to Jawaiian: Resituating History

While earlier African American musical genres like blues, jazz, funk,
soul, and rhythm and blues were never fully worked into the contempo-

rary Hawaiian music traditions (the rare exception being the jazz artist Richard Kauhi), they have resurfaced with the Jawaiian generation. African American artists from Otis Redding to Lionel Ritchie, from Tracy Chapman to Klymaxx, have had their songs recorded to Jawaiian beats. A few Jawaiian remakes of pop songs recorded by white artists have also been resituated. One example is Ho'onu'a's rendition of Stephen Bishop's 1970s hit "On and On." In Bishop's song, the heartbroken lover "puts on Sinatra and starts to cry," while in Ho'onu'a's version, he "puts on Bob Marley and starts to cry."[31] Thus Marley, the voice of reggae music, a powerful musical and cultural icon for the oppressed, displaces Frank Sinatra, a powerful musical and cultural icon in his own right. While it is likely that Ho'onu'a meant only to relate the classic pop tune of heartbreak and hope to a local youth audience, the replacement of Sinatra by Marley also works on a much deeper symbolic level.

From Traditional Hawaiian to Jawaiian *Mele*

Traditional Hawaiian *mele* (songs) have not escaped a Jawaiian rebirth, either. Classics such as "He 'Ono" (Ka'au Crater Boys), "Ku'u Wā Li'ili'i" (Valley Boys), "Hene Hene Kou Aka" (Israel Kamakawiwo'ole), "Hilo Hula" (Sean Na'auao), "Nani Ko'olau" (Robie Kahakalau), and more have been resurrected by contemporary and other recording artists. Traditional Hawaiian music aficionados and practitioners are not always happy with these very modern renditions of classic Hawaiian songs, again pointing to the fissures that occur in hybrid sounds. One example is the inclusion of "Ku 'u Pua (My Beloved Flower)" on O-shen's latest CD *Faya* (2005). A traditional Hawaiian song originally titled "Wai o ke Aniani (Crystal Waters)," the original mele expresses the composer's love for a woman, comparing her beauty to various delicate, fragrant, and favored *pua* (blossoms). One stanza, used in O-shen's version as well, states:

> E aloha a 'e ana au lā
> Aloha ku 'u pua ka pīkake lā
> E moani ke ala i ka poli lā
> 'Uhe 'uhene i ka wai o ia pua
>
> I offer up my affection
> How I love my pīkake (jasmine) blossom

> whose fragrance stirs the heart
> delighting in the nectar of this flower.
> (Wilcox et al. 2003, 270–71)

Each *paukū* (verse) of the original composition compares a woman to different fragrant flowers, suggesting either different qualities of that woman the composer admires, or even different women altogether! Thus is the nature of *kaona* (hidden or underlying meaning), which could be known by the entire community, or only to the composer. In O-shen's revamped Jawaiian version, the traditional flower names have been replaced with "naughtier," more youth-oriented botanical references, evoking a very different metaphorical context, one rooted in rebellious youth culture, rather than traditional ethnic culture. In O-shen's version, the cleverly veiled flower references are more blatant and openly suggestive, as he sings about the beloved but generic "pua nani" (pretty flower). Innocent enough, until one realizes that he's really singing about "punani," a vulgar slang reference to the vagina, corrupted from the term "pua nani," a more "polite" and poetic traditional reference. In subsequent verses, the fragrant flowers often fashioned into lei, the 'ilima, pua kenikeni, and lehua which are sung about in the original song are changed to the "pua pakalolo" (marijuana bud) and "pua melilewa" (a Papua New Guinean reference). When recontextualized, it changes the context and intent of the song entirely, a purposeful move on the part of the current performer. While the original composer expresses his love for a woman by admiring her beauty in a respectable way, the Jawaiian version expresses the desire to get stoned and have sex, values considered positive and perpetuated in circles of contemporary youth culture. While those "in the know" might share a few laughs at the clever turn of phrase, once again, indigenous perspectives are corrupted and devalued in a hybrid context. The danger lies in the assumption that the creation of a hybrid sound is an "innocent" or innocuous blending of the indigenous and Western, when, in actuality, the indigenous can be crushed, marginalized, destroyed.

One example is the young generation who perpetuates this new sound dismisses these complaints by arguing that they are just reflecting popular trends. However, there is more at stake than just musical preferences. Rather, it is a question of cultural erosion and the constant assault on Native Hawaiians and Native Hawaiian cultural forms. Historically, this has taken place through a dominant–oppressive relationship between the United States/Western world and Native populations. Today, the assault comes through global mass media, where Hawaiian youth, like youth around the globe, want to be part of what is hip and cool, rebellious and shocking. Mass media, however, teaches them, through MTV, that Native arts are not hip and cool. Thus, while more Hawaiian youth today play the ʻukulele, they are not playing traditional rhythms. This knowledge has eroded to such a point that at least one school, Kamehameha Schools, an educational institution founded to educate Native Hawaiian children, has included instruction on traditional "cha-lang-a-lang" styles of ʻukulele strumming in its music department curriculum.

Jawaiian Compositions and the Struggle for Originality

Although the Jawaiian sound has swept over and through these other musical genres, what really demonstrates the force of Jawaiian as a dynamic musical hybrid is the composition of original Jawaiian songs. More often than not, these *mele* draw on their Hawaiian roots not only through the use of instruments, but also in theme (song text). Traditional Hawaiian themes such as celebration of the land, which are not common in popular music from other familiar cultures (such as American culture), were the cornerstone of traditional Hawaiian chant and song and continue to be in the contemporary period. Hundreds of these *mele aloha ʻāina* and *mele pana* have been composed and sung in the Hawaiian language from the ancient past to the present.

With the overthrow of the Hawaiian monarchy in 1893, some of these mele aloha ʻāina (such as "Kaulana nā Pua") were evoked politically as Hawaiians struggled to regain sovereignty and hold on to their land. Not surprisingly, *mele aloha ʻāina* such as Harry K. Mitchell's "Mele o Kahoʻolawe" resurfaced in the Hawaiian language in the 1970s as Hawaiians protested the use of the sacred island, Kahoʻolawe, as a target for bombing practice by the U.S. military and its allies.[32] Mele aloha ʻāina were incorporated into Jawaiian songs too, such as Bruddah Walter Aipolani and Island Afternoon, "Hawaiian Lands" (1990). The chorus, "Keep Hawaiian lands in Hawaiian hands," has been used as a rallying cry in different land struggles over the past several decades, often appearing on bumper stickers and protest placards. The song also evokes the Hawaiian state motto, "*Ua mau ke ea o ka ʻāina i ka pono*," which is often translated as, "The Life of the Land is Perpetuated in Righteousness," indicating that the land lives when justice is served.

A decade later, the sovereignty movement is just as strong, and lyrics reflecting political views of *aloha ʻāina* are still being recorded and are still popular. Take, for example, Kaleilani Caceres's "Couldn't Take the Mana":

> They took the land
> They took aloha
> Overthrew the queen even though they didn't know her
> Suppressed *ikaika* (strength) and then *kūpuna* (elders)
> Broke the *ʻohana* (family)
> But they couldn't take the *mana* (spiritual strength). (Caceres 2001)

Many of these *mele kūʻē* reflect a thematic intertextuality that refer to other protest chants and *mele* going back a hundred years or more. As such, they are enriching the important tradition of our *kūpuna* (ancestors) and leaving a legacy for future generations of Hawaiians that demonstrates our history of resistance to American oppression and theft of land.

Mele pana have also consistently been represented in the Jawaiian sound from its inception. One of the best examples of the merging of Jawaiian styles with this traditional Hawaiian theme is Hōʻaikane's "Kailua–Kona." Rhythmically, "Kailua–Kona" is a classic Jawaiian song. Thematically, it is a classic Hawaiian *mele pana* with lyrics that celebrate *aloha ʻāina*:

> There is a place that is heavenly
> A place where life can be so free
> Where people work and live easily
> That is a place for you and for me
>
> Go up to the mountains or down to the sea
> Enjoy the view or eat sweet *ʻopihi*
> Work and play till the sun goes down
> Cruise the beach road to Kona town
>
> Play reggae music with the Hōʻaikane band
> Surf at Banyans by the Surf and White Sands
> Go north and south as for as you can go
> Go Mauna Kea to see the island snow.

chorus:

Kailua–Kona, where the air is clean

Kailua–Kona, where the grass is green

Kailua–Kona, where the fishing's fine

Kailua–Kona, it will blow your mind. (Hōʻaikane 1990)

The lyrics of "Kailua–Kona" are reminiscent of other, more traditional *aloha ʻāina* songs, such as "Aia i Kona (There in Kona)," "A Kona Hema i ka Lani (The Chief Is There at South Kona)," and "Kona Kai ʻŌpua i ka Laʻi (Kona of the Mirrored Seas [in the Calm])":

Hanohano ʻo Kona kai ʻōpua i ka laʻi

ʻŌpua hīnano kau i ka mālie

Puaʻi nā wai ka maka o ka ʻōpua

ʻAʻole nō ʻelua aʻe like aku ai

Me Kona kai ʻōpua, ke kai māʻokiʻoki

Ke kai malino aʻo Kona

Haʻaheo i ka mālie

O Kona kai ʻōpua i ka laʻi

Kilakila ʻo Hualālai

I ke kai malino aʻo Kona.

Grand is Kona of the clouds mirrored in the sea

Puffy white clouds nestled in the calm

Waters spill forth from the cloud banks

There's no other that can compare

With Kona of the mirrored seas, a sea of mingling hues

The calm seas of Kona

Proud indeed in the tranquility

Kona of mirrored seas in the calm

Majestic is Hualālai

The calm seas of Kona. (Wilcox et al. 2003)

Like "Kona Kai ʻŌpua i ka Laʻi," "Kailua–Kona" mentions specific (modern) place names (Banyans, White Sands), which highlight the fondness of the composer for those particular areas. Another traditional device *mele* employs is the concept of *pono*, or dualism, which links particular concepts with specific opposites. In the case of *mele pana*, these are usually geographical features. Common pairs are mountains and sea, windward and leeward, and east and west. These typically appear in a specific order, such as from the uplands to the sea, from windward to leeward, and from east to west. This is demonstrated in "Kailua–Kona" in the line, "Go up to the mountains or down to the sea."

This is but one example of the many skillfully written original Jawaiian compositions in existence today that perpetuate traditional Hawaiian themes in a modern context. In a 1992 article on Jawaiian music, Andrew Weintraub lamented that "a large part of the Jawaiian repertoire consists of covers (or 'versions') of reggae tunes" (Weintraub 1998). Yes, reggae and pop covers still prevail. However, as many of the examples cited in this chapter demonstrate, myriad original Jawaiian tunes have been composed since then, many of which reflect traditional Hawaiian values expressed with a reggae-inspired beat.

In the case of rap music, David Toop argues that cultural tweaks on rap follow "an age–old tradition of new immigrants [trying to fit in], but expressing it in a form that Hollywood tells us is exclusively Black and Hispanic" (Toop 1992, 188). But in Hawai'i, Native Hawaiian Jawaiian and rap artists are not "immigrants trying to fit in." Nor are they, as some critics allege, perpetuating a "weak" sound. By following in the footsteps of Hawaiian musicians of previous generations, they are drawing from their Native Hawaiian roots as much as they are incorporating African-diasporic sounds and resituating them in a Hawaiian context. This is something that has been successfully achieved by Old School, New School, and Next School Jawaiian artists.

Ha'ina 'ia mai ana ka puana (Conclusion)

> Jawaiian still rules, like it or not.
> — WAYNE HARADA[33]

Ha'ina 'ia mai ana ka puana. This is a standard phrase that ends traditional Hawaiian songs. It translates, "Thus my song (story) has come to an end." And what is the *ha'ina* (conclusion) of our sojourn with contemporary Hawaiian music? First, Hawaiian music is adaptable: It has survived transformations into choral, ballroom, jazz, slack key, falsetto, lounge sound, pop, rock, reggae, rap, and hip hop, drawing on its Hawaiian roots as much as on foreign influences. What this constant evolution demonstrates is that Hawaiian is a vital, living culture, and, "as with all other living cultures, the Hawaiian culture has always been and will continue to be in a state of evolution" (Stewart 2002). In an interview with the Native

Hawaiian musical icon "Aunty" Martha Hohu, Leslie Keli'ilauahi Stewart discusses this point. Despite her early training and perpetuation of a more traditional Hawaiian music, Aunty Martha echoes Stuart Hall's perspective on the dynamics of musical hybridity:

> Jawaiian music was inevitable. . . . There is so much mass communication today that it would be impossible for Hawaiian music to exist in isolation. And who would want Hawaiian music to be isolated? Do you really think guys like Israel Kamakawiwo'ole and Gabby Pahinui would be able to produce the kind of music they did if it wasn't for the introduction of those instruments [the 'ukulele and guitar]? (Stewart 2002, 46)

Another point worthy of consideration is that reggae and rap speak to young Native Hawaiians in a way that other music genres originating from *haole* cultures do not. Why have reggae and rap had such a strong influence on Jawaiian (and post-Jawaiian) music while other popular genres — disco, goth, techno, and punk, for example — have not? Jon Osorio thinks it is because those other forms of music are associated with and produced by dominant white culture, and that Native Hawaiian and Pacific youth identify more with oppressed peoples of color, such as those of the African diaspora, and thus relate better to their music. Perhaps the similar geographies and climates of Hawai'i and the Caribbean (hence, the term "island" music) has played a role in shaping the mix of Hawaiian and reggae; perhaps skanking to the more languid reggae tunes is comparative to, and reminiscent in some way of, Hawaiian hula. Perhaps the oral and storytelling nature of African American rap and its percussion-based bass beats resonate and are more appealing to Native Hawaiian youth who are mixing the rhythms of contemporary urban society with the storytelling and percussion-based drum beats of our Hawaiian ancestors.

It is likely that there are many reasons that reggae and rap have had such phenomenal impact on contemporary Hawaiian music and will continue to do so in the foreseeable future: the commonalities between Native Hawaiian and African-diasporic cultures as being people of color oppressed by white hegemony; the similarity of vibrant oral traditions that, according to some hip-hop scholars, underpin rap music through storytelling, or what is known locally in Hawai'i as "talking story." It is also possible, as Trisha Rose argues, that there is a preference for percussion-based music in African American hip hop because it resonates (pun intended) from deeper African roots (Rose 1994).

Native Hawaiian culture, too, is rooted in the resonant tones of the *pahu* drum, *pūniu* (knee drum), *ipu heke* (double gourd drum), and *kā ʻekeʻeke* (bamboo sections that emit a deep drum-like resonance). Finally, it is possible that cultures have developed out of our relationships to our respective environments, which is best demonstrated in our contemporary musics in musical influence and song forms.

The "double consciousness" of youth culture in exerting its own creativity by reflecting environments as young poets who are also rebelling should also be mentioned (Osumare 1999). While barriers or boundaries are often drawn along lines of race, color, gender, and even sexual preference, perhaps we should pay more attention to the boundaries we draw around ourselves in regard to musical preference, which marks our age and generational affiliations. Raised in the 1960s, the contemporary Hawaiian musician and composer Jon Osorio admits to being influenced by the Beatles and Bob Dylan.[34] As a composer who came of age in the 1980s, I am more inclined to be influenced by Madonna and Wham! or Bob Marley and UB40. Certainly, young Hawaiian composers such as the members of Sudden Rush are being influenced by hip hop and rap stars I cannot keep up with. And so it will continue.

Finally, and perhaps most important, is the message of the music, combined with the beat, that first attracted a Hawaiian audience to reggae. Reggae's attraction to such a diverse ethnic audience has been explained as "the music nurtur[ing] the consciousness of black people without denying the humanity of any people" (Potash 1997, xxii).

In Hawaiʻi, the message of the reggae, particularly in the early period, was as important as the beat. For Hula Records' Cindy Lance, "Back then, it wasn't the rhythm alone, it was the message; the message in reggae was closer to what was felt about getting the [Hawaiian] islands back — it was the message of freedom from oppression."[35]

Whether it is the message, the beat, or both that attracts a Hawaiian audience to reggae and Jawaiian music, it is clear that it, along with the growing popularity of rap music in Hawaiʻi, has played a key role in shaping the dynamic strand of this hybrid contemporary Hawaiian music. Jawaiian and post-Jawaiian rap have been successful in capturing the essence of Native Hawaiian and African-diasporic influences and mixing them into something new. While this melding of musics has not always been easy to negotiate, the artists drawn to experimenting with this hybrid sound have managed to carve a place for it.

Notes

1   The next example is probably the *leo kiʻekiʻe*, or falsetto, which some believe was adapted from the Mexican *vaqueros* (cowboys) who were recruited to Hawaiʻi to break horses and herd cattle. Whether they were responsible for introducing *leo kiʻekiʻe*, or not, they are credited for the development of *kī hōʻalu* (slack key). When the early vaqueros left Hawaiʻi, the Hawaiians did not know how to tune the guitars to the standard tuning and thus inadvertently created new tunings. Today, this is called slack key and is celebrated and studied around the world. (With the vaquero influence on Hawaiian society, *paniolo*, or cowboy songs, became a new genre of Hawaiian music.) Another example is the adaptation of the Portuguese *braguinha* into the Hawaiian *ʻukulele* in the late 1870s. Along with the steel guitar, the ʻukulele was popular in the second half of the nineteenth century through the 1950s.

2   Macka B, "Bob," on the CD *Roots Music, Volume 2: Private Beach Party* (Universal City, Calif.: Universal Music Special Markets, 1999).

3   Some international reggae stars who have performed in Hawaiʻi, often multiple times, are Ziggy Marley, Steel Pulse, Aswad, Yellowman, Inner Circle, Shabba Ranks, Alpha Blondy, Shaggy, Black Uhuru, Maxi Priest, UB40, Gregory Isaacs, Eddie Grant, and Third World. Artists who have become established in Hawaiʻi include Dread Ashanti, the Shakers, Natural Vibrations, Marty Dread, Sistah Sistah, Roots Natty Roots, Nā Mele Rasta, Island Irie, Rainbow Rastasan, Dub Version, and Jah Fire. Some performers have come and gone, while others have been around for a while. Examples not mentioned elsewhere in this article are Hauʻula, Puʻunui, Brother Nolan, Titus Kinimaka, Mataio Band, Three Scoops of Aloha, Leahi, Diane and da Boyz, Loco Moco Band, Hoalikelike, Hawaiian Time, Island Rhythms, Third Road Delight, Island Boyz, Pure Heart, Kaʻū, Colon, Imua, Three Plus, ʻEkolu, Valley Boys, Norm, the ʻOpihi Pickers, Malino, Kekai Boys, Lahaina Grown, and Nuff Said, just to name a few.

4   Two examples are the groups Hōʻaikane and Manaʻo Company, whose members Walter Tavares and Sean Naʻauao have continued on with successful Jawaiian projects.

5   For example, Hōʻaikane had released four traditional Hawaiian albums before its acclaimed Jawaiian breakthrough album, *A New Beginning* (Kahale Music, 1989).

6   Two examples are Justin and Bitty McClean, Shiloh Pa and Steel Pulses' Conrad Kelly.

7   Back cover, *Hawaiian Reggae*.

8   Amy Kuʻuleialoha Stillman, e-mail communication, May 22, 2002.

9   The Hawaiian Dictionary defines the word haole, in part, as, "white person, Caucasian; American, English; formerly, any foreigner, foreign, introduced of foreign origin, as plants." Samuel H. Elbert and Mary Kawena Pukui 1986, 58.

As Hawaiians became more familiar with different ethnicities and nations of origin, the word *haole* came to specifically refer to Caucasian people, and Western ways.

10 Composed in the nineteenth century as a *mele* for King David Kalākaua, "Heʻeia" is not a surfing song per se. However, it does incorporate the metaphor of surfing as a description of lovemaking and sexual prowess. This penchant for veiled meaning in traditional Hawaiian music is called *kaona*, and it is an important traditional poetic technique favored by Hawaiian poets. See Elbert and Mahoe 1972.

11 Local musician Peter Moon is often cited as an originator of the Jawaiian sound in Hawaiʻi. While his Peter Moon Band has recorded only one reggae song, a Jawaiian-inspired remake of Bob Marley's "Guava Jelly" (*Cane Fire*, 1982), he has lent support behind the scenes to other artists. For over twenty years, Moon organized the popular Kanikapila ("Music Jam") concert series at the University of Hawaiʻi, Mānoa, which showcased popular Hawaiian music, including "crossover" Jawaiian artists such as Brother Nolan and Kapena. The earliest local recording of a reggae-inspired tune, however, is Billy Kaui's "Mr. Reggae" (*Billy Kaui*, 1977).

12 Some examples are the rising popularity of Sudden Rush, B.E.T. (Big Every Time), and the emergence of Hawaiian artists O-shen and Chief Ragga as talented rap artists, as seen in a guest studio appearance on "urban contemporary" hip hop radio station "Da Bomb" 102.7 FM. O-shen and Chief Ragga (a.k.a. Jamin Wong, formerly of Hōʻaikane) performed an energetic, dynamic, and flawless original rap that was truly inspiring, giving the listening audience a promising preview of what may be coming in the new sound of contemporary Hawaiian music in the post-Jawaiian era (January 24, 2003).

13 The Hawaiian scholar George Kanahele defines "cha-lang-a-lang," a term for the sound the strings of a ʻukulele make when strummed back and forth, as a style or technique of playing the ʻukulele in which "a certain unmistakable sound" is produced (Kanahele 1979, xxix). This typically fast back-and-forth strumming style, sometimes done in double time, was common in Hawaiian music of the 1940s–60s among artists such as Genoa Keawe. It is considered a style of playing that is unique to Hawaiʻi. "Picking" is a technique of playing the steel guitar, slack-key guitar, and the ʻukulele, in which strings are plucked individually rather than strummed to create a distinct and unique sound.

14 Keala Kawaʻauhau, as quoted on Sudden Rush 1997.

15 Local with a capital L is evoked in Hawaiʻi-based scholarship to mean something more than just a geographic marker (i.e., local vs. global). See Candace Fujikane, "Introduction, Asian Settler Colonialism in Hawaiʻi." In *Whose Vision? Asian Settler Colonialism in Hawaiʻi*, ed. Russell Leong, special issue of *Amerasia Journal* 26, no. 2 (2000): xv–xxii.

16 See Fujikane 1994; Okamura 1980; Sumida 1991; Trask 2000; Yamamoto 1979.

17 Sudden Rush website, available at http://hawaii–nation.org/sudden-rush/html (October 7, 2002).

18 Jon Osorio, personal communication, May 11, 1999.

19 An excellent synopsis of this aspect of Hawaiian culture is found in Kameʻeleihiwa (1992).

20 Lilikalā Kameʻeleihiwa, personal communication, January 24, 1995.

21 The word "Kanak" is a shortening of *kanaka,* the Hawaiian word for person.

22 The CD anthology *Sessions: Summer/Winter, Volume 1* (Pearl City, Hawaiʻi: Polystar, 1996), brings together many of these surf-related tunes.

23 My transcription and translation.

24 Examples of remade reggae songs are "96 Degrees in the Shade" (Third World/Manaʻo Company); "Bend Down Low" (Bob Marley/Hōʻaikane); "Rub-a-Dub Style" (Michigan and Smiley/Hōʻaikane); "Pass the Kutchie" (Mighty Diamonds/Nā Wai Hoʻoluʻu o ke Ānuenue), "Red Red Wine" (UB40/Kapena). Examples of remade pop songs are "My Eyes Adored You" (Frankie Vallie/Justin); "Everything I Own" (Bread/ʻEkolu); "Make It With You" (Bread/Sean Naʻauao). An example of a remade Hawaiian song is "Kuʻu Wā Liʻiliʻi" (Lena Machado/Valley Boys). Original Jawaiian songs include "Molokaʻi Slide" (ʻEhukai); "Surf," "North Shore," "ʻOpihi Man" (Kaʻau Crater Boys), and "Lahaina Grown" (Lahaina Grown).

25 The lyrics for Bob Marley's "No Woman No Cry" are from www.bobmarley.com. The lyrics for Bruddah Walter Aipolani and Island Afternoon's version are transcribed from the CD *Hawaiian Reggae* (Honolulu: Platinum Pacific, 1990).

26 For a complete history, see Kameʻeleihiwa 1992.

27 "Sonny" refers to Sonny Kaniho, one of the first Native Hawaiins to sign up for DHHL land in the 1950s. A thorough historical account of the abuse of Hawaiian home lands is found in Susan Faludi, "Broken Promise: Hawaiians Wait in Vain," *Honolulu Star-Bulletin and Advertiser*, September 15, 1991, B1.

28 In 2003, Native Hawaiians commemorated 110 years since the overthrow, with new anthems of political protest, such as Sudden Rush's rap "Kūʻē (Resistance)."

29 Popular hits of the past few years not already mentioned are "Sharing the Night Together" (Dr. Hook/Fiji), "Somewhere over the Rainbow/What a Wonderful World Melody (Judy Garland and Louis Armstrong/Israel Kamakawiwoʻole), "Sweet City Woman" (Stampeders/Kapena), "Still Say Yes" (Klymaxx/Native Blend), "Three Times a Lady" (Lionel Ritchie/Sean Naʻauao), and "Master Blaster" (Stevie Wonder/Darryl Labrado).

30 The lyrics for Redding's "Sittin' on the Dock of the Bay" are from www.otisredding.com. The lyrics for Fiji's version are transcribed from the CD *Gratitude* (Honolulu: Ricochet Records, 1999).

31 Stephen Bishop, "On and On," on *Careless* (Uni/MCA, 1976). Hoʻonuʻa's version is on the anthology *Pride of the Islands III* (Honolulu: KCCN FM, 2000).

32 Harry K. Mitchell, "Mele o Kaho'olawe," on Olomana, *And So We Are* (Kailua, Hawai'i: Seabird Sounds, 1977).

33 Wayne Harada, "Jawaiian Sounds Remain Strong," *Honolulu Advertiser,* June 27, 2002.

34 Jon Osorio, personal communication, May 11, 1999.

35 Cindy Lance, personal communication, May 9, 1999.

CHAPTER FIFTEEN

Heartbreak

ROBERTA J. HILL

~~~~~~~~~~

Jean didn't scrub the friggin' bathroom. She's got a few more days before it's back to managing the office at Kelly's Insurance. I come in from getting groceries at Copps, and my sister is still staring at the snow splotched on the branches of the alder tree. Her eyes are so swollen she looks drugged. Looks like she never moved, not even after I left. When our eyes meet, her brown eyes darken from charcoal pain blotting her pupils. Lips puffy like a rubber blow-up ball and in gray sweats, well, she looks like shit. Not a bad-looking woman, but geez, theatrical as hell. We do heal from heartbreak. I holler from the en- trance — get off your freaking duff and do something, go out, get some work done, do dishes, vacuum, anything, get energy flowing, buy a dog and walk it, but she sniffles, moans, wraps her arms around her stomach. Tears pour down her cheeks. All last week she lay in bed in the morning, then sat the afternoons on the shut-in porch or at the kitchen table. She took two weeks off work to straighten out. Two whole weeks! Think of the money she lost and didn't even call in sick. Took it from her vacation. Heartbreak's a constant process. I can cook, shop, clean to help her through, but I'll need a week to get a better grip when she's gone.

I had to kick the door shut because she didn't even get up to help me with the two bags in my arms. I can't stop figuring it out. I am getting pissed. Seems only one force will stop her from going down into a gaseous pool of crap. That's you, Willie. You helped me feel strong and tender-hearted, but I won't pay all the rent. If she's going to live with me, she's got to support herself. Get in better shape by Monday for Kelly's Insurance. I'm going to puke if she brings it all up again. Geez, process. Telling you helps me because it's about life. Her life, his life, my life now she's here. You grew up with eyes in the back of your head. It'll never happen to you, this thing between an Indian woman and a black man. You are tough enough to stop it on a dime. But it's not unusual. Indians and blacks have been balling each other since the Olmecs. Four hundred years being enslaved together, being shipped and sold in Spain, Portugal, Angola, Ghana, the West Indies, go ahead, tell me there wasn't any loving going on.

I put celery in the fridge, holler through the gloom, "What you doing today? You gonna start smoking? Fridge could get cleaned. Your orange is green. It'll explode to dust if I touch it. Maybe get your tax stuff organized?"

"I'm going to call him." I hear her husky voice sheltering false hope. When I look at her, her bottom lip is trembling, seizing up in contortions the broken-hearted recognize. "I'm going to hurt forever and love him till the day I die." She takes a jerky breath, then looks through the trees. "It's been thirty-nine days since I wrote him and said how I felt. I wonder if he got it or thought it through." She wipes off a tear, then chokes. Her shoulders slope over her heart, and her back bows with one shoulder leaning left like she's been kicked in the chest.

"I hurt his feelings."

"He's an asshole, Jean." I shove two pints of lemon yogurt in the fridge, start folding bags. She pulls her fingers through tangles in her long brown hair, pulling the twisted hair gently apart. Not much gray for forty-one. "Think! You write to say he hurt you. He doesn't answer, not in one month, or maybe two, maybe never. He read it, ripped it up, laughed, went out for a scotch. Geez, get with it. He was a perfect example of an asshole, your first lesson in cross-cultural dating." I sit down in the chair across from her. You can almost smell the smoldering in her heart. Oh god, she hurt.

"He's angry because I know so much about him."

"Kind men don't protect themselves that much."

"He's had to move so much because of his job."

"He gets himself into shit and runs away." I cut off her wrongful reminiscing, but she flicks her eyes and smiles her toothbrush ad smile.

I envy her large, even teeth. What can I say? So you a thrush or bowl of mush? Gray morning light floods the kitchen, and I'm getting hungry for toast.

"We had fun together," she says, still dreaming. "We laughed for hours on our trip to Kender's Falls. We talked like we were meant to be. We drove north into mountains. He was working in Minneapolis when we met. We felt alive, so joyous. I still feel that sunshine. The piney woods, camp smoke, waking up in a golden dawn to birds chirping, he's curled up near me, his breath warming my neck. The lake and shore subdued in mist. Fog covered our car when he drove through forests. Trees faint as clouds that emerge in a marvelous soft green, melting before our eyes. Ah, Theresa, we walked under a waterfall, thundering in sunshine. We laughed and talked for hours. I felt so happy. I saw his happiness. We made love in the tent. Kissing his warm cheeks, touching his strong shoulders, feeling him hold me with a taut desire. Once I opened my eyes and he was looking at me. How I wanted." She stops to clear her throat. Her voice squeaks "to love him for. . . ." and, . . .

Holy moly, she's shrieking with pain, bursts out sobbing with piercing cries that surely are turning her sinuses to rocks. Tears streaming, she falls overboard again. Shameless. Not even caring how I feel watching her. No dignity. No demeanor. She reaches for tissues, blows three long blasts and smears her tears. Her pain is a throbbing drum in the kitchen. She curls knees to chest in those smudged gray sweats, immersed in grief. Pounce, my fuzzy cat, is mewing in her sleep in the next room.

Yes, Willie, I am older and know heartbreak's not easy. Reminds me how I loved Joel till my mind broke. Let my needs go, just turned numb with longing. She'll learn. Geez, I warned her not to go there when I met her fella a while ago. Handsome, intelligent, charming. Dreads all over his head down to his shoulders, sensitive mouth, full beard framing eyes so black they took the sheen of stone. I couldn't read them. Curly lashes. Polished obsidian, I thought, sharp-edged and lean, intelligent and purposeful. Couldn't tell how old until he started talking. Then I thought, yes, he is old, for a man that old you could hardly tell. Kept himself in good shape. He had to, knowing women even as he claimed not to know them. Always teasing about how little he knew! That's when you are in the presence of a real piece of art, deceiving and sweet as can be. He must have played women for years, probably grew up being shown how to please. Do this for me, child. Do that now and be sweet. Grew up having to act with charm, faking and sacrificing real feeling to survive. They buried the real spirit of him while they coached him how to create devastating charm.

But geez, we also had to please to survive. Turning on daddy charms. Making pretend selves to hide behind. When faking turns to habit, it gets hard to shut that fake self down. Does he feel what happens after he takes a woman like Jean for a ride, then cuts her off? A punishing man. Pissed at women. Remember Joyce? Charmed that Inuit man from Fairbanks and then, poor miserable slob, he wept when he came last time to see her. She shut him down like ice. Saw her doing that, but geez, couldn't do anything. So Jean showed up a month ago, looking confused. I was worried. I warned her not to sleep with him. She looked at me like I was a rotten incisor. I'd given up on love, or so she said.

Jean reaches for the phone and picks up the receiver, cradles it between her breasts as if the man's breath is going to come through any second. "If I call him, he may say he's been thinking of calling me and then we'll be together again. I just can't believe it's over. It didn't end well. I can't figure out what I did wrong. How can I make amends if I don't know what I did wrong?" She blows her nose. The snow whooshes down.

"Turn on a speaker 'cause I don't want to stand here in the dark." She punches on the speaker and closes her eyes, gathering courage or prayers. Then, after a deep sigh, she punches his numbers with a stiff forefinger. The answering machine comes on. Jean's leaving a message when, holy moly, Vincent breathes hello.

"Miss you," she burbles. "I needed to hear your voice and see how you were doing and if you're clearer 'bout your feelings."

"Hi, Sugar, how are you? I've already explained I've got a job in Manitoba for four months. I'm leaving in two–three days for oil exploration up north. Just me, a crew, and wolves. I don't have energy for this long-distance thing. Besides, I'm on permanent rebound. We talked this over a few months ago. Lovers never know each other. We did talk, didn't we?"

"Did you get my letter? We gave each other so much. I feel alive when you're with me."

"Awesome, that's awesome, but baby, I never give myself away. I told you that. I'd get flat, you see what I'm saying? We'd bore each other, start picking fights. Besides, I've never seen a man and woman stay in love for long. It don't happen in this world. Sugar, protect yourself now and stay the mystery you are."

"Vincent, I don't get it. I was good for you. You said so. I'll do whatever it takes. I'll be here waiting for . . ." She glances at me with sad red eyes. I'm shaking my head, waving my arms No! But his warm voice runs quick as hot cocoa through the speaker.

"Sugar, I'm a solipcist. Good at the game, never first string. Can't cut it. I don't know anymore what people mean when they talk feelings. I just move along, doing what I do. I don't feel nothing. No love, fear, grief. So, I don't get it. Why go on like this?"

"You can go solo, but please, let's get together again. I gotta see you sometime."

"Sure, baby, but don't burn out all your bulbs waiting, you see what · I'm saying?"

"When do you get back?" She stares at the floor like it might start shaking. His answer. Click. He hangs up. She hits redial with a trembling finger. The line is busy. Snow and wind rattle the window. She holds the receiver against her heart. It's bleeping. Frantic. She doesn't hear it. Outside the wind is coming through the branches sending silver flakes along the window pane near the table. We can feel wind coming through the sill. It isn't the best apartment, you know, but it works for us as home, two women, both divorced, getting their lives squared away so they can each find a new pattern.

I take the receiver and stop the buzz. She doesn't get it. I have to tell her. "Jean, you just trusted the wrong man. You are not wrong. You are beautiful, stupid as a guppy, but not wrong. He gave you every reason to trust him. He was sweet and called you every day. He told you he loved you and could not live without you. Yes, he didn't pay for much when you went out. You handled the whole paying thing for that trip you took because he was between jobs. Engineers don't always make that much money, I guess. Don't forget the rock he brought you from that beach in Ghana, when he went there for a job last May. Not a big rock, a pebble isn't a ruby or a peach moonstone, but hey, on the beach, he thought of you, picked up a stone and brought it all the way back — your favorite shade of pink. Did you see signs of a break-up?"

She rises from the chair to pour herself a glass of water. She swings her hair away from her face, taking a few sips before she sits down. Geez, if she keeps crying so hard, blood vessels are going to break on her nostrils. A varicose nose! Then she'll have something to cry about!

She holds her breath. "How will I ever meet someone as nice? I can't stop loving him. How can he be just a friend? What if . . . I never . . . see him again?"

She drinks more water, twists her neck, and puts her hands on her nape to rub away tension, then falls into reverie. When she speaks again, I realize she doesn't know I'm here for her.

"When he leaned above me, his dreads tickled my breasts. The way he tucked his arm under his head and looked into my eyes, his black eyes looking into mine, so sweet. Being together was like getting a present every morning. My heart shaped a pearl in his embrace. I want to hold him. He smelled like nutmeg. Ohhh, I feel such longing to keep on loving him. My heart's ripped out and it's worse . . ." She moans like Pounce when she senses no one's home. "It's worse than leaving Harry."

Oh god, I want to moan with her, but if two of us get to moaning, what will that do? I think of her divorce and Harry and yes, it's true. She is crying harder for Vincent whom she loved for six or eight months. She divorced Harry over a year ago. Harry, twenty years her husband. When she reached the ripe age of forty, Harry decided she was growing old! As if he didn't fathom this when they got married. He wanted youth. He wanted to take a young woman back home to Wolf Point. She couldn't believe it when she found that lady's panties in his suit pocket. Size five, sheer periwinkle blue, probably from Wicked Secrets. Harry never treasured her. But geez, commitment takes two rooted people, not gnats in the sun. My divorce forced me to get rooted.

You got to get over here, Willie, and help me straighten her up. She's beyond pathetic. Tell her she didn't deserve this pain. She needs to reframe the whole thing, beginning to end. I'm trying, but I'm no-where good as you. So I give her another picture, one that might spring her into action, you know, back in the flow of things.

"Earth to Jean," I say, sliding my chair closer now and touching her shoulder. I go on. "At this very moment, Vincent's kissing Louise now, telling her she's the world to him. He's saying marry me. He may marry her. Then what you gonna do? Be standing on the sidelines like a muddle head? He was putting smoke on you! He's going from woman to woman until he gets too old to attract a woman beautiful and loving as you. He'll find a woman and convince her she's the perfect one. He'll tell her he loves her."

"He has to leave town. For work. Didn't you hear? He's solo. I know you won't stop until you've had your say."

I go on. "On one level, he believes she's the perfect one to convince them both. But within a year or two after the marriage, he'll find another. He'll tell his wife he loves her, too, and will play yo-yo with her for some time. Then maybe he'll divorce her because she wasn't right. His job keeps him traveling. If they stay married, she won't know why, but she'll knock her brains out trying to keep the day he leaves from coming. Something in her will feel it under the bed when he falls asleep, like a fuzz ball that shuffles through the dark or some dazzling worry in the corner of her eye."

Jean's forehead waffles. She touches the glass to the table, watching me while she makes a wet ring form. "Nah!" she says.

I go on. "He'll punish her subtly with the implication he's leaving. If she believes and loves him, she'll grow gallstones or herniate a disk from being hypervigilant. He's not giving you or any woman anything. Each time he leaves a woman, he grows lonelier, till his spirit's frozen. He's going to die a petrified man. That's the consequence."

"Theresa, how unfair! How unkind! He wants love more than anything in the world. He simply dreads commitment. How can you say that? How do you know so much when you only laid eyes on him once? That's your ex you're talking about!"

She holds on to men who are not worth a hill of beans. She won't let go because we're the same. For twenty-seven years I lived with Joel. How I cried, yes, cried for three years during the divorce. Remember that, Willie? You helped me through. Patient, listening, firm. Now I'm glad to be free. We were trained to hold on, even when there was no emotional involvement or attention coming back. We never even knew it was supposed to! We didn't know our own needs for attention and consideration and a few crumbs of emotional nourishment. We been waiting with hands out for crumbs all our lives. But a woman's got to be kind to herself, get rooted to her own life, 'cause each time, love will come along. She has to grip her own kindness to her heart, get under her hurt to feel the anger at being played. Then she discovers self-protection. I will not give up, Willie. I'm going to keep trying, so I'm going on.

"It happens that way. A man can't do for you what you gotta do for yourself. Chant this with me, come on, try it: *I will not trade well-being for love. I will not trade well-being for love.* Chant till it's automatic. You see him again, think 'well-being,' smile and shine him on!"

She was hiccupping hard, tears still streaming. I know damn hollow burning grief like that. I burned up until I felt a frozen continent the size of Antarctica in my heart, yes. She was hiccupping away, her hands limp as two bratwursts before they're cooked, her mouth a prune. Geez, it must be lunchtime by now, but with heartbreak, you can't eat regular. That's why I don't think Vincent will ever feel heartbreak, because that man was set on eating regularly on his own schedule like a train or something.

I look at her with her long brown hair and her faint crow's feet, her youthful hands. I think of my own self, my strong black eyes and few wrinkles. We're not desert plants who only need a scant shower every year. Why must we hang on when love goes bad?

She sighs. The snow. Sometimes cozy, sometimes cold. Like allies, snowflakes whirl around and dash themselves against the pane. Her face is swollen with red splotches dotting her cheeks. Her nose has grown three sizes, and her eyes are jet streaks in clumps of damp lashes.

Her voice less mildly hoarse, she simpers, "I heard from Evelyn that his new woman is very pretty and has four children. I'm too old for children. Two months ago, we were together. How did he change in one night? He said, *It's over. We won't be lovers again.* I talk, and Indian women are supposed to be quiet. I'm energetic, and Indian women are patient, still as deer. She's Brazilian from São Paulo." Jean lifts her chin, holding it up, considering whether she can ever be as cosmopolitan and chic as a Brazilian woman from São Paulo with four young children.

She is balancing on the edge of catastrophe, unimaginable and deadening, the catastrophe of our colonization, of families broken apart, of love shattered generation after generation. We all suffered and were suffering the result of punishing histories, of being ripped from those we loved, of being unable to trust that love is vastly different from subjugation. Inheriting that suffering, we grow needy and angry when we feel afraid. We stand in our own shadows because we dare not feel utterly helpless. Jean is reaching the feeling carried by the millions of broken spirits before us, all crowding round. Yes, heartbreak begets nervous breakdowns, depression, suicide, and bad faith. She wants his love, Willie, but we know there's no story for it, no space to say this love has promise. I envy folks who inherit more stable patterns — black, Indian, whatever. They learn to keep love going. Maybe they have resources, jobs, or basic trust. Maybe no masters, overseers, or government policies ever separated them from each other. How do we heal generations of heartache? Tears now pooling in my eyes, I got to talk down grief, so I rub my face and get up to go to the counter. Jean doesn't believe we have blind spots.

"You didn't ask him about the Brazilian on the phone."

"He doesn't love her. He told me that when he said we won't be lovers again. He doesn't have the energy. He won't lie to me about it."

"But that's cruel! If he's got her, he can't have you, now can he? Don't throw yourself at him. She doesn't know about you. He's not going to raise children. She'll move closer, and he'll pull away. He'll need some space. He's putting smoke on her. She won't see it until she gets a whiff of the pretty woman who works with the crew up in Canada when he goes there to figure out how to get oil out of limestone."

"Shale."

"Does it matter?"

"Yes, everything about him matters, at least to me. He finds oil in shale, OK? You got it right?"

I take some bread out and make myself toast while she sits there. Silence gets me. The snow, the dreaming cat, the wedge of impatience and sad losses make me try again. "Reframe it. You didn't lose the only man you'll ever love. Love comes again. Come on, now, say it: *I won't trade well-being for love*. Say it until you learn the lesson. Check the next man out."

She is alert now, even as I'm feeling teary. She wipes her nose tenderly and blinks long and slow. I feel myself in the presence of an owl checking out movement before it lifts its noiseless wings. In a brilliant move, I start pounding a forty-nine on the counter, my palm lifting like a sassy drummer's stick. It was grace coming down to help us, ancestor inspiration!

When the dance is over, he'll be there, way a hi, way a hiiiii-yo,
Some black men are lovers, hope you get your share, way a hi, way a hiiiii-yo,
His dreads will come swinging on a southern breeze, way a hi, way a hiiii-yo,
Grown so long they're bouncing off his knees, way a hi, way a hiiii-yo.
Way a hi, way a hi, way a hiii-yo.

"You don't get it, do you?" She tucks her upper lip against her teeth. She might be pissed, but you know, Willie, I'm the hottest temper in the family. Sad. She can't take a tease about him.

"I love Vincent because he's Vincent. You never liked him. You told me he was a sleazy worm. You were jealous, say it, admit it. You never liked Harry, either. You are a judgmental bitch, thinking you know everybody's insides."

She is getting her dander up, mugging a frown like a three year old's.

"Going on with your psychology shit," she says, standing up and taking her glass to the sink, then settling into her chair like a gunslinger entering a new saloon in TV westerns.

"You flunked psychology! Admit it." She glares at me, her pain corkscrews in. I just look back, cool as I can, taking her all in. But my ears are getting hot, and my lips feel thin.

"You wouldn't know a dysfunction if it whupped you on the ass!" She stands up to slap her ass, then sidles over to where I'm standing at the counter. "You took one class—experimental rat maze, stop watch, count the beanies, screwball stuff. How do you know the motives of a man you never hardly spoke to? Even a psychologist's got to ask her client to tell his story."

She starts bouncing on the balls of her feet. Her eyes are glinting like hypnotizing hooks. I smell the drift of her Black Night perfume.

"I see what's going on," she shouts into my face, so close I could slap her. "He loved me. He loved me more than you, and you can't stand that!" I know that kind of pain. My neck and head are burning, and the room falls into hell.

"You want to scrap?" I say. "Look how he treated you. Yo-yo girl! You're too good for him—energetic and happy. People like you. He wasn't giving anything of himself at all. I tried to tell you to watch out. I had to wake up to see the same thing about myself with Joel. Really, I'm not down on you, but can't you see it for what it was?"

I am counting on you to get here soon, Willie, 'cause she irks me bad. I can't do this every day. She's got to regain some composure. I've settled my divorce and stay open to love, but there's all kinds of love in this world.

"You never liked my boyfriends. You told dad about Skip. You! Goody two shoes! You were the light in his eyes. You always got him to do what you wanted. He gave you the car and money and clothes. But me? He never paid attention to me! Always too busy. I wanted to light up his eyes, too!" She is waving her arms around, a snow snake full of gestures, now palms flat against her chest to point out how she got the short shrift, then punching toasted air. I get back to Vincent, the real crisis maker, not dad or our ex-hubbies.

"If Vincent was a concert," I say, "you're at the end of the second block in line waiting for a ticket."

"You always pick on men I love." She is glaring, her jaw grinding. She is winding up to lash pain on someone. I'm the only one here. The cat meows at the door and looks at both of us. How can she float like that, her eyes watching us? She carries her tail high and happy. I can hear her purring as she jogs over and rubs Jean's leg. Pounce is coiling herself around Jean's calf, chin to tail tip in a full body stroke.

"If Vincent was a book," I say, "you'd be living on a riverbank without a library card. If he was a fire, you'd be . . ." She's not one foot from me, closes in, her top lip stretched thin as a knife edge. I duck her swing. My heart's beating so hard I can't hear much. The punch misses, but my little sister's a magnet of fury, then she huffs and grabs her hand. I'm shaky and hot but straining to pay her my whole attention. Pounce meows long, loudly, dainty with her paws as she leaps to the counter and winds round my arm. Jean snorts and groans. She curses. Her fist nicked the cupboard. She shakes as a wave breaks through her, then looks at her split knuckle. The top of her right hand opens like a tiny mouth. The short, deep gash makes her hand shake as blood beads out and drips on the countertop. No wires fall out. Must be my sister. I grab hold her shoulder. She touches me with her left hand, lightly. When I back off, she's nursing her hand, the blood dripping down. I go to the sink for a wet rag.

She takes the cold cloth, wraps her wound, and flashes a smile that comes from a place I've never seen. A place from the blood inside us both, formed from love between a half-million ancestors.

"I didn't mean it, just wanted you to get off the pity pot."

She raises her left hand and swallows before she answers me.

"If loving him made a fire, I've still got sparks, flying in trees, wafting on breezes."

She leans into the counter with the white rag on her fist. She seems ancient and fragile as if her spirit found itself in the ocean at night or in a thick forest under a full moon. I feel something in the room, a change coming through her, a surrender to love, a giving from inside herself without expectations. She's feeling like you Lakotas say—*bloka*, the way a warrior feels when she's given up everything, when she's traveling a strong-heart road.

We look at each other. Two peas from one pod who follow a similar genetic code, ride down the same family road, and wear the same size jeans. Maybe our genes blink on and off in phases.

"Dad never stayed home," I whisper. "He loved us but he wasn't home much."

"Yeah, I'm starting to remember," she says, lifting the rag to check her wound. I don't know how long she'll hold this way, but she's that way now. *Bloka*, ready for anything, anything at all.

Afterword

ROBERT WARRIOR

~~~~~~~~

The conference that prompted much of what's included in this important collection was, according to every person with whom I have spoken who was in attendance, one of the most intriguing and oddest academic gatherings ever. Motley is one of the only ways to describe the group of scholars and other interested parties who gathered in Hanover, New Hampshire, in April 2000 for " 'Eating Out of the Same Pot': Relating Indian and Black (Hi)stories."

There were Indians, black people, black Indians, and white people in attendance, but that hardly captures the strange mix of identities that made up the group. Phenotype was the last criterion one could use to sort through who was whom. Someone with deep, dark brown skin might be black and Indian, while someone with blue eyes and light hair might be Native. Clothing was, for some who worked obviously to dress a particular part, a more predictable marker of identity. Yet even clothes and jewelry only served to highlight the instability and ambiguity of identity.

Someone wearing a gorget, feathers, beads, or ribbons in the morning might reappear in a sport coat or designer dress in the afternoon. College students in attendance, of course, defied convention at every turn. Regardless of identity, they wore dashikis, Doc Martens, turquoise, chinos, board shorts, and every sort of hairstyle imaginable, none of which provided a reliable guide to the identity of the person underneath.

Looking at the program ahead of time should have clued anyone who was planning to be there into the way the conference would have no easy polarities of difference (black–white, white–Native, black–Indian) around which to rally, and once at the conference, the noise of all the jewelry was something that we all could have gotten used to. But I doubt that anyone could have predicted the way this gathering to discuss the intersections of black and Indian experiences would generate such visceral feelings.

The emotions of this topic spilled over into everything that happened that weekend at Dartmouth. From the first panel to the last, the deep feelings of many participants dangled at or above the surface and came to be at least as important as the scholarship that was presented. Sometimes that seemed to come from giddiness that such a gathering could be and was actually happening. Sometimes it came from anger over issues of invisibility and ignorance. Sometimes it came from sadness over the sense of loss — of loved ones, of unrealized potential, of moments of hopefulness — that pervades the histories of black people and Indian people on this continent. Some people seemed to be bothered that so much was being made over it all. Whatever, the presence of emotion made "Eating out of the Same Pot" much different from the usual lifeless academic gathering where the most one can hope for is to hear a few new ideas, share a meal with an old chum, or make a new friend.

My role at the conference was something akin to my role here — commenting at the end on all that happened. At the conference, that required that I be at all of the sessions, which for the most part I was. Theda Purdue, who had also been asked to comment on what had transpired, spoke before me then was whisked off to the airport. Before escaping, she lobbed a few grenades — provocative comments about Cherokee slavery, a short excursus on Aristotle's views of humanity and how they have been used in the Americas against Indians and blacks. I used more of an approach-avoidance strategy, making some observations about how the conference had demonstrated the extent to which everyone who comes into such a discussion enters shifting terrain and how that had prompted many people there to seek surety where there was none to be had. At our best, we had used the situation to reveal the depth of the existential reality of what it means to think about what it has meant for Indian people and black people to share a history on this continent. At our worst, I said, some of us had fallen back on unconscious, uncritical, unexplored ways of dealing with the differences that were at the center of our gathering — suspicion, stereotypes, and even a disturbing strain of homophobic scapegoating (as if to say, "Well, here's something to agree on and rally around"). I concluded with a reading of an unexpurgated nonfiction story I wrote about being at the one-hundredth anniversary of the Wounded Knee Massacre in 1990 with a black and Narragansett law student I was friends with while in graduate school.

The question-and-answer session that followed devolved into a free-for-all in which a few members of the audience hurled inflammatory comments and shouted at each other. Eventually, some of this spilled outside, and at least one person had to be physically restrained. For my part, I slid down in my chair at the table I was sitting at on the stage and looked for an escape route. I wanted to be at the airport with Professor Purdue. I did manage to get off the stage and to the back of the room in time for the closing, which featured a group of Native women who sang "Amazing Grace" in several Native languages, then led the group in a couple of verses in English. It was a great idea, but it turned out to be a pretty somber rendition. I, for one, felt more wretched than saved and sensed that we were all more blind than we wanted to admit.

But for all the weirdness and the madness, the conference was incredibly important. In contrast to most academic gatherings in which it is hard to see what, if anything, is finally at stake, it was clear to everyone I have talked to about "Eating Out of the Same Pot" that we touched an incredibly important nerve. It changed the way many of us who were there think about this subject. What transpired at the conference has certainly inflected my work in this area. Most, if not all, work comparing Native and African American experience that has come out since has been affected.

This volume is a clear indication of the shifts in the field, and my hope is not so much that it will be a guide to the settled knowledge on the topic as that readers will find in it a marker of how to treat Afro-Native studies with the existential depth and anguish it deserves. Jennifer D. Brody, Tamara Buffalo, David A. Y. O. Chang, Robert Keith Collins, Roberta Hill, Sharon P. Holland, ku'ualoha ho'omanawanui, Deborah E. Kanter, Virginia Kennedy, Barbara Krauthamer, Tiffany M. McKinney, Melinda Micco, Tiya Miles, Celia E. Naylor, Eugene B.

Redmond, and Wendy S. Walters each explore aspects of why the realities of Afro-indigenous experience demand our best attention, our deepest thinking, and our most thorough engagement with neglected voices, unspoken oppression, and the haunting silences of those who most often have been relegated to the hidden spaces of this continent and our consciousnesses.

Rather than recapitulating what these able authors have already said in their contributions, I want to make one observation that readers might find helpful to ponder as they leave these pages. That is, in considering the conflicts that arise in the dynamics of comparing Native and black histories, I found myself again and again reminded of something I have written about elsewhere: the philosopher Raimundo Pannikar's formulation of a "diatopic hermeneutics" (Pannikar 1988, 130ff.), a formulation Walter Mignolo has reworked into "pluritopic hermeneutics" (Mignolo 1995, 11ff.).

According to Pannikar, "If we want to interpret another basically different philosophy we will have to attend to the school of that philosophy and immerse ourselves in its universe of discourse as far as is possible for us. We will have to overcome our parameters and plunge into a participatory process of which we may not be able to foresee the outcome" (Pannikar 1988, 133). The same, I would suggest, is true of finding the depth of comparison in a work like this one.

What is important about Pannikar's work here is that his notion of comparative work is helpful in avoiding a strictly relativist approach — you have your way of seeing things and I have mine — to difference. He achieves this, I think, by steering clear of dialogics in favor of diatopics. This focus on topos, or place, is especially apt for those of us seeking a way to understand and interpret what has been shared in the experiences of Indian and African people on this continent. The temptation, however, to focus on how we might promote dialogue risks losing both the ground upon which those experiences have taken place and the levels of feeling they provoke.

I like these essays exactly because they do not, as Pannikar says of most comparative work, accept "a priori some rules before the dialogue takes place" (Pannikar 1988, 32–33). They are, instead, an invitation to a diatopic hermeneutics that develops in the "existential encounter, an art as much a science, a praxis as much a theory. It is a creative encounter, and there is no blueprint for creativity" (Pannikar 1988, 132–34). For Mignolo, what guides this creative encounter is not the nihilistic retreat into language games of so much contemporary academic work, but ethical discourse. That move to the subject of ethics is part and parcel of overcoming the debilitations of cultural relativism and shifts the focus of the hermeneutic enterprise. As he says, "If the epistemological and ontological aspects of a pluritopic understanding could be dealt with in terms of relativism, its ethical dimension invites one to look at the configuration of power" (Mignolo 1995, 15).

My hope for this field of inquiry is that all of us who care about it will see books like this one as important crossroads on a long road ahead. Scholars, as usual, are in the position of having to try to catch up to the wave of experience that has found expression in the histories presented here and the contemporary realities that other pieces point toward. What seems clear is that, on the streets of this continent's inner cities and on the roads and pathways that cross indigenous enclaves around the world, the black people and red people will keep unfolding a history that crisscrosses, zigs, zags, and doubles back. I am glad that these editors and writers have helped us pick up the trail.

References

~~~~~~~

Abel, Annie Heloise. 1993 (1925). *The American Indian and the End of the Confederacy*. Lincoln: University of Nebraska Press.

———. 1992. *The American Indian as Slaveholder and Secessionist*. Lincoln, Neb.: Bison Books.

Adams, David Wallace. 1995. *Education for Extinction: American Indians and the Boarding School Experience, 1875–1928*. Lawrence: University of Kansas Press.

Alberro, Solange. 1981. "Beatriz de Padilla: Mistress and Mother." Pp. 247–56 in *Struggle and Survival in Colonial America*, ed. David G. Sweet and Gary B. Nash. Berkeley: University of California Press.

Apter, Emily. 1996. "Acting Out Orientalism: Sapphic Theatricality in Turn-of-the-Century Paris." Pp. 15–34 in *Performance and Cultural Politics*, ed. Elin Diamond. London: Routledge.

Archuleta, Margaret, Brenda Child, and K. Tsianina Lomawaima, eds., 2000. *Away from Home: American Indian Boarding School Experiences, 1879–2000*. Phoenix: Heard Museum.

Axtell, James. 1975. "The White Indians of Colonial America." *William and Mary Quarterly* 32 (3d series), no. 1 (January): 55–88.

Bailey, M. Thomas. 1972. *Reconstruction in the Indian Territory: A Story of Avarice, Discrimination, and Opportunism*. Port Washington, N.Y.: Kennikat Press.

Baker, T. Lindsay, and Julie P. Baker, eds. 1996. *The WPA Oklahoma Narratives*. Norman: University of Oklahoma Press.

Barrett, Ward. 1970. *The Sugar Hacienda of the Marqueses del Valle*. Minneapolis: University of Minnesota Press.

Barsh, Russel Lawrence, and Heather Steel. 2000. *New England Afro-Indians and Abolitionism: A Shared Struggle*. Paper presented at "Eating Out of the Same Pot: Relating Black and Native (Hi)stories." Symposium, Dartmouth College, Hanover, N.H. April 21, 2000.

Barth, Fredrik. 1969. *Ethnic Groups and Boundaries*. Boston: Little, Brown.

Bateman, Rebecca. 1991. "'We're Still Here': History, Kinship, and Group Identity among the Seminole Freedmen of Oklahoma." Ph.D. diss., Johns Hopkins University, Baltimore.

Beinart, Peter. 1999. "Lost Tribes: Native Americans and Government Anthropologists Feud over Indian Identity." *Lingua Franca* website, May–June 1999. Available at www.linguafranca.com (accessed November 12, 2000).

Beleña, Eusebio Buenaventura. 1787. *Recopilación sumaria de todos los autos acordados de la Real Audiencia y sala del crimen de esta Nueva España, y providencias de su superior gobierno; de varias reales cédulas y órdenes que después de publicada la Recopilación de Indias han podido recogerse así de las dirigidas á la misma audiencia ó gobierno, como de algunas otras que por sus notables decisiones convendrá no ignorar: por el doctor don Eusebio Buenaventura Beleña*. 2 vols. Mexico City: Viceregal government of Mexico.

Bellin, Joshua David. 2001. *The Demon of the Continent: Indians and the Shaping of American Literature*. Philadelphia: University of Pennsylvania Press.

Bennett, Herman L. 1993. "Lovers, Family and Friends: The Formation of Afro-Mexico, 1580–1810." Ph.D. dissertation, Duke University, Durham.

Benston, Kimberly. 2000. *Performing Blackness: Enactments of African American Modernism*. London: Routledge.

Bergland, Renee L. 2000. *The National Uncanny: Indian Ghosts and American Subjects*. Hanover, N.H.: University Press of New England.

Bittle, William E., and Gilbert Geis. 1964. *The Longest Way Home: Chief Alfred C. Sam's Back-to-Africa Movement*. Detroit: Wayne State University Press.

Bogle, Lori. 1994. "On Our Way to the Promised Land: Black Migration from Arkansas to Oklahoma, 1889–1893." *Chronicles of Oklahoma* 72 (Summer): 160–77.

Bowser, Frederick P. 1973. *The African Slave in Colonial Peru, 1524–1650*. Stanford: Stanford University Press.

Brennan, Jonathan, ed. 2003. *When Brer Rabbit Meets Coyote: African–Native American Literature*. Urbana: University of Illinois Press.

Brockington, Lolita Gutiérrez. 1989. *The Leverage of Labor: Managing the Cortés Haciendas in Tehuantepec, 1588–1688*. Durham, N.C.: Duke University Press.

Brodkin, Karen. 1999. *How Jews Became White Folks and What That Says About Race in America*. New Brunswick, N.J.: Rutgers University Press.

Brooks, James, ed. 2002. *Confounding the Color Line: The Indian–Black Experience in North America*. Lincoln: University of Nebraska Press.

———. 1998. "Confounding the Color Line: Indian–Black Relations in Historical and Anthropological Perspective." Special issue. *American Indian Quarterly* 22, nos. 1–2 (Winter–Spring): 123–258.

Buescher, Derek T., and Kent A. Ono. 1996. "Civilized Colonialism: *Pocahontas* as Neocolonial Rhetoric." *Women's Studies in Communication* 19, no. 2: 125–53.

Byfield, Judith. 2000. "Introduction: Rethinking the African Diaspora." Special issue. *African Studies Review* 43, no. 1 (April): 1–9.

———. 2001. "Tales from the Diasporan Frontier: The African Diaspora in Latin America." Paper presented at Dartmouth College, Hanover, N.H., January 22.

Caceres, Kaleilani. 2001. "Couldn't Take the Mana." On *Who I Am*. Kanaka Boogie Productions.

Calloway, Colin G., ed. 1997. *After King Philip's War: Presence and Persistence in Indian New England*. Hanover, N.H.: University Press of New England.

———. 1986. "Neither White nor Red: White Renegades on the American Indian Frontier." *Western Historical Quarterly* 17 (January): 43–66.

Campisi, Jack. 1991. *The Mashpee Indians: Tribe on Trial*. Syracuse, N.Y.: Syracuse University Press.

Carby, Hazel. 1987. *Reconstructing Womanhood: The Emergence of the Afro-American Woman Novelist*. New York: Oxford University Press.

Carney, Cary Michael. 1999. *Native American Higher Education in the United States*. New Brunswick, N.J.: Transaction Publishers.

Carney, George O. 1998. "Oklahoma's All-Black Towns." Pp. 147–59 in *African Americans on the Western Frontier*, ed. Monroe Billington and Roger D. Hardaway. Boulder: University Press of Colorado.

Carroll, Patrick J. 1991. *Blacks in Colonial Veracruz: Race, Ethnicity, and Regional Development*. Austin: University of Texas Press.

Carson, James Taylor. 1999. *Searching for the Bright Path: The Mississippi Choctaws from Prehistory to Removal*. Lincoln: University of Nebraska Press.

Carter, Clarence Edwin. 1958. "The Territorial Essays of the United States." Pp. 452–54 in *The Territory of Florida, 1824–1828*, Vol. 23. Washington, D.C.: U.S. Government Printing Office.

Carter, Kent. 1999. *The Dawes Commission and the Allotment of the Five Civilized Tribes, 1893–1914*. Orem, Utah: Ancestry.com.

———. 1991. "Deciding Who Can Be Cherokee: Enrollment Records of the Dawes Commission." *Chronicles of Oklahoma* 69, no. 2 (Winter): 174–205.

Cashman, Cheryl. 1991. "Toronto's Zanies." *Canadian Theatre Review* 67: 22–23.

Casmier-Paz, Lynn A. 2003. "Slave Narratives and the Rhetoric of Author Portraiture." *New Literary History* 34, no. 1 (Winter): 91–116.

Chang, David A. Y. O. 2002. "From Indian Territory to White Man's Country: Race, Nation, and the Politics of Land Ownership in Eastern Oklahoma, 1889–1940." Ph.D. diss., University of Wisconsin, Madison.

Child, Brenda. 1998. *Boarding School Seasons: American Indian Families, 1900–1940*. Lincoln: University of Nebraska Press.

Choctaw National Council. 1865. "An Act Temporarily Providing for Such Persons as Have Been to the Present Time Considered as Slaves," October 14. Records of the Choctaw Nation, microfilm roll CTN-9, Archives and Manuscripts Division, Oklahoma Historical Society, Oklahoma City.

Chrisman, Laura, Farah Jasmine Griffin and Tukufu Zuberi. 2000. "Introduction to Transcending Traditions Special Issue." *Black Scholar* 30 (Fall–Winter): 2–3.

Churchill, Ward. 1998. *Fantasies of the Master Race: Literature, Cinema and the Colonization of American Indians*. San Francisco: City Lights Books.

Cialdini, R. B. 1984. *Influence: How and Why People Agree to Things*. New York: William Morrow.

Clifford, James. 1988. *The Predicament of Culture: Twentieth-Century Ethnography, Literature, and Art*. Cambridge, Mass.: Harvard University Press.

Cope, R. Douglas. 1994. *The Limits of Racial Domination: Plebian Society in Colonial Mexico City, 1600–1720*. Madison: University of Wisconsin Press.

Crapanzano, V. 1977. "The Life History in Anthropological Field Work." *Anthropology and Humanism Quarterly* 2:3–7.

Crockett, Norman L. 1989–90. "Witness to History: Booker T. Washington Visits Boley." *Chronicles of Oklahoma* 67 (Winter): 382–91.

———. 1979. *The Black Towns*. Lawrence: Regents Press of Kansas.

Dannett, Sylvia G. L. 1964. *Profiles of Negro Womanhood, 1619–1900*. Negro Heritage Library. New York: American Book–Stratford Press.

Debo, Angie. 1991. *And Still the Waters Run: The Betrayal of the Five Civilized Tribes*, 4th ed. Princeton, N.J.: Princeton University Press.

———. 1961. *The Rise and Fall of the Choctaw Republic*, 2d ed. Norman: University of Oklahoma Press.

———. 1941. *The Road to Disappearance: A History of the Creek Indians*. Norman: University of Oklahoma Press.

———. 1940. *And Still the Waters Run: The Betrayal of the Five Civilized Tribes*. Princeton, N.J.: Princeton University Press.

Deloria, Philip J. 1998. *Playing Indian*. New Haven, Conn.: Yale University Press.

———. 1996. "'I Am of the Body': Thoughts on My Grandfather, Culture, and Sports." *South Atlantic Quarterly* 95, no. 2 (Spring): 321–38.

Deloria Jr., Vine. 1988 (1969). *Custer Died for Your Sins: An Indian Manifesto*. Norman: University of Oklahoma Press.

Deloria Jr., Vine, and Raymond J. DeMallie. 1999. *Documents of American Indian Diplomacy: Treaties, Agreements, Conventions, 1775–1979*, 2 vols. Norman: University of Oklahoma Press.

DeMallie, Raymond. 1998. "Kinship: The Foundation of Native American Society." Pp. 306–56 in *Studying Native America: Problems and Perspectives*, ed. Russell Thornton. Madison: University of Wisconsin Press.

Derrida, Jacques. 1998. *Archive Fever: A Freudian Impression*. Trans. Eric Prenowitz. Chicago: University of Chicago Press.

Dorris, Michael. 1988 (1987). *A Yellow Raft in Blue Water*. New York: Warner Books.

Diamond, Elin. 1997. *Unmaking Mimesis*. London: Routledge.

Dickason, Olive Patricia. 1997. *Canada's First Nations: A History of Founding Peoples from Earliest Times*. Toronto: Oxford University Press.

Dixon, Melvin. 1987. *Ride Out the Wilderness: Geography and Identity in Afro-American Literature*. Chicago: University of Illinois Press.

Dowd, Gregory Evans. 1992. *A Spirited Resistance: The North American Indian Struggle for Unity, 1745–1815*. Baltimore: Johns Hopkins University Press.

Drinnon, Richard. 1972. *White Savage: The Case of John Dunn Hunter*. New York: Schocken Books.

Drunkman, Steven. 1995. "Suzan-Lori Parks and Liz Diamond: Doo-a-diddly-dit-dit, an Interview with Steven Drunkman." *Drama Review* 39, no. 3: 56–73.

Du Bois, W. E. B. 1971. "The Field and the Function of the American Negro College." Pp. 51–69 in *W. E. B. Du Bois: A Reader*, ed. Andrew Paschal. New York: Collier Books.

———. 1904. *The Souls of Black Folk*. Reprint, Greenwich, Conn.: Fawcett, 1961.

Eastman, Charles Alexander. 1980 (1911). *The Soul of the Indian: An Interpretation*. Lincoln: University of Nebraska Press.

———. 1971 (1902). *Indian Boyhood*. New York: Dover.

Edmunds, R. David. 1984. *Tecumseh and the Quest for Indian Leadership*. Boston: Little, Brown.

———. 1983. *The Shawnee Prophet*. Lincoln: University of Nebraska Press.

Ehrenreich, Barbara. 2001. *Nickel and Dimed: On (Not) Getting By in America*. New York: Henry Holt.

Elbert, Samuel H., and Mary Kaurena Pukui. 1986. *Hawaiian Dictionary*, revised ed. Honolulu: University of Hawaii Press.

Elbert, Samuel H., and Noelani Mahoe. 1972. *Nā Mele o Hawai'i Nei, 101 Hawaiian Songs*. Honolulu: University of Hawaii Press.

Ellison, Ralph. 1986. "Going to the Territory." Pp. 120–144 in *Going to the Territory*. New York: Vintage International.

Erdrich, Louise. 1993. *Love Medicine*, rev. ed. New York: HarperCollins.

Erickson, Erik H. 1967. *Identity and the Life Cycle: Selected Papers, Psychological Issues*, Vol. 1, no. 1. New York: International Universities Press.

Faery, Rebecca Blevins. 1999. *Cartographies of Desire: Captivity, Race, and Sex in the Shaping of an American Nation*. Norman: University of Oklahoma Press.

Fanon, Frantz. 1967. *Black Skin, White Masks*. New York: Grove Press.

Farred, Grant. 2000. *Midfielder's Moment: Coloured Literature and Culture in South Africa*. Boulder, Colo.: Westview Press.

Farriss, Nancy M. 1984. *Maya Society under Colonial Rule: The Collective Enterprise of Survival*. Princeton, N.J.: Princeton University Press.

Fernando, S. H. 1994. *The New Beats: Exploring the Music, Culture, and Attitudes of Hip-Hop*. New York: Anchor Books.

Fogelson, Raymond D. 1982. "Self, Person, and Identity: Some Anthropological Retrospects, Circumspect, and Prospect." Pp. 67–109 in *Psychological Theories of the Self*, ed. Benjamin Lee. New York: Prenum Press.

———. 1998. "Perspectives on Native American Identity." Pp. 40–59 in *Studying Native America: Problems and Prospects*, ed. Russell Thornton. Madison: University of Wisconsin Press.

Foner, Eric. 1988. *Reconstruction: America's Unfinished Revolution*. New York: Harper and Row.

Forbes, Jack D. 1993. *Africans and Native Americans: The Language of Race and the Evolution of Red–Black Peoples*, 2d ed. Urbana: University of Illinois Press.

Foreman, Grant. 1932. *Indian Removal: The Emigration of the Five Civilized Tribes of Indians*. Norman: University of Oklahoma Press.

Foster, Laurence. 1935. "Negro–Indian Relationships in the Southeast." Ph.D. diss., University of Pennsylvania, Philadelphia.

Frieze, James. 1998. "Imperceptible Mutabilites in the Third Kingdom: Suzan-Lori Parks and the Shared Struggle to Perceive." *Modern Drama* 41: 523–32.

Fujikane, Candace. 1994. "Between Nationalisms, Hawaii's Local Nation and Its Troubled Racial Paradise." In *Critical Mass: A Journal of Asian American Cultural Criticism* 1, no. 2 (Spring/Summer): 23–58.

Fulweiler, Howard W. 2000. "Belonging and Freedom in Morrison's *Beloved*: Slavery, Sentimentality, and the Evolution of Conscious." Pp. 113–42 in *Understanding Toni Morrison's Beloved and Sula: Selected Essays and Criticisms*, ed. Solomon O. Iyasere and Maria W. Iyasere. New York: Whitston Publishing.

Fusco, Coco. 1995. *English Is Broken Here*. New York: New Press.

Gallaher, Art. 1951. "A Survey of the Seminole Freedmen." Master's thesis, Department of Anthropology, University of Oklahoma, Norman.

García Martínez, Bernardo. 1990. "Pueblos de Indios, Pueblos de Castas: New Settlements and Traditional Corporate Organization in Eighteenth-Century New Spain." Pp. 103–16 in *The Indian Community of Colonial Mexico*, ed. Arij Ouweneel and Simon Miller. Amsterdam: CEDLA.

Gates, Eddie Faye, ed. 1997. *They Came Searching: How Blacks Sought the Promised Land in Tulsa*. Austin: Eakin Press.

George, Nelson. 1998. *Hip Hop America*. New York: Penguin.

Gibson, Arrell. 1971. *The Chickasaws*. Norman: University of Oklahoma Press.

Gibson, Charles. 1964. *The Aztecs under Spanish Rule: A History of the Indians of the Valley of Mexico*. Stanford, Calif.: Stanford University Press.

Gilroy, Paul. 1993. *The Black Atlantic: Modernity and Double Consciousness*. Cambridge, Mass.: Harvard University Press.

Ginsberg, Elaine K. 1996. "Introduction: The Politics of Passing." In *Passing and the Fictions of Identity*, edited by Elaine K. Ginsberg. Durham, N.C.: Duke University Press.

Glissant, Edouard. 1989. *Caribbean Discourse*. Trans. J. Michael Dash. Charlottesville: University Press of Virginia.

Goble, Danney. 1980. *Progressive Oklahoma: The Making of a New Kind of State*. Norman: University of Oklahoma Press.

Goldstein, Warren. 1996. "Bender, Chief." In *Encyclopedia of North American Indians*, ed. Frederick Hoxie. Boston: Houghton Mifflin.

Gomez, Michael A. 1998. *Exchanging Our Country Marks: The Transformation of African Identities in the Colonial and Antebellum South*. Chapel Hill: University of North Carolina Press.

———. 1842 [1839]. *Elleanor's Second Book*. Providence, R.I.: B. T. Albro.

Green, Rayna. 1988. "The Tribe Called Wannabee: Playing Indian in America and Europe." *Folklore* 99, no. 1: 30–55.

———. 1975. "The Pocahontas Perplex: The Image of Indian Women in American Culture." *Massachusetts Review* 16, no. 4: 698–714.

Gregory, Stephen, and Roger Sanjek, eds. 1996. *Race*. New Brunswick, N.J.: Rutgers University Press.

Griffin, Catherine Carrie. 2000. "'Joined Together in History': Politics and Place in African American and American Indian Women's Writing." Ph.D. diss., University of Minnesota, Minneapolis.

Guth, Deborah. 2000. "A Blessing and a Burden: The Relation to the Past in *Sula*, *Song of Solomon*, and *Beloved*." Pp. 315–37 in *Understanding Toni Morrison's* Beloved *and* Sula: *Selected Essays and Criticisms*, ed. Solomon O. Iyasere and Maria W. Iyasere. New York: Whitston Publishing.

Hall, Stuart. 1991. "Old and New Identities, Old and New Ethnicities" and "The Local and the Global: Globalization and Ethnicity." Pp. 41–68 in *Culture, Globalization and the World-System: Contemporary Conditions for the Representation of Identity*, ed. Anthony D. King. Binghamton: Department of Art and Art History, State University of New York, Binghamton.

Hamilton, Kenneth Marvin. 1991. *Black Towns and Profit: Promotion and Development in the Trans-Appalachian West, 1877–1915*. Urbana: University of Illinois Press.

Harris, Melvin. 1964. *Patterns of Race in the Americas*. New York: Norton.

Hauptman, Laurence M., and James D. Wherry. 1990. *The Pequots in Southern New England: The Rise and Fall of an American Indian Nation*. Norman: University of Oklahoma Press.

Henslick, Harry. 1970. "The Seminole Treaty of 1866." *Chronicles of Oklahoma* 48, no. 3 (Fall): 280–93.

Herndon, Ruth Wallis. 2004. "'Who Died an Expence to This Town': Poor Relief in Eighteenth-Century Rhode Island." Pp. 135–62 in *Down and Out in Early America*, ed. Billy G. Smith. University Park: Pennsylvania State University Press.

Herndon, Ruth Wallis, and Ella Wilcox Sekatau. 1997. "The Right to a Name: The Narragansett People and Rhode Island Officials of the Revolutionary Era." Pp. 114–43 in *After King Philip's War: Presence and Persistence in Indian New England*, ed. Colin G. Calloway. Hanover, N.H.: University Press of New England.

Hertzberg, Hazel. 1971. *The Search for an American Indian Identity*. Syracuse, N.Y.: Syracuse University Press.

Hill, Robert A., ed. 1983–95. *The Marcus Garvey and Universal Negro Improvement Association Papers*. Berkeley: University of California Press.

Hollan, Douglas, and Jane Wellenkamp. 1994. "Methodological Developments in Psychocultural Anthropology." Pp. 3–10 in *Contentment and Suffering: Culture and Experience in Toraja*. New York: Columbia University Press.

Holland, Dorothy. 1992. "How Cultural Systems Become Desire: A Case Study of American Romance." Pp. 61–89 in *Human Motive and Cultural Models*, ed. Roy D'Andrade and Claudia Strauss. Cambridge: Cambridge University Press.

———. 2001. *History in Person: Enduring Struggles, Contentious Practice, Intimate Identities*. School of American Research Press.

Holland, Sharon P. 1994. "'If You Know I Have a History, You Will Respect Me': A Perspective on Afro-Native American Literature." *Callaloo* 17, no. 1 (Winter–Summer 1994): 334–50.

Holt, Thomas. 1999. "Slavery and Freedom in the Atlantic World: Reflections on the Diasporan Framework." Pp. 33–44 in *Crossing Boundaries: Comparative History of Black People in Diaspora*, ed. Darlene Clark Hine and Jacqueline McLeod. Bloomington: Indiana University Press.

Honey, Maureen. 1984. *Creating Rosie the Riveter: Class, Gender, and Propaganda during World War II*. Amherst: University of Massachusetts Press.

Hōʻaikane. 1990. "Kailua Kona." On *Island Irie*. Honolulu: Kahale Music.

hoʻomanawanui, kuʻualoha. 2005. "He Lei Hoʻoheno no nā Kau a Kau: Image, Metaphor, and Performance in Contemporary Hawaiian Poetry." *Contemporary Pacific* 17, no. 1 (Spring): 29–81.

Hoʻonuʻa. 1998. "Feel Good Island Music." On *Feel Good Island Music*. Honolulu: Island Style Records.

Hudson, Peter J. 1939. "Choctaw Indian Dishes." *Chronicles of Oklahoma* 17, no. 3: 333–35.

Idahosa, Pablo. 2000. Conversation with Tiya Miles. University of California Berkeley and York University Dissertation Workshop on African Diasporas. Sonoma, Calif., December 7–10.

Jackson, Deborah D., and Elizabeth E. Chapelski. 2000. "Not Traditional, Not Assimilated: Elderly American Indians and the Notion of Cohort." *Journal of Cross-Cultural Gerontology* 15, no. 3: 229–59.

Jackson, Papa Charlie. 1983 (1925). "The Faking Blues." P. 117 in *Blues Lyric Poetry: An Anthology*, ed. Michael Taft. New York: Garland Publishing.

Jeyifo, Biodun. 1997. "Determinations of Remembering: Postcolonial Fictional Genealogies of Colonialism in Africa." Pp. 111–28 in *Streams of Cultural Capital: Transnational Cultural Studies*, ed. David Palumbo-Liu and Hans Ulrich Gumbrecht. Stanford, Calif.: Stanford University Press.

Joseph, Miranda. 2002. *Against the Romance of Community*. Minneapolis: University of Minnesota Press.

Ka'aihue, Henry Kapono. 1992. "Broken Promise." On *Kapono*. Honolulu: PaMoKa Records.

Ka'au Crater Boys. 1996. "He 'Ono." On *Making Waves*. Honolulu: Roy Sakuma Productions.

Kahakalau, Robie. 1995. "Pi'i Mai Ka Nalu." On *Sistah Robie*. Honolulu: Kanai'a Records. The lyrics are from the liner notes and were translated by Kū Kahakalau.

Kalèik, Susan. 1984. "Ethnic Foodways in America: Symbol and the Performance of Identity." Pp. 37–65 in *Ethnic and Regional Foodways in the United States: The Performance of Group Identity*, ed. Linda Kell Brown and Kay Mussell. Knoxville: University of Tennessee Press.

Kamakawiwo'ole, Israel. 1993. "Hawai'i '78." On *Facing Future*. Honolulu, Hawai'i: Big Boy Record Company.

Kame'eleihiwa, Lilikalā. 1992. *Native Lands and Foreign Desires, Pehea La e Pono ai?* Honolulu: Bishop Museum Press.

Kanahele, George. 1979. *Hawaiian Music and Musicians*. Honolulu: University of Hawai'i Press.

Kanter, Deborah. 1992. "Viudas y vecinos, milpas y magueyes — el impacto del auge de la población en el Valle de Toluca: El caso de Tenango del Valle en el siglo XVIII." *Estudios demográficos y urbanos* 7: 19–33.

Kappler, Charles J, comp. 1904. *Indian Affairs: Laws and Treaties*, Volume 2: *Treaties*. Washington, D.C.: Government Printing Office.

Katz, William Loren. 1986. *Black Indians: A Hidden Heritage*. New York: Ethrac Publications.

Kaufman, Bob. 1965. "Dolorous Echo." In *Solitudes Crowded with Loneliness*, 31. New York: New Directions.

Kekaula, Robert. 1994. *Kanaka Attack*. Honolulu: Paradise Records.

Kelley, Robin D. G. 2000. "How the West Was One: On the Uses and Limitations of Diaspora." *Black Scholar* 30 (Fall–Winter): 31–35.

Kelly, John R. 1983. *Leisure Identities and Interactions*. London: Allen and Unwin.

Kickingbird, Kirke, Lynn Kickingbird, Charles J. Chibitty, and Curtis Berkey. 1999. "Indian Sovereignty." Pp. 1–64 in *Native American Sovereignty*, ed. John R. Wunder. New York: Garland.

Kidwell, Clara Sue. 1995. *Choctaws and Missionaries in Mississippi, 1818–1918*. Norman: University of Oklahoma Press.

Knight, Alan. 1990. "Racism, Revolution, and *Indigenismo*: Mexico, 1910–1940." Pp. 71–113 in *The Idea of Race in Latin America, 1870–1940*, ed. Richard Graham. Austin: University of Texas Press.

Konkle, Maureen. 2004. *Writing Indian Nations: Native Intellectuals and the Politics of Historiography, 1827–1863*. Chapel Hill: University of North Carolina Press.

Konrad, Herman. 1980. *A Jesuit Hacienda in Colonial Mexico: Santa Lucia, 1576–1767*. Stanford: Stanford University Press.

"Letter from Liberia, West Africa." 1996. Pp. 45 in *Indians and Intruders*, vol. 3, ed. Sharron Standifer Ashton. Norman, Okla.: Sharon Standifer Ashton.

Levy, Robert, and Douglas Hollan. 1998. "Person Centered Interviewing and Observation in Anthropology." Pp. 333–64 in *Handbook of Research Methods in Anthropology*, ed. Russell Bernard. Walnut Creek, Calif.: Altamira Press.

Lewis, David Levering. 1993. *W. E. B. Du Bois: Biography of a Race, 1868–1919*. New York: Henry Holt.

Lewis, Earl. 1999. " 'To Turn as on a Pivot': Writing African Americans into a History of Overlapping Diasporas." Pp. 3–32 in *Crossing Boundaries: Comparative History of Black People in Diaspora*, ed. Darlene Clark Hine and Jacqueline McLeod. Bloomington: Indiana University Press.

Lewis, Laura A. 2003. *Hall of Mirrors: Power, Witchcraft, and Caste in Colonial Mexico*. Durham, N.C.: Duke University Press.

Lionnet, Françoise. 1989. *Autobiographical Voices*. Ithaca, N.Y.: Cornell University Press.

Littlefield Jr., Daniel F. 1996a. *Seminole Burning: A Story of Racial Vengeance*. Jackson: University Press of Mississippi.

———. 1996b. "The Treaties of 1866: Reconstruction or Re-Destruction?" Pp. 97–109 in *Proceedings: War and Reconstruction in Indian Territory, a History Conference in Observance of the 130th Anniversary of the Fort Smith Council*. Fort Smith, Arkansas: Fort Smith National Historic Park.

———. 1980. *The Chickasaw Freedmen: A People without a Country*. Westport, Conn.: Greenwood Press.

———. 1977. *Africans and Seminoles: From Removal to Emancipation*. Westport, Conn.: Greenwood Press.

Lockhart, James, and Stuart B. Schwartz. 1983. *Early Latin America: A History of Colonial Spanish America and Brazil*. Cambridge: Cambridge University Press.

Loewenberg, Bert James, and Ruth Bogin, eds. 1976. *Black Women in Nineteenth-Century American Life*. University Park: Pennsylvania State University Press.

Lomawaima, K. Tsianina. 1994. *They Called It Prairie Light: The Story of the Chilocco Indian School*. Lincoln: University of Nebraska Press.

Lopez, Ian F. 1996. *White by Law: The Legal Construction of Race*. New York: New York University Press.

Lovett, Laura L. 2002. "African and Cherokee by Choice: Race and Resistance under Legalized Segregation." Pp. 192–222 in *Confounding the Color Line: The Indian–Black Experience in North America*, ed. James F. Brooks. Lincoln: University of Nebraska Press.

Mandell, Daniel R. 1998. "Shifting Boundaries of Race and Ethnicity: Indian–Black Intermarriage in Southern New England, 1760–1880." *Journal of American History* (September): 466–501.

———. 1996. *Behind the Frontier: Indians in Eighteenth Century Massachusetts*. Lincoln: University of Nebraska Press.

Martin, Cheryl E. 1990. "Popular Speech and Social Order in Northern Mexico, 1650–1830." *Comparative Studies in Society and History* 32 (April): 305–24.

———. 1985. *Rural Society in Colonial Morelos*. Albuquerque: University of New Mexico Press.

May, Katja. 1996. *African Americans and Native Americans in the Creek and Cherokee Nation, 1830s to 1920s: Collision and Collusion*. New York: Garland.

McCaa, Robert. 1984. "Calidad, Clase and Marriage in Colonial Mexico: The Case of Parral, 1788–1790." *Hispanic American Historical Review* 64 (August): 477–501.

McClinton, Rowena, trans. Forthcoming. *The Moravian Mission to the Cherokees: Springplace in the Gambold Years, 1805–1821*. Lincoln: University of Nebraska Press.

McMullen, Ann. 2002. "Blood and Culture: Negotiating Race in Twentieth-Century Native New England." Pp. 261–91 in *Confounding the Color Line: The Indian–Black Experience in North America*, ed. James F. Brooks. Lincoln: University of Nebraska Press

Medearis, Angela Shelf. 1991. *Dancing with the Indians*. New York: Scholastic.

Merrell, James H. 1984. "The Racial Education of the Catawba Indians." *Journal of Southern History* 50 (August): 363–84.

Meserve, John Bartlett. 1937. "The Perrymans." *Chronicles of Oklahoma* 15: 166–84.

Micco, Melinda B. 1995. "Seminoles and Freedmen: Forging a Seminole Nation." Ph.D. diss., University of California, Berkeley.

Mignolo, Walter. 1995. *The Darker Side of the Renaissance: Literacy, Territoriality, and Colonization*. Ann Arbor: University of Michigan Press.

Miles, Tiya. 2005. *Ties That Bind: The Story of an Afro-Cherokee Family in Slavery and Freedom*. Berkeley: University of California Press.

Milfort, Louis LeClerc. 1956. *Memoir: Or, a Cursory Glance at My Different Travels and My Sojourn in the Creek Nation*, ed. John Francis McDermott, trans. Geraldine de Courcy. Chicago: Lakeside Press.

Minerbrook, Scott. 1996. *Divided to the Vein: A Journey Into Race and Family*. New York: Harcourt Brace.

Mojica, Monique. 1991. *Princess Pocahontas and the Blue Spots*. Toronto: Women's Press.

Moraga, Cherríe. 2002 (1981). "From Inside the First World Foreword 2001." Pp. xv–xxxiii in *This Bridge Called My Back: Writings by Radical Women of Color*, ed. Cherríe Moraga and Gloria Anzaldúa. Berkeley, Calif: Third Woman Press.

Mörner, Magnus. 1967. *Race Mixture in the History of Latin America*. Boston: Little Brown.

Mörner, Magnus. 1966. "Los esfuerzos realizados por la Corona para separar negros e indios en Hispanoámerica durante el siglo XVI." Pp. 331–44 in *Homenaje. Estudios de filogia e historia literaria lusohispanas*. The Hague: Van GoorZonen.

———. 1965. "Separación o integración? En torno al debate dieciochesco." *Journal de la Societe des Americanistes* 54, no. 1: 31–45.

Morrison, Toni. 1998. *Paradise*. New York: Alfred A. Knopf.

———. 1992. *Playing in the Dark: Whiteness and the Literary Imagination*. Cambridge, Mass.: Harvard University Press.

———. 1990. "Unspeakable Things Unspoken: The Afro-American Presence in American Literature." Pp. 201–30 in *Modern Critical Views: Toni Morrison*, ed. Harold Bloom. New York: Chelsea House.

———. 1987. *Beloved*. New York: Alfred A. Knopf.

———. 1977. *Song of Solomon*. New York: Penguin Group.

Moses, Sharon K. 1998. "The Effects of a Dominant Hegemony on the Ethnogenesis of Contemporary American Indian Identity." *Northwest Anthropological Research Notes* 32, no. 2.

Mulroy, Kevin. 1993. *Freedom on the Border: The Seminole Maroons in Florida, the Indian Territory, Coahuila, and Texas*. Lubbock: Texas Tech University Press.

Murray, Timothy. 1994. "In Exile at Home: Tornado Breath and Unrighteous Fantasy in Robbie McCauley's *Indian Blood*." *Discourse* 16, no. 3: 29–45.

Na'auao, Sean. 1997. *Fish and Poi*. Honolulu: Fat Katz.

Nagel, Joanne. 1996. *American Indian Ethnic Renewal: Red Power and the Resurgence of Identity and Culture*. New York: Oxford University Press.

Nash, Gary B. 1995. "The Hidden History of Mestizo America." *Journal of American History* 82, no. 3: 941–64.

Naylor-Ojurongbe, Celia. 2002. "'Born and Raised among These People, I Don't Want to Know Any Other': Slaves' Acculturation in Nineteenth-Century Indian Territory." Pp. 161–91 in *Confounding the Color Line: The Indian–Black Experience in North America*, ed. James F. Brooks. Lincoln: University of Nebraska Press.

Ngugi wa Thiong'o. 1997. "Enactments of Power." *The Drama Review* 41, no. 3: 11–30.

Nolen, Curtis L. 1980. "The Okmulgee Constitution: A Step toward Indian Self-Determination." *Chronicles of Oklahoma* 58: 264–81.

Norton, John. 1970 (1816). *The Journal of Major John Norton*. Toronto: Champlain Society.

O'Brien, Jean M. 1997a. *Dispossession by Degrees: Indian Land and Identity in Natick, Massachusetts, 1650–1790*. Lincoln: University of Nebraska Press.

———. 1997b. "'Divorced' from the Land: Resistance and Survival of Indian Women in Eighteenth-Century New England." Pp. 144–61 in *After King Philip's War: Presence and Persistence in Indian New England*, ed. Colin G. Calloway. Hanover, N.H.: University Press of New England.

O'Dowd, Sarah C. 2004. *A Rhode Island Original: Frances Harriet Whipple Green McDougall*. Hanover: University Press of New England.

Okamura, Jonathan Y. 1994. "Why There Are No Asian Americans in Hawai'i: The Continuing Significance of Local Identity." *Social Process in Hawai'i* 35: 161–78.

Olaniyan, Tejumola. 1995. *Scars of Conquest/Masks of Resistance: The Invention of Cultural Identities in African-American and Caribbean Drama*. New York: Oxford University Press.

Omi, Michael, and Howard Winant. 1994. *Racial Formation in the United States from the 1960s to the 1990s*. 2d ed. New York: Routledge.

O-shen. 2005. "Ku'u Pua" on *Faya*. Honolulu: Cinnamon Red Records.

Osumare, Halifu. 1999. "African Aesthetics, American Culture: Hip Hop in the Global Era." Ph.D. diss., University of Hawaii, Mânoa.

Owens, Louis. 2001. *I Hear the Train: Reflections, Inventions, Refractions*. Norman: University of Oklahoma Press.

———. 1998. *Mixedblood Messages: Literature, Film, Family, Place*. Norman: University of Oklahoma Press.

Pa, Shiloh. 2002. "Leave Some Land." On *Leave Some Land*. Hanalei, Hawai'i: Poiboy Records. Chant by Kaleinani Kahaunaele. English lyrics from CD cover. Hawaiian lyrics translated by ku'ualoha ho'omanawanui.

Painter, Nell Irvin. 1992 (1977). *Exodusters: Black Migration to Kansas after Reconstruction*. New York: W. W. Norton.

Pannikar, Raimundo. 1988. "What Is Comparative Philosophy Comparing?" Pp. 116–36 in *New Essays in Comparative Philosophy*, ed. Eliot Deutsch and Gerald James Lawson. Princeton, N.J.: Princeton University Press.

Parks, Suzan-Lori. 1994. "The Death of the Last Black Man in the Entire World." Pp. 239–80 in *Moon Marked and Touched by the Sun: Plays by African American Women*, ed. Sydné Mahone. New York: Theatre Communications Group.

Pasquaretta, Paul. 2003. "African–Native American Subjectivity and the Blues Voice in the Writings of Toni Morrison and Sherman Alexie." Pp. 278–91 in *When Brer Rabbit Meets Coyote: African–Native American Literature*, ed. Jonathan Brennan. Urbana: University of Illinois Press.

Perdue, Theda. 2003. *Mixed Blood Indians: Racial Construction in the Early South*. Athens: University of Georgia Press.

———. 1979. *Slavery and the Evolution of Cherokee Society, 1540–1866*. Knoxville: University of Tennessee Press.

Piper, Adrian. 1996. "Passing for White, Passing for Black." Pp. 234–69 in *Passing and the Fictions of Identity*, ed. Elaine K. Ginsberg. Durham, N.C.: Duke University Press.

Plane, Ann Marie. 2000. *Colonial Intimacies: Indian Marriage in Early New England*. Ithaca, N.Y.: Cornell University Press.

Porter, Kenneth W. 1996. *The Black Seminoles: History of a Freedom-Seeking People*. Gainesville: University Press of Florida.

Porter, Kenneth W. 1933. "Notes Supplementary to 'Relations Between Negroes and Indians within the Present Limits of the United States.'" *Journal of Negro History* 18 (July): 282–321.

——. 1932. "Relations between Negroes and Indians within the Present Limits of the United States." *Journal of Negro History* 17 (July): 287–367.

Potash, Chris. 1997. *Reggae, Rasta, Revolution: Jamaican Music from Ska to Dub*. New York: Schirmer Books.

Prucha, Francis Paul. 1994. *American Indian Treaties: The History of a Political Anomaly*. Berkeley: University of California Press.

——. 1984. *Great Father: The United States Government and the American Indians*, Vol. 2. Lincoln: University of Nebraska Press.

Puhipau and Joan Landers, dir. 1993. *Act of War: The Overthrow of the Hawaiian Nation*. Honolulu: Nâ Maka o ka Āina Productions.

Quarles, Benjamin. 1961. *The Negro in the American Revolution*. Chapel Hill: University of North Carolina Press.

Quinn, Naomi. 1992. "The Motivational Force of Self-Understanding: Evidence from Wives' Inner Conflict." Pp. 90–126 in *Human Motive and Cultural Models*, ed. Roy D'Andrade and Claudia Strauss. Cambridge: Cambridge University Press.

Radhakrishnan, R. 1993. "Postcoloniality and the Boundaries of Identity." *Callaloo* 16, no. 4 (Fall): 750–71.

Red Bird Investment Company (Fort Smith, Ark.). 1905. "Red Bird Creek Nation, I.T. An Opportunity for the Colored Man." Brochure. Twine Collection, Western History Collections, University of Oklahoma, Norman.

Rigney, Barbara Hill. 1991. *The Voices of Toni Morrison*. Columbus: Ohio State University Press.

Riley, Patricia. 2003. "Wrapped in the Serpent's Tail: Alice Walker's African–Native American Subjectivity." Pp. 241–56 in *When Brer Rabbit Meets Coyote: African–Native American Literature*, ed. Jonathan Brennan. Urbana: University of Illinois Press.

Robinson, Amy. 1994. "It Takes One to Know One: Passing and Communities of Common Interest." *Critical Inquiry* 20, no. 4 (Summer): 715–36.

Rodriguez, Clara E.1994. "Challenging Racial Hegemony: Puerto Ricans in the United States." Pp. 131–45 in *Race*, ed. Steven Gregory and Roger Sanjek. New Brunswick, N.J.: Rutgers University Press.

Root, Maria P. P. ed. 2000. *Rethinking Racial Identity Development / We Are A People: Narrative and Multiciplicity in Constructing Ethnic Identity*. Philadelphia: Temple University Press.

Roosens, Eugene E. 1989. *Creating Ethnicity: The Process of Ethnogenesis*. Newbury Park: Sage Publications.

Rose, Trisha. 1994. *Black Noise*. Middletown, Conn.: Wesleyan University Press.

Sameth, Sigmund. 1940. "Creek Negroes: A Study in Race Relations." Master's thesis, University of Oklahoma, Norman.

Sanjek, Roger. 1994. "The Enduring Inequalities of Race." Pp. 1–17 in *Race*, ed. Steven Gregory and Roger Sanjek. New Brunswick, N.J.: Rutgers University Press.

Saunt, Claudio. 2005. *Black, White, and Indian: Race and the Unmaking of an American Family*. New York: Oxford University Press.

———. 1999. *A New Order of Things: Property, Power, and the Transformation of the Creek Indians, 1733–1816*. Cambridge: Cambridge University Press.

Schneider, Rebecca. 1997. *The Explicit Body in Performance*. London: Routledge.

Scholliers, Peter. 2001. "Meals, Food Narratives, and Sentiments of Belonging in Past and Present." Pp. 3–22 in *Food, Drink and Identity: Cooking, Eating and Drinking in Europe since the Middle Ages*. Oxford: Berg.

Seacole, Mary. 1988. *The Wonderful Adventures of Mrs. Seacole in Many Lands*, ed. Henry Louis Gates Jr. New York: Oxford University Press.

Sharpes, Donald K. 1995. "Princess Pocahontas, Rebecca Rolfe (1595–1617)." *American Indian Culture and Research Journal* 19, no. 4: 231–39.

Silko, Leslie Marmon. 1991. *Almanac of the Dead*. New York: Simon and Schuster.

Skidmore, Thomas E. 1972. *Black into White: Race and Nationality in Brazilian Thought*. New York: Oxford University Press.

Smedley, Audrey. 1993. *Race in North America: Origin and Evolution of a Worldview*. Boulder: Westview Press.

Smith, Bessie. 1998 (1930). "Work House Blues." Pp. 352–53 in *Blues Legacies and Black Feminism*, ed. Angela Y. Davis. New York: Vintage Books.

Smith, John. 1580–1631. *The True Travels, Adventures, and Observations of Captain John Smith, in Europe, Asia, Africke, and America, Beginning About the Yeare 1593 and Continued to This Present 1629, from the London Edition of 1629*. Richmond, Va.: Republished at the Franklin Press, W. W. Gray, Printer, 1819.

Snipp, C. Matthew. 1989. *American Indians: The First of This Land*. New York: Russell Sage Foundation.

Spickard, Paul R. 1992. "The Illogic of American Racial Categories." Pp. 12–23 in *Racially Mixed People in America*, ed. Maria P. P. Root. Newbury Park, Calif.: Sage Publications.

Spiderwoman Theatre. 1996 (1981). "Sun Moon and Feather." Pp. 297–309 in *Contemporary Plays by Women of Color*, ed. Kathy A. Perkins and Roberta Uno. London: Routledge.

Stampp, Kenneth Milton. 1956. *The Peculiar Institution: Slavery in the Antebellum South*. New York: Knopf.

Standing Bear, Luther. 1975 (1928). *My People the Sioux*. Lincoln: University of Nebraska Press.

———. 1976 (1933). *The Land of the Spotted Eagle*. Lincoln: University of Nebraska Press.

Stanley, Amy Dru. 1998. *From Bondage to Contract: Wage Labor, Marriage, and the Marker in the Age of Slave Emancipation*. New York: Cambridge University Press.

Starr, Floyd Favel. 1997. "The Artificial Tree: Native Performance Culture Research 1991–1996." *Canadian Theatre Review* 90: 83–85.

———. 1993. "Floyd Favel: 'They Thought ahead Seven Generations' Studies in Canadian Literature/Etudes en litterature canadienne. Interview by Greg Doran." *Studies in Canadian Literature* 18, no. 1: 139–51.

Sterling, Dorothy,ed. 1984. *We Are Your Sisters: Black Women in the Nineteenth Century*. New York: W. W. Norton.

Stewart, Leslie Keliʻilauahi. 2002. "Legacy of Music, Legacy of Love: The Gifts of Aunty Martha Kaumakaokalani Aʻoe Poepoe Hohu." *ʻŌiwi* 2: 43–47.

Stillman, Amy Kuʻuleialoha. 1998. "Hula Hits, Local Music and Local Charts: Some Dynamics of Popular Hawaiian Music." Pp. 89–103 in *Sound Alliances: Indigenous Peoples, Cultural Politics and Popular Music in the Pacific*, ed. Philip Hayward. London: Cassell.

Strong, Pauline Turner. 1999. *Captive Selves, Captivating Others : The Politics and Poetics of Colonial American Captivity Narratives*. Boulder, Colo.: Westview Press.

Sturm, Circe. 2002. "Blood Politics, Racial Classification, and Cherokee National Identity: The Trials and Tribulations of Cherokee Freedmen." Pp. 223–57 in *Confounding the Color Line: The Indian–Black Experience in North America*, ed. James F. Brooks. Lincoln: University of Nebraska Press.

Sturtevant, William C. 1971. "Creek into Seminole." Pp. 92–128 in *North American Indians in Perspective*, ed. Eleanor Burke Leacock and Nancy Oestreich Lurie. New York: Random House.

Sudden Rush. 2002. *ʻEa* (Sovereignty). Honolulu: Quiet Storm.

———. 1997. *Kūʻē* (Resistance). Hilo, Hawaii: Way Out West Productions.

———. 1995. "ʻOnipaʻa." On *Nation on the Rise*. Hilo, Hawaii: Wreckxshop.

Szasz, Margaret Connell. 1977 (1928). *Education and the American Indian: The Road to Self-Determination since 1928*. Albuquerque: University of New Mexico Press.

Taylor, William B. 1979. *Drinking, Homicide, and Rebellion in Colonial Mexican Villages*. Stanford, Calif.: Stanford University Press.

Teall, Kaye M. 1971. *Black History in Oklahoma: A Resource Book*. Oklahoma City: Oklahoma City Public Schools.

Thornton, Russell. 1998. "The Demography of Colonialism and 'Old' and 'New' Native Americans." Pp. 17–39 in *Studying Native America: Problems and Prospects*, ed. Russell Thornton. Madison: University of Wisconsin Press.

Thornton, Russell, and Peter M. Nardi. 1975. "The Dynamics of Role Acquisition." *The American Journal of Sociology* 80, no. 4: 870–85.

Todorov, Tzvetan. 1987. *The Conquest of America*. New York: Harper and Row.

Toop, David. 1992. *Rap Attack 2: African Rap to Global Hip Hop*. London: Serpent's Tail.

Trask, Haunani Kay. 2000. "Settlers of Color and 'Immigrant' Hegemony: 'Locals' in Hawai'i." In *Critical Mass: A Journal of Asian American Cultural Criticism* 1 no. 2 (Spring/Summer): 1–26.

———. 1993. *From a Native Daughter*. Monroe, Maine: Common Courage Press.

Troper, Harold Martin. 1972. "The Creek-Negroes of Oklahoma and Canadian Immigration, 1909–11." *Canadian Historical Review* 53: 272–88.

U.S. Congress. 1870. *Memorial of a Committee on Behalf of the Colored People of the Choctaw and Chickasaw Tribes of Indians*. 41st Cong., 2nd sess. S. Misc. Doc. 106.

———. 1873. *Investigation of Indian Frauds*. 42nd Cong., 3rd sess. H. Rpt. 98.

———. 1886. *Report of the Committee on Indian Affairs, United States Senate, on the Condition of Indians in the Indian Territory, and Other Reservations, etc.* 49th Cong., 1st sess., Sen. Rpt. 1278.

———. 1896. *Report of the Dawes Commission*. 54th Cong., 1st sess. S. Doc. 182.

U.S. Congress, Senate. 1930. "Claims of the Seminole Indians against the United States." *Hearing before the Committee on Indian Affairs*, Senate bill S.3041, 71st Cong., 2d Session.

———. 1978. "Distribution of Seminole Judgment Funds." *Hearing Before the United States Senate Select Committee on Indian Affairs*, S.2000 and S.2811, 95th Cong., 2d Session.

U.S. Department of the Interior. 1866. Office of Indian Affairs, Seminole Agency, Letters Received, January 30, M234. Washington, D.C.: National Archives Microfilm Publications. Microcopy *R23*.

U.S. Office of Indian Affairs. 1868. Annual Report of the Commissioner of Indian Affairs. Washington, D.C.: Government Printing Office.

———. 1869. *Annual Report of the Commissioner of Indian Affairs*. Washington, D.C.: Government Printing Office.

Valdés, Dennis H. 1987. "The Decline of Slavery in Mexico." *Americas* 44 (October): 167–94.

Van Alstyne, Richard W. 1960. *The Rising American Empire*. New York: W. W. Norton.

Vizenor, Gerald. 1994. *Manifest Manners: Postindian Warriors of Survival*. Hanover, N.H.: Wesleyan University Press.

Walker, Alice. 2000. *The Way Forward Is with a Broken Heart*. New York: Random House.

———. 1989. *The Temple of My Familiar*. San Diego: Harcourt Brace Jovanovich.

———. 1976. *Meridian*. New York: Pocket Books.

Wallace, F. C., and Raymond D. Fogelson. 1965. "The Identity Struggle." Pp. 365–406 in *Intensive Family Therapy: Theoretical and Practical Aspects*, ed. Ivan Boszomenyi-Nagy and James L. Framo. New York: Hoeber Medical Division, Harper and Row.

Washington, Booker T. 1908. "Boley, a Negro Town in the West." *Outlook* 88 (January–April): 28–31.

———. 1965. "Up from Slavery." Pp. 23–205 in *Three Negro Classics*, ed. Henry Louis Gates Jr. New York: Avon.

Weintraub, Andrew. 1998. "Jawaiian Music and Local Cultural Identity in Hawai'i." Pp. 78–88 in *Sound Alliances: Indigenous Peoples, Cultural Politics, and Popular Music in the Pacific*, ed. Philip Hayward. London: Cassell.

———. 1993. "Jawaiian and Local Cultural Identity in Hawai'i." *Perfect Beat* 1, no. 2 (January): 80–89.

Whipple, Frances H. (Green). 1838. *Memoirs of Elleanor Eldridge*. Providence, R.I.: B. T. Albro.

Wiggins Jr., William H. 1993. "Juneteenth: Tracking the Progress of an Emancipation Celebration." *American Visions* 8: 28–31.

Wilcox, Carol, Kimo Hussey, Vicky Hollinger, and Puakea Nogelmeier. 2003. "Kona Kai 'Ōpua [i ka La'i]." On *He Mele Aloha, a Hawaiian Songbook*. Honolulu: 'Oli'oli Productions.

Williams, Nudie Eugene. 1996. "Oklahoma: Genesis and Tradition of the Black Press." Pp. 267–96 in *The Black Press in the Middle West, 1865–1985*, ed. Henry Lewis Suggs. Westport, Conn.: Greenwood Press.

Wilson, Raymond. 1983. *Ohiyesa: Charles Eastman, Santee Sioux*. Urbana: University of Illinois Press.

Woodson, Carter G. 1920. "The Relations of Negroes and Indians in Massachusetts." *Journal of Negro History* 5 (January): 45–62.

Wright Jr., J. Leitch. 1986. *Creeks and Seminoles: The Destruction and Regeneration of the Muscogulge People*. Lincoln: University of Nebraska Press.

———. 1981. *The Only Land They Knew: The Tragic Story of the American Indians in the Old South*. New York: Free Press.

Wright, Michelle M. 2004. *Becoming Black: Creating Identity in the African Diaspora*. Durham, N.C.: Duke University Press.

Wright, Muriel H. 1958. "American Indian Corn Dishes." *Chronicles of Oklahoma* 36 (Summer): 155–66.

Yamamoto, Eric. 1979. "The Significance of Local." *Social Process in Hawaii* 27: 101–15.

Yellow Bird, Michael. 1999. "What We Want To Be Called: Indigenous Peoples' Perspectives on Racial and Ethnic Identity Labels." *The American Indian Quarterly* 23, no. 2.

Young, Elliot. 1998. "Red Men, Princess Pocahontas, and George Washington: Harmonizing Race Relations in Laredo at the Turn of the Century." *Western History Association* 29, no. 1: 48–85.

Zack, Naomi. 1995. *American Mixed Race: The Culture of Microdiversity*. Lanham, Md.: Rowan and Littlefield.

Contributors

~~~~~~~~~

Jennifer D. Brody is Weinberg College Board of Visitors Teaching and Research Professor at Northwestern University. She is currently working on a monograph titled, "The Style of Elements, the Elements of Style: Politically Performing Punctuation" (Duke University Press).

Tamara Buffalo is a visual artist and creative writer based in Minneapolis.

David A. Y. O. Chang is assistant professor of history at the University of Minnesota. He researches and teaches on the comparative history of race and nationalism, Native American and African American history, and the history of the American West and the American empire. Chang is currently writing a book on discourses and practices of race and nation in the conflict over land ownership in Indian Territory and Oklahoma.

Robert Keith Collins (Choctaw–African American) is a lecturer in Native American studies at the University of California, Berkeley, and a lecturer in anthropology at California State University, Fullerton. He received his Ph.D. in anthropology from the University of California, Los Angeles, in 2002. His chapter in this volume derives from his ongoing study of black Choctaws' lived experiences.

Roberta J. Hill (Oneida) is a poet, fiction writer, and scholar. A professor of English and American Indian studies at the University of Wisconsin, Madison, she has written two collections of poetry, *Star Quilt* (1984) and *Philadelphia Flowers* (1996). She is currently writing a biography of Dr. Lillie Rosa Minoka-Hill.

Sharon P. Holland is associate professor of African American studies at Northwestern University. She is the author of *Raising the Dead: Readings of Death and (Black) Subjectivity* (Duke University Press, 2000), which won the Lora Romero First Book Prize from the American Studies Association in 2002. She has published in the fields of African American studies, feminist studies, and queer studies and is currently at work on a second book project, "The Erotic Life of Racism."

kuʻualoha hoʻomanawanui is a Ph.D. candidate in English at the University of Hawaiʻi, Mānoa, specializing in Hawaiian literature, folklore, and mythology.

Deborah E. Kanter is associate professor of history at Albion College. She is currently working on *Hijos del Pueblo: Gender, Family and Community in Rural Mexico, 1730–1850* (forthcoming).

Virginia Kennedy is an adjunct professor of English at the University of Scranton, Scranton, Pennsylvania.

Barbara Krauthamer teaches nineteenth-century African American and women's history at New York University. She received her Ph.D. from Princeton University. She is completing a book manuscript on the contested meanings of black emancipation and citizenship in the Choctaw and Chickasaw nations.

Tiffany M. McKinney is an associate at the law firm of Skadden, Arps, Slate, Meagher and Flom, LLP, in New York City. She received a J.D. from New York University School of Law as a Root-Tilden-Kern Scholar and Junior Fellow in the Center for International Studies in 2001.

Melinda Micco (Seminole) is associate professor in ethnic studies at Mills College. Her research focuses on Native and African American communities.

Tiya Miles is assistant professor in the Program in American Culture, Center for Afroamerican and African Studies, and Native American Studies Program at the University of Michigan. She is author of *Ties That Bind: The Story of an Afro-Cherokee Family in Slavery and Freedom* (2005).

Celia E. Naylor is assistant professor of history at Dartmouth College. She was one of the coordinators of the conference "'Eating Out of the Same Pot': Relating Black and Native (Hi)stories," held at Dartmouth College in April 2000. She is in the process of revising for publication her dissertation, "More at Home with the Indians: African-American Slaves and Freedpeople in the Cherokee Nation, Indian Territory, 1838–1907."

Eugene B. Redmond teaches English and edits *Drumvoices Revue* at Southern Illinois University. He is poet laureate of East St. Louis, Illinois, and has published *Drumvoices: The Mission of Afro-American Poetry* (1976).

Wendy S. Walters is assistant professor of English at the Rhode Island School of Design, Providence. She has published articles on black performance and electronica with an emphasis on urban culture and is now investigating the relationship between concepts of diaspora and new media technologies.

Robert Warrior is associate professor of English and Native American studies at the University of Oklahoma, Norman. He received his Ph.D. from Union Theological Seminary in 1992. He is the author of *Tribal Secrets: Recovering American Indian Intellectual Traditions* (1995) and *The People and the Word: Reading Native Nonfiction* (2005), and coauthor of *Like a Hurricane: The Indian Movement from Alcatraz to Wounded Knee* (1996).

Index

The symbol n refers to a note; *p*, a photograph; *t*, a table.

baseball, 184–85
Bateman, Rebecca, 127–28
Battiest, Jane, 104–5, 119n2
Battles, Ryan, 152–53
Bea, Ms. (Choctaw informant),
 260–61, 265–68, 270–72
Begay, Leona R., 152, 156
Beloved (Morrison), 12, 18, 199–
 205, 216–17; Cherokee characters
 in, 203–5; ghostly Indian pres-
 ence in, 200–202, 204–5
Bender, Charles, 184–85, 186
Bennett, Herman, 165
Benston, Kimberly, 229
Bergland, Renee, 18, 200–201
Berryhill, Tobe, 87
B.E.T. (Big Every Time), 306n12
Betty (slave), 1–2
BIA. *See* Bureau of Indian Affairs
Big Daddy Morgan (character),
 212–13
bilingualism, 105–6, 113–14
biological determinants of race:
 blood quantum requirements as,
 87–88, 129–30, 133–35, 137–38,
 140, 144n17, 263–64, 268; gen-
 omic analysis and, 160–61; literary examinations of blood and
 purity in, 211–14; racial mixtures
 in colonial Mexico and, 173–74,
 176–77; racial phenotypes and,
 150–57, 218–25, 260–63, 265–72,
 321. *See also* identity issues
Black Indians (Katz), 197
Black Man with Watermelon (character), 250–53
blacks in the United States: all-black
 towns of, 5–9; citizenship status
 of, 14, 100–118; education of, 17–
 18, 185–95; emigration to Liberia
 of, 81, 84–85, 88–94; idealized
 views of Native life by, 9–13;
 Inter-National Afro-American
 League, 80–81; musical traditions
 of, 273–74; newspapers of, 5–6;

passing practices of, 165–67, 231;
 playing Indian and, 148–49;
 reclaiming Black-Native identities
 of, 157–59, 162n34, 162–63n35,
 163n36; religious practices of,
 105–6; rifts between Creek Freedmen and black migrants, 90–93;
 slavery as basis of black identity,
 129–30; transatlantic focus of, 3,
 22n8. *See also* biological determi-
 nants of race; Freedmen, Freed-
 people; identity issues
Blind I Can C, A (Buffalo), 18,
 221*p*, 225
blood quantum requirements. *See*
 biological determinants of race
Bob Marley and the Wailers, 277
Bogle, Lori, 5
Boley (town), 7, 91, 93
Bonga, George, 220
Bonnin, Gertrude Simmons, 189–90
Bowser, Frederick, 165
Branch of Acknowledgement and
 Research (BAR), 63–66
Brandy, Carolyn, 26–27
Brashears, Richard, 111
Brody, Jennifer D., ix, 14, 323
"Broken Promise," 294
Bronson, Ruth Muskrat, 193
Brown, William J., 52n5
Bruddah Walter Aipolani and Island
 Afternoon, 280, 281, 291, 293–94,
 299–300
Bruner band of Seminole, 124
Brushell, Moses, 67
Brushell, Tamar, 62, 67–69
Buffalo, Tamara, 18, 218–25, 221*p*,
 323
Buffalo Bill's Wild West Show, 191
buffalo soldiers, 10
Bureau of Indian Affairs (BIA):
 Certificate of Degree of Indian
 Blood cards, 137–38; education
 programs of, 189–90; federal rec-
 ognition process of, 63–66, 122;

Herndon, Ruth Wallis, 35–36
"Hidden History of Mestizo America, The" (Nash), 196–97
higher education, 17–18, 185–95, 211
Hill, Roberta, 20, 309–20, 323
hip hop, 19–20, 280, 281–82, 285–87. *See also* Hawaiian (Jawaiian) music
Hitchcock, Lone Wolf v., 182–83
Hōʻaikane, 277–78, 280, 281, 291, 294, 300–302, 305nn4–5
Hohu, "Aunty" Martha, 303
Holland, Sharon P., 14, 18, 197, 215, 323
Hollinger, David, 197
hoʻomnawanui, kuʻualoha, 19–20, 323
Hoʻonuʻa, 281, 291–92, 297
How We Became Human: New and Selected Poems (Harjo), 13
hula dance, 274–77

Idahosa, Pablo, 11
identity issues, 7, 33–34; bilingualism and, 105–6, 113–14; of Choctaw and Chickasaw Freedpeople, 100–118; of Choctaw and Chickasaw slaves, 104–7; emigrationist movements and, 96–98; food preparation and, 104–5; miscegenation and, 58–59; of mixed race / New people, 19, 33–34, 57–59, 125–26, 260–72; performances of reinvented history and, 228, 232–35, 239–49, 259n31; playing Indian and, 145–49, 157–59; race betrayal through sex and, 241–43, 258–59n29; racial phenotypes and, 150–57, 218–25, 260–63, 265–72; Radhakrishnan's multiple rootedness and, 197; reclaiming Black Native identities, 157–59, 162–63nn34–36; recognition and identification, 260–72;

religious practices and, 105–6; of Seminole Freedmen, 126–28; slavery as basis of black identity, 129–30; of wannabees, 145–49, 259n30, 260–61, 285–87. *See also* performance of history
"Identity Struggle, The" (Wallace and Fogelson), 264
Ill Semantics, 283
immigration. *See* migrations
Indian Boyhood (Eastman), 188
Indian Claims Commission, 122–23
Indian Gaming Regulatory Act, 64, 70
"Indian Love Call," 239
Indian Reorganization Act, 183
Indian Territory, 3, 4–9, 14–15; African American population in, 91, 107; all-black towns in, 5, 7–8, 91; alliances with Plains tribes and, 86; Civil War in, 106–7, 112, 132; emigration movements in, 80–81, 84–98; idealized views of, 7, 9–13; identity issues in, 100–118; Inter-national Afro-American League and, 80–81; migrations of slaves to, 9–13, 90–93, 132–33; nationalist movements in, 80–81, 83–94; recruitment of settlers to, 5–7; segregation policies in, 8–9; sovereignty and land allotments in, 81, 83–89, 102–4, 107–9, 115–16, 121, 182–83; tribal citizenship in, 100–118. *See also* Five Civilized Tribes; Freedmen, Freedpeople; Oklahoma
Indian Trade and Intercourse Act of 1790, 73
Indian Wars, 10
industrial education, 185–95
intermarriage, 32–34, 56n28, 58–59; antimiscegenation laws and, 58–59, 130, 144n12; maroon communities and, 127–30; race suicide

intermarriage (*continued*)
concerns and, 150–51; racial basis
of tribal membership and, 68–72,
263–64; in Seminole Nation,
127–28. *See also* biological determinants of race
Inter-national Afro-American
League, 80–81, 85–86, 96
Ioane, Skip, 294–95
Isparhecher (Creek), 86–88, 96,
98n9

Jackson, Andrew, 203
Jackson, Jacob B., 87
Jackson, Papa Charlie, 10
Jacobs, John, 27–28
James-Johnson, Shirlee, 153
Jawaiian music. *See* Hawaiian (Ja-
waiian) music
Jerome Commission, 183
Johnson, J. Coody, 93–94
Johnson, Lewis, 131, 134–35,
139–40
Johnson, Willard, 158
Journal of Negro History, 9–10
Juneteenth Day, 89–90

Kaʻaihue, Henry Kapono, 294
Kaʻau Crater Boys, 281, 289–90
Kahakalau, Robie, 277, 279
"Kailua-Kona, 300–302
Kamakawiwoʻole, Israel, 277, 283,
292, 294–95, 303
Kameʻeleihiwa, Lilikalā, 289
Kanter, Deborah, 17, 323
Kapena, 280–82
Katz, William Loren, 197
Kawaʻauhau, Keʻala, 283, 285
"Keep Hawaiian Lands in Hawaiian
Hands," 293–94, 299–300
Kekaula, Robert, 290
Keliʻilauahi, Leslie, 303
Kennedy, Virginia, 18, 323
King Kapisi, 283
King Philip's War, 35
Kiowa Nation, 182–83

Krantz, Wendy, 141
Krauthamer, Barbara, 14, 323
Kūʻē (Resistance), 289
"Ku ʻu Pua (My Beloved Flower),"
297–98

Ladd, James, 111
Land of the Spotted Eagle, The (Standing Bear), 191–92
Las Casas, Bartolomé de, 167–68
Latin America. *See* Mexico
Lavis, Rick, 136
Lee, R. C., 93
legal aspects of Native and African
American co-histories: access to
land, 171–73; antimiscegenation
laws, 58–59, 130, 144n12; Atoka
Agreement, 116–17; biological
determinants of racial identities
and, 129–30, 133–35, 137–38,
140, 144n17, 160–61; Curtis Act,
116–17; *Davis v. United States*,
137, 138; definitions of tribal
membership, 57–58, 100–118;
Goat v. United States, 133–34;
Indian Reorganization Act, 183;
Lone Wolf v. Hitchcock, 182–83;
*Mashpee Tribe v. Town of Mashpee et
al.*, 72–74; *Seminole Nation v. Gale
Norton*, 121–24, 143n1. *See also*
membership in tribes
LeGault, Helen, 62
Liberia, 81, 84–94, 115
Lincoln City (town), 95
Linthicum, Leslie, 155, 162n29
Lionnet, Françoise, 232
Lisa Mayo (character), 233–34,
255n8
literary representations of "other"
Americans, 196–217; ghostly
presence of Indians in, 200–205;
importance of tradition, land, and
ancestors in, 205–9; Morrison's
historical novels, 199–217; performance of colonial narratives, 226–

31; as peripheral peoples, 198–99; poetry, 27–29; race and land relationships of, 199–201; resistance of Eurocentric history of, 199–200; themes of racial isolation of, 211–16; "third space" Americans and, 196; women's communities in, 214–16

Littlefield, Daniel F., 103, 127

Lone Dupres (character), 215

Lone Wolf v. Hitchcock, 182–83, 187

Lopez, Ian, 129

Love, Clarence, 8–9

Love, Kiziah, 104

Love Medicine (Erdrich), 190–91

Lovett, Laura, 72

Lumbee tribe, 72

Lynch, Dorothea, 152

Mack, Connie, 184

Macon Dead, Jr. (character), 205–11, 213

Mahoe, Noelani, 275

Maine, United States v., 73

major league baseball, 184–85

Mana'o Company, 277–78, 280, 305n4

Mancera, Viceroy, 173

Mandell, Daniel R., 32–33, 53n9, 56n28

Mankiller, Wilma, 158

Mann, William Brayton, 37, 54–55n18

Manuel, Marcelino, 176

Marley, Bob, 29, 277, 283, 292–94, 297, 306n11

Marshall, John, 182

Martin, Cheryl, 170

Mary Magda (character), 215–16

Mashantucket Pequot band, 14, 62; federal recognition of, 62–63, 69–72; gaming casino of, 64, 70, 75n8; membership criteria of, 57–58; racial conflicts of, 57–58, 62–63, 70–72

Mashantucket Pequot Indian Claims Settlement Act, 69–72

Mashpee tribe, 72–74; in Civil War, 59; federal recognition of, 73–74; intermarriage of, 58, 74, 79n48

Mashpee Tribe v. Town of Mashpee et al., 72–74

McCaleb, Neil A., 69

McKinney, Tiffany M., 14, 323

McMullen, Ann, 32–33

Medearis, Angela, 11

membership in tribes, 125–26; of Afro-Mexicans, 164–78; blood quantum requirements and, 87–88, 129–30, 133–35, 137–38, 263–64, 268; of Chickasaw and Choctaw Freedpeople, 100–118, 125–26; definitions of, 14–17, 57–58; financial incentives of, 122–23; impact on federal recognition and, 57–58; Miss Navajo Nation debates and, 16–17, 150–57; of mixed-race children, 59; racial basis of, 68–74; requirements of, 57–58, 59, 62–63, 68–74; of Seminole Freedmen, 121–42; treaties of 1866 and, 107–10, 119n4, 121, 123, 143n2

Memoirs of Elleanor Eldridge (Whipple), ix, 14, 51–52n2; appeals for help in, 37–39, 54n17; cataloguing of terms in, 36–37; literary status of, 32; portrait of Elleanor and, 39p, 40; portrayal of Elleanor as black in, 40–43, 47–48, 53n14; portrayal of Elleanor's personal qualities in, 43–46; publication of, 31–32, 54n16; subscription appeals in, 38, 48–51; title page of, 54n17; trope of gendered violence in, 48. See also Eldridge, Elleanor

Menus Jury (character), 212, 214

Meridian (Walker), 11

"Message to the Wannabees (Be Hawaiian)," 285–87

Mexico, 17; access to land in, 171–73, 179n6; Afro-Mexicans in Toluca region of, 164–78, 179n2; castas, labels, and stereotypes in, 173–78, 179n3, 179n13, 180nn14–15; emigrations from Indian Territory to, 85–89, 95–96, 97, 126, 127; *hijos del pueblo* status in, 170–73; migrations to Alabama from, 89; passing as Indian in, 165–67; segregation policies in, 167–68, 170–71; slavery in, 167–69, 174–75, 180n16

Micco, Melinda, 16, 323

Mignolo, Walter, 324–25

migrations, 1–4; African return movement, 81, 84–95, 115, 119n6; to Canada, 95; escape routes for slaves and, 4; forced migration to Indian Territory, 122, 127, 143n9, 203–5, 266; idealized notions of freedom and, 9–13; from Indian Territory, 81–98; to Mexico, 85–89, 95–96, 97, 126, 127; of Native tribes, 14, 35–36, 106; from post-Reconstruction South, 4–5, 90–93; racial and national identities and, 96–98; recruitment of settlers and, 5–7; transatlantic focus of, 3, 22n8

Miles, Tiya, 323

Milkman Dead (character), 205–11

Millán, Victoriano, 175–76

missionaries, 105–6

Miss Navajo Nation debates, 16–17, 150–57, 161n5, 161n11, 162n29

Mitchell, Harry K., 299

Mitchell, Mrs. J. Orlando, 8

Mixedblood Messages (Owens), 200

mixed race issues. *See* biological determinants of race; identity issues

Mohegan tribe, 58; Civil War and, 59; federal recognition of, 67; gaming casino of, 64; Pequot War and, 61

Mojica, Monique, 18–19, 226, 228, 232, 234–35, 253n2. See also *Princess Pocahontas and the Blue Spots*

Molina, Antonio Trinidad, 171–72, 174, 179n8

Monacans tribe, 72

Montauk tribe, 58

Montezuma, Carlos, 189–90

Moon, Peter, 306n11

Morgan, Lewis Henry, 147

Mörner, Magnus, 178

Morrison, Toni, 12, 18, 196–217. See also *Beloved*; literary representations of "other" Americans; *Paradise*; *Song of Solomon*

Moses, Ruth, 53n10

Mossman, Bina, 289

Mulroy, Kevin, 127–28, 199

multiculturalism, 196–97

Muriel Miguel (character), 233–34, 255n8

music, 19–20, 25–30. *See also* Hawaiian (Jawaiian) music

Muskogee Comet newspaper, 5

Muskogee Nation. *See* Creek Nation

Muskogee Reds Baseball Club, xxii*p*

My People the Sioux (Standing Bear), 191

Na'auao, Sean, 290, 305n4

Nā Mele o Hawai'i Nei, 101 Hawaiian Songs (Elbert and Mahoe), 275

Narragansett tribe, 35, 50; intermarriages in, 32–34, 58; official designation of, as black, 35–36; Pequot War and, 61; racial and cultural identity of, 33–36

narrative tradition, 11–12, 226–31

Nash, Gary, 196–97

Nathan Dupres (character), 213–14

National Association for the Advancement of Colored People, 190

National Congress of American Indians, 158

nationalist movements, 80–81; African return movements, 81, 84–95, 115, 119n6; emigrations to Mexico and, 85–89; identity politics and, 96–98; Native sovereignty movements, 81, 83–89; pan-Indian nationalism, 89

Native culture: athletics and, 184–86; black views of, 9–13; education and, 185–95, 211; land allotments and, 81, 83–89, 102–4, 107–9, 115–16, 182–83; literary views of, 196–217; music and, 19–20, 273, 275, 297–99; political and cultural independence and, 22n8, 182–83; religious practices and, 105–6, 188; sachem families in, 60, 75n3; wannabees and, 147–48, 259n30, 260–61, 285–87; white views of, 10. *See also* biological determinants of race; performance of history; playing Indian

Native Joy for Real (CD), 29–30

Navajo Nation, 16–17, 150–61, 161n5, 161n11, 162n29

Navarrete, Antonio, 173

Nā Wai Hoʻoluʻu o ke Ānuenue, 280–81

Naylor, Celia, 16–17, 102, 323

Nector (character), 190–91

Nehru, Jawaharlal, 197

Nesian Mystic, 283

New England Indian communities: federal recognition of, 62–63, 66–75, 75–76n9; gaming casinos of, 64, 70, 73–74, 75n8; historic overview of, 58–62, 75n4; intermarriage of, 58–59, 74, 79n48; racial conflicts in, 62–66, 68–75; reservation administration of, 62

New People, 125–26

New York Tammany Society, 147

Ngugi wa Thiongʻo, 228

Nickel and Dimed: On (Not) Getting By in America (Ehrenreich), 38

Norton, Gale, 121–42

"No Woman No Cry," 293–94

O'Brien, Jean, 32, 33–34, 60

Occom, Samson, 190

O'Dowd, Sarah, 32–34, 51n1

Oklahoma: all-black towns in, 5; Jim Crow laws in, 8–9, 93, 96, 117, 127; land run in, 28; statehood of, 8, 28, 83, 91–92; UNIA activity in, 94–95. *See also* Indian Territory

Olmstead, George T., 110, 114–15

"Onipaʻa (Stand Firm)," 287–89

oral tradition, 11–12, 226–31

Orientalism, 230

Osage Nation, 195n3

Osceola, 28, 130

O-shen, 280, 306n12

Osorio, Jon, 287, 304

Osumare, Halifu, 280

Owens, Louis, 200

Pa, Shiloh, 292, 305n6

Painter, Nell Irvin, 4

Pamunkey tribe, 72

pan-Africanism, 81, 84–95, 115, 119n6

Pannikar, Raimudo, 324–25

Paradise (Morrison), 18, 199–200, 210–16; exploitation of land in, 212; racist values of colonizers in, 211–14; women's communities in, 214–16

Parks, Suzan-Lori, 19, 231–32, 250

Pasamoquate tribe, 73

passing, 165–67, 231

Pati, 280

Patriarchs of America, 7

Patterson, A. E., 6, 7–8

Paucatuck Pequot band: federal recognition of, 67, 68–69, 75–76n9, 78–79n28; racial conflicts in, 57–58, 62–63, 69, 75–76n9, 78–79n28

Paul D. (character), 202–5, 205

Pautucket Pequot band, 14

Peaches, Ivis Daniel, 154
Pembroke State College, 193
Pequots in Southern New England, The (Hauptman and Wherry), 70
Pequot tribes: federal recognition of, 62–63, 66–72; gaming casinos and, 64, 70; historic overview of, 59–62, 75n4; intermarriage and, 58; mixed-race issues of, 32–36, 40–43, 47–48, 53n11, 53n14, 53n15, 57–75; racial conflicts of, 62–63, 69
Pequot War, 61–62, 75n4
performance of history, 18–19, 226–53; authorship and, 229–33, 236, 253–54n4, 255n10; bipolar dialectics of, 235–36, 256nn12–13; colonial narratives in, 226–28; counter-mimicry in, 229; praxis/*métissage* in, 232; racial classifications and stereotypes in, 230–35; reinventions of history in, 228–35, 253n3, 254–55n6, 255n9; teleologies of death and extinction in, 250–53; "wannabee" performances in, 259n30. *See also* identity issues; playing Indian
Perryman family (Creek), 82–83, 87
"Perspectives on Native American Identity" (Fogelson), 261, 263
Peter Moon Band, 306n11
"Pi'i Mai ka Nalu (Surf's Up)", 279
Pilate (character), 205–10, 216
Piper, Adrian, 231, 253–54n4
Pitt, Lillian, 224–25
Plains Indians, 86
playing Indian, 145–62; at Boston Tea Party, 145–46, 148; Green's descriptions of, 145–47; historical examples of, 145–48; Miss Navajo Nation debates on, 150–57; notions of trickery and deception in, 160; racial politics of, 148–49; reclaiming Black Native identities and, 157–59, 162n34, 162–63n35,

163n36; wannabees and, 147–48, 259n30, 260–61, 285–87
Playing Indian (Deloria), 147–49
Playing in the Dark (Morrison), 201
Pocahontas, 236–39, 256n14, 256n15, 258–59n29. See also *Princess Pocahontas and the Blue Spots*
Pocahontas (Disney film), 256–57n17
Poetic Justice (CD), 29
poetry, 27–29
Porter, Kenneth W., 9–10, 127
Powhatan Confederacy, 237–38
Pratt, Richard Henry, 185–87, 189, 191
Princess Pocahontas and the Blue Spots (Mojica), 18–19, 226, 253n2; blue spots of identity in, 241, 257n21; Contemporary Woman No. 1 in, 240–42; Contemporary Woman No. 2 in, 241–42; historical legend of Pocahontas and, 238–39; Lady Rebecca Rolfe in, 244–47, 249; La Malinche/Malnali in, 241–43, 246–47; Matoaka in, 247–49; Mothers of Métis in, 241, 245–47, 257n22, 257n24, 258n26; Princess Buttered-on-Both Sides in, 239–40, 243–44, 248–49, 257n19, 258n25; reinventions of history in, 228, 232, 234–35, 239–49; Sacrificial Virgin and Musician in, 243–44; songs in, 239; Storybook Pocahontas in, 243–44; transformations of identity in, 239–49, 257n18, 259n31
Prophet, Caleb, 36
Prophet, Hannah, 43, 55–56n25
Prophet, Thomas, ix, xi, 32–35, 41, 52n5, 53n10
Purdue, Theda, 321

Quarles, Benjamin, 43

racial politics: of Afro-Mexicans, 164–78; of alliances between minorities, 59, 128–30, 132; of assumptions of racial purity, 125–26; of binary system of racial designations, 129, 165; in case law, 72–74; of Jim Crow period, 8–9, 72, 93, 117, 127; of legal and biological basis of racial identities, 129–30, 133–35, 137–38, 140, 144n17, 150–57, 160–61; of maroon communities, 127–30; of nationalist movements, 80–98; of passing and racial variability, 165–67, 231; of performance of colonial narratives, 228–31; of playing Indian, 148–49; of race betrayal through sex, 241–43, 258–59n29; of returns to Liberia, 84–85; of rifts between Creek Freedmen and black migrants, 90–93; of tribal definitions of membership, 68–72, 100–118; of uplift through education, 17–18; of white views of others, 10, 13, 72, 128

Radhakrishnan, R., 18, 196–97

Ramirez, Tish, 154

rap music, 19–20, 280–83, 285–93. *See also* Hawaiian (Jawaiian) music

Rayona (character), 12–13

Reagan, Ronald, 62–63

Reconstructing Womanhood: The Emergence of the Afro-American Woman Novelists (Carby), 53n11

Reconstruction in the Indian Territory (Bailey), 103

Red Bird Investment Company, 6–8

Red Bird (town), 5, 6–8, 95

Redding, Otis, 296

Redhouse, Mary, 30

Redmond, Eugene B., 13–14, 25–30, 323–24

reggae, 19–20, 274–80, 292–95, 304, 305n3. *See also* Hawaiian (Jawaiian) music

religious practices, 105–6, 188

Reverb-ber-ber-rations, 229

Revolutionary War, 41–43

Richards, Caleb, 283

Rigney, Barbara Hill, 197–98, 200, 215

Rising American Empire, The (Van Alstyne), 129

Robinson, Amy, 176

Robinson, Jackie, 184

Roe Cloud, Henry, 186–87, 190

Rolfe, John, 238, 256n14, 256n16, 258–59n29

Rolfe, Rebecca (Pocahontas), 238, 256n14, 256n16, 258–59n29

Rose, Trisha, 303–4

Ruby, Oklahoma (town), 210–16

Rushes Bear (character), 190–91

Sabastian, Roy, 66–67

sachem families, 60, 75n3

"Sacrificial Corn Maiden," 239, 258n25

Sam, Alfred, 92–94

Sameth, Sigmund, xv–xvi

Samuels, C. G., 93

San Pedro Xolostoc, 164

Santee Normal Training School, 188

Schneider, Rebecca, 229

scholarship goals, 3–4, 22–23n9

Scribe, 283

Seacole, Mary, 37, 46

Sebastian, Manuel, 62, 67–68, 78–79n28

Seed of Life (recording), 159

Sekatau, Ella Wilcox, 35–36

Seminole Nation, 16, 80–81, 83; benefit allocations of, 136–40, 144n22; *Davis v. United States* and, 137, 138; Dosar Barkus band of, 124, 136–37; election of 2000 and, 121–24; emigration of, to Mexico, 86; forced migration of, to Indian Territory, 122, 143n9; General Allotment Act and, 115–16; *Goat*

Tiya Miles is assistant professor in the Program in American Culture, Center for Afroamerican and African Studies, and Native American Studies Program at the University of Michigan. She is author of *Ties That Bind: The Story of an Afro-Cherokee Family in Slavery and Freedom* (2005).

Sharon P. Holland is associate professor of African American studies at Northwestern University. She is the author of *Raising the Dead: Readings of Death and (Black) Subjectivity* (Duke University Press, 2000), which won the Lora Romero First Book Prize from the American Studies Association in 2002.

Library of Congress Cataloging-in-Publication Data

Crossing waters, crossing worlds : the African diaspora in Indian country / edited by Tiya Miles and Sharon P. Holland.

v. cm.

Includes bibliographical references and index.

ISBN-13: 978-0-8223-3812-3 (cloth : alk. paper)

ISBN-10: 0-8223-3812-2 (cloth : alk. paper)

ISBN-13: 978-0-8223-3865-9 (pbk. : alk. paper)

ISBN-10: 0-8223-3865-3 (pbk. : alk. paper)

1. African Americans — Relations with Indians.
2. Blacks — North America — Relations with Indians. 3. Blacks — North America — Relations with Indians. 4. Blacks — North America — Migrations. 5. Blacks — Latin America — Migrations.
6. Indians — Mixed descent. 7. Ex-slaves of Indian tribes. 8. African diaspora. I. Miles, Tiya. II. Holland, Sharon Patricia.

E98.R28C76 2006

305.8996'073017497 — dc22

2006011042